DC

M000285135

Best Things

in

New York

are

Free

Revised Edition

Marian Hamilton

Foreword by Betsy Gotbaum

Illustrations by Ken Hamilton

The Harvard Common Press
Harvard & Boston, Massachusetts

The Harvard Common Press
535 Albany Street
Boston, Ma. 02118

Library of Congress Cataloging in Publication Data

Hamilton, Marian, 1949-

   The Best Things in New York are Free: over 1,000 attractions
   and activities that won't cost you a penny!/Marian Hamilton. —
   Rev. ed.

      p. cm.

Includes index.

ISBN 1-55832-031-8 (pbk): $10.95.

1. New York (N.Y.) — Description — Guide Books.

I. Title

F128.18.H347 1991 917.47'10443-dc20 90-27139 CIP

Please note that this book reflects as accurate information
as possible at the time of printing. However, nothing can
be done to ensure that free places will continue such a
liberal admission policy.

Cover design by Jackie Schuman.

Book design by Ken Hamilton.

10 9 8 7 6 5 4 3 2 1

Printed in United States of America.

Contents

Foreword

City of New York
Parks & Recreation

Everyone knows that New York is the center of the world when it comes to culture, communications and finance.

What everyone doesn't know is that amid the riches and glamour, the posh uptown eateries and the bright lights of Broadway exists another New York—a magical city brimming with wonderful, fascinating activities, and all of them are absolutely free.

As City Parks & Recreation Commissioner, I oversee more than 26,000 acres of parkland, which includes 15 miles of beaches, 511 tennis courts, a dozen bird-watching sanctuaries, 1,580 parks, 105 swimming pools, 21 major recreation centers, 842 playgrounds, 3 zoos, 709 ballfields and the list goes on. You can ice-skate, take a martial arts class, catch a free concert, hone up your boxing skills, swim in an Olympic-sized Art-Deco swimming pool, play boccie or treat yourself to a ride on our newly restored 1912 Carousel. And that's only the beginning.

For sports fanatics, this city is the ultimate health club—and the cheapest one, too. There is no greater pleasure I know than running around the reservoir in Central Park, taking in the magnificent views on a crisp, clear autumn morning.

Real New York'ers know how to get the best for less — it's practically a requirement for survival in this town!

But now, thanks to the fine research and up-to-the-minute information compiled in Marian Hamilton's book, anyone can access the magnificent "free" world of New York City.

Betsy Gotbaum
Commissioner

Preface

People said it couldn't be done; a book on free things in New York would prove to be a very small pamphlet indeed. But back in 1985, I proved them wrong. I spent one year on an adventure throughout the 5 boroughs and unearthed over 1,000 cultural and recreational freebies. Now, for this revised edition, I went back on the road again to find the many new free attractions and to check on the status of the ones in the last book. And the quality of N.Y.C.'s free entertainment has remained impressive and makes you realize that it doesn't have to cost an arm and a leg to entertain yourself and your family.

This guidebook is activity oriented. It's loaded with places and events by which you could entertain yourself for the entire year. In order to qualify for this book, a place had to be free at some time of the day (year) or to a special age group (like children or seniors). At the beginning of each entry, look for the admission policy. You can assume that any entry without any information on admission is always free.

Check out the Calendar of Events for ongoing cultural offerings by day and week. So if it's Tuesday at 2pm and you've got some spare time, you can discover what free regularly scheduled events are available.

Consult the Apple Rating System in the introduction to ensure you go to all the "musts" of the city.

Chapters are organized by interest category. Those interested in museums and art galleries can zero in on those sections, while music, theater and movie lovers can concentrate on their specialties. For those places offering regularly scheduled activities, consult the "Events" listing at the end of each entry.

Places in Manhattan are listed alphabetically first in each chapter, with the other four boroughs following in kind. If you're interested in Staten Island, you can find your cultural activities at the back of most chapters. The maps at the back will help you locate places of interest.

Some places, such as schools and universities, appear in more than one category when they offer a broad range of events (concerts, art shows, films, etc.).

Hope you have as much fun in New York City for free as I have had exploring all these attractions.

— *MARIAN HAMILTON*

Acknowledgements

This book would not have come about if it hadn't been for my extraordinary husband Ken, who encouraged, supported and helped out this venture enormously. Not only did he do the excellent illustrations, but he provided the technical expertise on the book's production and typesetting. He and my daughters, Michelle and Ashley, were great sports when they were enlisted to accompany me on my countless field trips.

A salute to the wonderful people who assisted in the research and production of the book: first and foremost, Rikki Hudes Michels, my assistant; Bruce Shaw and Alix Cooper, Harvard Common Press; Tony Vargas and Rachel Zimmerman, N.Y.C. Department of Parks and Recreation; Barbara Bergeron, copy editor; Marion Maienthau, art consultant; plus all those helpful people at the places mentioned in this book, especially the historical societies and libraries.

Introduction

Most people probably wouldn't believe that there's much to do in N.Y.C. for free. Sure, there are free concerts in the summer, but that's about it. And if there are free things, they must be pretty "crummy"; otherwise they would cost money.

Nothing could be further from the truth. This book is a tribute to the Big Apple's freebies. In fact, it is possible to entertain yourself (and with top-notch events) for an entire year without spending a cent! Such an itinerary would take you to our world-famous museums, art galleries, concert halls, theaters and special attractions.

Come on, N.Y.C. has got to be one of the most expensive cities to live in (no less visit). How can this be?

First, many places are able to offer free admission policies thanks to generous corporate subsidies (let's hear it for big business!). This is particularly true of concert halls and museums offering a special performance or free evening. Also, many companies actually have their own free museums or exhibits, such as IBM, AT&T Infoquest, Forbes Magazine and Con Edison.

Second, the N.Y.C. government provides excellent services for the city. As Commissioner Betsy Gotbaum stated in her Foreword, the Department of Parks & Recreation administers an amazing number of parks and recreational facilities and sponsors a potpourri of free activities including sporting events, nature walks, concerts, theater and festivals (consult their monthly calendar). Also, the 3 main library systems for the 5 boroughs offer more than just books. The libraries' monthly calendars of free events read like mini yellow pages. And then there are the Human Resource Department and the Department of the Aging with over 500 free Senior Centers. The Department of Cultural Affairs sponsors concerts, exhibitions and special festivities.

Third, N.Y.C. is home to some of the finest schools and colleges, which train our best musicians, actors, artists, dancers and and other performing arts professionals. And to earn their degrees, many students must perform over and over again in front of an audience. These free events offer you an opportunity to see our future stars.

Fourth, various places (such as theaters, concert halls and museums) offer freebies to "whet" your appetites in the hope that next time you'll come back and buy a ticket. Also, it's just downright good advertising. This is especially true for various cultural societies that want to engender a "good image."

Fifth, many nonprofit organizations (such as churches and some museums) don't have a fixed admission policy but instead ask for a donation, contribution or "suggested contribution." A "suggested contribution" means just that. Although such events are not "completely" free, there's nothing to stop you from contributing only 10¢ or 25¢. Many people don't realize that they have that option. This is particularly true for tourists or even a New Yorker who might otherwise shy away from going to a museum because it costs $5. Let's face it, most of us are suckers for a good bargain.

Sixth, many people don't realize that some places are free to specific age groups. So although there might be an admission fee for an adult, the children can go for free. There are also special freebies frequently for seniors or students.

And finally, free cultural life does exist outside Manhattan. There is a wealth of excellent free museums, parks and concerts available in all 5 boroughs.

Many New Yorkers don't often realize all the goodies (for free, of course) in their own backyard. Frequently people think they have to be "on vacation" to enjoy fully the sights and culture of a city. This is the guidebook that every New Yorker should own. Also, visitors don't have to worry about taking out a second mortgage to entertain themselves once here.

N.Y.C. also offers a wealth of free information; here are a few of the organizations that provide up-to-date cultural calendars and brochures: **New York Convention & Visitors Bureau** (2 Columbus Circle or 207 W. 43rd St. (Broadway & 8th Ave.), (212) 397-8222, Mon-Fri 9am-6pm, Sat-Sun 10am-6pm) and the **New York State Division of Tourism** (write or call for free info—97 Washington St., Albany, N.Y. 12245, (800) 342-3810 or (212) 949-9300).

And let's not forget the various daily newspapers (not free) that list free events, including the *Daily News*, *New York Post* and *The New York Times*; and the weekly newspaper, *The Village Voice*. You may also try the weekly magazines (also not free), which include *New York Magazine* and *The New Yorker*. In addition, there are several free guides, *Where*, *City Guide* and *Quick City Guide*, available in about 60 hotels (ask the concierge for one).

Many people know that N.Y.C. has become known as "The Big Apple." For those of you who are curious about the phrase's origin, it was an expression used during the 1920s and 1930s, especially by jazz musicians, as a way of saying they were playing in the big time ("There are many apples on the tree, but when you pick N.Y.C., you pick the Big Apple.").

So now you're ready to take a "bite" out of the Big Apple without having to pay for the entire fruitstand!!

The Core Places

(The "Musts" of the Big Apple)

Some free places in N.Y.C. are better than others; here's a guide to the best (rating system: ♦♦♦♦ —world class, ♦♦♦ —excellent, ♦♦ —very good, ♦ —good):

♦♦♦♦ (World Class)
American Museum of Natural History
The Bronx Zoo
Brooklyn Botanic Gardens
Brooklyn Museum
Central Park
Ellis Island Immigration Museum
Frick Museum
Lincoln Center for the Performing Arts
Metropolitan Museum of Art (MMA)
Museum of Modern Art (MoMA)
Statue of Liberty
World Financial Center

♦♦♦ (Excellent)
American Museum of Immigration
AT&T Infoquest Center
Battery Park City
Central Park Zoo
The Cloisters
Cooper-Hewitt Museum
Forbes Magazine Galleries Museum
Guggenheim (Solomon R.) Museum
IBM Gallery of Science and Art
Museum of the City of New York
New York Botanical Gardens
New York Public Library, 42nd St. Central Research Library
Isamu Noguchi Sculpture Garden
Prospect Park
Richmondtown Restoration
Rockefeller Center
7th Regiment Armory
Snug Harbor Cultural Center
South Street Seaport
United Nations
Whitney Museum of American Art
World Trade Center

♦♦ (Very Good)
American Crafts Museum

Bartow-Pell Mansion
Bronx Museum of the Arts
Brooklyn Bridge
Brooklyn Children's Museum
Cathedral Church of St. John the Divine
City Hall & Governor's Room Museum
Columbia University
Empire State Building
Equitable Building
FAO Schwarz Toy Store
Flushing Meadow/Corona Park
Gracie Mansion
IBM Garden
International Center of Photography (ICP)
Jamaica Bay Wildlife Refuge
J. Pierpont Morgan Library
Museum of American Folk Art
Museum of Broadcasting
National Academy of Design
New York Aquarium
New York Hall of Science
The New-York Historical Society
New York Public Library for the Performing Arts
New York Stock Exchange
Queens Museum
Riverside Church
Rockaway Beach
St. Bartholomew's Church
St. Patrick's Cathedral
St. Peter's Church
Staten Island Children's Museum
Staten Island Ferry
Trinity Church
Trump Tower
Waldorf-Astoria
Wave Hill
Whitney Museum of American Art at Philip Morris
Woolworth Building

 (Good)
Alley Pond Environmental Center
Asia Society
Alice Austen House, Museum & Garden
Bowne House
Brighton & Manhattan Beach
Brooklyn Academy of Museum (BAM)
Brooklyn Arts Cultural Association (BACA)
Brooklyn Historical Society & Museum
Carnegie Hall
Center for African Art

Central Synagogue
Chrysler Building
Chung-Cheng Gallery
Church of the Transfiguration
Citicorp Center
Clay Pits Park
Clove Lakes Park
Commodities Exchange (COMEX)
Cooper Union
Empire-Fulton Ferry Park
Fashion Institute of Technology (F.I.T.)
Federal Hall National Memorial
Federal Reserve Bank of New York
Fire Museum
Forest Park
Fraunces Tavern
Grace Church
Grand Central Terminal
Grand Hyatt Hotel
Grey Art Gallery & Study Center
Headquarters Museum
High Rock Environmental Center
Hispanic Society of America
Hunter College Leubsdorf Gallery
International Center of Photography Midtown
Jamaica Arts Center
Japan House
Juilliard School of Music
Lladro Museum & Gallery
MetLife Gallery
Morris-Jumel Mansion
Municipal Arts Society
El Museo del Barrio
Museum of American Piano
National Arts Club
New Museum of Contemporary Art
New York Marriott Marquis
New York Police Department Museum
New York University
Nikon House
Old Merchants House
PaineWebber Gallery
Park Avenue Atrium
Pelham Bay Park
Players Club
P.S. 1 — Project Studio 1
Jacob Riis Park
Theodore Roosevelt Birthplace
St. Paul's Church
St. Thomas Church

Salmagundi Club
Schomburg Center for Black Studies
Seagram Building
Abigail Adams Smith Museum
Socrates Sculpture Park
South & Midland Beaches & FDR Boardwalk
Staten Island Zoo
Steuben Glass Gallery
Studio Museum of Harlem
Supreme Court of New York
Temple Emanu-el
Whitney Museum of American Art at Equitable
Whitney Museum of American Art Downtown
Woodlawn Cemetery

Calendar of Events

As some things change occasionally, it's best to check before setting out (see index for listings). Please note that some events do not take place every week and are indicated; for schools, (SY) indicates that events occur during the "School Year." Consult the special Calendar of Events under For the Kiddies for for programs exclusive to children.

MONDAY-FRIDAY

All Day:	Gallery Talks at the American Mus. of Natural History (Tue-Sun), IBM Gallery of Science & Art, Metropolitan Mus. of Art (Tue-Sun).
9am	CBS Studios—Joan Rivers taping (Mon-Wed).
10am	Columbia Univ.—Tour (mid May-Aug).
10:15am	MMA—Highlights Tour (Tue-Fri). Supreme Court of N.Y.—Tour.
11am	New York Public Lib. at 42nd St.—Tour. Cathedral Ch. of St. John's—Tour (Tue-Sat).
12Noon	Henry George School—Occ. film or discussion. Park Ave. Plaza—Music (Mon-Sat, til 3pm). MoMA—Gallery Talk (exc. Wed).
12:15pm	Brooklyn College—Occ. Humanities program (SY). J. Pierpont Morgan Lib.—Slide lecture (exc. Mon). Quaigh Theater—1-act play (donation). World Financial Center—Occ. entertainment.
12:30pm	Queens College—Occ. concert (SY). Whitney Mus. at Equitable—Gallery Talk (Tue-Fri).
1pm	CBS Studios—TV taping Joan Rivers (Mon-Wed). CBS Studios—TV taping Geraldo Riveria (Tue-Thu). The Cloisters—Garden Tour (May-Jun, Sep-Oct, exc. Mon). MoMA—Gallery Talk (exc. Wed).

1:15pm	MMA—Highlights Tour (Tue-Fri).
1:30pm	Whitney Mus.—Gallery Talk (Tue-Fri).
2pm	Columbia Univ.—Tour (mid May-Aug).
	National Mus. of Amer. Indian—Video.
	NYPL, 42nd St.—Tour.
	Trinity Ch.—Tour.
2:30pm	Whitney Mus.—Gallery Talk (Tue-Thu).
	Whitney Mus. at Equitable—Gallery Talk (Tue-Fri).
3pm	CBS Studios—TV taping Geraldo Riviera (Tue-Thu).
	The Cloisters—Gallery talk (exc. Mon).
	Columbia Univ.—Tour (Sep-mid May).
	MoMA—Gallery talk (exc. Mon).
3:15pm	MMA—Highlights Tour (Tue-Fri).
3:30pm	Whitney Mus.—Gallery Talk (Tue-Fri).
4pm	NYPL for Perf. Arts—Concert or performance (Sep-May).
6pm	NYPL, 42nd St.—Occ. lecture or reading.
6:30pm	World Financial Center—Occ. entertainment.
7pm	New York Bar Assn.—Occ. lecture (Mon-Thu, Sep-Jun).
	Queens College—Occ. lecture.
	World Financial Ctr.—Occ. entertainment.
7:30pm	New Dramatists Workshops—Readings several eves. (Sep-May).
8pm	Christ & St. Stephens—Occ. classical concert (Mon-Wed).
	Cornelia St. Cafe—Entertainment (Sun-Thu).
	Delacorte Theater, Central Pk.—Theater (Jul-Labor Day).
	Lincoln Center, Damrosch Pk.—Summer entertainment.
	Mannes School of Music—Occ. concert (Oct-May).
	N.Y. Academy of Science—Monthly lecture.
9pm	Red Spot Outdoor Theater—Multi-media show (above 40°).

MONDAY

12noon	Olympic Tower—Pianist.
	Pace Univ.—Film (most Mon, some fee).
12:10pm	St. Paul's—Classical concert.
12:20pm	875 3rd Ave.—Piano playing.
12:30pm	Mark Goodson Theater—Concert (Oct-Jun).
	Whitney Mus. at Philip Morris—Gallery Talk.
	Whitney Mus. Downtown—Gallery Talk.
1:30pm	Queens Borough Lib.—Movies for Seniors.
2:30pm	Donnell Lib.—Concert (most Mons).
	Mid-Manhattan Lib.—Tour
3pm	Pace Univ.—Film (most Mons, some fee).

	York Univ. — Lecture (2nd Mon, SY).
6pm	Donnell Lib. — Occ. lecture or reading (Oct-May).
	7pm
	CSC Rep — Play reading (Spring & Fall).
7:30pm	NY Stage & Film — Staged reading (Spring & Fall).
	Frank Silvera Workshops — Play reading.
	Speak Easy — Open reading.
	Winthrop Field — Summer concert.
8pm	Actors Playhouse — Play (Oct-Aug, exc. Hols).
	St. Mark's — Poetry reading (Oct-Jun, donation).
	Trump Village Camera — Occ. workshop.
	Ubu Rep Theater — Reading (most Mons, Oct-Jun).
9pm	Mona's — Open Mike.
	Pace Univ. — Film (most Mons, some fee).

TUESDAY

Free Museums: Brooklyn Historical Soc. & Mus. (noon-5pm), Cooper-Hewitt Mus. (6-9pm), Guggenheim Museum (6-8pm), International Center of Photography (6-8pm), Jewish Mus., National Academy of Design (6-8pm), The New-York Historical Soc.

12noon	Barnard College — Concert (most Tues, SY).
	Donnell Lib. — Film (Oct-Jun).
	Empire-Fulton Ferry Pk. — Entertainment (Summer).
	Galleria Atrium — Music.
12:15pm	Grace Bldg. — Concert (late Jun-Labor Day).
12:30pm	Crystal Pavilion — Piano playing.
	Fraunces Tavern — Occ. lecture.
	Rockefeller Ctr. — Outdoor concert (May-Aug).
12:45pm	Trinity Ch. — Noonday Concerts.
1pm	Ch. of the Incarnation — Seniors club.
	Middle Collegiate Ch. — Seniors club.
1:30pm	Mus. of Broadcasting — Tour.
2pm	Christ Ch. — Game day (2nd of month).
	City College — Occ. concert (SY).
2:30pm	Donnell Lib. — Film (Oct-Jun).
	J. Pierpont Morgan Lib. — Tour.
3pm	Seagram Bldg. — Tour.
4pm	Long Island Univ. — Jazz (once a month, SY).
5:30pm	St. Thomas — Evening song (Oct-May).
6pm	Donnell Lib. — Occ. lecture or reading (Sep-May).
	School of Tai Chi — Introductory class.
6:15pm	Cooper-Hewitt Mus. — Occ. gallery talk.
	Whitney Mus. — Gallery talk.

6:30pm	Riverside Church—Carillon & organ recital (Summer).
7pm	CBGB's—Theater workshop.
	Fort Tryon Pk.—Entertainment (Jul-Aug).
	Mosaic Books—Open reading (1st of month).
7:30pm	Books & Co.—Occ. reading (Spring & Fall).
8pm	American Theater of Actors—Play reading.
	Columbia Univ.—Occ. film (fee, SY).
	Fordham Univ., Bronx—Film (SY).
	Life Cafe—Poetry reading (exc. Summer).
	Lincoln Center, Alice Tully—Occ. Juilliard concert (SY).
	Performance Space 122—Open movement series.
	Washington Sq. Pk.—Occ. concert (Jul-Aug).
10pm	Columbia Univ.—Occ. film (fee).

WEDNESDAY

9:45am	Lincoln Ctr.—Occ. open rehearsal of Philharmonic (fee).
10:30am	St. Vincent's Hosp.—Blood pressure screening (monthly).
12noon	Barnard College—Concert (most Wed, SY).
	Community Ch.—Group socializing.
	Olympic Tower—Pianist.
	Pace Univ.—Occ. entertainment (SY).
	Queensborough Comm. College—Concert (SY).
12:10pm	St. Thomas Ch.—Sung Eucharist.
12:15pm	Continental Atrium—Concert.
	CUNY Graduate School—Occ. concert (Summer).
	John St. Unit. Meth. Ch.—Occ. concert.
12:20pm	875 3rd Ave.—Piano playing.
12:30pm	Brooklyn Borough Hall—Tour.
	Donnell Lib.—Jazz (Sep-Jun).
	Federal Hall Nat. Mem.—Concert.
	Grace Ch.—Organ recital (mid Sep-May).
	Grand Central Term.—Tour by MAS.
	IBM Garden—Concert by Juilliard.
	Marble Collegiate Ch.—Lunch for seniors ($1).
	St. Peters Ch.—Concert (most Weds, Oct-Apr, donation).
	Whitney Mus. Downtown—Gallery talk.
	Whitney Mus. Philip Morris—Gallery talk.
1pm	Juilliard School—Student concert (Oct-May).
2pm	NYPL for the Perf. Arts—Tour.
	Isamu Noguchi Sculpture Garden—Tour.
	Lower East Side Tenement Mus.—Special Program.
	Place des Antiquaires—Lecture.
2:30pm	Mid-Manhattan Lib.—Tour.
	J. Pierpont Morgan Lib.—Gallery talk.

5:30pm	Henry George School—Seminar series (May).
	Wetlands Preserve—Workshop (2nd Wed).
6pm	CBGB's—Open mike.
	Roberto Clemente Park—Concerts (Summer).
	Columbia Univ.—Occ. lecture (Architecture).
	Harkness Atrium—Occ. concert.
	YIVO Institute—Occ. lecture.
6:30pm	Jefferson Mkt. Lib.—Occ. poetry workshop,
	N.Y. Studio School—Lecture (SY).
7pm	Frank Silvera Workshop—Writers seminar.
7:30pm	Brooklyn Hts. Esplanade—Occ. concert (Summer).
	Carl Schurz Pk.—Concert (Jun-early Aug).
	3rd St. Music School—Faculty concert (SY).
8pm	A Different Light—Reading (Sep-mid Jun).
	ABC No Rio—Occ. open mike (donation).
	Great Kills Pk.—Occ. concert (Jul-Aug).
	Manhattan College—Film (twice a month, SY).
	St. Mark's Ch.—Poetry reading (Oct-Jun).
9pm	Columbia Univ.—Film (Summer).
	Conference House—Outdoor film (alternate Wed, Summer).

THURSDAY

Free Museum: Mus. of Modern Art (5-9pm).

12noon	Barnard College—Concert (most Thu, SY).
	Bronx Comm. College—Club Hour (SY).
	Donnell Lib.—Film (Oct-June).
	Pace Univ.—Occ. entertainment.
	St. Mark's Ch.—Concert (Jul).
	3rd St. Music School—Outdoor concert (Jun-Jul).
12:05pm	Columbia Univ., St. Paul's—Organ recital (Oct-Nov, Feb-Apr).
12:10pm	St. Paul's Ch.—Classical concert.
12:15pm	City College—Concert (SY).
12:30pm	Crystal Pavilion—Piano playing.
1:30pm	Rockefeller Ctr.—Concert (May-Aug).
2:30pm	J. Pierpont Morgan Lib.—Tour.
3pm	Frick Mus.—Occ. lecture (fee).
5:30pm	MoMA—Gallery talk.
	St. Thomas Ch.—Sung evening prayer (Oct-May).
6pm	Coney Island—Concert (Summer).
	Donnell Lib.—Occ. workshop.
	MoMA—Adult workshop (fee).

6:30pm	Donnell Lib.—Occ. book discussion.
	Pratt Institute—Occ. lecture (may be on Mon, SY).
7pm	City College—Occ. concert (SY).
	MoMA—Gallery Talk.
	Port Authority Bus. Term.—Concert.
7:30pm	Books & Co.—Reading (Spring & Fall).
	CBGB's—Open improvisation.
	Midwood Field—Concert (Jul-Aug).
8pm	Columbia Univ.—Bach series (end May-Jun).
	Columbia Univ.—Occ. film (fee, SY).
	Columbia Univ., Deutsches Haus—Occ. lecture (SY).
	Columbia Univ., Maison Française-Film (alt. Thu, Oct-Dec, Feb-May).
	Fordham Univ., Bronx—Film (SY).
	Off-Center Theater—Play reading (occ. breaks).
	Three Lives & Co.—Occ. reading.
10pm	Columbia Univ.—Occ. film (fee, SY).
	International House—Cultural evening (twice a month).
10:30pm	Fordham Univ., Bronx—Film (SY).

FRIDAY

10am	Ch. of the Covenant—Senior program (fee).
11am	Washington Hts. Institute—Cultural program (Oct-May).
12noon	Galleria Atrium—Music.
	H.H. Lehman College—Lecture (Oct-May, exc. Hols).
	Jamaica Arts Ctr.—Jazz (Summer).
12:30pm	Grand Central District—Tour.
	Whitney Mus.—Gallery talk.
	Whitney Mus. Downtown—Gallery talk.
	Whitney Mus. Philip Morris—Gallery talk.
2:30pm	Mid-Manhattan Lib.—Tour.
	J. Pierpont Morgan Lib.—Gallery talk.
	Whitney Mus.—Gallery talk.
4pm	NYU, Institute of Fine Arts—Lecture (Oct-Dec, Feb-Mar).
5pm	Temple Emanu-el—Organ recital.
6:30pm	Christ Ch.—Film series (1st of month).
7pm	Barnard College—Occ. concert (may be Thu).
	City College—Occ. concert.
	Maison Française—French films (donation).
7:30pm	New School—Film series (fee).
	Washington Sq. Pk.—Folk dancing (til 10:30pm, mid Jun-Labor Day).
8pm	Bloomingdale House of Music—Concert (SY).

China Institute—Open house (Sep-Jun).
Columbia Univ., Casa Italiana—Film (donation, SY).
Cooper Union—Entertainment (some fee, SY).
Grace Ch.—Occ. choral work.
Great Kills Pk.—Occ. concert (Jul-Aug).
La Mama/La Galleria—Reading.
Lincoln Ctr., Alice Tully—Occ. Juilliard concert.
NYU—French film (most Fri, SY).
Prospect Pk.—Concert (Summer).

9pm   Columbia Univ., St. Paul's—Coffeehouse (Oct-Nov, Feb-early May).
Cupping Room Cafe—Entertainment (til 1pm).
Educational Alliance—Lecture ($1 inc. coffee).

SATURDAY

10am   Hostos College—Workshop (Spring & Fall).
NYU—Films (SY).

11am   Cathedral Ch. of St. John—Tour.
NYPL, 42nd St.—Tour.

12noon   The Cloisters—Special program.
N.Y. Transit Mus.—Films.
Park Ave. Atrium—Music (til 3pm).
Riverside Ch.—Carillon recital.

12:30pm   Canarsie Pier—Occ. concert (Summer).

1pm   Central Pk., The Dairy—Concert (Jun-Aug).
The Cloisters—Garden tour (May-Jun, Sep-Oct).
Henry George School—Lecture (SY).
MoMA—Gallery talk.
N.Y. Botanical Gardens—Tour (Apr-Oct).
NYU-Film (SY).
Whitney Museum at Equitable—Gallery talk.

1:30pm   Central Pk., The Dairy—Family Workshop

2pm   Battery Pk.—Folk dancing (weather permitting, til 6pm).
Brooklyn Mus.—Workshop.
Central Pk., King Jagiello Statue—Folk dancing (til dusk, Apr-Fall).
The Cloisters—Special program.
Hebrew Arts School—Monthly concerts.
National Mus. of Amer. Indian—Video or perf.
NYPL, 42nd St.—Tour.
Isamu Noguchi Sculpture Garden—Tour.
Public Theater—Documentary.
Queens Mus.—Film.
Theodore Roosevelt Birthplace—Concert.
Snug Harbor—Tour.

	Trinity Ch.—Tour.
	Whitney Mus.—Gallery talk.
2:30pm	Donnell Lib.—Occ. showcase.
	NYPL for the Perf. Arts—Concert or perf. (Sep-May).
3pm	MoMA—Gallery talk.
	N.Y. Botanical Gardens—Tour (Apr-Oct).
	NYU—Film (SY).
	Frank Silvera Workshop—Theater (Sep-Jun).
	Wave Hill—Occ. tour.
3:30pm	Whitney Mus.—Gallery talk.
4pm	Speak Easy—Poetry reading (alt. Sat, donation).
7:30pm	CBGB's—Music ($3).
8pm	Central Pk., Delacorte Theater—Theater (Jul-Labor Day).
	Cornelia St. Cafe—Entertainment.
	La Mama/La Galleria—Reading.
	McBurney Y—Indian powwow (4th Sat of month).
	Prospect Pk.—Concert (Summer).
9pm	Columbia Univ., St. Paul's—Coffeehouse (Oct-Dec, Feb-early May).
	Cupping Room Cafe—Entertainment (til 1am).
	Red Spot Side Theater—Multi-media show (above 40 degrees).

SUNDAY

10am	Great Kills Pk.—Nature walk (Jul-Aug).
10:30am	St. Martin's Ch.—Carillon recital.
10:45am	Church of the Ascension—Music.
	Soc. for Ethical Culture—Music.
11am	Clay Pits Pk.—Occ. walking tour.
12noon	The Cloisters—Gallery talk.
	Lower East Side Tenement Mus.—Special Program
12:15pm	Marble Collegiate Ch.—Coffeehouse.
	Riverside Ch.—Tour (Sep-Jun).
	St. Thomas Ch.—Tour.
12:30pm	Ch. of the Transfiguration—Tour &/or coffeehouse (exc. Hols).
	Grace Ch.—Tour (Oct-Jun).
12:45pm	Cathedral Ch. of St. John—Tour.
1pm	Brooklyn Botanic—Tour (Mar-mid Nov).
	Central Pk., The Dairy—Concert (Jun-Aug).
	The Cloisters—Garden tour (May-Jun, Sep-Oct).
	Crotona Pk.-Tour (most Sun).
	Fort Tilden—Tour (Jul-Aug).

	MoMA—Gallery talk.
	N.Y. Botanical Gardens—Tour (Apr-Oct).
	Prospect Pk.—Tour.
	Queens Borough Lib.—Film.
	Snug Harbor—Tree tour (Jun-Aug).
1:15pm	Wave Hill—Occ. walk.
1:30pm	Central Pk., The Dairy—Family workshop
2pm	Anthology Film Archives—Film (may be at 3pm).
	Battery Pk.—Folk dancing (weather permitting, til 6pm).
	Bronx Mus. of the Arts—Occ. film.
	Brooklyn Mus.—BACA concert (Oct-May, may be at 3pm).
	Center for African Art—Tour.
	Central Pk., The Dairy—Tour (Apr-Sep).
	Central Pk., King Jagiello Statue—Folk dancing (til dusk, Apr-Fall).
	Roberto Clemente Pk.—Concert (Summer).
	Jewish Mus.—Family program.
	Public Theater—Documentary
	Queens Mus.—Special event (most Sun).
	Snug Harbor—Tour.
	Trinity Ch.—Tour.
	Van Cortlandt Mansion—Tour.
	Whitney Mus.—Gallery talk.
2:15pm	Wave Hill—Tour.
2:30pm	Donnell Lib.—Occ. concert or film (Sep-May).
3pm	Abyssinian Ch.—Occ. music (Oct-Jun).
	Anthology Film Archives—Film (may be at 2pm).
	Bloomingdale House of Music—Concert (SY).
	Brooklyn Botanic Gardens—Concert (Jul-Aug).
	Christ & St. Stephens—Occ. concert (Sep-May).
	1st Presb. Ch.—Vocal concert.
	Forest Pk. Bandshell—Concert (mid Jun-Sep).
	Hamilton Grange—Occ. concert.
	Hebrew Arts School—Occ. faculty concert (SY).
	Hebrew Union College—Occ. lecture (SY).
	MoMA—Gallery talk.
	Mona's—Reading.
	Mus. of City of N.Y.—Gallery talk &/or concert (Oct-Apr).
	N.Y. Botanical Gardens—Tour (Apr-Oct).
	Riverside Ch.—Carillon recital.
	World Financial Center—Occ. entertainment.
3:30pm	Whitney Mus.—Gallery talk.
4pm	Grace Ch.—Occ. choral work.
	La Mama/La Galleria—Music (2nd Sun).

	Madison Ave. Presb. Ch.—Occ. chamber music (Oct-May, donation).
	Mosaic Books—Reading.
	Queens Botanical Gardens—Occ. concert.
	St. Bart's—Occ. concert (Fall & Spring, donation).
	St. Thomas Ch.—Evening song (Oct-May).
4:30pm	Backfence—Poetry reading (Aug-Jan).
4:45pm	St. Patrick's—Organ recital.
5pm	Holy Trinity Lutheran—Bach vespers (late Oct-Easter).
	Mus. of City of N.Y.—Special program.
	Nicholas Roerich Mus.—Concert (1st of month).
	St. Peter's—Jazz vespers.
5:15pm	St. Thomas Ch.—Organ recital (exc. Jun-Sep & Dec).
5:30pm	Wetlands Preserve—Workshop.
6pm	Baldwin Piano—Occ. piano recital.
	H.H. Lehman College—Concert (Summer).
6:30pm	Flushing Meadow—Occ. Summer Concert.
7pm	Irish Arts Center—Occ. music and dance.
	St. Peter's—Concert (most Sun).
7:30pm	Christ & St. Stephen's Ch.—Occ. music.
8pm	CBGB's—Reading.
	Central Pk., Delacorte Theater—Theater (Jul-Labor Day).
	Ch. of the Ascension—Occ. sacred music.
	Columbia Univ.—Occ. film (fee).
	Cornelia St. Cafe—Entertainment.
	Prospect Pk.—Concert (Summer).
	West Bank Cafe—Entertainment.
10pm	Columbia Univ.—Occ. film (fee).

For the Movers

To enjoy the freebies of N.Y.C., you must first get there. Sorry, can't help on free planes, trains or subways (unless it's New Year's Eve), but if you're driving into one of the boroughs, then you're in luck as there are many free bridges. Within a borough it's pretty easy—walking, running or bicycling will serve you admirably and cheaply; see "For the Birds" for parks that afford you these opportunities without your having to endure the traffic.

"For my part, I travel to go anywhere, but to go. The great affair is to move."

— ROBERT LOUIS STEVENSON

Here's a list of the free bridges into Manhattan:

Broadway—225th St.
Brooklyn ♣♣ (see below for details)
Alexander Hamilton (179th St.)
Macombs Dam (155th St.)
Madison (138th St.)
Manhattan (Canal St.)
145th St.
Queensborough—59th St.
Third Avenue (130th St.—one way from The Bronx to Manhattan)
University Heights (207th St.)
Washington (181st St.)
Williamsburg (Delancey St.)
Willis Ave. (125th St.—one way from Manhattan to The Bronx)

Remember, many toll bridges can be crossed on foot or by bicycle for free.

Note that the **Brooklyn Bridge** ♣♣ is a masterpiece of engineering design and beauty. Completed in 1883 by John Roebling and his son, Washington, after 16 arduous years of construction and many lost lives (including John's), this was the longest suspension bridge until 1903. Using innovative techniques, such as caissons and steel cables, this bridge provided a necessary link between Brooklyn and Manhattan. With its cascade of delicate-looking cables, this bridge is a work of art that can be appreciated from afar or from a pedestrian walkway.

The prize for the "best bargain" in the transportation category must be awarded to the **Staten Island Ferry**. ♣♣ For 50¢ round trip (cars $2.50), you get a 5-mile, 25-minute cruise in N.Y. Harbor from Battery Park, Manhattan, to St. George, S.I. This voyage provides you with extraordinary views of Governor's Island, the Statue of Liberty, Brooklyn, New Jersey, the Verrazano Narrows Bridge and, best of all, the skyline of Manhattan. Begun in the mid-1800s by the young Cornelius Vanderbilt, the ferry was the start of the "Commodore's" fortunes. The ferry runs 7 days a week, 24 hours a day; for information call (212) 806-6940.

For the Culture Vultures

Nowhere in the world can one find such a diverse offering of museums as in N.Y.C. The city boasts museums dedicated to art, history, culture, natural history, special interest groups and hobbies. You can visit world-class museums, such as the Metropolitan Museum of Art or the Museum of Modern Art; the incomparable American Museum of Natural History; outstanding historical houses like the Abigail Adams Smith, Kingsland House or Bartow-Pell; museums on African art, immigration, the fire and police departments, museums for children (big and small) and those focusing exclusively on coins, American Indians, TV or films. We even have the world's largest museum, in the South Street Seaport.

Associated with many museums are marvelous special programs, including tours, gallery talks, lectures, films, special holiday celebrations and children's programs, above and beyond the gallery outpourings. Though many museums are free (or have a free evening), some have a suggested admission fee. Remember that "Suggested Contribution" means just that — nobody will be turned away for offering 25¢ or less (though you may get one of those looks!).

> *"Layer upon layer, past times preserve themselves in the city until life itself is finally threatened with suffocation; then in sheer defense modern man invents the museum."*
>
> — *LEWIS MUMFORD*

ALTERNATIVE MUSEUM
17 White St. (at 6th Ave., 3 blocks S. of Canal St.).
☎ *(212) 966-4444.*
Hours: *Tue-Sat 11am-6pm. Closed Jul-Aug.*
Attractive modern galleries provide alternative space from the established museums for U.S. and international artists who want to address the social, political and humanitarian issues of our times. Look for the "Annual Day of the Dead" exhibit.
Events: *Concerts with collaborating composers and musicians (fee).*

AMERICAN CRAFT MUSEUM 𝒹𝒹
40 W. 53rd St. (5th-6th Aves.).
☎ *(212) 956-3535.*
Hours: *Tue-Sun 10am-5pm (Tue til 8pm). Closed Mon, July 4th, Thanksgiving, Christmas & New Year's.*
Free Admission: *Children under 12. Otherwise Adults $4.50, Students & Seniors $2.*
Groups: *By appt. only.*
Tours: *Tue evening and Sat mornings or by appt.*
In the age of mass production, it's comforting to know that American handcrafted works still remain a vibrant art form. In fact, this museum's primary aim is to demonstrate artistic excellence in handcrafted design and achievement. Changing exhibitions revolve around 20th C. crafts in many media and art forms, including glass, wood, clothes, jewelry, metal, paper and pottery; many will take your breath away. The 3-story modern gallery space with graceful wooden staircases has the tallest interior museum wall, which is the backdrop for many large hanging pieces and can be seen from the street. A selection from the permanent collection is on display in a showcase on the lower level.
Events: *"Meet the Artist" demos, Tue evening lectures about the exhibition, films and family workshops.*

AMERICAN MUSEUM OF IMMIGRATION 𝒹𝒹𝒹
(See Statue of Liberty under this chapter.)

AMERICAN MUSEUM OF NATURAL HISTORY 𝒹𝒹𝒹𝒹
Central Pk. W. at 79th St.
☎ *(212) 769-5800.*
Hours: *Mon-Sun 10am-5:45pm (Wed, Fri-Sat til 9pm). Closed on Thanksgiving and Christmas.*
Free Admission: *Fri & Sat evenings. Otherwise pay-what-you-want, suggested contribution: Adults $4, Students & Seniors $2. Planetarium & NatureMax (each): Adults $4, Seniors $3 & Children $2.*
Student Tours: *Weekdays before 1pm by appt. only.*
Highlight Tours: *Mon-Sun from 10:15am-2:30pm & Wed at 6:30pm (Jul-Aug). Meet at Info Desk on 1st floor, 769-5566.*
This place is too good to be true! An absolute wealth of goodies await the undaunted visitor of any age. Billed as the "largest museum of its kind," this natural history museum will transport you to dozens of fascinating empires and animal kingdoms. Its 40 halls contain over 35

million items with special attractions including a 1,300-year-old Sequoia tree; a 94-foot diving blue whale; a safari showcasing through African mammals; the 563-carat Star of India Sapphire; the Stegosaurus, an exact replica of a spiked-tail dinosaur; the Tyrannosaurus, one of the two dinosaur skeletons in the world; and the 31-metric-ton Ahnighito, the largest meteorite ever retrieved.

You will be enchanted by fabulous displays of birds, mammals, dinosaurs (a must), fish, reptiles, amphibians, and the cultures and history of the Asians, Africans and the American Indians. A recent addition is the Margaret Mead Hall of Pacific Peoples. Don't miss the truly spectacular gems and mineral collections. A highlights tour is highly recommended (see "For the Tourists").

The NatureMax Theater is not free, but it's an absolute must for all. Its 4-story screen and surround-sound make movie-going a new experience. Call 496-0900 for daily timetable.

The Library, containing over 400,000 volumes, is considered the most valuable resource on natural history in the U.S.

Events *(Call the main number for a recording of events or consult the free monthly publication, "Rotunda"): An amazing program of lectures, classes, workshops and film festivals every week.*

AMERICAN NUMISMATIC SOCIETY
Audubon Terr., Broadway at 155th St.
☎ *(212) 234-3130.*
Hours: *Tue-Sat 9am-4:30pm, Sun 1-4pm. Library closed on Sun.*

Mainly for coin enthusiasts, the museum has one of the most important collections of special coins, medals and decorations in the world, particularly from the U.S. The main focus is on study and research. The library offers 70,000 items, including books, periodicals, manuscripts and pamphlets of a numismatic nature.

THE ASIA SOCIETY ♣
725 Park Ave. (70th-71st Sts.).
☎ *(212) 288-6400.*
Hours: *Tue-Sat 11am-6pm, Sun noon-5pm. Closed Mon & Hols (summer hours may vary).*
Free Admission: *Only on occasional evenings. Otherwise Adults $2, Students & Seniors $1.*

Now housed in a beautiful red granite Park Avenue edifice (1981, Edward Larrabee Barnes), this museum is dedicated to increasing American understanding of Asia and its culture. Through its fine arts collection, bequeathed by John D. Rockefeller 3rd, those interested in Oriental art will enjoy selections from its 250 items covering the past two centuries of Asian art. The exhibit includes monumental bronze statues, figurines, busts, stoneware, ceramics, hanging scrolls and wood carvings from such countries as Java, Cambodia, Nepal, Tibet and Korea as well as China and Japan. Temporary exhibitions augment the cultural experience and have featured Japanese calligraphy and painting and photographs of China.

Events *(some free): Theater, dance, music, films, puppetry, courses, lectures and workshops.*

BLACK FASHION MUSEUM
155 W. 126th St. (Lenox Ave. & Adam Clayton Powell Jr. Blvd.).
☎ *(212) 666-1320.*
Hours: *Mon-Fri noon-6pm by appt. only.*
Admission: *By contribution.*

Affiliated with the Harlem Institute of Fashion, this museum features clothing and fashion items designed and executed by Black and minority designers, dressmakers, tailors and milliners. Exhibitions last about 6 months and have covered such themes as costumes from Black theater and films, the contribution of Blacks to fashion (1865-1965); costumes for America's best-dressed women and men; and bridal gowns by Black designers. Although the shows are generally good, the museum's brownstone is in need of additional refurbishing and tends to distract the eye.

Events: *Fashion shows and block parties, especially during Harlem Week; and special children's programs.*

THE CENTER FOR AFRICAN ART ✦

54 E. 68th St. (Park & Madison Aves.).

☎ (212) 861-1200.

Hours: Tue 10am-8pm, Wed-Fri 10am-5pm, Sat 11am-5pm, Sun noon-6pm. Closed Mon.

Suggested Admission: Adults $2.50, Seniors & Students $1.50.

Groups: By appt. only.

Tours: Sun at 2pm.

This center is the only museum in New York presenting changing exhibitions of African art. Three shows a year will reflect the varying artistic styles of African tribal cultures. It is housed on 3 floors of two restored turn-of-the-century townhouses; many of the original architectural and decorative details have been retained, including a white-marbled vestibule and foyer, leaded windows, decorative ceilings, marble fireplaces and wood panelling galore.

As the museum has no permanent collection (like the Metropolitan Museum of Art's Rockefeller wing), visits here during the year will provide a varied visual palette. Past shows have featured selections from the Musée de l'Homme in Paris (a fairly encyclopedic survey of tribal treasures), "Igbo Arts: Community and Cosmos" (Nigerian masks, textiles and jewelry) and "Art of the Guro" (Ivory Coast masks, figure sculpture, pulleys, weavings and jewelry).

Events: *Lecture and film programs accompany the exhibitions; rentals available (fee).*

CITY HALL & GOVERNOR'S ROOM MUSEUM ✦✦

City Hall Park at Broadway & Murray St.

☎ (212) 566-8681/566-5097. For a hotline on upcoming committee hearings, 566-3917.

Hours: Mon-Fri 10am-3:30pm.

Tours: Mon-Fri 10am-3:30pm by appt. only (2 weeks in advance).

As City Hall has been the home of city government since 1811, it is worth the trip to see the beauty of this French Renaissance and Neoclassical landmark designed by François Mangin and John Mc-Comb, Jr. Originally marble was only on the southern facade, as the rest of the building was not visible from within the city limits and no one thought the additional marble necessary. However, in 1959, a major $2 million renovation replaced the marble with limestone and granite all around, making City Hall far more visually democratic to all New York neighborhoods. A figure of Justice is appropriately perched on top of the cupola.

The outstanding interior feature is the magnificent ornate rotunda. Two marble staircases wind their way to the 2nd floor, where Abraham Lincoln was laid in state for one day (23,000 people filed by). On the 2nd floor is the museum in the Governor's Room. Once the official room

of visiting New York Governors, the main attraction now is the collection of life-sized portraits of our founding fathers painted by John Trumbull. Antique furniture, some attributed to Duncan Phyfe, is also on display, with Washington's desk a highlight.

Make your way into the City Council Room with its impressive mahogany panelling and dais carved with the 10 Commandments. It was decorated in the 1890s in an ornate European style, which serves as a contrast to the American Federal style of other rooms. The imposing, decorative ceiling of "New York Receiving Tributes of the 5 Boroughs" and the marvelous wall portraits (especially of General Lafayette by Samuel F.B. Morse) undoubtedly provide artistic distractions for many bored politicians!

Then explore the Public Hearing Room, done in Federal-style architecture with simple but elegant benches and dais, life-sized portraits and busts. The meetings are open to the public; a calendar is printed before the meetings and anyone can voice his opinion. There are occasional exhibits about N.Y.C. on the 2nd floor rotunda balcony, sponsored by the Arts Commission, which publishes an excellent free guidebook detailing the architectural attributes of the building. By all means, try to take the free tours (See "For the Tourists").

THE CLOISTERS ♦♦♦
Fort Tryon Park.
☎ *(212) 923-3700.*
Hours: *Tue-Sun & Hols 9:30am-5:15pm (Mar-Oct), Tue-Sun & Hols 9:30am-4:45pm (Nov-Feb). Closed Mon & some Hols.*
Free Admission: *Children under 12 acc. by an Adult. Otherwise a suggested contribution: Adult $6, Seniors & Students $3.*
Groups: *By appt. only (fee). Some free services are extended to N.Y.C. school groups, N.Y. State disabled groups and N.Y.C. senior groups from neighborhood centers.*
Gallery Tours: *Tue-Fri at 3pm, Sun at noon. Garden tours on Tue-Sun at 1pm (May-Jun, Sep-Oct).*

This branch of the Metropolitan Museum of Art, dedicated to art of the Middle Ages, is ideally cloistered away on the tip of northern Manhattan overlooking the Hudson River. This monastery-like museum was actually assembled in 1938 from sections of European cloisters, a chapter house and other religious architectural pieces from the 12th to 15th C. The artwork includes the famous Unicorn tapestries, 12th and 13th C. Spanish frescoes, illuminated manuscripts, stained glass, sculpture, enamels, ivories and fabulous goldwork. Medieval background music will transport you to the days of the knights in shining armor. Don't miss the flower and herb gardens, which grow 200 species of plants of the Middle Ages.

Events: *Special programs (not for groups) on Sat at noon & 2pm (check Hol weekends) featuring gallery talks, lectures or films; and occasional concerts.*

CON EDISON ENERGY MUSEUM
145 E. 14th St. (W. of 3rd Ave.).
☎ *(212) 460-6244.*
Hours: *Tue-Sat 10am-4pm. Closed Hols.*
Groups: *By appt. only.*

Through pictures, models, antiques and interactive exhibits, learn the history of electricity and new ways of developing energy. A working, scaled-down model of Edison's 1882 Pearl Street Station and experiments on how electricity affects our lives are illuminating! Of particular interest are the antique electrical inventions made possible and inspired by Edison, such as toasters, sewing machines, fans, "ice boxes," engines and coffee percolators. Old advertising also reveals how housework was revolutionized. A film from historical photos depicts N.Y.C. life at the turn-of-the-century.

The highlight is a fascinating replica of the underground network of pipes and cables which provide the basic services that we all take for granted. A question-and-answer board covers basic topics on electricity, perhaps of greater interest to the kids. Be sure to pick up or write for their excellent free walking tour through Edison's "1st District," the square mile in the Financial District to receive the first electricity.

THE COOPER-HEWITT MUSEUM 🍎🍎🍎

2 E. 91st St. (at 5th Ave.).
☎ *(212) 860-6868.*
Hours: *Tue-Sat 10am-5pm (Tue til 9pm), Sun noon-5pm. Closed Mon & major Hols.*
Free Admission: *Tue 6-9pm for all and always for Children under 12 acc. by an Adult. Otherwise Adults $3, Seniors & Students $1.50.*
Groups: *By appt. only.*
Tours: *Occasional Tue at 6:15pm. Gallery talks and tours for the visually impaired.*

As the Smithsonian's National Museum of Design, this is an absolutely superb place to while away the hours. Begun in 1897 by the Hewitt family as a museum for Cooper Union (founded by Peter Cooper, their grandfather), the collection was given over to the Smithsonian in 1967. In 1976, the museum moved into the old Andrew Carnegie mansion (a splendid vestige of how the rich used to live), complete with stunning Scottish oak panelling, leaded-glass windows by Tiffany and Art Deco chandeliers. It was built in 1901 by Babb, Cook & Willard for Carnegie, the industrialist and philanthropist who wanted "the plainest and most roomy house in N.Y.C." With 64 rooms, he certainly got the latter! A beautiful and spacious garden must be visited, especially in the spring when the overhanging wisteria are in bloom.

Solely dedicated to the decorative arts and the design process, the museum is proud of its collection of over 165,000 decorative art objects, such as furniture, ceramics, glass, metalwork, wallpaper, woodwork, prints, embroidery and textiles that cover 3,000 years of different cultures. The changing exhibitions are excellent and usually drawn from the museum's own works, including a large drawing and print collection. With more than one interesting show at a time, there's bound to be something you will have designs on. Favorite shows have featured the American picture palace, the evolution of writing implements, the story of buttons, the grand old luxury liners, the Fabergé collection, the doghouse and contemporary fabrics.

The Doris & Henry Dreyfuss Study Center and Library houses 50,000 books including rare volumes on design and marvelous collections of periodicals, pictures and book plates (by appt. only).

Events: Summer garden concerts on some Tue at 6 or 7pm; courses, lectures and symposia (fee) with tuition-free monitorships offered for each class; walking tours of N.Y.C. (fee); and children's programs on Sat-Sun, featuring puppet shows, workshops or talks (fee).

DYCKMAN HOUSE
204th St. & Broadway.
☎ *(212) 304-5450.*
Tours: By appt. only.

The only 18th C. colonial Dutch house surviving in Manhattan, this 1783 farmhouse was built by the Dyckman family, who owned 300 acres in the surrounding Inwood area. With a fieldstone foundation, this brick and wood house has a typical Dutch gambrel roof, spring eaves and porch. The interior rooms portray colonial life of the 18th C. with period furniture, clothing, kitchen implements and children's toys. Behind the house is a small garden, smokehouse and military shed used by the British during the Revolutionary War. Thanks to the Metropolitan Historic Structures Association, this historic house has been undergoing necessary renovations.

ELLIS ISLAND IMMIGRATION MUSEUM 🍎🍎🍎🍎
Hudson River across from Battery Park. Ferry leaves from Battery Park, South Ferry.
☎ *(212) 363-6304, 269-5755 (ferry).*
Hours: Daily 9am-5pm for Museum. Ferry runs every 45 minutes in winter (9:30am-3pm) and every half hour in summer (9am-4pm). Subject to change; call to confirm.
Free Admission: To the Museum. For the ferry, Adults $6, Children $3.

Although the author has bent the rules, as the ferry ride is never free, you could consider a stopover at Ellis Island free if you're going to the Statue of Liberty (one ferry stops at both for one fare!). The ferry ride is also a great way to see lower Manhattan. At any rate, a trip to Ellis Island, which opened in 1990 after an eight-year, $156 million restoration program, would be an invaluable and emotional experience.

Through the handsome portals of this French Renaissance building passed 12 million immigrants during the first 20 years of this century. Once called "The Island of Tears," Ellis Island determined whether those who staked their life savings could remain in this country and try to start a new life. Today the museum pays tribute to the potpourri of nationalities and cultures through huge photos of people and families, oral histories, displays of different countries' clothing and treasures, and piles of immigrants' baggage. Exhibit rooms recount the history of immigration through maps, charts and political cartoons. The important roles of the steamship and railroad companies are revealed; advertising posters proclaim the advantage of one ship over another. It's fascinating to examine the ships' manifestos and the immigrants' papers. The painstaking experience of getting processed at Ellis Island comes to life, especially if you were among the unfortunate ones "detained." Special Inquiry Rooms were used for testing one's mental and medical well-being. Photos depict the arduous laboring life of the immigrants once in America.

A 39-minute film containing live old footage and a photo montage tells the emotional story of many immigrants and should not be missed. A walk through the massive Registry Room with its sparkling Guastavino ceiling tiles underscores the awesomeness of the experience for many. Talkphones dotted throughout the museum reveal additional info, especially many people's own stories. A computer monitor for the American Immigration Wall of Honor can access those who chose to honor their family's heritage here.

But no matter where you walk, you will undoubtedly be touched by the faces of those "yearning to breathe free."

FEDERAL HALL NATIONAL MEMORIAL
26 Wall St. (at Broad St.).
☎ *(212) 264-8711.*
Hours: *Mon-Fri 9am-5pm. Closed Sat-Sun & Hols.*
Tours: *By appt. only.*

This Greek Revival building with impressive classic colonnades and a stunning rotunda is a fitting tribute to the site on which George Washington was inaugurated as the first President. Actually rebuilt in 1842 as the new Customs House, it now serves as a historical memorial. With exhibits of memorabilia marking the birth of our nation and the Washington inauguration, this is a good place to learn about our early democratic roots. There are occasional exhibits in the rotunda balcony.
Events: A classical or jazz concert on Wed at 12:30pm (sponsored by the American Landmarks Festival) in the rotunda; and a collection of historical films for loan or on-premises viewing.

FIRE MUSEUM ú
278 Spring St. (Hudson & Varick Sts.).
☎ *(212) 691-1303.*
Hours: *Tue-Sat 10am-4pm. Closed Mon, Sun & Hols.*
Admission: *By contribution.*
Groups: *By appt. only. For school children, tours include a movie, lecture and coloring books.*

This 2-story firehouse-turned-museum pays homage to all those valiant hook-and-ladder companies. On the 1st floor, antique horse-drawn fire engines and carriages dating back to 1857, fire-fighting equipment and old photos will douse you with a colorful, historical insight into the trials and tribulations of early firefighting. The 2nd floor further fires up your interest with excellent memorabilia, including additional fire engines, uniforms, hats, badges, shields, engine plates, ribbons and companies' medallions. An informative exhibit on the history of fire insurance reveals old policies dating as far back as 1661 and international fire insurance insignias or marks, signifying insured houses that would yield a bonus for firefighters if saved. A display case chronicles early fire extinguishers. A collection of Currier & Ives engravings immortalizes 19th C. firefighting. Photos, prints and old photos reveal the horrors of some of the worst fire disasters.
Events: Party rentals.

FORBES MAGAZINE GALLERIES MUSEUM ú ú ú
62 5th Ave. (at 12th St.).
☎ *(212) 620-2389.*
Hours: *Tue, Wed, Fri-Sat 10am-4pm.*
Groups: *Thu reserved for advance group tours only.*

Thanks to the late Malcolm Forbes's joie de vivre and insatiable taste for excellence, works of art and childlike acquisitions, we have this cultural gem. Enter the dazzling display of the Fabergé collection of over 200 jeweled fantasies and luxury objects. The highlights are the 12 Imperial Easter Eggs commissioned by the last two Russian tsars. Drift over to the Forbes fleet of 500 antique toy boats and then review the 12,000 miniature soldiers on parade. Presidential memorabilia, miniature historic rooms, trophies, dioramas, paintings and posters add historic interest. A Picture Gallery of changing exhibits will round off this real find.

FRANKLIN FURNACE
112 Franklin St. (W. Broadway & Church St.).
☎ *(212) 925-4671.*
Hours: *Tue-Sat noon-6pm. Closed Sun & Mon.*

As the name suggests, this artist-run museum provides some hot stuff! It claims to have the largest U.S. collection of published artists' works appearing in books, periodicals, postcards, pamphlets and records. As the space (in a converted warehouse) is somewhat small, the museum has only a limited portion on display at any given time. The installations incorporate printed material into the creative process and are usually quite innovative.
Events: *Performance art off-site (fee).*

FRAUNCES TAVERN
54 Pearl St. (at Broad St.).
☎ *(212) 425-1778.*
Hours: *Mon-Fri 10am-4pm.*
Suggested Admission: *Adults $2.50, Children & Seniors $1.50.*
Groups: *By appt. only.*

This museum of early American history and culture is located in an early 18th C. Georgian house (with 19th C. renovations). Originally built in 1719 as the private residence of Étienne de Lancey, an influential N.Y.C. citizen, it was converted into the Queen's Head Tavern in 1762 by a West Indian, Samuel Fraunces. A watering hole popular with George Washington, this was the site of his farewell to his generals in 1783 after the successful Revolutionary War. Today, the first floor remains a popular dining spot.

Above the restaurant, the museum contains interesting room restorations, especially the Long Room of the olde tavern. A Visitor's Orientation Exhibit illustrates the history of the tavern. A Bill of Rights Exhibit explains its constitutional importance. Displays of artifacts and antiques from colonial life give insight into the times. A 12-minute slide show, "A Colonial Seed Grows a Big Apple," is shown for school groups. This tavern is not off-limits for children; in fact, it's particularly recommended for younger school children studying this period.
Events: *Changing exhibitions with free lectures on many Tue at 12:30pm; and special Hol celebrations on Washington's Birthday and July 4th.*

THE FRICK COLLECTION 🍎🍎🍎🍎

1 E. 70th St. (at 5th Ave.).
☎ *(212) 288-0700.*
Hours: *Tue-Sat 10am-6pm, Sun 1-6pm. Closed Mon, New Year's, Jul 4th, Thanksgiving, Dec 24th & 25th.*
Admission: *Adults $3, Seniors & Students $1.50. Note: Children under 10 not allowed; those under 16 must be accompanied by an Adult.*
Groups: *By appt. only.*

The author is definitely taking liberties with this entry as this museum is, at the time of writing, not free to anyone. However, this personal favorite comes strongly recommended and is reasonable in cost. Once the home of Henry Clay Frick (1849-1919), the Pittsburgh coke and steel magnate, this magnificent 1914 mansion by Thomas Hastings (N.Y. Public Library architect) is modelled both inside and out in the grand 18th C. European style.

The interior highlight is the garden court, a classical Roman atrium, attractively manicured with flowers and greenery surrounding a central marble fountain. A skylight illuminates the garden court as you are transported to the glories of Europe. If that's not enough, the glories of Mr. Frick's art collection will transport you from one fabulous painting or sculpture to the next. Masterpieces by Vermeer, Rembrandt, Renoir, Constable, El Greco, Turner, Whistler, Titian, Van Dyck and Gainsborough adorn the dark wood-panelled walls. Boucher and Fragonard have their own exclusive rooms. Decorative arts, including 18th C. furniture, Sèvres porcelain, 16th C. enamel plates, triptyches and oriental rugs harmoniously complement the setting. Visit this gem in the spring when the blossoming magnolia trees are gorgeous.
Events: *Occasional lectures on Thu at 3pm and summer concerts on Sun at 5pm or Wed at 5:30pm (tickets required, write for 2 free tickets on the 3rd Mon before the event with a self-addressed, stamped envelope).*

THE SOLOMON R. GUGGENHEIM MUSEUM 🍎🍎🍎

1071 5th Ave. (88th-89th Sts.).
☎ *(212) 360-3513/3500.*
Hours: *Closed until Fall 1991. Call for hours once reopens.*
Free Admission: *Tue 5-8pm. Call for new fees.*

Currently undergoing a rebuilding program, Frank Lloyd Wright's architectural masterpiece, the "giant snail," caused quite a controversy upon completion in 1959 due to its unique design. Now it is considered

to be a major landmark of New York's art world. With its new addition, the museum will be able to exhibit even more of its great artwork and dynamic changing shows, which represent primarily art of the last 100 years.

HAMILTON GRANGE MUSEUM
287 Convent Ave. (141st-142nd Sts.).
☎ *(212) 283-5154.*
Hours: *Wed-Sun 9am-5pm.*
Groups: *By appt. only.*

Wanting a retreat from the "hostile" world of the city, Alexander Hamilton had this Federal-period country retreat built in 1802 by John McComb, Jr. (the City Hall co-architect). Hamilton, the first Secretary of the Treasury (hence his appearance on the $10 bill), was able to enjoy it for only 2 years before his death in 1804 in a duel with Aaron Burr. This memorial houses modest period furniture, clothing and monies (of course) as well as exhibits of maps and pictures recounting Hamilton's life in the Revolutionary War and in the formation of the government. You will also learn about his tragic death. A 10-minute film on Hamilton is worth seeing. Take a moment to walk around the garden.
Events: *Occasional concerts on Sun at 3pm; Mozart Festival in the summer sponsored by the American Landmarks Festival; colonial craft demos; and Christmas tree decorations.*

HEADQUARTERS MUSEUM ♿
National Society of Colonial Dames, 215 E. 71st St. (2nd & 3rd Aves.).
☎ *(212) 744-3572.*
Hours: *Groups only by appt. Mon-Fri 10am-noon for School Groups and in the afternoon for Adult Groups.*
Free Admission: *For School Groups only. Adults Groups pay nominal fee.*

Can you imagine a Manhattan townhouse built without any bedrooms on purpose! This unique house, built in 1828-30 by Richard Henry Dana, was intended from the very beginning to serve as a museum and headquarters for the National Society of Colonial Dames in the State of N.Y. Employing architecture and furniture of the 18th & 19th C., this "historical house" recreates the best of colonial life. Highlights include the Virginian entrance hall; a waiting room with pine mantel, panelling and handpainted Chinese wallpaper; a ballroom with an 18th C. English mantel and a musician's gallery; a dining room with Palladium windows; and a withdrawing room with exquisite Chippendale design. The rooms are complete with fine examples of Queen Anne, Chippendale and Sheraton furniture, oriental rugs, paintings and a superb collection of porcelain (look for the bird cages and shaving bowl) and Delftware.

As the museum is open only to groups at present, a strong emphasis is placed on its educational programs, especially for the children (see "For the Kiddies"). While the children's programs stress colonial life, the adult ones explore the design aspects of the architecture and furniture.

THE HISPANIC SOCIETY OF AMERICA 🍎
613 W. 155th St. (Audubon Terr. at Broadway).
☎ *(212) 926-2234/690-0743.*
Hours: *Tue-Sat 10am-4:30pm, Sun 1-4pm (Museum), closed Mon & Hols; Tue-Fri 1-4:30pm, Sat 10am-4:30pm (Library).*
Groups: *By appt. only, 926-2234 ext. 254.*

Situated at Audubon Terrace, this society, founded in 1904, offers a museum and reference library on Hispanic culture, specializing in Spain and Portugal. The main attraction is the 2-tier main court, intricately decorated in terra cotta with a Spanish/Moorish flavor. Arches embrace the art treasures of Velazquez, El Greco and Morales. Archaeological finds include a comprehensive ceramic and pottery collection, Hispanic silver work and Spanish furniture, with the Indo- Portuguese 17th C. cabinets as a highlight. A side chapel offers a sanctuary to 15th-17th C. painting and objects. Murals of Spanish festivals and costumes by Sorolla immortalize the early 1900s in Spanish provinces. Beautiful arabesque wall tiling can be admired throughout this villa-like museum.

A library of 100,000 books on Spanish and Portuguese art, history and literature is on the premises.

IBM GALLERY OF SCIENCE AND ART 🍎🍎🍎
Madison Ave. at 56th St., Concourse level.
☎ *(212) 745-6100.*
Hours: *Tue-Sat 11am-6pm. Closed Sun & Mon.*
Groups: *By appt. only, 745-5214.*
Gallery Talks: *Throughout the day, vary by exhibition.*

Not many corporations can boast of having their own museum, no less one so tastefully done, but IBM certainly can. In a modern new Madison Avenue skyscraper (1983, Edward Larrabee Barnes), an enormous concourse-level gallery offers diverse, professional art exhibitions and at least one major science show a year; shows change about every

8-10 weeks. You won't be disappointed whatever the shows may be; past favorites have revealed Mexican art, contemporary Swedish design, "lensless photography," Impressionists and Post-Impressionists of the Harvard University Museum and American folk art. From time to time, IBM's own fine art collection will be on display. Topical audio-visual programs supplement the displays.

In the IBM lobby, be sure to check out their NYCulture monitors for up-to-date cultural happenings around time. Also, for a delightful respite, visit the adjacent IBM Bamboo Garden (see "For the Lobbyists").

INTERNATIONAL CENTER OF PHOTOGRAPHY (ICP) ♠ ♠
1130 5th Ave. (at 94th St.).
☎ *(212) 860-1777.*
Hours: *Tue noon-8pm, Wed-Fri noon 5pm, Sat-Sun 11am-6pm. Closed Mon.*
Free Admission: *Tue 5-8pm for all and for N.Y.C. school groups. Otherwise Adults $3, Students $1.50 & Seniors $1.*
Groups and Guided Tours: *Tue-Fri 10am-2pm by appt., 860-1485.*

Visualize a museum solely dedicated to the eyes of the camera and you have the ICP, the first of its kind in the city. Exhibitions of up-and-coming and established photographers provide a constant visual feast. In the screening room, films are shown in conjunction with the photo exhibitions. Past shows have chronicled the works of Henri Cartier-Bresson, Berenice Abbott, Bill Brandt, Ansel Adams and Norman Parkinson. Photographs of famous artists and personalities from the permanent collection pop up occasionally.

The museum is housed in a landmark neo-Georgian townhouse (1914, Delano & Aldrich) built for Willard Straight, a banker and *New Republic* founder. You will notice the row of "bulls' eye" windows under the roof's cornice as they are particularly unique.

A Resource Library is open to researchers and students.

INTERNATIONAL CENTER OF PHOTOGRAPHY
MIDTOWN ♠
1133 Ave. of Americas at 43rd St.
☎ *(212) 768-4680.*
Hours: *Tue-Sun 11am-6pm (Thu til 8pm). Closed Mon.*
Free Admission: *To School Groups. Otherwise Adults $3, Students & Seniors $1.50.*

For interesting photographic exhibitions midtown, focus in on this branch of the ICP, with its modern multi-level gallery space. The 7-10 shows yearly are generally thematic (such as the photographs of faith healing or photojournalism in America) or one-person shows (Man Ray or the aerial photography of Marilyn Bridge). A selection from the ICP's permanent collection is on display on a rotating basis. The Screening Room presents contemporary video, films about artists and documentaries about the photographer(s) on display.
Events: *Lectures and educational programs.*

JEWISH MUSEUM
The New-York Historical Society, 170 Central Pk. W. (76th-77th Sts.).
☎ *(212) 399-3430.*
Hours: *Sun, Tue-Thu 10am-5pm, Fri 10am-3pm. Closed Sat, Mon & Hols.*
Admission: *Tue "Pay-what-you-want." Otherwise Adults $4.50, Seniors $3, Children $1 with access to The New-York Historical Society also.*
  Portions of the 1st and 2nd floors of The New-York Historical Society have been set aside to house the Jewish Museum, which is undergoing renovation on 5th Ave. Exhibitions change every 3 months and portray a Jewish theme or some connection to Jewish life, ideas or events.
Events: *Education programs and family activity center on Sun 2-4pm.*

LLADRO MUSEUM AND GALLERY ✦
43 W. 57th St. (5th-6th Aves.).
☎ *(212) 838-9352/9356.*
Hours: *Tue-Sat 10am-5:30pm.*
  The name Lladro is synomous with fine hand-crafted porcelain figurines. At this retail store, a 3-floor museum houses the best of Lladro's craft over the past 50 years. Each display case reflects a particular theme, such as horses, ballerinas, angels, playful puppies, feathered friends, professional people, sports or man and the sea. Some outstanding pieces include Don Quixote, an antique auto, a hansom carriage and a bull scene. The start-to-finish artistic process can be seen in several displays as well as in a 23-minute video entitled "Clay, Color & Fire."
  The 5th floor hosts changing contemporary art exhibits every 2-3 months, usually on a Spanish theme or by Spanish artists.

LOWER EAST SIDE TENEMENT MUSEUM
97 Orchard St. (Broome & Delancey Sts.).
☎ *(212) 431-0233.*
Hours: *Tue-Fri 11am-4pm, Sun 11am-3pm.*
Free admission.
  Housed in an 1863 tenement, this Museum is the first to preserve this early type of immigrant slum dwelling. Its mission is to present and interpret the immigrants' experiences on the Lower East Side through gallery exhibitions (photos, newspaper articles and cartoons, documents and memorabilia), a 20-minute video, lectures, walking tours and special programs. Probably the most interesting aspect of the building is the hallway, which truly reveals the feeling of tenement life with its peeling paint, fuse boxes and darkness. Pick up a brochure and learn about the history of 97 Orchard Street as well as the Lower East Side.
Events: *Programs most Sun at noon, 1 & 2pm (fee), and special series on Wed at 2pm.*

METROPOLITAN MUSEUM OF ART ✦✦✦✦
5th Ave. & 82nd St.
☎ *(212) 535-7710/879-5500.*
Hours: *Tue-Thu & Sun 9:30am-5:15pm, Fri-Sat 9:30am-8:45pm. Closed Mon & some Hols. Due to shortage of guards, some galleries are open*

only part of the day.
Free Admission: *Children under 12 acc. by an Adult.   Otherwise suggested contribution, Adults $6, Students & Seniors, $3.*
Groups: *By appt. only, 570-3711. Educational groups, 288-7733.*
Tours: *An excellent highlights tour on Tue-Fri at 10:15am, 1:15 & 3:15pm and tours of different collections and wings; consult kiosk in Great Hall or call 879-5500 ext. 3791.*
Gallery Talks: *Several lectures daily, consult kiosk.*
Films: *Consult 879-5500 ext. 2036 and film flyer at kiosk and Uris Center.*
Great Hall Info Kiosk: *For listings of monthly lectures, gallery talks, concerts, gallery hunts, special exhibitions and children's programs (See "For the Kiddies").*

As one of the largest art museums in the Western Hemisphere and one of the world's greatest, this museum is a must, requiring many visits. The MMA houses over 3.3 million works of art providing a comprehensive survey from the ancient civilizations of Egypt, the Near East, Greece and Rome as well as architecture, paintings, drawings, sculpture, costumes, musical instruments, and decorative arts of the Middle Ages to the 20th C. Possessing one of the world's best collections of European paintings, the MMA also boasts the most comprehensive collection of American art, including many famous drawings, paintings, decorative arts and sculptures. The primitive art collection, thanks to Nelson A. Rockefeller's generous bequest, offers a vast selection of Oceanic, African and Pre-Columbian art. The museum's special changing exhibitions are always first rate, whether blockbusters like "The Vatican Collection," "The Treasures of Tutankhamen," and "Van Gogh in Arles" or "Costumes from the Napoleonic Era."

Founded in 1870 by a group of influential N.Y.C. civic leaders and artists, the MMA was intended to encourage the study of fine arts and the ultimate incorporation of that high ideal into everyday life. The museum's construction evolved over a century with the first 1880 brick structure by Calvert Vaux and Jacob Wrey Mould facing into Central Park. That was conbined into a 1902 French Beaux-Arts monument (à la the N.Y. Public Library) by Richard Morris Hunt and his son with flanking north and south wings added by George B. Post (McKim, Mead & White) from 1911 to 1926. Notice the uncarved blocks of stone above the main entrance; lack of funds curtailed the intended allegorical carvings of the important civilizations in the history of art. The modern glass-walled additional wings were added by Roche, Dinkeloo & Associated (Ford Foundation architects) in 1975 as the Lehman Wing, in 1979 as the Sackler, in 1982 as the Rockefeller, in 1983 as the American, in 1987 as the Wallace, and in 1990 as the Petrie. The interior Great Hall and the Grand Staircase reflect the collaborative talents of the Hunts and Post. The 2-story Great Hall with skylit domes and its massive arched balcony is impressive, especially due to its changing floral exhibits. Free chamber music concerts fill the Great Hall with dulcet tones on Friday and Saturday nights.

The Galleries: For those seeking guidance on what to select from the museum's broad artistic menu, recommendations include the Charles Engelhard Court and the Little Dining Room (Frank Lloyd Wright) of the American Wing (plus the American paintings); the 19th C. European paintings; the Temple of Dendur (Egyptian, the Sackler Wing); the Egyptian jewelry and the Archaeological Room; the Astor Court (the Asian Wing); the Equestrian Court of Arms and Armor; the 18th C. Syrian room reconstruction (Nur ad-Din); the Cantor Roof Garden; and 20th C. American and European art in the Wallace Wing.

The Robert Lehman Collection (*ground & lst floors*): In an attempt to recreate Robert Lehman's N.Y.C. townhouse, special period rooms and galleries revolving around a central garden were built in 1975 to house his and his parents' fine collections. The highlights feature 14th-16th C. Italian paintings (Botticelli, Bellini), Dutch (Memling, Rembrandt), Spanish (El Greco, Goya) and 19th & 20th C. French (Ingres, Renoir, Monet, Bonnard, Balthus, Degas, Cézanne, and the Fauves). Decorative arts feature Italian majolica (19th C. glazed earthenware), Venetian glass, enamels, bronze and furniture.

European Sculpture & Decorative Arts (*ground & 1st floors*): One of the museum's largest collections, with 60,000 items from the beginning of the Renaissance through the early 20th C., it covers sculpture, woodwork and furniture, ceramics, glass, metalwork (including jewelry), horological (time) and mathematical instruments, tapestries and textiles. The collection's strength reveals Italian Renaissance sculptural pieces; French and English furniture and silver; Italian majolica; impressive ceramics from 16th C. French workshops of Rouen, Marseilles and Strasbourg and porcelain from Sèvres; Dutch Delft; German stoneware and English Wedgwood Room. Room reconstructions from palaces and mansions recreate 18th C. French salons, a 16th C. Spanish patio and 2 Neoclassical English rooms by Robert Adam (the tapestry room from Croome Court and the dining room from Lansdowne House). The textile collection is by appt. only.

The Costume Institute (ground floor): Dedicated to collecting, preserving and presenting clothing from the 17th C. to the present, this Institute with over 30,000 holdings features changing exhibitions of regional costumes as well as fashion and designer wear. Past favorites have featured the designs of Yves Saint-Laurent, "Man and His Horse" and "Costumes from the Napoleonic Era."

The American Wing (1st and 2nd floors): The Charles Engelhard Court is bedecked with 19th and 20th C. sculpture and architectural items, including exceptional stained glass by Louis Comfort Tiffany and John LaFarge, a cast-iron staircase by Louis Sullivan and a replica of Augustus Saint-Gaudens's "Diana" (the old Madison Square Garden controversial nude). The American 18th-20th C. gallery houses some of the best, including John Singleton Copley, Gilbert Stuart, John Trumbull, the Hudson River School painters, Winslow Homer and Thomas Eakins. Period rooms from the late Colonial days (1730-1820) adorn both floors with excellent examples of Chippendale and Queen Anne furniture as well as the classic living room from the Little House by Frank Lloyd Wright. Decorative arts include pewter, silver, coins, cases, candlesticks, glass and ceramics. With the addition of the Henry R. Luce Center, the museum's entire American collection is now on view.

Arms & Armor (lst floor): Mounted knights on horseback from 15th and 16th C. Germany, Italy, England and Spain regally parade their armor (some weighing over 60 lbs.) in the Equestrian Court. Swords, daggers, guns and rapiers are among the encyclopedic collection of offensive and defensive arms from Europe, the Near East, the Far East and America.

Egyptian Art (1st floor): This is one of the finest and most comprehensive American collections of Egyptian art. With 45,000 items dating from 3000 B.C. to A.D. 700, it traces the pre-dynastic period to the Byzantine, featuring reconstructions of tombs and chapels, sarcophagi, alabaster objects, relief carvings, pottery and jewelry. Highlights include the architectural monuments of the Temple of Dendur in the Sackler Wing (given to the U.S. in appreciation of its contribution to restoring the monuments submerged by the waters of the Aswan High Dam) and the Tomb of Perneb; the archaeological room depicting burial rites from Thebes with painted, decorative coffins, burial objects and mummies; jewelry from Middle to New Kingdoms; portrait sculpture from the Middle Kingdom and sculpture of Queen Hatshepsut.

Greek & Roman Art (lst & 2nd floors): Stretching from the pre-Greek to the fall of the Roman Empire, this collection finds its strength in its Cypriot sculpture, Greek painted vases, Roman portrait busts and wall paintings, glass, jewelry and Hellenic silverware. Its archaic Attic sculpture, including marvelous examples of male nudes or "kouros," is considered the finest outside of Athens. Of an excellent set of black and red Greek vases, the prize is "Red-Figured Calyx-Krater" by Euphronios (painter) and Euxitheos (potter); allegedly it was bought by the museum for $1 million. Roman sculpture and wall painting are best revealed in the cubiculum of Boscoreale, a Roman 40-30 B.C. villa buried at Pompeii in A.D. 79.

Medieval Art *(lst floor)*: Profiling the 4th to 16th C. Middle Ages in Europe, the Medieval Hall houses early Christian and Byzantine silver, enamel, glass, ivory and jewelry, and Romanesque and Gothic metalwork, stained glass, sculpture, enamel and ivory; all are approached through the stunning decorative wrought-iron Spanish Choir Screen of 1763. A strong collection of 14th-16th C. Belgian tapestries is hung here as well as at The Cloisters, the MMA's uptown branch dedicated solely to Medieval art. At Christmas, a fabulous tree with an 18th C. crèche is placed here.

The Michael C. Rockefeller Wing: *The Art of the Pacific Islands, Africa and the Americas (lst floor)*: Its African collection has a strong emphasis on wooden sculpture and masks by the Dogons, Bamana and Senufo of Mali and bronze sculpture from Benin (Nigeria). Funerary carvings, masks, wooden figures and totem poles represent the cultures of Asmat, New Guinea, Melanesia and Polynesia. The lands of Mexico and Central and South America reveal Pre-Columbian stone objects, gold and ceramics, while there are native arts and crafts from the Eskimos and American Indians.

Ancient Near Eastern Art *(2nd floor)*: Covering 6000 B.C. to A.D. 626, this collection explores ancient Mesopotamia, Iran, Syria and Anatolia with its strength in Sumerian stone sculpture, Mesopotamian jewelry, Achaemenid and Sasanian silver and goldwork as well as Assyrian reliefs and statues from the Palace of Ashurnasirpal II in the Sackler Gallery.

Drawings: Prints & Photographs *(2nd floor)*: The print collection boasts major contributions by almost every important printmaker, with a specialty in 15th C. German, 18th C. Italian and 19th C. French. Based on Alfred Stieglitz's collection, the Photography Department continues to grow by the acquisition of works by important international artists. An impressive collection (over 12,000 items) of illustrated books, drawings, posters and trade cards is represented here.

European Painting *(2nd floor)*: With 3,000 works from the 12th to 19th C., the collection is strongest in Italian Renaissance (Raphael, Fra Filipo Lippi, Botticelli, Bellini, Titian, Tintoretto, Veronese), Dutch (Van Eyck, Bosch, Bruegel the Elder, Rubens, Van Dyck, Hals, Rembrandt and Vermeer) and French (Poussin, Fragonard, David, Delacroix, Daumier, Manet, Degas, Cézanne, Monet, Renoir, Gauguin, Rousseau, Seurat, Toulouse-Lautrec). There's a fine showing of Spanish (El Greco, Goya, Velazquez), British (Hogarth, Reynolds, Gainsborough, Turner, Constable) and German (Dürer, Holbein the Younger) masterpieces. The 19th C. collection is perhaps unrivalled!

Asian Art *(2nd floor)*: This collection features paintings, sculpture, ceramics, bronzes, jades, decorative arts and textiles from Asian cultures ranging from 2000 B.C. to the 19th C. It is known to be the finest collection of Chinese Buddhist sculpture outside China. A main attraction is the Astor Court, the Chinese Garden Court modelled on a scholar's court in the Garden of the Master of Fishing Nets in Soochow, a city noted for its garden architecture. Also highly regarded are the major Chinese painting collection (Douglas Dillon galleries), the Ming dynasty furniture, Japanese screens, lacquer ware, Indian and Southeast Asian bronze sculptures, and Japanese and Tibetan 17th-19th C. robes.

Islamic Art (2nd floor): Tracing the spread of Islam from the 7th to the 19th C., this collection demonstrates the diversity of cultures. Highlights include glass, jewelry and metalwork from Egypt, Syria and Mesopotamia, royal miniatures from the courts of Persia and India, classical 16th and 17th C. carpets, a 14th C. Iranian mosaic Mihrab (mosque niche) and an 18th C. Syrian room reconstruction of the Ottoman period (Nur al-Din).

Musical Instruments (2nd floor): Founded in 1942, this collection is to the tune of over 4,000 musical works covering 6 continents from prehistoric times to the present. The main performers include European courtly instruments of the Middle Ages through the Renaissance, the oldest piano, rare violins and harpsichords, instruments made from precious materials and a typical violin maker's workshop. The music from these instruments can be heard on available audio equipment.

Twentieth Century, The Lila Acheson Wallace Wing (1st & 2nd floors): Chronicling paintings, sculpture, works on paper and decorative arts since 1900, this collection concentrates on the School of Paris (Matisse, Picasso, Derain, Braque, Modigliani, Bonnard) and the various American schools of art, including "The Eight" (the rebels: Prendergast, Sloan), the "Stieglitz Circle" (O'Keeffe, Hartley, Demuth, Dove), the Abstract Expressionists (Pollock, Gorky, de Kooning, Motherwell), the Color Field painters (Kelly, Still, Stella, Noland) and the Pop Artists (Lichtenstein, Rosenquist). Sculpture is represented in the works of Brancusi, Archipenko and Giacometti. Also, Art Nouveau and Art Deco furniture and metalwork can be seen.

Iris & B. Gerald Cantor Roof Garden: For a commanding view of Central Park and midtown Manhattan, visit this roof garden during May to October. Monumental 20th C. sculpture adds to the already wonderful experience.

Carroll & Milton Petrie Wing: This new sculpture garden court and adjacent galleries reveal 17th and 18th C. European sculptures; many have not been seen in many years.

Events: Lectures, classes, concerts (most at a fee); and see "For the Kiddies" for more events.

J. PIERPONT MORGAN LIBRARY ♦♦

29 E. 36th St. (at Madison Ave.).
☎ *(212) 685-0008.*
Hours: Tue-Sat 10:30am-5pm, Sun 1-5pm. Closed Mon, Hols, Sun in Jul and all of Aug.
Suggested Admission: Adults $3, Children & Seniors $1.
Groups: By appt. only.
Tours: Tue & Thu at 2:30pm (history and library), Wed & Fri at 2:30pm (exhibitions).

This 1906 Italian Renaissance mansion by McKim, Mead & White served as the library of its wealthy namesake. It is rich in marble, ornate wooden carvings, Flemish tapestries, decorative ceilings, antique furni-

ture and a fabulous collection of rare books, manuscripts, drawings and etchings dating back to the Middle Ages. Besides the changing exhibitions, the centerpieces of this extraordinary museum are the two rooms focusing on the written word: the study and the library.

The study is draped in rich, red Damask wallpaper with early Italian religious paintings, ornate bronze and glass bookshelf doors and an impressive carved wooden desk and ceiling.

The library has multi-tiered stacks of rare books under a painted ceiling of delightful female and muse figures depicting mythological scenes. The rare books, including a Gutenberg Bible of 1455, the first edition of the Coverdale Bible of 1535, the "Coptic Acts of the Apostles" (5th C. Egyptian and considered the earliest surviving Christian miniature), beautifully illustrated old church manuscripts and books with gorgeous jewel-studded bindings, are frequently available for viewing, as are other books, manuscripts or letters usually relating to the current exhibit. Try not to miss the bejeweled Stavelot Triptych (claiming to contain part of the True Cross).

The changing exhibitions cover a broad range of artistic works usually relating to libraries or the written word. Previous exhibits have featured the world of William Blake, Holbein and the court of Henry VIII and "Symbolic Animals, Monsters & Demons in Antiquity & Middle Ages."

Events: *Lunchtime recorded slide lectures Tue-Fri at 12:15pm, occasional readings and evening lectures.*

MORRIS-JUMEL MANSION ♿

1765 Jumel Terr. (160th-162nd Sts. & Edgecombe Ave.).
☎ *(212) 923-8008.*
Hours: *Tue-Sun 10am-4pm.*
Free Admission: *N.Y.C. public schools student. Otherwise Adults $3, Seniors & Students $1.*
Tours: *By appt. only. Fact sheets available in 7 different languages.*

This beautiful 1765 Georgian mansion served as the summer residence for the Englishman Robert Morris and his family, who owned 130 acres from the Harlem to the Hudson Rivers with this house overlooking the entire estate. During the Revolutionary War, Washington set up headquarters here in 1776 and fought the successful battle of Harlem Heights. In 1777, the British took over with General Clinton at the helm; later the Hessians moved in. After the war, the mansion changed ownership frequently and became the Calumet Hall tavern in 1790. Over the next 20 years it fell into disrepair. Then Stephen Jumel, a wealthy French wine merchant and importer, bought it for his family's country home and made extensive renovations with wallpaper and fine furniture imported from Paris (some pieces were acquired from the Bonaparte family). Mr. Jumel's untimely death in 1832 has often been attributed to his wife (leaving her the "richest widow in the country"); some believe his ghost still haunts the house. In 1833, Mme. Jumel went on to marry the 72-year-old Aaron Burr, although the marriage lasted only 6 months. In the 1850s, Mme. Jumel became more and more eccentric; she died in 1865. In 1903, the Daughters of the American Revolution saved the mansion from demolition.

Today the interior rooms reflect the 100 years of the different families and styles. The drawing room depicts the Morrises with late 18th C. English furniture and Chinese wallpaper. The front parlor (where Mme. Jumel and Aaron Burr were married) houses American Empire furniture. Napoleonic objects and Empire furniture adorn the Jumel bedroom, while Burr's bedroom contains late Federal pieces including his law office desk. The basement kitchen cooks up the Morris lifestyle. The 3rd floor presents on a rotating basis items from the museum's collection, including Mme. Jumel's fantastic obituary. As the house is on an acre and a half, you can walk along the tree-lined paths to see the rose and colonial gardens.

Events: *Occasional public programs including performances, exhibitions and the annual Historic House Festival (spring).*

EL MUSEO DEL BARRIO ⬤

1230 5th Ave. (104th-105th Sts.).
☎ *(212) 831-7272/369-4096 (Educ.).*
Hours: *Wed-Sun 11am-5pm. Closed Mon, Tue & some Hols.*
Free Admission: *Children under 12 with Adult. Suggested Admission: Adults $2, Students & Seniors $1.*
Bilingual Tours: *Wed-Fri 11am-2pm for groups by appt. only.*

As the only U.S. museum exclusively representing Puerto Rican and Latin American culture, this museum plays an important role in the surrounding community, particularly for children. There are always 2 or 3 different exhibitions of contemporary Puerto Rican and Latin artists plus one gallery featuring only photography, with all exhibitions lasting about 4-6 months. The main attraction is the collection of 16th to 20th C. Santos, saints made from wood, decoratively painted and always associated with a special story.

Events: *Special programs for children 5-10 on some Sun at 2:30pm; occasional lectures and concerts (la Pena) for adults.*

MUSEUM OF AMERICAN FOLK ART ⬤⬤

Eva & Morris Feld Gallery, Two Lincoln Center (Columbus Ave. at 65th St.).
☎ *(212) 977-7298/7170.*
Hours: *Daily 9am-9pm.*
Tours: *By appt. only, 595-9533.*

What a surprise to find whirligigs, weathervanes, carousel animals, painted trade signs and quilts in this modern, multi-level folk art museum across from Lincoln Center, the only museum in N.Y.C. open daily from 9am to 9pm. Enter into the Garden Court with its tasteful seating area and sculptural folk art. The impressive St. Tammany weathervane presides over the Atrium, from which four wings fan out. The two-story East Wing with skylights houses larger works, while the North Wing is devoted to small-scale works from the permanent collection of American folk art, including folk painting, decorative arts and sculpture. The South Wing presents changing shows, everything from Japanese folk art and American folk art painters to a quilt festival. This is a great place to step back in time, with or without a timed visit to Lincoln Center.

The museum's library contains more than 8,000 volumes and 200 periodicals.

Events: *Symposia, workshops, lectures and demonstrations.*

MUSEUM OF AMERICAN ILLUSTRATION

Society of Illustrators, 128 E. 63rd St. (Lexington & Park Aves.).
☎ *(212) 838-2560.*
Hours: *Mon-Fri 10am-5pm, Tue til 8pm. Closed in Aug.*

This showcase for the Society of Illustrators offers the best in the world of illustration. Founded in 1901 by William Glackens, N.C. Wyeth and Charles Dana Gibson (major figures in the art world), the Society today serves the professional community in the creative communication arts. Original artwork by comic artists, cartoonists, caricaturists and

poster artists is always fun to see as is the Society's own collection of over 1,000 contemporary and historic turn-of-the-century illustrations. The annual juried competition for students in May is excellent.
Events: Spring and fall lectures and classes (nominal fee).

MUSEUM OF ARMENIAN DIOCESE
St. Vartan's, 630 2nd Ave. (34th-35th Sts.).
☎ *(212) 686-0710.*   \
Hours: Mon-Fri 3am-5pm, Sat & Sun noon-6pm. Call first.
This small museum features occasional exhibits of an Armenian artist or theme. While you're there, visit the sanctuary of St. Vartan's (see "For the Believers").

MUSEUM OF BROADCASTING ♣♣
1 E. 53rd St. (off 5th Ave.). Moving Sep '91 to 25 W. 52nd St. (5th-6th Aves.).
☎ *(212) 752-7684/4690.*
Hours: Tue-Sat noon-5pm, Tue til 8pm. Closed Sun-Mon.
Suggested Admission: Adults $4.50, Students $3.50, Seniors & Children under 13 $2.50.
Groups: By appt. only.
Tours: Tue at 1:30pm.
Wouldn't it be great to watch old TV programs of *your* choice at will? It's possible at this one-of-a-kind museum that channels old programming to the public. Since 1975, this museum has been collecting, preserving, interpreting and exhibiting radio and TV programs. The 15,000-program radio collection includes radio's beginnings with FDR's 1920 broadcast as V.P. candidate, eyewitness accounts of the *Hindenburg* disaster, Edward R. Murrow's "This is London" WWII broadcasts, as well as news, historic, cultural, political and entertainment shows. The 25,000 TV cassettes feature highlights of such greats as Sid Caesar, Ed Sullivan, "Alfred Hitchcock Presents," "M*A*S*H," etc.
TV programs can be viewed at one of 23 2-person consoles (up to 100 consoles in new building) on a first-come basis. The 63-seat theater has daily screenings of various old TV shows. The archives collection contains rare radio scripts and NBC radio programming from 1927 to 1969.
Events: Lectures and seminars (fee).

MUSEUM OF MODERN ART (MoMA) ♣♣♣♣
11 W. 53rd St. (5th & 6th Aves.).
☎ *(212) 708-9400.*
Hours: Fri-Tue 11am-6pm (Thu til 9pm). Closed Wed & some Hols.
Free Admission: Thu 5-9pm (pay-what-you-want) and always for Children under 16 acc. by an Adult. Also free for N.Y.C. H.S. Students. Otherwise Adults $7, Students and Seniors $4.
Groups: By appt. only, 708-9685.
Library & Study Centers: By appt. only.
Gallery Talks: Weekdays (exc. Wed) at noon, 1 & 3pm, Thu at 5:30 & 7pm, Sat-Sun at 1 & 3pm, 708-9795.

Films: *Free tickets available at 11am for same-day shows (consult calendar).*

To see the world's best collection of modern art, the renovated MoMA (Cesar Pelli & Gruen Associates, 1984) is a new "high" in museum-going. Founded in 1929 with the intention of encouraging people's appreciation of the modern creative statement, today MoMA's collection of over 100,000 items includes everything from painting, sculpture, design, drawings, prints and photographs to the film media. The architectural focal point is the glass-enclosed 4-story Garden Hall with escalators and balconies overlooking the splendid sculpture garden with its greenery, reflecting pools and sculpture. Though the gallery rooms tend to be somewhat stark (so the artwork can speak for itself), the public spaces are bright and airy.

The 2nd and 3rd floors house chronologically the **Department of Painting and Sculpture** collection with such well-known favorites as van Gogh's "The Starry Night," Matisse's "Dance," Picasso's "Les Demoiselles d'Avignon," Wyeth's "Christina's World," and Mondrian's "Broadway Boogie Woogie." Special galleries were designed for Monet's "Water Lilies" and Matisse's "Swimming Pool." The 2nd floor begins with Post-Impressionism, Fauvism, Cubism (particularly Picasso), Futurism, Constructivism, Matisse's "Water Lilies," the Picasso gallery, Dadaism and Surrealism. A special Brancusi room features 10 works from 1908 to 1933. The Russian School adorns the 2nd floor stairwell.

Continuing on the 3rd floor is American art of the 1920s with Hopper, Wyeth, O'Keeffe, and Stuart Davis to American Surrealism with Dubuffet and Pollock through the late 1940s and 50s. Matisse cutouts and "The Swimming Pool" introduce the New York School and the Abstract Expressionists, such as Motherwell, Rothko, Gottlieb and de Kooning. Then Pop, Minimalism and Conceptualism are represented by Johns, Rauschenberg, Kelly and Noland. The museum's strength is also reflected in its coverage of each artist, as it possesses 63 Picassos, 36 Matisses and 21 Mirós.

The **Department of Photography** gallery is located on the 2nd floor; it is the largest such collection in the world, with 15,000 photos. In keeping with the spirit, its strength lies with 20th C. photographers, although it does cover the entire history of photography dating back to 1840 (which few museums can claim). The collection features examples of all the greats, including Ansel Adams, Diane Arbus, Eugène Atget, Bill Brandt, Walker Evans, Edward Steichen and Edward Weston.

The **Prints and Illustrated Books Department** on the 3rd floor offers changing selections from its collection of 40,000 items. This department features the works of such masters as Beckmann, Dubuffet, Johns, Klee, Matisse, Munch, Picasso and Villon. The **Department of Drawings** is also represented on this floor with selections from its 6,000 works in pencil, ink, charcoal, watercolor, gouache, collages and mixed media. Its collection includes Cézanne, Redon, Seurat, Dubuffet, Ernst, Klee, Kupka, Matisse, Schwitters, Johns, Pollock and Rauschenberg.

The **Department of Architecture & Design** offers insight into the evolution of modern architecture, thanks to drawings and models by Wright, Kahn, Mies van der Rohe, Le Corbusier, Rietveld and Johnson.

The history of design begins with furniture and accessories of the 19th C. Viennese style, the Arts & Crafts movement, Art Nouveau, de Stijl, the Bauhaus, Scandinavian and Italian designs up through the computer. Hovering above the escalator is a small helicopter, and nearby a Cisitalia sports car makes inroads in industrial art.

As the first museum department to recognize the motion picture as an art form, the **Department of Film** began collecting in 1935. Today it has 2 Titus Theaters on the lower level (seating 217 and 460) in which to present its 8,000 films, the strongest international collection in the U.S. Films are shown daily (no extra charge); tickets can be collected starting at 11am for same-day shows. Also the "Cineprobe" evenings introduce the works of independent and experimental filmmakers, while "New Directors/New Films" (additional fee) offers those by up-and-coming directors.

Besides departmental exhibitions, the museum sponsors temporary ones including such blockbusters as shows on Cézanne, Picasso and Klee.

Events: *Family talks (ages 5-10 + parent) on Sat at 10am and adult workshops on Thu at 6pm (fee); classic documentaries for children on some Sat at 11:15am; short courses (mainly at a fee); video and slide programs on the exhibits and written material for visiting groups; lectures, talks and films.*

MUSEUM OF THE AMERICAN PIANO ♪

211 W. 58th St. (7th Ave. & Broadway). May move in 1992.
☎ *(212) 246-4646.*
Hours: *Tue-Fri noon-4pm.*
Suggested contribution: *Adults $2.50, Seniors & Students $1.50.*

Thanks to a knowledgeable curator, you can be attuned to the history of the American piano at this small but interesting museum. The walls are lined with lithographs and pictures of old pianos (including a 16th C. spinet and the pianos of such famous composers as Schuman, Beethoven and Mahler) as well as industrial tools, jigs and piano parts. Of particular interest are the experimental action models, designed by engineers trying to improve upon the hammer-striking mechanism of the piano. Best of all, though, are the dozen examples of 19th C. square and upright pianos, many restored and in working order. In fact, if you are lucky enough to play piano, you are invited to try out the ivories.

Events: *Recitals (when move to larger quarters).*

MUSEUM OF THE CITY OF NEW YORK ♪♪♪

5th Ave. at 103rd St.
☎ *(212) 534-1672.*
Hours: *Tue-Sat 10am-5pm, Sun & Hols 1-5pm. Closed Mon, Thanksgiving, Christmas, New Year's.*
Admission: *Suggested contribution, Adults $4, Seniors & Children $2, Families $6.*
School Tours: *Tue-Fri mornings, grades K-12 by appt. only.*
Self-Guided Tours: *Tue-Fri afternoons for adults and children ($1 per child).*

Guided Tours for Adult Groups: *Tue-Fri afternoons, 15 or more per group by appt. only ($4 per person).*
Gallery Talks: *Sun at 3pm.*

What a wonderful place for all ages to learn about the history of N.Y.C. and the country. Founded in 1923, it was the first American museum dedicated to the history of a major city. The museum's U-shaped, neo-Georgian building (1932, Joseph H. Freedlander) with its impressive white marble ornamentation on the reddish brick facade is appealing to look at.

The museum offers a wide range of permanent exhibits including a reconstructed Dutch fort; dioramas of historical city scenes; the history of the Stock Exchange; firefighting equipment; splendid antiques of everything from model clipper ships, Duncan Phyfe furniture, kitchen implements and toys to silver pieces; and the Worth collection of antique clothing. The room reconstructions from olde N.Y.C. homes (e.g., John D. Rockefeller's 5th Avenue home) are excellent. Don't miss the 25-minute multi-media slide show on the Big Apple's history with its terrific photography or the antique doll houses (see "For the Kiddies" for further details).

Events: *Occasional concerts on Sun at 3pm (Oct-Apr) for adults with an informal gathering with the artists afterwards; special Sun at 5pm programs for adults and children including jazz, mime, theater and music (fee); a selection of different walking tours of the city on some Sun (Apr-Oct, fee); and fine children's activities (see "For the Kiddies").*

THE NATIONAL ACADEMY OF DESIGN ❝❝
1083 5th Ave. (89th-90th Sts.).
☎ *(212) 369-4880.*
Hours: *Tue noon-8pm, Wed-Sun noon-5pm. Closed Mon and legal Hols.*

Free Admission: *Tue 5-8pm. Otherwise Adults $2.50, Students &
Seniors $2.*

    Dwarfed by the nearby Cooper-Hewitt and Guggenheim Museums,
this esteemed Academy resides in a beautiful 5th Avenue townhouse.
Its dedication to the arts dates back to 1825 when there existed no art
galleries or art schools in N.Y.C. Its main role was as a drawing society,
concentrating on helping art students and promoting the arts of painting, sculpture, architecture and engraving. Many well-known artists,
such as Winslow Homer, John Singer Sargent and Thomas Eakins, have

been members. Membership in the Academy requires, in addition to a fair amount of talent, that each member donate a portrait of himself and representative art work. Consequently, the Academy has the largest collection of American portraits with over 3,000 paintings, 600 sculptures and 3,500 drawings, prints and photographs. Changing exhibitions include selections from the collection as well as outside shows and an annual competition of members' works.

Events: *Classes offered at the Fine Arts School, 3 E. 89th St. (fee); and occasional lectures and symposia.*

NATIONAL MUSEUM OF THE AMERICAN INDIAN
Smithsonian Institution, Audubon Terr., Broadway at 155th St. (moving to the Customs House in lower Manhattan in 1992).
☎ *(212) 283-2420.*
Hours: *Tue-Sat 10am-5pm, Sun 1-5pm. Closed Mon & Hols.*
Free Admission: *Always for American Indians and for the annual spring events. Otherwise Adults $3, Seniors & Students $2.*
Groups: *By appt. only.*

Founded in 1916 by George G. Heye, this museum is dedicated to collecting, preserving and studying the culture and life of the original people of North, Central and South America dating back to 10,000 B.C. With 3 floors of costumes, artwork, basketry, jewelry and archaeological finds, this museum is the largest of its kind. Each Indian tribe is represented separately by native costumes and cultural artifacts. Of particular interest are "the story of wampum," the Indian's technique of beading, the "Buffalo bundle," the peace pipes, the story of weapons and "the scalp," the Pueblo "kachinas," the Navajo jewelry, the basketry of the Arizona Indians, Eskimo ivory art and Pre-Columbian art.

Events: *Native American arts and crafts; video showings on some Tue-Sat at 2pm; artist-in-residence program; traditional Native American performances on some Sat at 2pm; and annual spring event.*

THE NEW MUSEUM OF CONTEMPORARY ART ♦
583 Broadway (Houston & Prince Sts.).
☎ *(212) 219-1222.*
Hours: *Wed-Sun noon-6pm (Fri & Sat until 8pm). Closed Mon, Tue & all major Hols. Breaks between shows, so call before going.*
Suggested Admission: *Adults $3.50, Students, Artists & Seniors $2.50.*

A wonderful maze of small rooms and multi-level galleries throws new light onto contemporary art in Soho. The New Museum presents many exciting and totally unencumbered exhibitions in all media. Four special shows a year on the main floor last about 6 weeks (with a 2-week break) and cover a wide variety of contemporary artists who have not yet received critical acclaim. The "on-view" lobby area features 3-week shows of young, emerging artists whose works are viewed and selected for immediate showing. By contrast, the special exhibits on the main floor are usually thematic and planned a year in advance.

Events: *Occasional lectures, performances, films and symposia (some free); and a Youth Program for 3rd to 5th graders in N.Y.C. public schools, call Educ. Dept.*

THE NEW-YORK HISTORICAL SOCIETY ♠♠
170 Central Pk. W. (76th-77th Sts.). Jewish Museum housed here as well until 1993 (see Jewish Museum).
☎ *(212) 873-3400.*
Hours: *Tue-Sun 10am-5pm; Library: Tue-Sat 10am-5pm and Mon-Fri 10am-5pm (summer).*
Admission: *Tue "Pay-what-you-want." Otherwise Adults $4.50, Seniors $3, Children $1.*
Groups and Tours: *By appt. only.*

Many people probably think that this is a place where scholars endlessly spew out dates, and they are completely unaware that a fantastic museum resides here. Founded in 1804 for the collection, preservation and dissemination of history about N.Y.C., New York State and the Union, this treasure house of Americana makes history dance before your very eyes.

The outstanding permanent collection includes antique furniture, household utensils, toys and dolls, paperweights, firefighting equipment and tools. Fine examples of American portrait paintings are by Charles Willson Peale, Gilbert Stuart, John Trumbull, Benjamin West and John Singleton Copley. Original watercolors of Audubon's birds seem to be everywhere. A gorgeous collection of Tiffany stained-glass lamps, windows and other works of art can be found on the 2nd floor. While The Jewish Museum is in residence, some exhibits may not be available for viewing.

A library of 600,000 volumes including manuscripts, pamphlets and prints is particularly great for American history students. It has the best collection of 18th C. New York newspapers, genealogical material, local history on each state and letters of G. Washington.
Events: *"Why History?" annual program, occasional lectures, concerts and films. (some fee)*

NEW YORK POLICE DEPARTMENT MUSEUM ♠
235 E. 20th St. (2nd-3rd Aves.).
☎ *(212) 477-9753.*
Hours: *Mon-Fri 9am-3pm. Closed summer.*
Groups: *Tours for all ages by appt. only.*

N.Y.C.'s boys in blue offer a colorful array of police memorabilia dating back to the force's inception in 1663. There are display cases with fabulous antique pistols and guns including Al Capone's machine gun, a WWI Spandau aircraft gun and a valuable Lüger. A marvelous collection of antique uniforms, caps, medals, badges, handcuffs, billy clubs and old communication devices, such as telephones, experimental transmitters, telegraphs and a switchboard, brings the policeman's world into better view. Old photos decorate the walls. One special display reveals the frightening weaponry of today's youth gangs.

One of the more interesting exhibits is the story of crime detection before fingerprinting; there are also detailed descriptions of fingerprinting with examples of how detectives cracked tough cases by using those unique grooves on our fingers and hands!

You will learn about the workings of the specialty divisions, like ballistics, bomb squad, crime scene unit and emergency (bridge jumpers). Definitely worthwhile, especially with a guided tour (see "For the Tourists").

NEW YORK PUBLIC LIBRARY FOR THE PERFORMING ARTS 🍎🍎
(See "For the Bookworms.")

NEW YORK UNEARTHED
17 State St. (at Pearl St.).
☎ *(212) 363-9372*
Hours: *Mon-Fri noon-6pm. Sat hours may begin.*

In the shadow of Lower Manhattan's mighty skyscrapers is New York Unearthed, an archaeological museum dedicated to digs of New York City. A branch of the South Street Seaport Museum, this "find" presents 10 dioramas of the history of New York City and some of its archaeological mementos, including flints, bones, ceramics, glass, china, clay pipes and even a pair of false teeth. The displays feature such topics as lunchtime around 1950, a tenement in the 1880s, Washington Square in 1850, an 18th C. silversmith shop, taverns in the 1700s and Native American life.

Downstairs, you can watch the preservation process in progress, as many archaeological pieces are being worked on. An 8-minute video about digs and 7" segments of unexcavated walls with peek-a-boo windows are also on view.

OLD MERCHANT'S HOUSE 🍎
29 E. 4th St. (Lafayette St. & the Bowery).
☎ *(212) 777-1089.*
Hours: *Sun 1-4pm. Closed Aug.*
Free Admission: *Children under 12 acc. by an Adult. Otherwise Adults $2, Students & Seniors $1.*
Tours: *Sun 1-4pm or weekday tours by appt. only for groups of 20-50.*

Built in 1832 as a Federal-style row house, this house became the residence of Seabury Tredwell, a successful hardware merchant, in 1835. The house stayed in the family until 1933 when Tredwell's youngest daughter, Gertrude, died at 93. After extensive renovations, today it is a museum reflecting Tredwell's lifestyle in the 1830s. Knowledgeable guides take you on a 30-minute tour of the first 3 floors. Of special interest are the kitchen, the Greek Revival parlor rooms and the bedrooms, all filled with stunning period furniture. Display cases of antique clothing, fans, combs, shoes, gloves and shoeboxes reveal the fashion of the times. As there really aren't too many easily accessible landmark homes like this in Manhattan, it is worth the small admission fee.

NICHOLAS ROERICH MUSEUM
319 W. 107th St. (Broadway & Riverside Dr.).
☎ *(212) 864-7752.*
Hours: *Tue-Sun 2-5pm. Closed Mon.*

Admission: *Donation.*

In a tribute to Nicholas Roerich, a Russian artist, philosopher, scientist and humanitarian who believed that "Art will unify humanity," this townhouse museum has a permanent collection of his work which includes his paintings and published works. The 3 floors of exhibit space also include a community gallery for established and up-and-coming artists and artisans.

Events: *Monthly art exhibits; and concerts or recitals on 1st Sun of month at 5pm and poetry readings.*

THEODORE ROOSEVELT BIRTHPLACE ●

28 E. 20th St. (Broadway & Park Ave. S.).
☎ *(212) 260-1616.*
Hours: *Wed-Sun 9am-5pm. Closed Mon & Tue.*
Free Admission: *Children under 16, Seniors & School Groups. Otherwise $1.*
Groups: *By appt. only.*

This memorial to the only U.S. President born in N.Y.C. is a fascinating place to visit, especially for history buffs. Part of the tour includes the reconstructed Gothic Revival brownstone of TR's birthplace; some of the Victorian furniture is original. The main attractions are the displays and exhibits of TR's memorabilia, including pictures, photos, writings, books, diaries, political cartoons and presidential paraphernalia. Also of interest was TR's love of nature and his role in conservation. Clearly he was a splendid man; so speak softly and no big sticks allowed!

Events: *Classical music concerts every Sat at 2pm; occasional free lectures.*

SCHOOL OF VISUAL ARTS MUSEUM

209 E. 23rd St. (2nd-3rd Aves.).
☎ *(212) 679-7350.*
Hours: *Mon-Thu 9am-8:30pm, Fri-Sat 9am-4:30pm (Oct-Apr). Closed Sun & Hols. Call first.*

The professional showcase for the SVA is this one-room gallery, which hosts 5 exhibits a year. Contemporary American painting, sculpture, prints or photos are the visual offering. Past exhibits have featured Rauschenberg, Warhol and Noland, but not all the artists are in that league. Openings are available to the public; call Public Relations for dates.

THE ABIGAIL ADAMS SMITH MUSEUM ●

421 E. 61st St. (1st & York Aves.).
☎ *(212) 838-6878.*
Hours: *Mon-Fri 10am-noon for groups, Mon-Fri noon-4pm and Sun 1-5pm for general public.*
Free Admission: *Children under 12. Otherwise Adults $2, Seniors & Students $1.*
Groups: *By appt. only in mornings.*

Most people do not know about this magnificent stone coach house

in Manhattan and have probably passed it many times unwittingly. Surrounded by a stone wall and manicured shrubs, it's well disguised. Built in 1799 on the 23-acre estate of Abigail Adams (daughter of the 2nd President) and her husband, William S. Smith (aide to Washington), it is now run by the Colonial Dames of America who purchased the house in 1924 and restored the rooms to the Federal period. The checkered history of this coach house comes alive thanks to the informative guides, who take you through the 9 rooms of colonial antiques.

A delightful 18th C. style garden awaits you behind the house. It's worth a stopover in the spring just to relax among the fragrant tulips and lilacs.

Events: *Special programs 2nd Sun of month (Sep-May) feature lectures, concerts, walking tours or children's workshops; and rentals (fee).*

SOUTH STREET SEAPORT MUSEUM 🍎🍎🍎
At Fulton St. between Water & South Sts.
☎ *(212) 669-9424/9400.*

This recently renovated 11-block area, reminiscent of the South Street Seaport's heyday in the 19th C. with its restored Federal row houses, a replicated fish market and piers (with anchored sailing ships), is the world's largest museum.

As the first port for N.Y.C., the harbor between what is now the Battery and the Brooklyn Bridge was a thriving port, especially from 1800 to 1870. Landfills or "water lots" built up the area of South Street (the original shoreline was at Pearl St.) with warehouses and markets, and the place bristled with activity from the dock loaders and street vendors. In 1814, Robert Fulton began his Fulton Ferry steamboat service to Brooklyn, which increased the importance of the harbor. But with the advent of the oceanliner in the late 19th C. and its need for deeper waters, South Street was replaced by docks along the Hudson River. The area was never to be the same again.

In the early 1960s, a systematic series of urban-renewal-erected

office buildings on South Street threatened to destroy the remaining vestiges of harbor life. But the South Street Seaport Preservation began its campaign in 1967 to save the 11 blocks around the Brooklyn Bridge. The committee's perseverance paid off and the result was unveiled in 1984.

The focal points are the piers and the restored "village" (secluded from traffic) at Fulton and Pearl Streets, which offers food, entertainment, shopping, history, museums and tours. It is important to note that the museum, tours (particularly of the harbor ships), lectures and South Street Seaport film are all at a rather high tariff. But you can walk around and soak up the great atmosphere for free. Street entertainment abounds in nice weather. Guaranteed you won't get away without a nosh at the New Fulton Market and Pier 17, excellent places to have lunch or dinner as everyone can select his own snack and there's generous seating available. Be sure to check out the following freebies —

Bowne & Co. Stationers
211 Water St.
☎ *(212) 669-9451.*
Hours: *Daily 10am-5pm.*
One of the first printing companies (1775) in N.Y.C., this reconstructed shop is complete with old presses, type sorts and stamps; written placards describe the printing process. Free printing demos are given throughout the day.

New Fulton Market
At Fulton St., between Water & South Sts.
☎ *(212) 732-7678.*
Hours: *Mon-Sun 10am-10pm.*
This 1983 replica of the 1882 New Fulton Market (where wholesale food was sold until the 1960s, now at Hunt's Point) has 4 floors of restaurants and food stalls with temptations of ethnic food from curries to knishes. Beekman pushcarts sell wares in and outdoors as in the 1800s.

The Piers
East River & Fulton St.
Pier 16 has been transformed into one large floating museum,

permanently anchored with turn-of-the-century vessels: the 1911 *Peking* (the interior is part of the museum tour for a fee), the 1893 wooden fishing schooner *Lettie G. Howard*, the small wooden tugboat *W.O. Decker*, the 1885 3-mast tail ship *Wavertree*, the 1925 steam ferry *Major General William H. Hart*, the 19th C. 2-mast schooner *Pioneer*, the 19th C. paddlewheeler *Andrew Fletcher*, the steamboat *DeWitt Clinton* and the 1908 *Ambrose Lightship*. The Seaport Line Harbor Cruise offers daytime and evening boat trips (fee) lasting from 90 minutes to 3 hours depending upon the cruise, (212) 406-3434. The pier also hosts the enoyable "Summerpier" concerts on most Sat at 8pm (Jul & Aug, times may change); pick up tickets 2 hours before at the box office. Pier 17 is a striking 3-story glass and steel pavilion jutting out 400 feet into the East River with 120 shops, cafes and restaurants. A deck overlooking the East River is the ideal resting spot.

Schermerhorn Row
Between Water & South Sts. at Fulton St.
    This row of renovated 1811 Federal brick warehouses now houses trendy stores.

Titanic Lighthouse
At Pearl & Fulton Sts.
    This is the site of the original shoreline and it honors "those lost on the disastrous trip on the *Titanic*."
Events: *Free outdoor concerts in summer, Hol celebrations and international festivals.*

STATUE OF LIBERTY ♦♦♦♦
Liberty Island, N.Y.C. Harbor.
☎ *(212) 732-1286/269-5755 (ferry).*
Hours: *Ferries leave from Battery Park, South Ferry, every 45 minutes in winter (9:30am-3pm) and every half hour in summer (9am-4pm). Subject to change; call to confirm. American Museum of Immigration open daily 9:15am-5pm.*
Free Admission: *To the Museum & Statue; however, the ferry costs: Adults $6, Children 11 and under $3 (trip includes Ellis Island). Group rate for 25 or more.*

    Impressively guarding N.Y. Harbor, Ms. Liberty must unquestionably be the most famous statue or piece of sculpture in America. Thanks to Frédéric Auguste Bartholdi, a French sculptor, and the generosity of the French people who wanted to pay tribute to the freedom and liberty of America, this present found its home in 1886. Topped by a spiked crown, Ms. Liberty holds the Declaration of Independence in her left hand and the famous torch in her right (305 feet above sea level), while her feet are breaking the shackles of tyranny. As the statue itself is 151 feet high with a 35-foot waistline and weighs 225 tons, it's not surprising that Bartholdi faced many structural difficulties, some of which were solved only after consulting with Alexandre Gustave Eiffel (who had already tackled his Tower).

    What's always spectacular is the view from her crown; when you gaze out into the fabulous harbor, the ascent up 171 stairs is worth the effort. (The torch has been closed to visitors since 1916.)

Your journey should also include a stroll around the lovely grounds, especially the sculpture garden with bronze statues, which pays tribute to the supporters and creators of the statue. Let us not forget Emma Lazarus, the American poet whose famous 1883 poem includes the passionate line, "Give me your tired, your poor, your huddled masses yearning to breathe free...." There's no doubt that Ms. Liberty was an inspiration to all those turn-of-the-century immigrants who arrived in N.Y. Harbor by the shipload.

THE STUDIO MUSEUM OF HARLEM ¢
144 W. 125th St. (Lenox Ave. & Adam Clayton Powell Jr. Blvd.).
Hours: *Wed-Fri 10am-5pm, Sat-Sun 1-6pm. Closed Mon & Tue.*
Free Admission: *Wed for Senior Citizens. Otherwise Adults $2, Children, Seniors & Students $1.*
Group Tours: *By appt. only on Wed-Fri 10:30am-3pm, Sat 1-5pm.*

Serving as a principal center for the study of Black art, this museum offers wonderful changing exhibitions on contemporary and historical African, Caribbean and American art. Set against attractively designed modern galleries, previous shows have featured Haitian art, African masks, Black contemporary sculpture, James VanDerZee photos of the Harlem Renaissance of the 1920s and 30s, and Black American quilts.

Emphasis is also placed on special programs. The artist-in-residence programs allow tour groups to observe the creative process in the artist's studio. A yearly co-op school program sends artists into the schools to guide children creatively. The best student artwork is then displayed at the art gallery at ACP State Office across the street.

Their latest addition is a new gift shop. An adjacent sculpture garden will feature changing exhibits once it's completed in 1992.
Events *(some for a fee): Puppet shows, concerts, symposia, lectures, gallery talks, storytelling with dance and music, poetry involving both children and adults; and films.*

TRINITY CHURCH MUSEUM
74 Trinity Pl. (at Broadway & Wall St.).
☎ *(212) 602-0847/0848.*
Hours: *Mon-Fri 9:45-11:45am, 1-3:45pm, Sat 10am-3:45pm, Sun 1-3:45pm. Not open during concerts.*

While at Trinity Church (see "For the Believers"), you might drop in on this one-room museum tracing the church's history, evolution and contribution to society. Diaries, photos, artifacts and descriptions are competently arranged; a 10-minute slide show illuminates the parish's history. An illustrated timeline traces the life of the parish and the city from the 17th C. to the present.

UKRAINIAN MUSEUM
203 2nd Ave. (12th-13th Sts.).
☎ *(212) 228-0110.*
Hours: *Wed-Sun 1-5pm.*
Free Admission: *Children under 6. Otherwise Adults $1, Seniors & Students $.50.*

Not the most inviting greeting awaits you as you must negotiate an apartment building with a buzzer system. Inside the museum are modest changing exhibits on Ukrainian culture and history. A festive permanent collection features ceramics, metalwork and costumes. The highlight is the annual Ukrainian Easter Egg exhibition (early Mar), lasting for several months.
Events: *Annual Easter Egg workshops for children, spring and summer workshops, traditional Christmas & Hol ornaments.*

WHITNEY MUSEUM OF AMERICAN ART 🍎🍎🍎
945 Madison Ave. (at 75th St.).
☎ *(212) 570-3600/3676.*
Hours: *Tue 1-8pm, Wed-Sat 11am-5pm, Sun & Hols noon-6pm. Closed Mon & National Hols.*
Free Admission: *Tue 6-8pm for all and for all N.Y.C. Secondary School Groups, College Students & Children under 12 acc. by an Adult. Otherwise Adults $5, Seniors $3.*
Gallery Talks: *Tue-Thu at 1:30, 2:30 and 3:30pm (Tue also at 6:15pm), Fri at 12:30 & 2:30pm, Sat-Sun 2 & 3:30pm.*

Don't be put off by the somewhat austere exterior of this museum. This 5-story inverted wedding cake with irregularly shaped windows, completed by Marcel Breuer in 1966, offers an excellent view of 20th C. American art.

As early as 1915, Gertrude Vanderbilt Whitney offered young artists the chance to meet and display their work in her Greenwich Village studio. She encouraged them by buying their work, which became the nucleus of her 1931 Whitney Museum. Today, after several relocations, the museum still remains the primary salon and supporter of contemporary American art, especially with its all-important biennial show.

The changing exhibitions cover a wide range of American art with an

emphasis on the 20th C., particularly living artists. The museum boasts one of the world's foremost collections of the works of Calder, de Kooning, Gorky, Hopper, Nevelson and Noguchi. Since film and videotape are part of the modern art scene, there are frequent shows dedicated to those media. Of the permanent collection a favorite is the Calder circus, which must not be missed. Also be sure to find the little village by Simonds, tucked away in the staircase corners.

Events: *Occasional lectures, films and summer concerts; an Artreach program introduces N.Y.C. children to art.*

WHITNEY MUSEUM OF AMERICAN ART AT EQUITABLE CENTER &

787 7th Ave. (at 51st St.).
☎ *(212) 554-1113/1000.*
Hours: *Tue-Fri 11am-5pm (Thu til 7:30pm), Sat noon-5pm. Closed Sun, Mon & major Hols.*
Gallery Talks: *Tue-Fri at 12:30 & 2:30pm, Sat at 1pm.*

In the lobby of the impressive Equitable Center (see "For the Lobbyists") is the one-room North Gallery of the Whitney Museum with its 5 changing exhibitions. The Whitney's branches carry on the museum's mission of showing 20th C. American artists with an emphasis on living ones.

WHITNEY MUSEUM OF AMERICAN ART AT PHILIP MORRIS & &

120 Park Ave. (at 42nd St.).
☎ *(212) 878-2453/2550.*
Hours: *Mon-Sat 11am-6pm, Thu eve until 7:30 (Gallery). Mon-Sat 7:30am-9:30pm, Sun 11am-7pm (Sculpture Garden).*
Tours: *By appt. only.*
Gallery Talks: *Mon, Wed & Fri at 12:30pm.*

Imagine being greeted by a 10-foot-high icebag, a giant typewriter eraser or a crushed-up automobile! That or something equally monumental awaits you in the impressive sculpture garden of the Philip Morris building. With an attractive combination of glass, granite and greenery, this 2-story enclosed pedestrian plaza provides a modern backdrop for 20th C. American artists, such as Claes Oldenburg, Alexander Calder, John Chamberlain and Louise Bourgeois. And better yet, you can sit and relax among the sculpture and eat your lunch. An adjacent gallery offers 6 different exhibits during the year with an emphasis on painting, drawing and sculpture. Bravo for Philip Morris and their support of the arts.

Events: *Informal mid-day and evening performances.*

WHITNEY MUSEUM OF AMERICAN ART DOWNTOWN AT FEDERAL RESERVE PLAZA &

Lower level, 33 Maiden La.
☎ *(212) 943-5657/5655.*
Hours: *Mon-Fri 11am-6pm. Closed major Hols.*
Gallery Talks: *Mon, Wed & Fri at 12:30pm.*

For a cultural escape from the world of high finance, a visit to this branch of the Whitney Museum of American Art will pay a big return. Exhibits change every 2 to 3 months and can either be loan shows or thematic group ones, drawing upon the Whitney's vast art reserves. Though the gallery space is only one large room, it's well-lit and always interesting.

YESHIVA UNIVERSITY MUSEUM
Pollack Library, 2520 Amsterdam Ave. (at 185th St.).
☎ *(212) 960-5390.*
Hours: *Tue-Thu 10:30am-5pm, Sun noon-6pm (Sep-Jul).*
Free Admission: *Children under 3. Otherwise Adults $3, Children under 16 $1.50.*

This museum has one major show a year on either a historic, fine arts or philosophical Jewish theme. Past exhibits have included wedding symbols, children's books, a retrospective of a Zionist painter and the art of celebration (the building of a town and sukkot with facades from 18th C. engravings). In the East gallery, changing exhibitions present the works of photographers and painters on contemporary Jewish themes. The 4th floor contains 10 synagogue models, representing different cultures.

The Bronx

BARTOW-PELL MANSION ♥♥
Shore Rd., Pelham Bay Pk. (opposite Pelham Split Rock clubhouse).
☎ *(212) 885-1461.*
Hours: *Wed, Sat-Sun noon-4pm.*
Free Admission: *Children under 12. Otherwise Adults $2.*
Group Tours: *By appt. only.*

This pleasing stone mansion, built in 1836 for Robert Bartow, is the third house on the site where Thomas Pell lived after buying the surrounding land from the Indians in 1654. Bought by the city in 1888, the house was restored in 1914 by the architects Delano & Aldrich for the International Garden Club, which has maintained it ever since.

With splendid examples of furniture and accessories from the Federal period (1810-40), the rooms are filled with treasures, many on loan from the Metropolitan Museum of Art. Each room has its own book, which describes in great detail every item contained within. The highlights include: the entrance foyer with its graceful elliptical staircase and mahogany bannister; the Greek Revival drawing and dining rooms with American and French Empire furniture; the library with its mahogany and rosewood piano circa 1830; the red bedroom with an Aubusson 19th-C. rug and canopy sleigh bed draped with red and grey satin and crowned with a "couronne de lit"; and the upstairs reception room containing a N.Y. Empire settee with symmetrical hammer arms and carved-leaf and rosette decorations. The entire house is really marvellous.

The backyard has a terraced garden with a lily pond.

BRONX MUSEUM OF THE ARTS ✦✦
1040 Grand Concourse (at 165th St.).
☎ *(212) 681-6000.*
Hours: *Mon-Thu & Sat 10am-4:30pm, Sun 11am-4:30pm. Closed Fri.*
Free Admission: *Children under 12. Otherwise Adults $2, Seniors & Children $1.*
Group Tours: *By appt. only (fee).*

Founded in 1971 to stimulate the community's appreciation of the visual arts, this museum houses multiple galleries, a sculpture garden, a classroom, a cable-TV production studio, a darkroom and a computer graphics lab. The galleries feature changing, top-notch exhibitions with an emphasis on 20th C. and contemporary art, community art groups and shows of or about the Bronx. In addition, the museum's outreach program has established various satellite galleries around the borough and provides art classes in public schools.
Events: *Free films on some Sun at 2pm, workshops, classes and camp (fee).*

MARITIME MUSEUM AT FORT SCHUYLER
SUNY Maritime College, Fort Schuyler.
☎ *(212) 409-7200.*
Hours: *Mon-Fri 9am-4pm, Sat-Sun noon-4pm (Sat-Sun only in Sep-May).*

The Maritime Museum commemorates 2 important events at Fort Schuyler: first, the building of the fort in 1856 for protection of N.Y.C., and second, the founding of the school in 1874. Exhibits reveal the history and importance of the U.S. Merchant Marine and other sea-going governmental agencies, ships and companies that have played a role in international trade, and the Alumni Hall of Fame. Ship memorabilia include flags, wheels, bells, paintings and photos. The twenty-three ship models on view range from sailing, merchant vessels to modern freighters and tankers.

POE COTTAGE MUSEUM
Poe Pk., Grand Concourse & E. Kingsbridge Rd.
☎ *(212) 881-8900.*
Hours: *Wed-Fri 9am-5pm, Sat 10am-4pm, Sun 1-5pm.*
Free Admission: *Children under 12 acc. by Adult and during Poe week in Apr. Otherwise $1.*
Tours: *By appt. only.*

In 1846, Edgar Allan Poe, the famous mystery/horror short story writer and poet, moved to this simple white colonial English/Dutch house (built in 1812 for sharecroppers). His wife was dying of tuberculosis and they thought the "country" air might help; sadly, she died that first summer. In poverty, Poe remained here with his mother-in-law and wrote several works, including parts of "Annabel Lee" (the tribute to his wife) and "The Bells" until his mysterious death in 1849.

This small cottage with period furniture is a tribute to Poe's poor but

productive life in the Bronx. Be sure to hook up with the caretaker, who gives tours and makes the house come alive. Also, upstairs there's an 18-minute audio-visual show that traces Poe's days in Manhattan and the Bronx.
Events: Poe week in Apr and free concerts in Poe Pk. Bandshell in summer.

VALENTINE-VARIAN HOUSE
Museum of Bronx History, 3266 Bainbridge Ave. (Van Cortlandt & 208th Sts.).
☎ *(212) 881-8900.*
Hours: *Sat 10am-4pm, Sun 1-5pm. Weekdays by appt only. Closed Hols.*
Free Admission: *Children under 12 acc. by an Adult. Otherwise Adults $1.*

This landmark colonial English fieldstone farmhouse was built in 1758 by Isaac Valentine, a local blacksmith. During the Revolutionary War, the Valentine family evacuated and the English took up residence. Then, in 1791, Isaac Varian, a successful farmer, bought the house with 260 acres of land; the house remained in the Varian family until 1964.

Today this handsome stone landmark is administered by the *Bronx County Historical Society,* which sponsors a variety of exhibitions in celebration of the Bronx with material from its library and photo/postcard collections. The Colonial room with its original wooden floorboards and a remodeled fireplace contains placards, posters and maps, which trace the history of the Bronx.
Events: Exhibits, lectures, tours, demonstrations of colonial crafts, outdoor art shows and concerts.

VAN CORTLANDT MANSION HOUSE
Van Cortlandt Pk., near Broadway & N. 242nd St.
☎ *(212) 543-3344.*
Hours: *Tue-Fri 11am-3pm, Sun 1-5pm. Closed Sat & Mon.*
Free Admission: *Children under 12 and school groups by reservation. Otherwise Adults $2 and Seniors $1.50.*
Groups: *By appt. only ($2/person).*
Tours: *Sun at 2pm.*

This 1748 Georgian landmark served as the manor house for Frederick Van Cortlandt's wheat plantation, which supported local artisans, craftsmen, indentured servants and slaves. During the Revolutionary War, Washington allegedly planned strategy with the French General Rochambeau from this house and then went on to launch his triumphant 1783 liberation march to Manhattan.

Today the mansion sits in the SW corner of Van Cortlandt Park. Nine rooms have been restored to Dutch/English days of the American Revolution with fine examples of 18th and 19th C. antique furniture, memorabilia and documents. In nice weather, visit the traditional knot garden in the back.
Events: A Colonial Festival (early May) with crafts and craftsmen demonstrating their trades; lectures and concerts.

Brooklyn

BROOKLYN CHILDREN'S MUSEUM 🍎🍎
(See "For the Kiddies.")

BROOKLYN HISTORICAL SOCIETY & MUSEUM 🍎
128 Pierrepont St. (at Clinton St.).
☎ *(718) 624-0890.*
Hours: *Tue-Sat 10am-4:45pm (Library), Tue-Sun noon-5pm (Museum). Student program upon appt. on Tue-Fri 9, 10 or 11am.*
Free Admission: *Tue noon-5pm (Museum). Otherwise Adults $2.50, Children $1 (Museum & Library).*

Founded in 1863, this Historical Society is housed in an attractive, eclectic building (1878, George B. Post) with fine terracotta ornamentation. The main attraction is the splendid wood-panelled library with its old-fashioned wooden writing tables and overhanging balcony with wooden-carved bannisters. The 125,000 books, primarily on the history of Brooklyn and genealogy, are housed in striking diagonally-panelled wooden stacks. An imposing grandfather clock adds telling charm to the already perfect library atmosphere.

The new museum features the Shellens Gallery of Brooklyn History with permanent exhibits profiling 5 important landmarks and symbols—the Brooklyn Bridge, Coney Island (memories of the boardwalk and a wax museum), the Brooklyn Navy Yard, the Brooklyn Dodgers and Hall of Fame and famous Brooklynites (the "Honeymooners" stage set). Changing exhibits reveal the history of Brooklyn and the development of various communities. Past exhibits have included Black churches in Brooklyn, Italian street festivals, the history of the Fulton ferryboat and Dutch homesteads.

Events: *Noonday programs with Church of St. Ann's (fall & spring) featuring guided tours, films or lectures; evening lectures; and Genealogy Society meeting on 1st Sat at noon.*

BROOKLYN MUSEUM 🍎🍎🍎
Eastern Pkwy. at Washington St.
☎ *(718) 638-5000.*
Hours: *Mon, Wed-Fri 10am-5pm, Sat, Sun & Hols 10am-5pm. Closed Tue, Thanksgiving, Christmas, New Year's.*
Free Admission: *Children under 12 acc. by an Adult. Otherwise suggested contribution: Adults $4, Students $2, Seniors $1.50.*
Groups & Tours: *By appt. only, ext. 221.*

In the great classical tradition, this 1897 McKim, Mead & White architectural masterpiece offers a grand backdrop with 5 floors for the art treasures of the ages. Started in 1823 as a library to encourage young men to "use" their leisure time productively, it became the Brooklyn Institute of Arts & Sciences in 1843, thanks to Augustus Graham, a local distiller.

The exterior sculptures are works of art. Look for Daniel Chester French's "Manhattan" and "Brooklyn" (originally guarding the Manhat-

tan Bridge until 1963), now serving as sentries at the main entrance. Also, the frieze is resplendent with the world's greatest thinkers and artists.

On the **1st floor** you will find art, ceremonial objects, masks and dolls of the American Indians, Oceania and African cultures. The Frieda Schiff Warburg sculpture garden, built in 1966, contains souvenirs from demolished N.Y.C. buildings saved by the Anonymous Art Recovery Society, including pieces from the old Penn Station. The **2nd floor** houses the Oriental galleries and the changing exhibits from the print collection (14th C. to present).

The **3rd floor** is dedicated to the excellent Egyptian collection, considered one of the finest in the world, thanks to the generous bequest of C.E. Wilbour. Don't miss the rose-colored sarcophagus of 2500 B.C. and a gilded wood and silver sarcophagus for a sacred ibis. Galleries of ancient civilizations, such as Greek, Roman and Assyrian, complement the Nile treasures.

The **4th floor** features the Decorative Arts. Highlights are the 19th and 20th C. galleries including Tiffany lamps and glass European furniture, American and European costumes and Art Deco crafts; and the 17th-19th C. American period rooms, including such highlights as the Moorish Room from John D. Rockefeller, Sr.'s Manhattan townhouse and the 17th C. Dutch colonial home of Jan Martense Schenck of Brooklyn.

The **5th floor** holds American and European painting and sculpture. Of special interest are the 18th and 19th C. American painters ranging from the Hudson River to the "Ashcan" schools. A veritable palette of changing shows is in the Rotunda.

See "For the Bookworms" for the museum's library facilities.

Events: *"What's up" workshops for children 8-12 on Sat & Sun at 2pm; special school programs (some fees), ext. 221; "Arty Facts" programs for children 4-12 on Sat; special Hol workshops; and BACA concerts on Sun at 2pm (Oct-May, sometimes at 3pm) featuring classical music or recitals.*

HARBOR DEFENSE MUSEUM
Ft. Hamilton, off Ft. Hamilton Pkwy. & 101st St.
☎ *(718) 630-4349.*
Hours: *Mon, Thu-Fri 1-4pm, Sat 10am-5pm. Closed all Hols except Memorial Day, July 4th & Labor Day.*
Tours: *By appt. only.*

Housed in the 1829 "caponier" (built to protect the entrance into the fort), the museum serves as a chronicle of 18th and 19th C. history of the armed forces. Displays include old armaments such as an 1883 Gatling gun and a 24-pound Howitzer, a Civil War cannon; military dress and paintings dating back to the Revolutionary War; and life-like dioramas, featuring Long Island battles and the "Battle That Never Was." For school groups, a demonstration on loading a cannon is included.

LEFFERTS HOMESTEAD
Prospect Pk., Flatbush Ave. near Empire Blvd.
☎ *(718) 965-6505.*
Hours: *Wed-Sat & Hols noon-4pm, Sun noon-5pm.*
Groups & Tours: *By appt. only.*

This 1778 traditional Dutch house with dormer windows and gambrel roof belonged to Peter Lefferts, a wealthy farmer who lived on Lefferts Avenue amid Dutch farmland. Donated to the city in 1981, the house was moved into Prospect Park and today is run by the Daughters of the American Revolution.

Containing some fine examples of 18th & 19th C. furniture and accessories, it is worth a short visit. Of special interest are the 2 impressive wooden Dutch "Kas" used for storing linen and china in the hallways; the interesting collection of trundle, canopy and sleigh beds; such personal items as a shaving bowl (notice the neck indentation), antique clothing, fans and combs; and the spinning wheels, weaving accessories and quilting frames. The outside garden is planted with kitchen and medicinal herbs used in colonial times.
Events: *Craft fairs, classes, workshops and Hol programs and decorations.*

NEW YORK TRANSIT MUSEUM
Beneath Boerum Pl. & Schermerhorn St.
☎ *(212) 330-3060/3063.*
Hours: *Tue-Fri 10am-4pm, Sat 11am-4pm.*
Free Admission: *N.Y.C. transit workers. Otherwise Adults $1.15 and Seniors & Children 55¢.*

Recreating commuting life in a 1936 subway car, this museum reveals subway memorabilia dating back over a century. Antique turnstiles, equipment, 18 classic subway cars and changing exhibits will be part of the "moving" experience.

Events: *Films on Sat from noon-3pm and workshops for kids on Sat from noon-2pm.*

PIETER CLAESEN WYCKOFF HOUSE MUSEUM
Clarendon Rd. & Ralph Ave.
☎ *(718) 629-5400.*
Hours: *Fri-Sun noon-5pm (Apr-Nov), noon-4pm (Dec-Mar) or by appt.*
Admission: *Special rate for school groups. Otherwise Adults $2, Seniors & Students $1.*

As the oldest building in N.Y.C. (circa 1652), this popular stopping place for travelers is an excellent example of colonial Dutch/American architecture with its sloping roof, double Dutch door, carved fishtail shingles and fieldstone foundation. Owned by the Wyckoff family (originally wealthy and influential farmers) for over 250 years and today administered by family members, it has been restored to the 1652-1819 period.

The oldest section, the kitchen, is of particular interest, with its exposed wattle and mud insulation (including corn cobs and acorns) and a restored jambless fireplace. The parlor features some good examples of Dutch and Federal furniture.

Events: Lectures, craft workshops, children's reading hours and outdoor community programs (including free concerts) on the impressive lawn.

Queens

BOWNE HOUSE 🍎
37-01 Bowne St., Flushing.
☎ *(718) 359-0528.*
Hours: *Tue, Sat & Sun 2:30-4:30pm.*
Free Admission: *School classes by appt. Otherwise Adults $2, Seniors & Children $1.*

The oldest house in Queens, John Bowne's 1661 "salt box" house (with additions in 1680 and 1696) remains an architectural gem with its original pegged floors, hand-hewn beams and 17th and 18th C. furniture, pewter, artifacts, portraits and documents belonging to the family. In the kitchen of this house, Bowne allowed the Quakers to hold their meetings, thereby taking a direct stand against Peter Stuyvesant's religious intolerance. The house remained in the family for 9 generations until 1954 when it was purchased by the Bowne Historical Society.

Ongoing tours guide you past some superb antiques including a Chippendale secretary, a lady slipper table, a variety of chairs (check out the "gout" one, the forerunner of a wheelchair), kitchen implements, footwarmers and hot water bottles, antique plates and a "Worth dress." An exhibition of olde maps, photos and drawings describes the house and the community.

Events: Auction in Mar, craft demos in spring, 1st Tue of month appreciation day (fee) and free candlelight tour in Dec.

FRIENDS MEETING HOUSE
137-16 Northern Blvd. (E. of Main St.), Flushing.
☎ *(718) 358-9636.*
Hours: *1st Sun of month from 2-4pm or by appt. Sun service at 11am.*
Built from 1694 to 1719, this simple Quaker house of worship is the oldest meeting house in continuous use in the city. This landmark has retained its fine examples of American Colonial architecture. A guided tour takes you into the austere meeting room containing only benches where you learn about the Quakers, their history and their fight for religious freedom. A small cemetery in the back can also be visited.

THE GODWIN-TERNBACH MUSEUM
Queens College, Paul Klapper Hall, Kissena Blvd. (off L.I.E. exit 24).
☎ *(718) 520-7129.*
Hours: *Undergoing major reconstruction, reopens Fall 1991. Call for further information.*
The Godwin-Ternbach Museum collection contains over 2,000 objects with a strong emphasis on ancient glass and 20th C. drawings, watercolors and prints.

KING MANOR HOUSE
150-03 Jamaica Ave. (King Pk. & 153rd St.), Jamaica.
☎ *(718) 291-0282. Number may change.*
Under renovation until Dec '91. Until then free monthly tours by the Urban Rangers usually on the last Sun of month at 2pm; tours include the architecture of the house, the restoration project and the history and life of Rufus King and his family. Upon reopening, several historic period rooms will provide a backdrop for special events and receptions.

KINGSLAND HOUSE
143-35 37th Ave., Flushing.
☎ *(718) 939-0647.*
Hours: *Tue, Sat & Sun 2:30-4:30pm.*
Free Admission: *Only for exhibit openings (4x a year). Otherwise Adults $2, Seniors & Students $1.*
This house was built in 1774 for Charles Doughty, a well-to-do farmer; its Dutch and English architectural styles include a gambrel roof, central chimney and arched and half-moon windows (the latter believed necessary by the Dutch to ward off evil spirits). Doughty, a humanitarian, was the first community person to enfranchise his servant in 1799. His daughter married Joseph King, an English sea captain, who bought the house from his father-in-law in 1801.
Today the house is the showcase for the Queens Historical Society, which assembles 4 special exhibits a year on American history, such as a past favorite of dolls from colonial days to the 1950s. One room is exclusively dedicated to the photographic documentation of the house's move in the late 1960s. There is a one-room reconstruction, a Victorian parlor complete with all the trimmings. A small reference library with books on Queens and N.Y. history is available upon appt.
Check out the weeping beech tree in the backyard, which is beautiful

in all seasons. The oldest of its kind, it was planted in 1846 by Sam Parsons, a nurseryman, who procured a cutting from the gardens of a Belgian Baron. The tree's beauty was so revered that the city decided to buy up the surrounding land and preserve it as a park.

NEW YORK HALL OF SCIENCE 🍎🍎
(See "For the Kiddies.")

ISAMU NOGUCHI GARDEN MUSEUM 🍎🍎🍎
32-37 Vernon Blvd. at 10th St., Long Island City.
☎ *(718) 721-1932, 204-7088.*
Hours: *Wed & Sat 11am-6pm (Apr-Nov).*
Suggested Contribution: *$2.*
Tours: *Wed & Sat at 2pm.*

Twelve galleries and a delightful garden reveal over 300 works, models, pieces of furniture and photographs spanning the 60 years of this world-renowned and creative Japanese-American sculptor, who died in 1988. Working in everything from basalt and marble to metal, Noguchi captured the beauty inherent in the materials through artistic form and varied textures. His innovations in furniture ranged from sculptural table bases to paper lamps. A visit to this museum is worth the pilgrimage to Long Island City.
Events: *A 50-minute video on Noguchi's life plays every hour.*

QUEENS COUNTY FARM MUSEUM
73-50 Little Neck Pkwy., Floral Park.
☎ *(718) 347-3276.*
Hours: *Mon-Fri 9am-5pm (grounds all year), Sat-Sun noon-5pm (Apr-Sep).*
Group Tours: *By appt. only Mon-Fri 10am-1pm ($2).*

This landmark 7-acre farm with an 18th C. colonial farmhouse is the last "authentic working farm in N.Y.C." The farmhouse combines a unique blend of Dutch and early English Colonial architecture. Of particular interest are the original hand-split shingles, floor boards, hand-made nails, window sashes and the restored Victorian parlor room. The outbuildings feature 3 greenhouses, a wagonshed, a cowbarn and a henhouse. Sheep, chicken, ducks and geese add to the local color, making this place more interesting for young children. The farm resides on 53 acres with a nature preserve and trails (of interest to all).
Events *(most at a fee): Educational programs for children including demos, workshops and classes in colonial crafts; antique car show (late Apr); Rites of Spring Festival (late May); Thunderbird American Indian Dancers Festival (end of Jul); summer drop-in center for children; Queens County Fair (Sep); and Children's Fall Festival (late Oct).*

QUEENS MUSEUM 🍎🍎
N.Y. State Bldg., Flushing Meadow, Corona Pk., Flushing.
☎ *(718) 592-5555/9700.*
Hours: *Tue-Fri 10am-5pm, Sat-Sun noon-5:30pm. Closed Mon.*
Free Admission: *Children under 5 acc. by an Adult; includes free parking. Otherwise suggested contribution: Adults $2, Seniors &*

Students $1.
Gallery & Group Tours: *By appt. only.*

On permanent display is the incredible Panorama of New York City of the 5 boroughs, which is the largest architectural scale model (9,335 square feet) in the world. Every street, apartment building, brownstone, park, pier and airport (with planes landing and taking off) is meticulously detailed. You stand above the city and look down upon it from many different vantage points. The city lights sparkle when nightfall descends every few minutes.

In addition there are several galleries, which feature a wide variety of exhibitions changing every 10 weeks. Past favorites were life-size puppets, Michelangelo drawings, streamlined designs and a juried competition.

Events: *Films on Sat at 2pm; special events on most Sun at 2pm relating to the exhibit; Sun "drop-in" workshops from 1-4pm (school year) for the whole family; guided tours and workshops for school groups by appt.; and "Art on Site" workshops on Tue & Thu at 1:30pm in summer (fee).*

QUEENS MUSEUM AT BULOVA CORPORATE CENTER
75-20 Astoria Blvd. (77th St. & 25th Ave.), Jackson Hts.
☎ *(718) 899-0700.*
Hours: *Mon-Fri 7am-7pm, Sat 10am-4pm.*

As the Queens Museum's first satellite gallery, the West Concourse has 4 timely solo exhibitions of emerging artists. The Atrium Lobby displays 6 plaster-cast sculptures on loan from the MMA.

TELEPHONE PIONEER MUSEUM
88-11 165th St., Jamaica.
☎ *(718) 523-3764.*
Group Tours: *By appt. only.*

As caretakers of telephone memorabilia, the Pioneers (an association of telephone employees with 18 or more years of service) have recalled more than 100 different types of telephones and switchboards for their hands-on museum. Younger children can touch, play and learn to use these phones without racking up valuable message units on your own phone. The museum also presents various films on the telephone's history, how to use telephones and what the Telephone Pioneers do.

Staten Island

ALICE AUSTEN HOUSE, MUSEUM & GARDEN ♦
2 Hylan Blvd., Rosebank.
☎ *(718) 816-4506.*
Hours: *Thu-Sun noon-5pm.*
Suggested Contribution: *$2.*
    With an excellent view of N.Y. Harbor and the Verrazano Bridge, this charming restored 17th C. Dutch farmhouse with Victorian frills was the home of Alice Austen, a pioneer in photography in the 1890s. She received a camera from an uncle and took over 8,000 photos from 1884 to 1934; she recorded the life and times of Victorian Staten Island and New York City. As a tribute to her talents, changing photo exhibitions line the rooms on the first floor; only occasionally, however, do we actually get to see the wonderful photos by Alice Austen. A Victorian parlor with period furniture recreates Alice's home life. An informative, 20-minute videotape narrated by Helen Hayes reveals many of Alice's photographs.
Events: *Two antique fairs (spring & fall), Victorian tea (Jun), Photo Day (Jun), Nautical Festival (Aug), Halloween Party, Christmas open house, family programs, lectures and concerts.*

CONFERENCE HOUSE
Billopp House, foot of Hylan Blvd., Tottenville.
☎ *(718) 984-2086.*
Hours: *Wed-Sun 1-4pm (Apr-Sep); Wed-Sun at 1pm (Oct-Mar).*
Free Admission: *Children under 6. Otherwise Adults $1, Children & Seniors 50¢.*
    This 1680 national landmark was the meetinghouse for the unsuccessful peace conference in 1776 between British Lord Howe and 3 representatives of the Continental Congress (Benjamin Franklin, John Adams and Edward Rutledge) in an attempt to prevent the Revolutionary War. Today this stone house offers period furnishings, a 17th C. kitchen and beautiful rolling lawns down to the waterfront.
Events: Summer concerts.

GARIBALDI-MEUCCI MUSEUM
420 Tompkins Ave., Rosebank.
☎ *(718) 442-1608.*
Hours: *Tue-Fri 9am-5pm, Sat-Sun 1-5pm.*
Admission: *By donation.*
    This 1840 National landmark was owned by Antonio Meucci, a struggling scientist from Italy, who claimed to have developed his telephone in 1857 (long before Bell) but because of lack of funds and the loss of his temporary patent, he never got the due credit he was due. From 1851 to 1853, Giuseppe Garibaldi lived here in exile with the Meuccis while working for Italian unity and making candles to raise money. In fact, Garibaldi went on to liberate Southern Italy after leaving S.I. As a result of this rich Italian history, 5 small rooms feature

memorabilia, paintings and photos in tribute to Garibaldi and his relatively unknown inventor-friend, Meucci. Downstairs, don't miss the chair and piano made from willow branches by Meucci. Upstairs is the Garibaldi bedroom with period furniture. A 30-minute videotape about Garibaldi is available upon request.

MUSEUM OF STATEN ISLAND
75 Stuyvesant Pl., St. George (moving to Snug Harbor in 1991).
☎ *(718) 727-1135.*
Hours: *Mon-Sat 9am-5pm, Sun 1-5pm.*
Free Admission: *On Mon to all and always to children under 5. Otherwise Adults $2.50, Children $1.50.*
  Founded in 1881 and today run by the S.I. Institute of Arts & Science, this showcase offers changing exhibitions on art, science, the history of S.I. and natural history with a permanent collection of prints on 19th C. Americana. A public reading room for the museum library and archives is by appt. only.
Events: *Occasional free lectures and slide shows; Sun afternoon films (fee), tours and talks (fee) and birthday parties (fee).*

THE JOHN A. NOBLE COLLECTION
270 Richmond Terr., New Brighton. Soon to move to Snug Harbor, "D" Bldg.
☎ *(718) 447-6490.*
Hours: *Wed-Sat 1-5pm and by appt.*
  John A. Noble was considered by some a gifted lithographer and artist, who immortalized the American maritime industry from 1928 to 1983. His home, "Opossum Acre," today serves as a museum, archive and study center for maritime art and history. Art, lithographic stones and photos reveal a *noble* love of the sea. (Regrettably, the author was not able to visit.)

RICHMONDTOWN RESTORATION VILLAGE ⚑⚑⚑
Richmond Rd. at Clarke Ave. & Arthur Kill Rd., Greenbelt.
☎ *(718) 351-1611/9414 (Groups).*
Hours: *Wed-Fri 10am-5pm, Sat-Sun 1-5pm. Closed Mon-Tue.*
Free Admission: *"Christmas in Richmondtown" on 2nd Sun in Dec and always for Children under 6. Otherwise Adults $4, Seniors & Students $2.50.*
Group Guided Tours: *Upon request ($1.75 per person). Self-guided tours last about 2 hours.*
  To see what N.Y.C. colonial life was like in the 1700s, make a pilgrimage to this restored village; you will be pleasantly surprised. This 96-acre historic restoration (N.Y.C.'s only one), located at the actual village of Richmond (which dates back to 1690), contains 26 buildings and sites (14 interiors are currently open to the public). Of particular interest are the old courthouse, Voorlezer's House (oldest public school in U.S.), Lake-Tysen House, Stephen's House & General Store, Boehm-Frost House and the Bennett House (check out the wonderful doll collection).

On-site guides clad in colonial garb offer historical background and reenact the daily crafts of the early colonists, such as pottery making, baking, carpentry, basket weaving and harness making. The Transportation and S.I. Historical Society Museums feature exhibits of furniture, costumes, tools, photography, horse-drawn vehicles and firefighting equipment. The entire place, though, is a museum! Visit the Greek Revival Third County Courthouse (1837) to get a brochure and a personal orientation for your self-guided tour.

Events: Militia Day (spring); County Fair & Old Home Day (fall); Candlelight tours (Dec); Christmas Festival on 2nd Sun in Dec; Hol workshops for families in mid-Dec at 4-7pm; and free lectures, concerts and public performances.

SNUG HARBOR CULTURAL CENTER ♩♩♩

1000 Richmond Terr., Livingston.
☎ *(718) 448-2500.*
Hours: *Daily 8am-dusk (Grounds), Wed-Sun noon-5pm (Exhibits).*
Free Admission: *Except Newhouse Center $2.*
Tours: *Sat & Sun at 2pm from Visitors Center. Tree tours on Sun at 1pm (Jun-Aug).*
Group Tours: *By appt. only (fee). Workshops for school groups (fee).*

Originally a retirement refuge for sailors dating back to 1851, this 80-acre cultural center offers lovely grounds and 28 impressive historical buildings reflecting diverse architectural styles, including Greek Revival, Beaux-Arts, Gothic and Empire. Architect Minard Le Fever designed the original buildings like those of ancient Greece to commemorate the birthplace of democracy. As the county's largest renovation project over the past many years, this center houses botanical gardens, parks, museums, galleries and performing arts centers.

Most of the art galleries (Newhouse Center for Contemporary Art, Gallery III and Atelier Gallery) showcase contemporary artists or S.I. community groups with exhibitions changing every 4-6 weeks. The S.I. Botanical Gardens (see "For the Birds"), S.I. Children's Museum (see "For the Kiddies") and the Art Lab, an art school for children and adults, reside here as well. The Veterans' Memorial Hall, formerly the Chapel, is an intimate recital hall (seats 200) for the performing arts, while the 1892 Music Hall, one of N.Y.C.'s oldest legitimate theaters, will seat 600 when it opens in 1992. Catch a ride on the trolley bus, a historic reproduction that runs on compressed natural gas, which provides a 10-minute ride from the S.I. Ferry Terminal to the Center (children free, adults $1).

Events: Jazz festival (Feb), outdoor summer concerts featuring the N.Y. Philharmonic and Metropolitan Opera, annual outdoor sculpture festival (Summer), Art Lab camp for ages 6-12 (fee), afterschool art scene (fee),"Annual Gift Gathering" (early Dec), seminars and lectures.

STATEN ISLAND CHILDREN'S MUSEUM AT SNUG HARBOR ♩♩

(See "For the Kiddies.")

STATEN ISLAND FERRY MUSEUM
St. George Terminal.
☎ *(718) 727-2508.*
Hours: Mon-Thu 9am-2pm.

This small tribute to the S.I. Ferry is a worthwhile diversion while waiting for the ferry. Ferryboat paraphernalia abounds including models, an old turnstile, wheels, engineer's dials, a fire gong and wooden patterns for machine casting. Pictures of old ferryboats and destroyers adorn the walls. Probably the most interesting aspect is the model River Town of North America constructed by Harry Cotterel, Jr., a historian, who during his life took pictures of famous people's homes, old buildings and ferryboats in America. In retirement he built wooden replicas from these photos, featuring houses and shops in New England clapboard, log cabin and Georgian styles. In addition, you'll see Poe's garden house, Jack London's saloon, Betsy Ross's house, Abe Lincoln's and Stephen Foster's birthplaces. Quite an interesting undertaking.

For the Artists

Noncommercial art galleries are plentiful in N.Y.C. Located in cultural centers, schools, institutes, companies, churches and municipal buildings, they provide us with valuable artistic showcases. In most cases, admission is free. Generally the galleries offer changing exhibitions in an attempt to provide a wide variety of artistic themes. Occasionally, new shows are launched by an opening, which presents the artist(s) and refreshments.

Please consult "For the Lobbyists" and "For the Society-Goers" for additional places with art galleries.

> *"All that is good in art is the expression of one soul talking to another, and is precious according to the greatness of the soul that utters it."*
>
> — *JOHN RUSKIN*

AMERICAN ACADEMY AND INSTITUTE OF ARTS AND LETTERS
155th St. & Broadway, Audubon Terr.
☎ *(212) 368-5900.*
Hours: *Tue-Sun 1-4pm (mid Nov-mid Dec, Mar-early Apr & mid May-mid Jun).*
Groups: *By appt. only.*

To be elected to this Academy for achievement in the arts and literature is considered the highest honor in the country; the list of previous members reads like an artistic "Who's Who." Dating back to 1898, the Academy continues to present awards and prizes to distinguished artists as well as to sponsor public exhibitions of artwork and manuscripts. The main spring event features works of newly elected members and award recipients; the fall show reveals members' works and those from the Academy's permanent collection (especially Childe Hassam). The Academy resides in a Neoclassical McKim, Mead & White building at Audubon Terrace, which in itself is an architectural achievement.

AMERICAN INDIAN COMMUNITY HOUSE GALLERY
708 Broadway (4th St. & Astor Pl.).
☎ *(212) 598-0100.*
Hours: *Tue-Sat noon-6pm.*

This cultural center annually presents 5 or 6 rotating exhibitions of contemporary and historical American Indian art from North and South America. Past shows have displayed Canadian Eskimo art, Hopi-Navajo crafts, Andean weaving and the works of native women artists. Exhibition space is also provided for artists who might otherwise not have a N.Y.C. showcase.

AMERICAN INSTITUTE OF GRAPHIC ARTS (AIGA)
1059 3rd Ave. (at 62nd St.).
☎ *(212) 752-0813.*
Hours: *Mon-Fri 9:30am-4:30pm. Call first.*

Since 1914 this nonprofit professional trade organization has sponsored competitions, exhibitions, publications and educational events in an attempt to promote excellence in graphic design. AIGA sponsors four yearly competitive exhibitions, frequently held at other locations, such as the Low Library at Columbia University. However, AIGA itself has hosted shows featuring book covers, book displays, corporate communications (annual reports, logos, etc.), posters and political art. The membership library, open to public researchers, offers books and periodicals on graphic design and production.

THE ARCHITECTURAL LEAGUE OF NEW YORK
Urban Center, 457 Madison Ave. (at 51st St.).
☎ *(212) 753-1722.*
Hours: *Mon-Sat 10am-5pm. Closed Hols.*

This nonprofit organization was founded in 1881 by architect Cass Gilbert (Woolworth Building and U.S. Customs House) to promote communication among architects, artists and design professionals. The League sponsors exhibitions (some at the Urban Center, some at museums), lectures, conferences, tours, books, guides and maps.

ART STUDENTS LEAGUE OF NEW YORK
(See "For the Knowledge Seekers.")

ARTS INTERACTION
Gallery 12, Washington Hts. & Inwood Council for Arts, 711 W. 168 St. (W. of Broadway).
☎ *(212) 927-5004.*
Hours: *Mon-Fri 10am-4pm.*

Opened in 1979, this nonprofit organization makes community members more aware of the cultural attractions in their own backyard. Gallery 12 offers monthly exhibitions featuring arts and crafts primarily from local groups, often quite homespun.

Events: *Slide & sound shows, plays, poetry readings, festivals, seniors' programs, cultural workshops and outdoor summer concerts at Fort Tryon & J. Hood Wright.*

BARUCH COLLEGE GALLERY
(See "For the Knowledge Seekers.")

THE BOARD OF JEWISH EDUCATION
426 W. 58th St. (off 9th Ave.).
☎ *(212) 245-8200 ext. 339.*
Hours: *Sun-Thu 11am-4pm.*
Groups: *By appt. only.*

All 5 floors of this Jewish educational board building have been turned into a showcase for professional and amateur artwork of the young and old. Every wall and cranny features something to gaze at, either oils, watercolors, charcoals, collages, crafts or sculpture. In the spring and summer, the annual children's show presents topical artwork.

CAMERA CLUB OF NEW YORK
853 Broadway, (14th St.), 2nd fl.
☎ *(212) 260-7077.*
Hours: *Mon-Fri noon-5pm.*

This camera club focuses on monthly photographic shows; twice a year (spring & Dec), members' works are displayed.

CASTILLO CULTURAL CENTER
500 Greenwich St. (Spring & Canal Sts.), room 201.
☎ *(212) 941-5800.*
Hours: *Mon-Sat 10am-10pm, Sun noon-6pm.*

This collective of over 70 artists/writers/performer-activists provides an environment for *free art* for political or nonpolitical purposes with no fear of censorship. A gallery reveals interesting monthly exhibits. The video facilities produce a weekly cable show, and offers hands-on training with video cameras and editing. Opportunities for furniture

CITY GALLERY

making and graphic design are available. A theater presents Off-Off-Broadway plays (fee), which are always provocative.

CATHEDRAL CHURCH OF ST. JOHN THE DIVINE
(See "For the Believers.")

CBGB'S
(See "For the Matinee Idlers.")

CENTER FOR THE MEDIA ARTS
(See "For the Knowledge Seekers.")

CHEMICAL GALLERY
(See Chemcourt under "For the Lobbyists.")

CINQUE GALLERY
560 Broadway (near Pine St.).
☎ *(212) 966-3464.*
Hours: *Wed-Sat 1-6pm.*
A nonprofit corporation founded by 3 leading Black artists (Romare Bearden, Ernest Crichlow and Norman Lewis), Cinque Gallery exists to "encourage, assist and exhibit" the works of young, aspiring minority artists.

CITY COLLEGE OF NEW YORK GALLERIES
(See "For the Knowledge Seekers.")

CITY GALLERY
2 Columbus Circle (58th St. & 8th Ave.), 2nd fl.
☎ *(212) 974-1150 ext. 27.*
Hours: *Mon-Fri 10am-5:30pm. Closed Hols; call for occasional weekend hours.*
This small gallery sponsored by the N.Y.C. Department of Cultural Affairs offers varied exhibitions on city life and culture with the occasional N.Y.C. community group thrown in. Previous shows have centered on such themes as contemporary photos of the Lower East Side, N.Y.C.'s WPA artists, children's book illustration, Beijing and 17 city printmakers. As this gallery is located at the N.Y. Convention & Visitors Bureau, be sure to look for the free pamphlets and maps of the city.

THE CLOCKTOWER
108 Leonard St. (Lafayette St. & Broadway), 13th fl.
☎ *(718) 784-2084, (212) 233-1096.*
Run by the Institute for Contemporary Art, this clocktower gallery has "wound" up on the 13th floor (the elevator only goes to 12) of this 1870 landmark, renovated by McKim, Mead & White in the 1890s with the important addition of the clocktower. This gallery chimes out with one-person shows. This place is definitely for the hardy art admirer, as the gallery space continues up another flight of stairs to the 14th floor. Once there, you can climb a narrow spiral staircase to the clocktower and see its workings. A good setting for an Alfred Hitchcock thriller!

COLUMBIA UNIVERSITY
(See "For the Knowledge Seekers.")

COOPER UNION HOUGHTON GALLERY
(See "For the Knowledge Seekers.")

CORK GALLERY, AVERY FISHER HALL
Lincoln Center, Concourse Level.
☎ *(212) 580-8700.*
Hours: *Mon-Sat 10am-10:30pm, Sun noon-10:30pm.*
    During the intermission at Lincoln Center wend your way down to see this gallery, one of the largest free public ones in the city. Exhibi-

tions change frequently and can be sketchy, depending upon which show is up (about 26 a year!), though most are quite professional. Definitely worth a quick interlude to get you away from the crowds.

CREATIVE TIME, INC.
☎ *(212) 619-1955.*
This nonprofit organization was founded in 1973 to help visual and performing artists find exhibition and performance space around the city.

CUNY GRADUATE SCHOOL AND UNIVERSITY CENTER
(See "For the Knowledge Seekers.")

DANCE THEATRE WORKSHOP (DTW)
219 W. 19th St. (7th-8th Aves.), 2nd fl.
☎ *(212) 691-6500.*
Hours: *Mon-Fri 10am-6pm, Sat 1-6pm, Sun by appt. (mainly Sep-Jun).*
For artwork on motion or dance, bob over to the DTW gallery for their creative diversions.

EDUCATIONAL ALLIANCE
(See "For the Knowledge Seekers.")

80 WASHINGTON SQUARE EAST GALLERIES
NYU, 80 Washington Sq. E. (W. 4th St. & Washington Pl.).
☎ *(212) 998-5747.*
Hours: *Tue 11am-7pm, Wed-Thu 11am-6pm, Fri-Sat 11am-5pm (Sep-mid May); Mon-Fri 11am-5pm (mid May-Jul). Closed Aug.*
This charming townhouse on Washington Square Park reveals 8 galleries for exhibitions of everything from painting, sculpture, ceramics and photography to glassmaking. As NYU graduate students in studio art are required to have at least one public showing for their degree, this offers an ideal space for their debut. The annual juried competition of small works (no larger than 12" in any dimension) takes place in Feb. Ask to be put on their mailing list to be invited to openings. Don't forget to visit the Grey Art Gallery around the corner at 33 Washington Place (see separate listing).

EMANUEL MIDTOWN YM-YWHA PHOTOGRAPHIC GALLERY
344 E. 14th St. (1st-2nd Aves.), 2nd fl.
☎ *(212) 674-7200.*
Hours: *Sun-Thu noon-8pm, Fri noon-4pm. Closed Sat & major Jewish Hols & breaks between shows.*
Since 1972 this gallery has been lining walls in corridors and small rooms with photos by emerging photographers or retrospectives of well-known ones. This Y also has reputable dance and theater performances (fee) and programs for seniors.

EMPIRE STATE COLLEGE, SUNY
(See "For the Knowledge Seekers.")

FASHION INSTITUTE OF TECHNOLOGY (F.I.T.) ⚫
Shirley Goodman Resource Center ("E" Bldg.), 227 W. 27th St. (7th & 8th Aves.).
☎ *(212) 760-7760/7848.*
Hours: *Tue-Fri noon-8pm, Sat 10am-5pm. Closed Sun, Mon & Hols. Call first.*

For those unfamiliar with this fashion and design school, this is a real find and worth incorporating into your cultural circuit. The Newhouse Gallery displays student, faculty and invitational work on fashion, design and advertising. The gallery rooms are large, modern and attractively designed—a wonderful backdrop for any artistic endeavor.

The students' works are not to be underestimated as they are always interesting and provocative. Visit Building "C" for additional displays of students' design drawings.

FEDERAL OFFICE BUILDING
26 Federal Plaza (Broadway between Worth & Duane Sts.), lobby.
☎ *(212) 264-9290.*
Hours: *Mon-Fri 7:30am-5:30pm. Closed Hols.*

Paintings, photos and sculpture make up the changing monthly exhibitions for this "living buildings program," the use of federal office space for shows by local independent artists or art groups.

FEDERAL RESERVE BANK
(See "For the Tourists.")

FORDHAM UNIVERSITY AT LINCOLN CENTER
(See "For the Knowledge Seekers.")

ABRAHAM GOODMAN HOUSE
(See the Hebrew Arts School under "For the Knowledge Seekers.")

GREY ART GALLERY & STUDY CENTER ⚫
NYU, 33 Washington Pl. (off Washington Sq. E.).
☎ *(212) 998-6780.*
Hours: *Tue, Thu & Fri 11am-6:30pm, Wed 11am-8:30pm, Sat 11am-5pm.*

As NYU's fine arts showcase, the Grey Gallery offers colorful professional exhibitions to the general public. Occupying the site of the first fine arts academy in America, begun by Samuel F.B. Morse (yes, the inventor as well as artist) in 1835, this studio was popular with many artists, such as Winslow Homer and George Inness. From 1924 to 1942, A.E. Gallatin established a "Gallery for Living Art," which served as one of the few public windows for abstract art.

Keeping in the Gallatin tradition, the gallery today concentrates on American artists from the 1940s to the present in painting, drawing and photography; exhibitions change every 8 weeks. Also around the corner visit 80 Washington Square East Galleries (see separate listing).

HEBREW UNION COLLEGE—JEWISH INSTITUTE OF

RELIGION
(See "For the Knowledge Seekers.")

HENRY STREET SETTLEMENT
Louis Abrons Arts for Living Center, 466 Grand St. (at Pitt St.).
☎ *(212) 598-0400/766-9200.*
Hours: *Mon-Sat noon-6pm and before all performances. Call first.*
   This cultural center serves a "rainbow community" of Blacks, Asians, Hispanics and Jews. Its dedication to enriching the life of the Lower East Side dates back almost 100 years to the spirit of its founder, Lillian Wald, "a fighter for food for the soul as well as the body." That nourishment is achieved in part by offering monthly exhibitions of promising and talented contemporary artists, especially minorities and women. With an impressive theater, the Henry Street Settlement offers sterling programs in music, dance and theater; most are at a fee, although occasionally they'll throw in a free one. The center also sponsors a varied program of workshops and classes for the neighborhood.

HIGH SCHOOL OF ART & DESIGN
1075 2nd Ave. (at 57th St.), lobby.
☎ *(212) 752-4340 ext. 31.*
Hours: *Spring show in May. Call for hours.*
   Student, alumni and faculty artwork illustrates the breadth of talent at this school.

HUDSON GUILD
441 W. 26th St. (9th-10th Aves.)
☎ *(212) 760-9806.*
Hours: *Mon-Fri 11am-5pm.*
   The Joe & Emily Lowe Art Gallery sponsors changing exhibits every 2 months of local and well-known Chelsea artists.
Events: *Book fair (3rd week in Oct), theater performances (some fee) and aerobics.*

HUNTER COLLEGE LEUBSDORF GALLERY 🍎
Lexington Ave. at 68th St. (S.W. corner in Hunter College West).
☎ *(212) 772-4991.*
Hours: *Mon-Sat noon-5pm. Closed Sun and mid Jun-mid Sep.*
   This modern multi-leveled showcase for contemporary art and art theory presents the creative talents of established professional artists, not students. Monthly exhibitions have generally been well done and have featured such shows as the drawings of Tony Smith, photos of jazz musicians, minimalists and serialists. See "For the Knowledge Seekers" for info on the other three Hunter College galleries.

INTERNATIONAL TYPEFACE CORP. (ITC CENTER)
2 Hammarskjold Plaza (866 2nd Ave., 46th-47th Sts.), 3rd fl.
☎ *(212) 371-0699.*
Hours: *Mon-Fri noon-5pm (Tue until 8:30pm). Call first.*

For good shows of graphic and typographic design come see this gallery sponsored by the International Typeface Corp. About 6 shows a year may feature newspaper design, typographic contests or calligraphy with an occasional slide show. Free copies of their newspaper, *U&LC*, are available.

KAMPO CULTURAL CENTER
31 Bond St. (Lafayette St. & Bowery).
☎ *(212) 228-3063.*
This cultural center is primarily for community artists and performers. The gallery presents 4 exhibitions a year covering all visual arts.
Events: *Theater, dance and lectures all for a fee.*

LA MAMA/LA GALLERIA
(See "For the Matinee Idlers.")

MARYMOUNT MANHATTAN COLLEGE GALLERY
(See "For the Knowledge Seekers.")

MASTER EAGLE GALLERY
40 W. 25th St. (Broadway & 6th Ave.).
☎ *(212) 924-8277.*
Hours: *Mon-Fri 9:30am-4pm.*
Groups: *By appt. only.*
This engraving company carves out an artistic niche for the best in graphic art and design. Two good-sized rooms act as the gallery with 6 shows a year ranging from original art for children's book illustrations (Dec & Jan), cartoon art, calligraphy and Japanese art to the Andy Awards (advertising design). Business, school and community groups can arrange a visit, which will include a lecture and a film on the preparation process for printing.

METLIFE GALLERY ◆
24 E. 24th St. (Madison Ave.), main fl.
☎ *(212) 578-2723/2037.*
Hours: *Mon-Sat 10am-6pm.*
The MetLife Gallery presents 5 exhibits yearly on diverse themes and artistic media; many are top-notch loan shows. Previous ones have featured video art, hands-on exhibits and children's art in this large one-room gallery. Be sure not to miss the outstanding WPA murals in the lobby by 3 generations of Wyeths, depicting historical American scenes using Wyeth family members as models.

MIDDLE COLLEGIATE CHURCH, 7TH & 2ND PHOTO GALLERY
(See "For the Believers.")

MUNICIPAL ART SOCIETY (MAS) ◆
Urban Center, 457 Madison Ave. (at 51st St.).
☎ *(212) 935-3960.*

Hours: *Mon-Sat 11am-5pm. Closed Hols. Call first.*

What better goal could a society have than wanting to make N.Y.C. a "more livable city"? Started in 1892 with the intention of adorning public places with art, statues, murals and fountains, the MAS has since expanded its role to include improving and preserving our architectural heritage and visual aesthetics. MAS has become the watchdog over our physical city and a force to be reckoned with in the courts, with developers and city planners. It has played an essential role in saving and obtaining landmark status for Grand Central, Radio City Music Hall, Tweed Courthouse, Lever House, St. Bart's and the Villard Houses (the Society's home and the lobby of the Helmsley Palace). MAS guards against skyscrapers obstructing valuable sun and air space and adamantly opposes the construction of "sliver buildings." It also helped to ban soft-coal burning within the city limits and supported Rockefeller Center, an unpopular project at the time.

The MAS sponsors exhibitions on aspects of N.Y.C., such as Rockefeller Center's birthday celebration, the Brooklyn Bridge centennial, the buildings of Philip Johnson and the history of housing from 1880.

Take a moment to admire the Urban Center's Villard Houses. Built in 1883-85 for the railroad magnate and journalist Henry Villard, they provide a superb example of a High Renaissance palazzo by McKim, Mead & White.

MAS's 40-page *Guide to Lower Manhattan* with 5 tours originating from Foley Square is given free to those on jury duty (or can be purchased at the Urban Center). The Information Exchange is a reference library and clearinghouse on urban issues (see "For the Bookworms").

Events: *Occasional evening programs of seminars, lectures, panel discussions or films (some at a fee) pertaining to the exhibit; classes (fee); a free Wed at 12:30pm walking tour of Grand Central Terminal (see "For the Tourists"); occasional mid-day talks generally on Thu; and weekend walking tours of N.Y.C. (fee).*

NATIONAL ARTS CLUB ♣
15 Gramercy Pk. S. (Irving Pl. & Park Ave. S.).
☎ *(212) 475-3424.*
Hours: *Mon-Sun noon-6pm (vary by exhibition). Closed Jul & Aug.*

This elegant 1884 Victorian Gothic townhouse remodeled by Calvert Vaux was once the residence of Samuel Tilden, the 1876 Democratic presidential candidate who lost to Rutherford B. Hayes. Today it's a private club (dating back to 1898) for artists and patrons. Their exhibitions, generally of a high caliber, include a members' show in Dec-Jan as well as a roster of other professional ones.

NATIONAL INSTITUTE FOR ARCHITECTURAL EDUCATION
30 W. 22nd St. (5th-6th Aves.), 6th fl.
☎ *(212) 924-7000.*
Hours: *Mon-Fri 10am-4pm, Sat 11am-5pm.*

This Institute's good-sized gallery constructs 6 changing exhibitions a year relating to architecture through drawings, models and

photographs.
Events: *Competitions for fellowships.*

NATIONAL URBAN LEAGUE—GALLERY 62
500 E. 62nd St. (at York Ave.).
☎ *(212) 310-9000.*
Hours: *Mon-Fri 10am-4pm. Closed Sat, Sun & Hols and between shows.*
Group Tours: *By appt. only.*

Next door to a gas station and almost on the FDR Drive seems an unlikely place to find a little art gallery. The 6 exhibitions a year in the lobby feature the works of minority artists. The League provides valuable services for minorities, including career training, voter registration, healthcare, housing, crime prevention and prison reform.

NEW SCHOOL ART COLLECTION
65 5th Ave. (13th-14th Sts.).
☎ *(212) 741-5690/5667.*
Hours: *Mon-Fri 10am-4:30pm (school term).*

The art collection of the Albert A. List family adorns the first 3 floors of this New School building. Some interesting paintings and sculptures by lesser-known artists should be viewed in a cursory fashion. The lobby provides a comfortable respite and student environment. For a delightful outdoor sculpture garden, visit the New School's main location at 66 W. 12th St.

NEW YORK STUDIO SCHOOL GALLERY
(See "For the Knowledge Seekers.")

NIKON HOUSE
620 5th Ave. (at Rockefeller Center).
☎ *(212) 586-3907.*
Hours: *Tue-Sat 9:30am-5:30pm. Closed Sun, Mon & some Hols. Call first.*

Situated on the English side of the Channel Gardens at Rockefeller Center, the Nikon House takes excellent photographs and presents them on a monthly basis. A full line of Nikon equipment can be examined in the presence of their technical staff.
Events: *Free lunchtime workshops on 35 mm photography.*

NYU PHOTO CENTER GALLERY
NYU Tisch School of the Arts, 721 Broadway, (Washington Pl. & Waverly St.), 8th fl.
☎ *(212) 998-1930.*
Hours: *Mon-Fri 10am-6pm, Sat noon-5pm (mid Sep-May with Hol breaks). Call first.*

NYU's Photography Department develops photographic shows by either professionals or student/faculty works. Don't be dissuaded if there's no sign on the ground floor or if the elevator is temperamental, as the shows can be worthwhile.

OFFICE OF MANHATTAN BOROUGH PRESIDENT
Municipal Bldg., 1 Centre St., Room 19 South.
☎ *(212) 669-8300.*
Hours: *Mon-Fri 10am-5pm.*

Along the walls of this hallowed (and well-trodden) corridor, you will find a brief cultural respite from the otherwise political scene. Monthly art exhibitions are governed by photos, paintings, drawings or any hanging medium of Manhattan artists, community groups or on a Manhattan theme, all in the interest of patronizing up-and-coming artists.

Also take a moment to appreciate the substantial Municipal Building, home of the city's administrative agencies, which was built in 1913 by William A. Kendall of McKim, Mead & White. Incorporating the need for skyscraper construction and a new subway station, plus the popularity of classical architecture, the architect achieved a successful blend. A grand and innovative 3-floor open plaza once received traffic from Brooklyn and was called "The Gate of the City." A floodlit, 20-foot copper statue of "Civic Fame" by Adolph Weinman proudly tops it off.

PAINEWEBBER ART GALLERY 🍎
1285 Avenue of Americas (51st-52nd Sts.).
☎ *(212) 713-2162.*
Hours: *Mon-Fri 8am-6pm.*
Groups: *By appt. only.*

This showcase for N.Y.C. nonprofit cultural groups presents quarterly exhibitions covering diverse themes in all media.
Events: *Special holiday Toy Soldiers in front of PaineWebber.*

PAINTING SPACE 122
409 E. 9th St. (off 1st Ave.).
☎ *(212) 533-4624.*
Hours: *Thu-Sun noon-6pm.*

A small (very small) ground-floor room of a converted public schoolhouse has about 10 exhibits a year featuring up-and-coming artists.

PARSONS SCHOOL OF DESIGN
(See "For the Knowledge Seekers.")

PEN & BRUSH
16 E. 10th St. (5th Ave. & University Pl.).
☎ *(212) 475-3669.*
Hours: *Tue-Sun 1-4pm (Sep-May). Closed Mon. Call first.*

This art and literary club offers exhibitions of crafts, paintings, drawings or sculpture in the small living room of this brownstone, where the club has been located since its inception in 1893.
Events: *On 4 evenings a month, free lectures on art or writing or a concert (which follows dinners that are not free); and prose & poetry seminars, workshops and arts & crafts courses.*

ADAM CLAYTON POWELL JR. STATE OFFICE BUILDING
163 W. 125th St. (Lenox Ave. & Powell Blvd.).
☎ *(212) 864-4500.*
Hours: *Mon-Fri noon-3pm.*

Black and Hispanic artwork lines the walls of this State office building, lending a cultural contrast to the business at hand. Administered by the Studio Museum of Harlem, the exhibitions have featured a wide range of art, including shows on emerging African-American and Latino artists, community groups and works from the permanent collection. Each show lasts about 10-12 weeks with a 2-week break between shows.

PRATT MANHATTAN GALLERY
Puck Bldg., 295 Lafayette St. (at E. Houston St.), 2nd fl.
☎ *(212) 925-8481.*
Hours: *Mon-Sat 10am-5pm.*

This professional showcase of Pratt Institute (Brooklyn) presents thematically lively monthly exhibitions dedicated to painting, sculpture, architecture and graphic arts. Eight thoughtful shows a year feature a combination of student and professional artists.

The Puck Building, a 9-story landmark in Romanesque Revival style, was the home to *Puck*, a satirical weekly of American life, which was published from 1887 to 1918; today it has been transformed into commercial condo space and the Pratt Manhattan Gallery. A delightful golden statue of the building's namesake stands perched over the entrance, holding a crayon as a staff in one hand and a mirror in the other.

SALMAGUNDI CLUB 🍎
47 5th Ave. (11th-12th Sts.).
☎ *(212) 255-7740.*
Hours: *Mon-Fri 1-5pm.*

This oldest professional art club in the U.S. (founded in 1870) occupies a grand 1852 Italianate brownstone with all the cozy trimmings (wood panelling, fireplaces, spiral staircases). A classy living room for members is off limits but can be peeked into. Exhibitions, however, are very much open to the public, featuring the club's own collection, members' handiworks, the American Watercolor Society juried competition and the spring auction. An art archive is available only upon permission.

Events: *Bi-monthly lectures & demos by member artists or invited speakers.*

SCHOMBURG CENTER FOR RESEARCH IN BLACK CULTURE
(See "For the Bookworms.")

SCHOOL OF VISUAL ARTS — STUDENT GALLERIES
(See "For the Knowledge Seekers.")

SCULPTURE CENTER
167 E. 69th St. (Lexington & 3rd Aves.).
☎ *(212) 879-3500.*
Hours: *Tue-Sat 11am-5pm. Closed Mon, Sun & Jul-Aug.*
Founded in 1929, this sculpture school has been chiseling out talented artists ever since. Its gallery provides alternative space for emerging and mid-career sculptors. Installations and student works are exhibited in Jun.
Events: *Workshops, children's classes and performances.*

TRAPHAGEN SCHOOL OF FASHION
☎ *(212) 673-0300.*
This school of design and interior decoration is trying to establish an ethnic costumes museum in Soho in 1992. Call for info.

TWEED COURTHOUSE
(See "For the Exhibitionists.")

URBAN CENTER
(See Municipal Art Society in this chapter.)

WOMEN'S INTERART CENTER
549 W. 52nd St. (at 11th Ave.).
☎ *(212) 246-1050.*
Hours: *Mon-Fri 1-6pm (may vary by show) and before each performance.*
Begun in 1969, this center promotes and provides a showcase for the works of independent women in all artistic disciplines including new media. Located off the beaten track, this multi-arts center, through its gallery, theater and workspaces for artists, encourages the blending and integration of art forms. The gallery has about 8 exhibitions or installations a year, focusing on painting, sculpture, photography, ceramics, performance art and videotape by artists around the country. Music, dance and theatrical productions are performed here (fee).

WORLD FINANCIAL CENTER ♦♦♦♦
(See "For the Lobbyists.")

YMCA
(See "For the Knowledge Seekers.")

The Bronx

Art galleries displaying professional and student works can be found at Fordham University at Rose Hill, Hostos Community College, Herbert H. Lehman College and Manhattan College; please consult "For the Knowledge Seekers" for details.

Brooklyn

Art galleries displaying professional and student works can be found at Kingsborough Community College, Long Island University, N.Y.C. Technical College and Pratt Institute; please consult "For the Knowledge Seekers."

BROOKLYN ARTS & CULTURAL ASSOCIATION (BACA) 
111 Willoughby St. (Bridge & Duffield Sts.).
☏ *(718) 596-2222/783-3077.*
Hours: *Tue-Fri noon-6pm, Sat 1-6pm and during performances Thu, Fri & Sat nites. Closed Sun, Mon & Jul-Aug.*
Opening reception usually on 1st Fri of show from 6 to 8pm.

This active arts and cultural center sponsors 2 galleries featuring exhibitions for 4-week stints by contemporary artists on a wide range of themes, such as a holiday toy show, body sculpture, women in the arts and video shows. Their annual Juried Miniature Exhibit blooms in spring. The New Contemporary Theater presents generally avant-garde performances of music, dance and theater (fee). Ask to be put on their mailing list for their great brochure of cultural happenings in Brooklyn.
Events: *Free "Summerseries" concerts in Brooklyn parks.*

BROOKLYN BOTANIC GARDENS EXHIBITS AT STEIN-HARDT CONSERVATORY
(See "For the Birds.")

BROOKLYN HEIGHTS ARTS PROMENADE ART SHOW
Brooklyn Heights Promenade at East River.
☏ *(718) 783-4469.*
Brooklyn's oldest outdoor art exhibit is sponsored by BACA twice a year.

GRAND ARMY PLAZA, THE MEMORIAL ARCH GALLERY
(See Prospect Park under "For the Birds.")

HISTORIC BROOKLYN BRIDGE ANCHORAGE
Brooklyn Bridge, Cadman Plaza W. & Front St.
☏ *(212) 619-1955, (718) 855-7882.*
Hours: *Thu-Sun 11am-6pm (summer).*

In the "cavernous vaults" of the Brooklyn Bridge is one exhibition each summer of large-scale installation works sponsored by Creative Time; it's quite a unique experience to see art inside a bridge!

KINGS BAY YM-YWHA GALLERY
Meinhard Bldg., 3495 Nostrand Ave. & Ave. V.
☏ *(718) 648-7703.*
Hours: *Mon-Thu 8:30am-9pm, Fri 9am-4pm, Sun 9am-5pm. Closed Sat & Hols.*

Monthly exhibits feature primarily local artists working in all artistic media. "Meet the Artist" receptions are usually held on Sun 1-3pm.

OLLANTAY CENTER FOR THE ARTS
87-03 Northern Blvd., Jackson Hts.
☎ *(718) 565-6499.*
Hours: *Call for details.*
   This center is interested in the promotion and preservation of Latin American culture in N.Y.C., especially Queens. Exhibitions include both Hispanic and non-Hispanic artists. The Ollantay Traveling Theater offers Spanish and English theater in Queens.
Events: *Workshops and folk art programs.*

PROSPECT PARK BOATHOUSE GALLERY
(See "For the Birds.")

THE ROTUNDA GALLERY
Brooklyn War Memorial, Cadman Plaza W. at Orange St. Moving Fall '91 to 1 Pierpont Plaza.
☎ *(718) 875-4031.*
Hours: *Tue-Fri noon-5pm, Sat 11am-4pm.*
School Groups: *By appt., 855-7882.*
   Sponsored by The Fund, this gallery presents Brooklyn-affiliated artists' works in 4 different shows a year.
Events: *Courses for school groups.*

YMCA OF BROOKLYN
30 3rd Ave. (Atlantic Ave.), 2nd fl.
☎ *(718) 875-1190.*
Hours: *Mon-Fri 9am-6pm, Sat by appt.*
   This Y features exhibits of local artists every 2-3 months with opening receptions.

Queens

Art galleries displaying professional and student works can be found at Queens, Queensborough Community and York Colleges; please consult "For the Knowledge Seekers."

CENTRAL QUEENS YM & YWHA
67-09 108th St. (67th Rd. & 67th Ave.), Forest Hills.
☎ *(718) 268-5011.*
Hours: *Mon-Thu 9am-9:45pm, Fri 9am-3pm, Sun 9am-6:45pm. Closed Sat & Hols.*
   This Y has a complete gym, an Olympic-sized pool, classes, the Heresi Jewish Heritage Library, social services for new Russian immigrants and an art gallery featuring quarterly shows on Jewish themes and local artists.
Events: *Free trial classes, weekly children's storytelling for ages 2 1/2-5 on Thu at 1:15pm and lectures for seniors.*

CHUNG-CHENG GALLERY ☀
St. John's University, Grand Central & Utopia Pkwys., Jamaica.
☎ *(718) 990-6581.*
Hours: *Mon-Fri 10am-6pm, Sat-Sun 10am-4pm. Closed Thanksgiving. Call first.*
Groups: *By appt. only.*
This cultural showcase for the Institute of Asian Studies of St. John's is housed in the Sun Yat Sen Hall, which was modeled after the Great Peace Palace of the Forbidden City of Beijing. Specializing in Oriental art, the gallery displays items from its permanent collection of over 1,000 pieces from 7th C. to contemporary Chinese porcelain, painting, calligraphy, photography, clothing, stamps, currency, sculpture and Japanese artworks. There are also about 8 to 10 special exhibitions yearly.

Some highlights of the permanent collection (thanks to Harry Goebel, a N.Y. lawyer, plus later donations) include Ming dynasty jade seals, an amazing jade elephant (worth its weight in gold!), 19th C. imperial robes, sake bottles with splendid glazes, Satsuma ceramic ware (most important in the 19th C.), ivory netsukes, Ming dynasty landscape paintings and a priceless imperial Chinese painting set of the late 1600s. About 200 pieces are on display at any given time. The special exhibitions are primarily on Oriental art; however, 2 or 3 feature community shows of all kinds.
Events: *Movies, lectures, performing arts and demos.*

FLUSHING ARTS COUNCIL GALLERY
137-35 Northern Blvd. (W. of Main St.), Flushing.
☎ *(718) 463-7700.*
Plans for Gallery space in 1992.
Housed in the renovated 1862 Flushing Town Hall, a Gothic Revival delight, this nonprofit Arts Council plans to have gallery space available in 1992 to show the works of good contemporary artists, with a preference for those living in Queens. A theater for performances is also on the drawing board. The Council continues to collaborate with other organizations to sponsor art exhibits around Queens.

To obtain the Council's excellent "CultureCalendar," call for a complimentary copy (membership is reasonable).
Events: *Many free events, especially summer concerts around Queens.*

LANGSTON HUGHES COMMUNITY LIBRARY & CULTURAL CENTER
(See "For the Bookworms.")

JACKSON HEIGHTS ART CLUB
35-64 79th St. (off 37th Ave.), lower level.
☎ *(718) 939-7111.*
Hours: *Sat-Sun 1-4pm.*
This club sponsors indoor monthly exhibits of members' works in oils, pastels, acrylics and watercolors and outdoor art shows (Jun & Sep). Children's artwork is also displayed.

Events: Inexpensive art classes for adults and children.

JAMAICA ARTS CENTER ⚫

161-04 Jamaica Ave., Jamaica.
☎ *(718) 658-7400.*
Hours: *Mon-Sat 10am-5pm (some exhibits vary the hours).*
Groups: *By appt. only. School groups can arrange a participatory session with an artist.*

Begun in 1872 to provide downtown Jamaica with a cultural center, JAC has certainly succeeded. By offering art exhibitions, music programs, outreach programs, workshops and classes (most at a fee), JAC is a valuable community arts resource center. Three different gallery exhibitions are shown concurrently: one of a "museum-oriented" thematic nature, one by community groups and one by the collective artistic wisdom of 7 Black artists in the co-op gallery.

JAC sponsors an impressive portfolio of classes and workshops (3 semesters a year) for all ages (some free). At the theater, children's storytelling with puppets is a big hit. Jazz is offered at the Black Box Theater by the Jamaica Arts Jazz Ensemble; jazz sessions are held on Fri from noon-2pm (Jun-Aug) at the nearby Farmers' Market.

P.S. 1—PROJECT STUDIO ONE ⚫

46-01 21st St. (46th Rd. & 46th St.).
☎ *(718) 784-2084/2.*
Hours: *Wed-Sun noon-6pm. Closed Jul-mid Sep.*

A classic example of Romanesque Revival architecture, this 1892 school building (the oldest in Queens) was slated to be scrapped in 1976 until the Institute for Art & Urban Resources took it over. This nonprofit arts organization turned the building into the largest alternative space (50,000 sq. feet) in North America, representing over 3,000 artists in 3 shows yearly. Past shows have projected the images of "New York, New Wave," abstract painting of the 1960s and "Expressions, New Art from Germany." A tremendous amount of space for artist's studios and installations is available.
Events: Video, film, fashion shows and performances.

SOCRATES SCULPTURE PARK

(See "For the Birds.")

Staten Island

Art galleries displaying professional and student works can be found at the College of Staten Island and Wagner College; please consult "For the Knowledge Seekers."

For the Gallery Hoppers

In the world of commercial art galleries, "Gallery hopping" can be an enjoyable free cultural sport, especially as New York City is blessed with an exuberance of art dealers. But keep in mind a few rules of the game.

First, you don't have to be a wealthy art collector to play. Everyone is welcome. In fact, clearly 90% of most gallery "gawkers" probably have no intention of buying a thing. Since many galleries represent the works of contemporary artists, gallery hopping exposes you to the mainstream of contemporary art. Also, note that most galleries are closed in Aug or open by appointment only.

Second, don't be afraid to ask questions or to request to see additional works of an artist that are not on display.

Third, be aware that some galleries are either dealer-run (representing many artists for their mutual profit) or co-op artist-run (to profit the artists only). In the latter case, the artist may in fact be "manning" the gallery and can certainly answer questions.

And last, don't be too shy to ask for a free copy of the *Gallery Guide*, the industry's Bible, which lists what's going on and includes detailed maps; it lists exhibition openings in the back of the magazine. Traditionally, galleries show the works of one artist each month with a group exhibition in the Summer. Each new show is typically launched by a reception for the Artist(s) during the first week of the month. The public is welcome. Frequently refreshments are served.

As there are hundreds of different commercial galleries, each with its own specialty, the following list highlights the important or unique galleries worth visiting in the 3 major gallery locations: Soho, 57th Street and Madison Avenue (or above 57th Street).

> *"Every portrait that is painted with feeling is a portrait of the artist, not the sitter."*
>
> — OSCAR WILDE

Soho

BROOKE ALEXANDER
59 Wooster St. (Spring & Broome Sts.), 2nd fl.
☎ (212) 925-4338.
Hours: Tue-Sat 10am-6pm.
Specialty: Paintings, drawings, sculpture by contemporary artists.

PAMELA AUCHINCLOSS GALLERY
558 Broadway, (Prince & Spring Sts.), 2nd fl.
☎ (212) 966-7753.
Hours: Tue-Sat 10am-6pm.
Specialty: Works by contemporary American and European artists.

DAVID BEITZEL GALLERY
102 Prince St. (corner of Greene St.), 2nd fl.
☎ (212) 219-2863.
Hours: Tue-Sat 10am-6pm.
Specialty: Contemporary artists in all media.

MARY BOONE GALLERY
417 W. Broadway (Prince & Spring Sts.).
☎ (212) 431-1818.
Hours: Tue-Sat 10am-6pm.
Specialty: Contemporary American and European artists.

JANET BORDEN INC.
560 Broadway (corner Prince St.), 6th fl.
☎ (212) 431-0166.
Hours: Tue-Sat 11am-5pm.
Specialty: Works by contemporary photographers.

LEO CASTELLI
420 W. Broadway (Prince & Spring Sts.), 2nd fl.
☎ (212) 431-5160.
Hours: Tue-Sat 10am-6pm.
Specialty: Paintings, drawings, sculpture by established contemporary artists.

PAULA COOPER GALLERY
155 Wooster St. (Houston & Prince Sts.).
☎ (212) 674-0766.
Hours: Tue-Sat 10am-6pm.
Specialty: Contemporary paintings, sculpture, drawings, prints and photography.

THE DRAWING CENTER
35 Wooster St. (Broome & Grand Sts.).
☎ (212) 219-2166.
Hours: Tue-Fri 10am-6pm (Wed til 8pm), Sat 11am-6pm.

Specialty: *Exhibitions of old masters and contemporary drawings.*

RONALD FELDMAN FINE ARTS
31 Mercer St. (Grand & Canal Sts.).
☎ *(212) 226-3232.*
Hours: *Tue-Sat 10am-6pm, Mon by appt.*
Specialty: *Modern and contemporary art, including Russian artists.*

BARBARA GLADSTONE
99 Greene St. (Prince & Spring Sts.).
☎ *(212) 431-3334.*
Hours: *Tue-Sat 10am-6pm.*
Specialty: *Contemporary artists, many Europeans in all media.*

JOHN GOOD GALLERY
532 Broadway, (Prince & Spring Sts.), 2nd fl.
☎ *(212) 941-8066*
Hours: *Tue-Sat 10am-6pm.*
Specialty: *Contemporary artists in all media.*

JAY GORNEY MODERN ART
100 Greene St. (Prince & Spring Sts.).
☎ *(212) 966-4480.*
Hours: *Tue-Sat 10am-6pm.*
Specialty: *Works mainly by conceptual and installation artists.*

THE HELLER GALLERY
71 Greene St. (Spring & Broome Sts.).
☎ *(212) 966-5948.*
Hours: *Tue-Sat 11am-6pm.*
Specialty: *Contemporary glass artists.*

NANCY HOFFMAN GALLERY
429 W. Broadway (Prince & Spring Sts.).
☎ *(212) 966-6676.*
Hours: *Tue-Sat 10am-6pm.*
Specialty: *Contemporary paintings, sculpture and works on paper.*

LORENCE-MONK GALLERY
568 Broadway (corner Prince St.), 11th fl..
☎ *(212) 431-3555.*
Hours: *Tue-Sat 10am-6pm.*
Specialty: *Contemporary artists in all media.*

CURT MARCUS GALLERY
578 Broadway (corner Prince St.), 10th fl.
☎ *(212) 226-3200.*
Hours: *Tue-Sat 10am-6pm.*
Specialty: *Contemporary artists, mainly painting, sculpture and photography.*

METRO PICTURES
150 Greene St. (corner Houston St.).
☎ *(212) 925-8335.*
Hours: *Tue-Sat 10am-6pm.*
Specialty: *Contemporary artists in all media.*

MAX PROTETCH GALLERY
560 Broadway (corner Prince St.), 2nd fl.
☎ *(212) 966-5454.*
Hours: *Tue-Sat 10am-6pm.*
Specialty: *Contemporary American paintings, ceramics and architectural drawings.*

TONY SHAFRAZI
130 Prince St. (corner Wooster St.), 5th fl.
☎ *(212) 274-9300.*
Hours: *Tue-Sat 10am-6pm.*
Specialty: *Works in all media by emerging and established artists.*

STALEY-WISE
560 Broadway, (corner Prince St.), 6th fl.
☎ *(212) 966-6223.*
Hours: *Tue-Sat noon-5pm.*
Specialty: *20th C. photography, including Hollywood, fashion and portraiture.*

STARK GALLERY
594 Broadway (Houston & Prince Sts.), 4th fl.
☎ *(212) 925-4484.*
Hours: *Tue-Sat 10am-6pm.*
Specialty: *Contemporary American and European artists.*

STUX GALLERY
155 Spring St. (Wooster St. & W. Broadway), 2nd & 3rd fls.
☎ *(212) 219-0010.*
Hours: *Tue-Sat 10am-6pm.*
Specialty: *Contemporary painting, sculpture and photography.*

EDWARD THORP GALLERY
103 Prince St. (corner Greene St.), 2nd fl.
☎ *(212) 431-6880.*
Hours: *Tue-Sat 10am-6pm.*
Specialty: *Contemporary American and European paintings and sculpture.*

BARBARA TOLL FINE ARTS
146 Greene St. (Houston & Prince Sts.).
☎ *(212) 431-1788.*
Hours: *Tue-Sat 10am-6pm.*
Specialty: *Contemporary American and European artists in all media.*

JOHN WEBER GALLERY
142 Greene St. (Houston & Prince Sts.), 3rd fl.
☎ *(212) 966-6115.*
Hours: *Tue-Sat 10am-6pm.*
Specialty: *Contemporary painting, sculpture and photography; also contemporary aboriginal artists.*

WITKIN GALLERY, INC.
415 W. Broadway, (Prince & Spring Sts.), 4th fl.
☎ *(212) 925-5510.*
Hours: *Tue-Sat 11am-6pm.*
Specialty: *Historic and contemporary photographs and books.*

57th Street

ASSOCIATED AMERICAN ARTISTS
20 W. 57th St. (5th-6th Aves.), 6th fl.
☎ *(212) 399-5510.*
Hours: *Tue-Sat 10am-6pm.*
Specialty: *Old master and contemporary prints and works on paper.*

BLUMHELMAN GALLERY
20 W. 57th St.,(5th-6th Aves.), 2nd fl.
☎ *(212) 245-2888.*
Hours: *Tue-Sat 10am-6pm.*
Specialty: *Modern and contemporary American and European painting and sculpture.*

GRACE BORGENICHT GALLERY
724 5th Ave. (at 56th-57th Sts.), 8th fl.
☎ *(212) 247-2111.*
Hours: *Tue-Fri 10am-5:30pm, Sat 11am-5:30pm.*
Specialty: *Modern and Contemporary artists.*

ANDRE EMMERICH GALLERY
41 E. 57th St. (Madison & Park Aves.), 5th & 6th fls..
☎ *(212) 752-0124.*
Hours: *Tue-Sat 10am-5:30pm.*
Specialty: *Contemporary American and European art as well as also classical antiquities.*

MARIAN GOODMAN GALLERY
24 W. 57th St., (5th-6th Aves.), 4th fl.
☎ *(212) 977-7160.*
Hours: *Tue-Sat 10am-6pm.*
Specialty: *Contemporary painting, sculpture and prints by American and European artists.*

SIDNEY JANIS GALLERY
110 W. 57th St. (6th-7th Aves.), 6th fl.
☎ *(212) 586-0110.*
Hours: *Mon-Sat 10am-5:30pm.*
Specialty: *20th C. and contemporary art.*

KENNEDY GALLERIES, INC.
40 W. 57th St. (5th-6th Aves.), 5th fl.
☎ *(212) 541-9600.*
Hours: *Tue-Sat 9:30am-5:30pm.*
Specialty: *American paintings, sculpture and prints from the 18th, 19th & 20th C.*

KENT FINE ART
41 E. 57th St. (Madison & Park Aves.), 3rd fl.

☎ *(212) 980-9696.*
Hours: *Tue-Sat 10am-5:30pm.*
Specialty: *Contemporary and modern artists.*

JAN KRUGIER GALLERY
41 E. 57th St., (Madison & Park Aves.), 6th fl.
☎ *(212) 755-7288.*
Hours: *Tue-Sat 10am-5:30pm.*
Specialty: *19th & 20th C. European and American artists.*

MERRIN GALLERY
724 5th Ave. (56th-57th Sts.), 3rd fl.
☎ *(212) 757-2884.*
Hours: *Tue-Sat 10am-5pm.*
Specialty: *Ancient and medieval art.*

ROBERT MILLER GALLERY
41 E. 57th St. (Madison & Park Aves.), 2nd fl.
☎ *(212) 980-5454.*
Hours: *Tue-Sat 10am-5:30pm.*
Specialty: *Modern and contemporary painting, sculpture and photography.*

THE PACE GALLERY
32 E. 57th St. (Madison & Park Aves.), 2nd fl.
☎ *(212) 421-3292.*
Hours: *Tue-Sat 930am-5:30pm, Sat 10am-6pm.*
Specialty: *20th C. painting, sculpture, drawings and prints.*

HOLLY SOLOMON GALLERY
724 5th Ave. (56th-57th Sts.), 5th fl.
☎ *(212) 757-7777.*
Hours: *Mon-Sat 10am-6pm.*
Specialty: *Works in all media by contemporary artists.*

JACK TILTON GALLERY
24 W. 57th St. (5th-6th Aves), 3rd fl.
☎ *(212) 247-7480*
Hours: *Tue-Sat 10am-6pm.*
Specialty: *Contemporary painting, drawings and sculpture.*

ZABRISKIE GALLERY
724 5th Ave. (56th-57th St.), 12th fl.
☎ *(212) 307-7430.*
Hours: *Mon-Sat 10am-5:30pm.*
Specialty: *Early 20th C. and contemporary works including photography and large scale sculpture.*

Above 57th Street

GAGOSIAN GALLERY
980 Madison Ave. (76th-77th Sts.).
☎ *(212) 744-2313.*
Hours: *Tue-Sat 10am-6pm.*
Specialty: *Museum-quality exhibits by 20th C. artists.*

HIRSCHL & ADLER FOLK
851 Madison Ave. (71st-72nd Sts.), 2nd fl.
☎ *(212) 988-3655.*
Hours: *Tue-Fri 9:30am-5:30pm, Sat 9:45am-4:45pm.*
Specialty: *19th C. American folk art and furnishings.*

HIRSCHL & ADLER GALLERIES
21 E. 70th St. (5th & Madison Ave.).
☎ *(212) 535-8810.*
Hours: *Tue-Fri 9:30am-5:15pm, Sat 9:30am-4:45pm.*
Specialty: *American art from 18th C. to present and European art and decorative arts.*

HIRSCHL & ADLER MODERN
851 Madison Ave. (71st-72nd Sts.), 2nd fl.
☎ *(212) 744-6700.*
Hours: *Tue-Fri 9:30am-5:30pm, Sat 9:30am-5pm.*
Specialty: *Contemporary American and European art.*

KNOEDLER & COMPANY
19 E. 70th St. (Madison & 5th Aves.).
☎ *(212) 794-0550.*
Hours: *Tue-Fri 9:30am-5:30pm, Sat 10am-5:30pm.*
Specialty: *Contemporary American and European art.*

SALANDER-O'REILLY GALLERIES
20 E. 79th St. (5th & Madison Ave.).
☎ *(212) 879-6606.*
Hours: *Mon-Sat 9:30-5:30pm.*
Specialty: *Contemporary, 19th C. and old masters paintings.*

For the Auctioneers

If you've never been to an auction, you'll find it mildly enjoyable to attend at least one even if you don't have the slightest interest in buying anything. By selecting either Christie's or Sotheby's, you will be gavel gazing in particularly classy and pleasant surroundings. For most auctions, previews are held several days before so you get the chance to examine the goods (as that's not possible on the day); check newspapers for details. Just remember, if you're there to watch, keep your hands down!

> *"I will give thrice so much to any well-deserving friend; but in the way of a bargain, mark me, I will cavil on the ninth part of a hair."*
>
> — WILLIAM SHAKESPEARE

CHRISTIE'S
502 Park Ave. (59th-60th Sts.).
☎ *(212) 546-1000.*

WILLIAM DOYLE
175 E. 87th St. (Lexington & 3rd Aves.).
☎ *(212) 427-2730.*

LUBIN GALLERIES
30 W. 26th St. (Broadway & 6th Ave.).
☎ *(212) 924-3777.*

MANHATTAN GALLERIES
221 W. 17th St. (7th & 8th Aves.).
☎ *(212) 727-0370.*

PHILLIPS
406 E. 79th St. (at 1st Ave.).
☎ *(212) 570-4830.*

SOTHEBY'S
1334 York Ave. (at 72nd St.).
☎ *(212) 606-7245.*

SWANN GALLERIES
104 E. 25th St. (at Lexington Ave.).
☎ *(212) 254-4710.*

For the Exhibitionists

Besides art, N.Y.C. is an active and vital center for business, government, commerce and education. Places like the United Nations, the Courts and the Stock Exchanges offer behind-the-scenes glimpses and special collections, which provide valuable and interesting information. Also dotted around the city are special exhibitions on such things as books, history, ships and new cars. There's even one dedicated to the wide variety of locks.

Though this chapter covers only Manhattan, check out the colleges and universities (see "For the Knowledge Seekers") in the other boroughs for various exhibits, especially the Bronx Community College for its Hall of Fame and Manhattan College for its collection of vacuums! Check Floyd Bennett Field in Queens under "For the Birds" for an exhibition on aviation.

"Things seen are mightier than things heard."

— ALFRED, LORD TENNYSON

THE ARSENAL GALLERY
830 5th Ave. (at 64th St.), 3rd fl.
☎ *(212) 360-1309.*
Hours: *Mon-Fri 9:30am-4:30pm. Closed Hols. Call first.*

This solid stone and cast-iron edifice, built from 1847 to 1857, served as the nation's archives for out-of-date Revolutionary War munitions. In 1869 the American Museum of Natural History made its first home here. Today the Arsenal extends its arms to the N.Y.C. Department of Parks & Recreation, which sponsors monthly exhibitions featuring paintings on the environment, photos of N.Y.C., Christmas wreaths or N.Y.C. teachers' art. While in the first floor lobby, check out the wall decorations of life in the 1800s and the 1848 newspaper article.

BELVEDERE CASTLE
(See Central Park listing in "For the Birds.")

THE BMW GALLERY
320 Park Ave. (at 51st St.).
☎ *(212) 319-0088.*
Hours: *Mon-Tue, Thu-Fri 11am-6pm, Wed noon-8pm, Sat noon-6pm.*

At the Park Avenue showroom of BMW are changing exhibits by artists in all media and displays of their exclusive cars and motorcycles.

CASTLE CLINTON
Battery Pk.
☎ *(212) 344-7220.*
Hours: *Daily 8:30am-5pm. Closed Christmas.*
Groups: *By appt.*

Built in 1811 during "fortification fever" (in anticipation of the War of 1812) on what was then an island, this landmark has served the city in many ways over the years: as an entertainment center, an immigration depot, an aquarium, but never as an active fort. In 1842, Samuel F.B. Morse introduced the first wireless telegraph here and in 1850, Jenny Lind (the Swedish nightingale) sang here with tickets selling as high as $225. Seven million immigrants passed through these portals between 1855 and 1890 before the larger Ellis Island took over. Then the aquarium was housed here from 1896 to 1941. The fort was saved from demolition by the National Parks Service and reopened in 1976.

Today the circular red sandstone structure with 8-foot-thick walls punctuated with gun ports contains a courtyard and several small rooms, which recount the fort's history through displays and reconstructions. After the visit, the best bit of all is that you can get recharged in the surrounding Battery Park with its ideal situation facing New York harbor (see "For the Birds").

MARY CELESTE EXHIBIT
45 Wall St., 10th fl.
☎ *(212) 943-1800.*
Hours: *Mon-Fri 8:30am-4:30pm. Call for appt.*

Located on the Atlantic Companies' executive floor, this historical tribute to the mystery of the *Mary Celeste* is not as interesting as the actual tale. As this Insurance Company is the only remaining insurer of the ship's 1872 cargo, the room contains an insurer's rolltop desk, a model of the ship and some memorabilia from the fateful journey. The marine library and the executive dining room are part of the tour. The best part, though, is the mysterious story of this abandoned ship. Knowing that, abandon the tour.

CENTRAL PARK 🍎🍎🍎🍎

(See separate listings under the Arsenal Gallery and The Dairy; also see Central Park under "For the Birds.")

COMMODITIES EXCHANGE (COMEX) 🍎
4 World Trade Center, 9th fl.
☎ *(212) 938-2018.*
Hours: *Mon-Fri 9:30am-3pm.*
Tours: *By appt. only (5 or more).*

A Visitors Gallery takes you into the world of crude oil, gold, silver, coffee, sugar, cotton and orange juice futures. From a perch above the exchange floor, you have an excellent view of each exchange's ring where buyer and seller negotiate prices by outcries. You really must see this to believe it! Go toward the end of the day when the exchanges are closing to see the last-minute pandemonium. A prearranged tour with slide show can be set up for 10am, 11am or 2:15pm and it's worthwhile as the wall displays really do not explain what's happening. Don't be disappointed at not seeing pork bellies, as they're traded in Chicago.

THE CON EDISON CONSERVATION CENTER
405 Lexington Ave. (main floor of Chrysler Bldg. at 42nd St.).
☎ *(212) 599-3435.*
Hours: *Mon-Fri 9am-5pm (mid May-mid Oct) and Tue-Sat 9am-5pm (mid Oct-mid May).*

Want to know how to cut down on your electric bill? Want to know how to insulate your home properly? Want to know if you have the right size air-conditioner for your room? These and more probing questions can be explored at this exhibition of energy-saving ideas on heating and cooling, appliances, air-conditioning, weatherization and lighting. An information center with brochures on energy conservation (including comic books and tips for seniors) probably makes this place more interesting for those with high electricity bills. A good advertising job on Con Edison's behalf, nonetheless. Check out the Chrysler Building while you're here (see "For the Lobbyists").

THE COURTS
(See separate listings under the N.Y. Surrogates Court, the Supreme Court of N.Y., Tweed Courthouse and the U.S. Courthouse.)

"Bird-nesting" or sitting in on trials can be interesting, provided you get a good trial (try the U.S. Courthouse or the Supreme Court of N.Y. at Foley Square). For a listing of what's being tried, consult the last page of the *Law Journal* or check the court calendar at the Information

Desk. Easier yet, ask the security guard what he recommends! Once inside the courtroom, you can stay as long as you want.

A historical aside—at one time Foley Square (a few blocks north of City Hall) provided fresh water from its "collect" (pond) for the colonists, but after becoming polluted, the area was filled in to provide valuable real estate. Today several buildings have basement pumps for eliminating the water from these deep underground springs. So it can be said that at times the lawyers are truly treading on dangerous ground!

THE DAIRY
Central Park, S. of 65th St. Transverse between the Zoo and Carousel.
☎ *(212) 397-3156.*
Hours: *Sat-Thu 11am-5pm, Fri 1-5pm (closes 1 hour earlier in winter).*

This decorative, cutesy-looking Victorian folly (once the park's milk bar for children in the 1870s) has been renovated to serve as a Visitors Center. The Dairy enriches our lives by having several exhibitions a year on some aspect of Central Park, such as the park's history, the rebuilding process of the Zoo or the Carousel. An audio-visual slide show on the history of the park is self-activating. Nothing too earth-shattering, but probably interesting for the kids.

Events: *Occasional free guided park tours by Urban Park Rangers usually on Sun at 2pm (Apr-Sep); concerts Sat, Sun & some weekdays at 1pm (Jun-Aug); family workshops for children 5-7 on Sat or Sun from 1:30-3pm (reservation needed); performances for all ages; and a self-guided walking tour of Central Park (fee).*

THE FEDERAL RESERVE BANK GALLERY
(See "For the Tourists.")

GENERAL MOTORS (GM) BUILDING
767 5th Ave. (58th-59th Sts.), lobby.
☎ *(212) 418-6100.*
Hours: *Mon-Fri 9am-6pm, Sat 10am-6pm.*

Check out the General Motors new car offerings without a high-pressure salesman breathing down your neck! Sticker prices and brochures are available. Romping around inside the cars is allowed.

GOTHAM BOOK MART
41 W. 47th St. (5th-6th Aves.).
☎ *(212) 719-4476.*

You certainly wouldn't expect to find this gem in the otherwise sparkling diamond district, but for the past 70 years this place has been a refuge for those particularly looking for new or used books on 20th C. literature. It has also over the years been the relief headquarters for many needy writers, such as Henry Miller. Don't be dismayed at the utter clutter of the bookshelves as the capable staff can miraculously help to sort it out.

On the 2nd floor are exhibitions, usually relating to books and featuring young writers and illustrators. At Christmas, this showcase branches off to include antique Christmas tree ornaments placed on a tree and in display cases, some for sale and some Dresden classics. In the summer, rare and unusual postcards are on view (it's the owner's hobby). The decorative store sign says "Wise Men Fish Here," and this really is quite a catch.

Events: *Occasional readings and publication parties open to the public.*

GRANT NATIONAL MEMORIAL (GRANT'S TOMB)
122 St. & Riverside Dr.
☎ *(212) 666-1640.*
Hours: *Wed-Sun 9am-4:30pm.*
Groups: *By appt. only.*

Incorporating the ideas of famous Greek and Roman mausoleums, this massive tribute to a Civil War General and our 18th President stands proudly on a bluff overlooking the Hudson River. It's 150 feet high and is made from 8,000 tons of granite. Completed in 1897 by architect John Duncan and sculptor J. Massey Rhind, this grand final resting place seems somewhat inappropriate for a man who considered himself shy, unassuming and uncomfortable with pomp and ceremony. At any rate, appreciate the exterior ornamentation with figures representing Victory and Peace, upholding the inscription "Let Us Have Peace" (referring to Grant's 1868 pledge of amnesty for Confederate leaders and protection for freed Blacks).

Inside, the magnificent marble and limestone rotunda is flanked on either side by sculptural reliefs and exhibits of the life and times of Ulysses S. Grant. The bronze busts in the crypt are of Grant's favorite generals: Sherman, Sheridan, Thomas and MacPherson.

Take time to enjoy the colorful and undulating mosaic benches surrounding the memorial. In this artwork done by the community in the early 1970s (this author shared in this wonderful experience), you

will see everything from world leaders, the Statue of Liberty (you really have to look for that), Michelangelo's "Creation," Matisse dancers, to cowboys and Indians, animals, trees and much more.

Events: *The annual celebration of Grant's birth on Apr 27th; the Jazzmobile and Dancemobile (summer).*

THE GROLIER CLUB
47 E. 60th St. (Madison & Park Aves.).
☎ *(212) 838-6690.*
Hours: *Mon-Sat 10am-5pm (Oct-Jun). Occasional summer exhibits. Closed Hols.*

Founded in 1884 for the purpose of improving the quality of book production, design and illustration, this club continues that quest through 5 to 6 public shows a year of the best in manuscripts, books and drawings of the past and present. Recent exhibitions have featured the life of Washington Irving and the relics of writers. A library for scholars, collectors and students offers tomes on the history of book production.

HOYA CRYSTAL GALLERY
450 Park Ave. at 57th St.
☎ *(212) 223-6335.*
Hours: *Mon-Sat 10am-6pm.*
This sparkling gallery/store displays designer and museum glass pieces.

MANHATTAN SAVINGS BANK
385 Madison Ave. (at 47th St.).
86th St. & 3rd Ave.
☎ *(212) 688-3000.*
Hours: *Mon-Fri 8:30am-3pm.*
Monthly exhibits featuring photography, paintings or crafts are quite varied. A comfortable lounge with a piano player makes this a pleasant respite to bank on!

JOHN M. MOSSMAN LOCK COLLECTION
Mechanics Institute, The General Society of Mechanics & Tradesmen, 20 W. 44th St. (5th-6th Aves.).
☎ *(212) 840-1840.*
Hours: *Mon-Fri 10am-4pm. Closed in Jul & at other times. Call first.*
You have probably never seen so many different types of locks before. The variety of new and antique locks (like time, key, dial and padlocks) is staggering. Of particular interest is "the very complicated lock." This exhibit, however, is not displayed well—everything is crammed together. An accompanying book by John M. Mossman, a past president of the society, offers insight into the mystery of how the locks work.

NEW YORK PUBLIC LIBRARY, 42ND STREET CENTRAL RESEARCH LIBRARY ♦♦♦
5th Ave. & 42nd St.
☎ *(212) 661-7220/869-8089/340-0849.*
(See "For the Bookworms.")

NEW YORK STOCK EXCHANGE ♦♦
11 Wall St. (Visitors Gallery at 20 Broad St.), 3rd fl.
☎ *(212) 656-3000.*
Hours: *Mon-Fri 9:15am-4pm (temporarily closed, call to see if reopened).*
Groups: *Of 15 or more by appt. only.*
For an excellent opportunity to learn about our private enterprise system, you can dabble in this stock exchange without losing your shirt! Self-guided tours explain the market's procedures and the meaning of the electronic data. Information boards offer hands-on experience and answer frequently asked questions. Display cases with antiques bring to life the history of the exchange. A film shown every half-hour offers a multi-media experience.

The main attraction undoubtedly is the Visitors Gallery overlooking the exchange floor. A tape recording (in several languages) describes

activities on the floor and the cast of characters. The hubbub and noise is quite overwhelming! You will be impressed by the number of electric monitors and screens spewing out endless stock quotations. All in all, it's very well presented. Go early to avoid the groups.

N.Y. SURROGATES COURT
(a.k.a. Hall of Records), 31 Chambers St.
☎ *(212) 374-8233.*
Hours: *Mon-Fri 9am-5pm.*

This handsome Beaux-Arts landmark was built by John R. Thomas at the turn of the century and was originally called the Hall of Records. Today it houses some surrogate judges' chambers, which are open to the public, as well as the Municipal Archives and Reference Library.

It's worth a moment to pop inside and admire the entrance foyer and lobby. The arched mosaic ceiling of the foyer depicts ancient gods and zodiac signs. The 2 sculptural groupings above the doorway represent the "Consolidation of New York" and "Recording the Purchase of Manhattan Island." The baroque 4-story lobby of luscious multi-colored marble is topped by a skylight, all inspired by the Paris Opera. Display cases house historical exhibitions from time to time. Some of the judges' chambers are worth visiting just for the magnificent mahogany panelling.

ROCKEFELLER CENTER ❅ ❅ ❅
5th-6th Aves., from 48th-51st Sts.
☎ *(212) 698-8676.*
Hours: *Mon-Fri 9am-4:30pm (exhibit on concourse level), Mon-Sun for Rockefeller Center grounds.*

Once of the world's largest privately owned commercial centers (before being sold to the Japanese corporation, Mitsubishi Estate Ltd. in 1989), this complex offers 22 buildings for business, entertainment and sheer pleasure. With 66,000 employees and another 175,000 visitors daily, the Center's population is beaten only by 64 U.S. cities. As one of the first buildings to emphasize the human element, the Center provides a wonderful maze of gardens, fountains and rooftop greenery to make the view pleasant for all around.

John D. Rockefeller negotiated with Columbia University for the lease to the property in the late 1920s, intending it as the site of the Metropolitan Opera House. However, as the Depression set in, the opera company couldn't make the commitment and backed out. Left with a yearly $3 million lease, Rockefeller took a bold and inspired plunge by deciding to build a business and entertainment complex. Even after terrible reviews from the press when the architectural models were presented in 1931, John D. persevered. From 1931 to 1940, a team of architects (Hood & Fouilhoux; Reinhard & Hofmeister; Corbett, Harrison & MacMurray) fulfilled his dream.

The Channel Gardens (separating the French and British buildings) with their ever-changing floral displays majestically lead you down the garden path from 5th Avenue to the focal point, the central esplanade with sunken plaza encircled by colorful flags of UN-member nations. A bronze sculptural "Prometheus" smiles down on ice skaters in winter and outdoor diners in summer. Art Deco buildings of all sizes surround the central arena with one of the highlights, the 70-floor GE building at 30 Rockefeller Plaza, directly behind the fiery God of mankind. Check out the fabulous wall and ceiling murals allegorically depicting the building of the Center. Stand in the lobby and look up at the massive bodies straddling the pillars.

On the Concourse level, find the exhibit room (you may need to consult the guard) to learn more about the history and the prolific artwork at the Center. Display cabinets with photos, original floorplans, memorabilia and an impressive model are fascinating. A 15-minute videotape on the Center's construction seen through the eyes of a junior architect, Walter Kilham, is fascinating.

Events: *See "For the Tourists" for tours (fee); a aummer outdoor music program on Tue & Thu 12:30-1:30pm (May-Aug) in McGraw-Hill Park (49th-50th St. & 6th Ave.), 664-4000; free tickets for NBC-TV shows (see "For the Film Buffs"), 664-4000; the Christmas tree lighting ceremony (early Dec); an excellent tour of Radio City Music Hall leaves from 30 Rockefeller Plaza about every 30 minutes Mon-Sun 10:15am-4:45pm for Adults $6.50 and Children under 6 $3.25 (reservations required for groups of 18 or more; 632-4000).*

SONGWRITERS' HALL OF FAME
Temporary Address: Symphony Cafe, 950 Eighth Ave. (at 56th St.). Plans for permanent museum location in the works.
☎ *(212) 319-1444.*

Until a permanent museum is established, the walls of the Symphony Cafe sing out in tribute to those who made musicals possible, with memorabilia from the Songwriters' Hall of Fame. The singing and dancing worlds of the songwriter and his music are remembered by Gene Kelly's dancing shoes, Fred Astaire's top hat and cane, Ted Lewis's clarinet and cane, Elvis Presley's guitar pick, Hoagy Carmichael's mouthpiece and Julie Andrews's guitar from *The Sound of Music.* Relics of the early music-making machines will include a wind-up phonograph, playasax, playapiano converter and an 1890 Kimball parlor organ. Tin Pan Alley dioramas portray the flavor of that well-known Manhattan address. Old sheet music, photos, records and letters of songwriters and artists add a very personal touch.

STEUBEN GLASS ♦
717 5th Ave. (at 56th St.).
☎ *(212) 752-1441.*
Hours: *Mon-Sat 10am-6pm.*

Outstanding designs in glass can be clearly seen in the gallery/store of Steuben. Be sure to find the museum-quality pieces in the back.

SUPREME COURT APPELLATE DIVISION
27 Madison Ave. (at 25th St.).
☎ *(212) 340-0477.*
Hours: *Mon-Fri 9am-5pm, except Hols.*

Pick up a brochure at the Information Desk to learn about the amazing architectural and sculptural details of this building (inside and out). When the architect, James Brown Lord, built this Neoclassical courthouse in 1900, he spent over one-third of the $683,000 budget for artwork. The lobby has recently had a facelift, which makes the elaborate gold-leaf ceilings, mural friezes and honey-colored Carrara marble even more handsome. Exhibitions on famous Americans, like Aaron Burr and Boss William Tweed, are on display and last 6 months each. Check out the courtroom; a red cherry oak judges' bench and the skylit dome with stained-glass windows of famous lawyers are striking.

SUPREME COURT OF NEW YORK ♦
Foley Sq., 60 Centre St.
☎ *(212) 374-8524/4780.*
Hours: *Mon-Fri 9am-5pm.*
Tours: *Mon-Fri 10:15am for groups (4th graders and up) or individuals by appt. only.*

This bastion of justice resembling a Roman temple, built in 1927 by Guy Lowell, reflects Beaux-Arts classicism at its finest. Above the pediment are 3 statues representing Law, Equity and Truth by Frederick Warren Allen and the inscription of Washington's words, "The True Administration of Justice is the Firmest Pillar of Good Government."

Inside, the decorative dome recounts the "Story of Law" with colorfully painted scenes of great lawgivers over the centuries (done as a WPA project in the 1930s).

In the rotunda, there's always an interesting historical exhibition from the County Clerk's Archives. Previous shows (about 2 per year) have displayed documents, letters, drawings and old photos of Alexander Hamilton and the tricentennial celebration of the city's courts. An informative brochure accompanies each exhibit. For wall scenes of New York life in colonial days in the 1930s, check out Jury Assembly Room 452.

In addition, you really should consider hooking up with the tour to learn more about our judicial system (see "For the Tourists").

TWEED COURTHOUSE
(a.k.a. Old N.Y. County Courthouse), 52 Chambers St.
Hours: *Mon-Fri 9am-4:30pm.*

This building was begun in 1861 but, due to the misappropriation of $10 million by the powerful and notorious Tammany leader, Boss Tweed, it wasn't completed until 1878. John Kellum, the architect, mixed Romanesque and Renaissance Revival styles quite grandly. Having once served as the county and city courthouse, today it houses municipal offices.

The interior rotunda is of interest with its multi-tiered balconies with arches and windows, illuminated by an octagonal skylight. An art gallery showcases the work of city agencies and community groups and is sponsored by the Art Commission (a wonderful organization that ensures the physical beauty of our city through outdoor sculpture and commissions—check out their book, *Manhattan's Outdoor Sculpture*).

UNITED NATIONS ♦♦♦
United Nations Plaza (1st Ave. between 42nd-43rd Sts.).
☎ *(212) 963-1234.*
Hours: *Mon-Fri 9am-5pm, Sat, Sun & Hols 9:15am-5pm. Children under 12 must be acc. by an Adult.*
Tours: *Daily 9:15am-4:45pm (fee, see below for details).*

McMillan
OCT '83

Want to take a trip out of the U.S. and never leave Manhattan? Then visit the United Nations, an organization of sovereign nations striving to maintain worldwide peace, harmony and security through international cooperation. Chartered in 1945, it was not until 1950-52 that the United Nations occupied its permanent home on the East River. Thanks to John D. Rockefeller, Jr.'s $8.5 million offer to purchase the slum area between 42nd-48th Sts. in 1946, we have the UN in Manhattan. It was designed in the International Style by a team of 11 architects headed by the American Wallace K. Harrison, with assistance from LeCorbusier of France and Oscar Niemeyer of Brazil. The construction was financed by an interest-free loan of $67 million from the United States government. The focal point quickly became the Secretariat building (544 feet high), the splendid green-tinted glass and steel skyscraper, the first of its kind in N.Y.C. to deviate from the wedding-cake style (or setbacks). Be sure to walk around the grounds so you can appreciate all facets of the building, the riverview garden and artwork from around the world situated on its 18 acres.

Once inside, the right side of the lobby reveals the UN pendulum, the magnificent stained-glass window (entitled "Peace") by Marc Chagall located in front of the Meditation Chapel and a display case containing a moon rock. To the left side of the entrance is a model of the Soviet satellite "Sputnik I." Beyond the information desk is an exhibit area, frequently with shows of children's artwork from around the world. A Visitors Guide brochure can be obtained at the Information Desk. The concourse level should be approached at your own risk as there are some wonderful souvenir shops and bookstores.

If you are interested in seeing the UN in action, ask the security guards if the Security Council is meeting, as occasionally its meetings are open to the public; children under 12 are not allowed at the official meetings. Prearranged briefings on the UN and current issues are available for groups of 20 or more (for high school students and older) on Mon-Fri by calling 693-7710.

For a comprehensive understanding of the UN and a behind-the-scene's glimpse of all the facilities, take the one-hour guided tour (daily 9:15am-4:45pm); it is well worth its tariff (Adults $5.50, Students $3.50, Seniors $4.50—Children under 5 not permitted). The tour takes you past artwork and displays not otherwise accessible, such as the amazing Chinese ivory carving of the Chengtu-Kunming railroad (made from 8 elephant tusks, weighting 330 pounds and having taken 150 artists over 2 years to complete); the Japanese Peace Bell, cast from coins and metal donated by people of 60 nations; the Security Council Chamber mural by Per Krohg; and a gripping exhibit on the destruction wrought upon Hiroshima by the atomic bomb. Tours are given in 25 different languages, and reservations are recommended for tours other than in English and for groups of 15 or more (963-4440).

Around the corner from the Gift Shop (where the tour ends), consult the Public Inquiry Unit, which provides information, brochures and documents on the UN. A guide will answer any questions.

U.S. COURTHOUSE
Foley Sq., 40 Centre St.
☎ *(212) 791-1140.*
Hours: *Mon-Fri 10am-noon, 2-5pm (courts), Mon-Fri 9am-5:30pm (exhibits).*
Tours: *For groups of 20 or fewer, by appt. only.*

The architects, Cass Gilbert and his son, completed this building in 1935 in the grand Roman Revival style of a classic temple. However, it doesn't take long to bring you back to the 20th C., thanks to the 32-story granite monstrosity perched on top. For group tours of the Courthouse, see "For the Tourists" or, better yet, take the tour organized by the Supreme Court of New York.

For the Lobbyists

As N.Y.C. is known for its skyscrapers, what better free thing to do than admire them! Thanks to recent city legislation, many developers have been "encouraged" to build public atriums, plazas or arcades into their skyscrapers (it affords them valuable additional floors). Whatever the motivation, it serves the public well. Many of these spaces are attractively furnished with chairs and tables, greenery and some artwork. You can even bring your lunch. Frequently, free entertainment is provided.

"Architecture is inhabited sculpture."

— CONSTANTIN BRANCUSI

ALWYN COURT
58th St. & 7th Ave.

Terracotta serpents, dragons and gargoyles leer out at you from all sides of this extraordinarily ornate apartment building. This co-op features an impressive trompe l'oeil by Richard Haas, which "creates" an interior Roman atrium (not easily accessible to the public).

AMERICAN TELEPHONE & TELEGRAPH (AT&T)
550 Madison Ave. (55th-56th Sts.).
☎ *(212) 644-7000.*
Hours: *Mon-Fri 9am-5pm.*

Inspired by a Florentine Palace, this 37-story "Post Modern" Neoclassical skyscraper by Philip Johnson and John Burgee was completed in 1984. In sharp contrast to its stark but sleek neighbor, the IBM Building, this building is replete with ornamentation.

The 5-story arch with rose window, the circular cubiculum of the crown (the distinctive notch cut-out in the top), the latticework of the rose-gray granite walls, the Gothic golden-arched lobby ceiling, the 24-foot bronze statue ("The Spirit of Communication") and the attractive black-and-white geometric marble flooring are just the beginning. Be sure to take the elevator (lined with onyx panels) to the sky lobby, 77 feet high, peeking out behind the rose window. White-veined Carrara marble is everywhere, including the floor, the walls, the arches and the second-story crenelated balustrades.

The main building is connected to a 4-story annex by a glass-covered "through park" arcade. A free museum, the AT&T Infoquest Center (see "For the Kiddies"), is in the annex building. Street-level twin loggia offer generous public seating with tables and greenery.

THE ANSONIA HOTEL
2108 Broadway (73rd-74th Sts.).

This French chateau-like Renaissance landmark, built in 1904 by Graves & Duboy with the help of Stanford White, was intended as the most elegant residential hotel in the country. This 17-story H-shaped apartment hotel quickly became dubbed "the wedding cake of the West Side" as its confection of ornate turrets, gargoyles, carvings, balconies with intricate grillework and mansard roof was a visual delectation.

To attract the "right" people, there were lots of attractions, like lavish dining rooms, a lobby with gilded decor, 3 swimming pools in the basement, the first air-conditioning system in N.Y.C., a linen service and the availability of fresh eggs (thanks to W.E.D. Stokes, the original owner, who had a small chicken farm on the roof). And the "right" people did live here, including Florenz Ziegfeld, Enrico Caruso, Arturo Toscanini, Babe Ruth and Theodore Dreiser. Today this residential hotel still retains its exterior grandeur, although the lobby has lost its splendor. However, near the 74th Street lobby entrance there are photos of and articles about the good ole days at the Ansonia.

BOWERY SAVINGS BANK
130 Bowery (Grand & Broome Sts.).
Hours: Mon-Thu 8:30am-3pm, Fri 8:30am-6pm, Sat 9am-noon.
The interior of this L-shaped Beaux-Arts landmark (1894, McKim, Mead & White) is bedecked with classical Corinthian columns and a truncated, skylit-domed ceiling decorated with ornate grillework and recessed gold-leaf rosettes. It certainly makes waiting in line a lot more palatable.

CHANIN BUILDING
122 E. 42nd St. (at Lexington Ave.).
Hours: *Mon-Sun 24 hours.*
This 1929 Art Deco skyscraper by Sloan & Robertson is a visual picnic, inside and out. The terracotta carvings particularly on the 4th floor depict tropical vegetation and sea monsters, while a sculptured bronze band separates the exterior 3rd & 4th floors. Skyscraper miniatures can be seen on the Lexington Avenue buttresses near the flagpole. The interior lobby exudes richness with its Istrian marble and superbly crafted Art Deco bronzework. The bas-reliefs on the elevator doors and mailboxes, the "jeweled" clocks and the ornate radiator grilles (done in the building's theme, "New York, City of Opportunity") are the highlights.

CHELSEA HOTEL
222 W. 23rd St. (7th-8th Aves.).
☎ *(212) 243-3700.*
This Victorian Gothic landmark with decorative wrought-iron balconies, turrets, gables and dormers was the city's earliest co-op apartment, built in 1884 by Hubert & Pirsson. The first building to have a penthouse, it became a hotel in 1905 and attracted many literary types, such as Arthur Miller, Dylan Thomas, Thomas Wolfe and O'Henry (William Sydney Porter). The lobby sports an impressive teakwood fireplace with a carved mantelpiece held up by ferocious rams and gargoyles; above is a bas-relief depicting the arts. The artistic spirit is continued with painting, montages, sculptures and decorative crafts. In the window is a papier-mâché sculpture representing the hotel's famous residents.

CHEMCOURT
277 Park Ave. (47th-48th Sts.).
☎ *(212) 310-7366.*
Hours: *Mon-Sun 24 hours.*
This block-wide 3-story greenhouse is the city's largest (12,500 sq. feet); its sumptuous greenery surrounds white marble cascading waterfalls. At the 48th St. entrance, don't get in the way of "Taxi" (by J. Seward Johnson), a life-sized sculpture of a businessman hailing a cab. Look for the concerts at Christmas. In the lobby, the very small Chemical Gallery offers changing art exhibitions from the corporate collection.

CHRYSLER BUILDING 🍎
405 Lexington Ave. (at 42nd St.).
Hours: *Mon-Fri 9am-5pm.*

Take time to examine the Art Deco facade of this superb N.Y.C. landmark. As a visual tribute to the automobile, each building setback

glorifies the machine in some fashion; at the 4th level are gargoyles shaped like radiator caps and brickwork wheels of a 1929 Chrysler.

As it was Walter Chrysler's wish to build the tallest building, his architect, William Van Alen, worked in secrecy on the building's spire. In fact, when the tower reached 925 feet, everyone assumed it was finished, including the 2 architects working on the 40 Wall Street building who added 2 feet to theirs to claim the "world's tallest" title. Then, to everyone's amazement, the Chrysler Building's chromium spire was raised through the roof to the height of 1,048 feet, making it the tallest. It held the distinction for one year, until the Empire State Building was completed in 1931 at 1,250 feet.

The lobby is splendid with its beautiful African marble floors and wood-inlaid elevator doors of striking geometric patterns. On the ceiling is one of the world's largest murals (97 by 100 feet), painted by Edward Trumbull, and appropriately representing transportation at work. And let's not forget the gorgeous, sunburst spire that illuminates the skyline at night for all to enjoy.

CITICORP CENTER ♥
153 E. 53rd St. (Lexington & 3rd Aves.).
☎ *(212) 559-2330.*
Hours: *Mon-Fri 7am-midnight, Sat 8am-midnight & Sun 10am-midnight.*

Completed in 1977 by Hugh Stubbins & Associates, the 48-floor skyscraper (affectionately called the "Giant Eraser") rests impressively on massive 115-foot columns and provides public space in an enclosed atrium. St. Peter's Church (which originally owned much of the land) is unobtrusively incorporated into the center. The Market (or atrium) offers a pleasant setting for resting your weary bones and, on select evenings, listening to concerts. It's a desirable snack spot as you can bring your own or else give in to the scrumptious temptations surrounding you. A special excursion must be taken to neighboring St. Peter's as it's an architectural masterpiece (see "For the Believers").
Events: *Full range of concerts, kid's programs and shows whose times change monthly; consult the info line above.*

CRYSTAL PAVILION
805 3rd Ave. (at 51st St.).
Hours: *Mon-Sat 8am-11pm.*

This multi-level atrium of chrome and matte-grey granite with escalator walkways offers several public seating areas. The central atrium affords a view of the small raised stage and the glass-enclosed elevator with flashing lights; stores and restaurants line the lobby.
Events: *Piano music on Tue & Thu from 12:30-2:30pm.*

DAILY NEWS BUILDING
220 E. 42nd St. (2nd-3rd Aves.).
☎ *(212) 949-1234.*
Hours: *Mon-Sun 24 hours.*

The main attraction of this 1930s landmark (Howells & Hood, architects) is the lobby with the world's largest rotating globe with distances and sizes of the solar system and planets. Bronze lines in the floor show the direction of American cities and the distance from N.Y.C. The walls are covered with provocative old front-page blow-ups, maps, time clocks, the solar system and wind directional signs. A photographic exhibition changes every 2 months.

875 5TH AVENUE
875 5th Ave. (46th-47th Sts.).
☎ *(212) 986-4676.*
Hours: *Mon-Sun 7am-midnight.*
   This classy small-scale shopping mall and atrium is done in peach-colored marble punctuated by criss-cross escalators and an exterior glass elevator. The highlight is the colorfully-geometric, 1,600-square-foot stained-glass ceiling, one of the largest in N.Y.C. Limited seating is on the lower level.

875 3RD AVENUE
875 3rd Ave. (52nd-53rd Sts.).
Hours: *Mon-Sat 7am-11pm, Sun & Hols 11am-7pm.*
   This 3-level atrium provides public seating throughout, though the street level has the least. The lower level, the Market, has tables and chairs in the center with take-out eateries all around. The upper level, or balcony, is the quietest spot for relaxing, though not when the piano playing occurs.
Events: *Piano playing on Mon & Wed at 12:20pm.*

EMPIRE STATE BUILDING ✔✔
350 5th Ave. (33rd-34th Sts.).
☎ *(212) 736-3100.*
Hours: *Mon-Sun 9:3am-midnight.*
   Built in 1931 by Shreve, Lamb & Harmon, this world-famous building remained the tallest for many years until it was overtowered by the World Trade Center in 1970. Though the observation tower is never free (Adults $3.50, Children $1.75), the lobby is open for observation. Traces of Art Deco can be seen throughout, but the most appealing sight is of the stained-glass panels of the 7 wonders of the ancient world. An eighth panel proudly boasts the Empire State Building. Magnificent bas-reliefs enhance the building exterior. On the concourse level is the Guinness World Record Exhibition (Sun-Thu 9am-8pm, Fri-Sat 9am-10pm) for a fee, 947-2335. Better to appreciate from afar this 102-story, 1,250-foot building with its captivating evening light show.

EQUITABLE CENTER ✔✔
6th-7th Aves., 51st-52nd Sts.
   The Equitable Center is comprised of the Equitable Tower at 787 7th Avenue, designed by Edward Larrabee Barnes, and the PaineWebber Building at 1285 Avenue of Americas, designed by Skidmore, Owings and Merrill. Art exhibits and sculpture abound, not only at the Whitney Museum branch (see "For the Culture Vultures") and the PaineWebber Art Gallery (see "For the Artists"), but throughout the center.

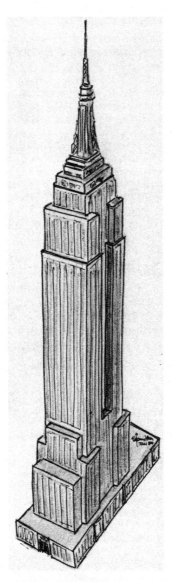

EMPIRE STATE BUILDING

In the Equitable Tower, Roy Lichtenstein's monumental "Mural with Blue Brushstroke" dominates the lobby, under which is Scott Burton's "Atrium Furnishment," a 40-foot semi-circular green-marble bench with 4 pink onyx lights and a circular table with aquatic plants. In the corridors, 10 extraordinary panels entitled "America Today" by Thomas

Hart Benton were commissioned by the New School for Social Research in 1930 and depict the many facets of America that Benton saw on his trips through the country's back roads. Originally the murals hung in the boardroom of the New School; this project influenced the mural program established by the WPA during the Depression to employ artists. On the other side of the corridor is Paul Manship's "Day," a bronze Art Deco sculpture designed in 1938 by the sculptor who did "Prometheus" at Rockefeller Center's sunken esplanade.

At mid-block, the Galleria connects the two buildings. Note the 6 geometric wall drawings by Sol LeWitt; the "Young Elephant" and "Hare on Bell" by Barry Flanagan are located at either end. Take a peek into the restaurant "Palio" to see Sandro Chia's dazzling and powerful mural of the famous Italian horse race at Palio. In front of the PaineWebber Building, a "Pair of Urban Plazas" by Scott Burton offer functional, sculptural tables, benches and stools.

FORD FOUNDATION
320 E. 42nd St. (1st-2nd Aves.).
☎ *(212) 573-5000.*
Hours: *Mon-Fri 9am-5pm.*

Opened in 1967, this modern skyscraper (designed by Roche & Dinkeloo Associates) was one of the first atrium buildings in the city. An 11-story glass-enclosed greenhouse with a zig-zag skylight houses a terraced garden with mature trees and thousands of plants landscaped around a central pond of aquatic life. There is no seating here, so it's really only for "look-see."

GALLERIA ATRIUM
115 E. 57th St. (Park & Lexington Aves.).
☎ *(212) 751-9649.*
Hours: *Mon-Fri 8am-10pm, Sat-Sun 8am-8pm.*

Built in 1975 under the new zoning law for public spaces, this edifice contains offices, luxury apartments, a health club and a classy atrium. Attractively designed stores and multi-level glass-enclosed offices with overhanging plants overlook the central atrium, which has limited public seating and a restaurant. During nice weather, the front awning rolls back and the front becomes open.
Events: *Lunchtime concerts on most Tue & Fri year round.*

GRAND CENTRAL TERMINAL ✦
89 E. 42nd St. (Lexington & Vanderbilt Aves.).
Tours: *Wed at 12:30pm; call Municipal Art Society, 935-3960.*

This impressive Beaux-Arts landmark train station was built in 1913 (architects, Warren & Wetmore and Reed & Stem) for Cornelius "Commodore" Vanderbilt, the wealthy ferryboat entrepreneur. He embarked upon this massive project in order to make way for electrified trains and to unite lower and upper Park Avenue, as the open train yards for the steam engine trains were no longer needed. Also (and probably the main reason), he hoped to build more commercial space. From 1903 to 1913, William J. Wilgus and Reed & Stem dealt effectively with engineering obstacles and successfully made innovations. They developed an impressive stacked tunnel system with ramps; semi-circular tracks for trains to enter along one side and to exit the other; and a 2nd-story viaduct to reroute Park Avenue traffic.

Viewed best from the south on Park Avenue, the splendid facade is triumphantly topped by a sculptural grouping, "Transportation," with Mercury (Roman God of Commerce) surrounded by Minerva (Goddess of Arts) and Hercules (Greek God of Strength and Courage). Underneath the clock stands a statue in tribute to the "Commodore." The inside, however, is fairly plain. Its massive stone walls and columns have very little decoration as the architects were not sure what effect the trains' vibrations would have on artwork. The vaulted celestial ceiling with zodiac signs in the main rotunda provides a star-studded view of the solar system as if you were looking down on it and not looking up from earth!

The 1-hour tour on Wed at 12:30pm (see "For the Tourists") takes you behind the scenes of this station, which accommodates about 100,000 passengers daily.

GRAND HYATT HOTEL ⚫
42nd St. & Lexington Ave.
☎ *(212) 883-1234.*

In the Hyatt tradition of attractively designed hotels, this one is certainly no disappointment. Built by Gruzen & Partners in 1980, it employs the original steel cage of the Commodore Hotel but embellishes it with rich bronze glass.

The gorgeous 4-story lobby immediately captivates you with a multi-tiered Italian rose marble fountain surrounded by greenery. Up a few steps in the main area, comfortable, luscious brown banquettes and chairs allow you to soak in the warm atmosphere. An attractive gold chrome spiral staircase carries you to the cantilevered, glass-enclosed bar overhanging 42nd Street. The lobby restaurant (not free, however) serves some of the best croissants in town. A piano player serenades you at the breakfast hour and starts up again at 1pm, while a trio plays in the evening.

HARKNESS ATRIUM
61 W. 62nd St. (Broadway & Columbus Ave.).
☎ *(212) 371-8511.*

This high-tech multi-colored, multi-leveled atrium beckons the Lincoln Center visitor, although seating is limited and somewhat austere. ***Events:*** *Performances of dance or music on most Wed from 6 to 7:30pm (not Hols).*

HARLEY HOTEL
42nd St. (2nd-3rd Aves.).
☎ *(212) 490-8900.*

This modern hotel (1981, Emery Roth & Sons) has a small, attractive lobby with really no seating area except for a bar. However, the bathroom in the rear of the lobby is particularly appealing as the ladies' room has some of the best freebies (shoe polisher, sewing kit). A small tip for the attendant is a nice touch.

HELMSLEY PALACE HOTEL
Madison Ave. between 50th-51st Sts.
☎ *(212) 888-7000.*

Luckily for us, this new hotel or "palace" (1980, Emery Roth & Sons) had no choice but to preserve the classic High Italian Renaissance exterior of the landmark Villard Houses (1885, McKim, Mead & White), which serves as its Madison Avenue entrance. This grand courtyard with lighted trees is a regal welcome.

However, after that it's all down hill! With 51 stories stacked remorselessly on top, the hotel reeks of architectural confusion. To make matters worse, inside you are greeted by an unbelievably ostentatious lobby with heavy red-and-gold carpeting, elaborately ornate gold banisters and highly polished rose marble walls and columns. Happily, remnants of the Villard craftsmanship can be found again in the Gold Room Bar with its John LaFarge murals of music and drama. Very little seating is available in the lobby, but the mezzanine is better equipped, with seats and bathroom facilities.

HILTON HOTEL
6th Ave. between 53rd-54th Sts.
☎ *(212) 586-7000.*

This active Hilton lobby offers lots of hubbub and little seating. However, if you are in need of various services, such as airline reservations, Broadway theater tickets, limos or free entertainment guides, this is a good place to find them all together. Bathrooms are located on the mezzanine ballroom floor, accessible by escalators.

IBM GARDEN 🍎🍎
The Bamboo Court, Madison Ave. at 56th St.
☎ *(212) 407-3500.*
Hours: *Mon-Sat 8am-10pm.*

This 68-foot-high, glass-enclosed garden (11,000 sq. feet) with a saw-toothed skylight between the IBM Building and Trump Tower is a serene resting place. The garden consists of 45-foot-high bamboo trees, potted plants and flowers that change seasonally. There are tables and chairs interspersed among the greenery for public seating (brown bags allowed). Also, computer terminals make available the NYCulture program, a computerized guide to cultural attractions.

The 43-story IBM skyscraper, built by Edward Larrabee Barnes in 1983, is a five-sided masterpiece of grey-green polished granite. Housed on the concourse level is the IBM Gallery of Science & Art, which should not be missed (see "For the Culture Vultures").

Events: *Excellent concerts by the Juilliard School of Music on Wed at 12:30pm.*

LEVER HOUSE
390 Park Ave. (53rd-54th Sts.).
☎ *(212) 906-4685.*
Hours: *Mon-Fri 10am-5pm, Sun & Hols 1-5pm (except in summer). Closed Sat, July 4th, Labor Day, Christmas & New Year's Day.*

Designed by Skidmore, Owings & Merrill in 1952, this "glass house" is one of the first stainless steel and glass skyscrapers to be built in a style reminiscent of LeCorbusier. The glass-enclosed lobby sets a desirable stage for fine arts and special exhibitions (12 per year). Past shows have featured Japanese flower arrangements, the history of cartoons, advertisements and an annual juried sculpture competition. In May, selected works of public school children are on display. An absolute must during the Christmas season is the famous Christmas Carousel, which first appeared in 1953 and is as delightful as ever.

NEW YORK BANK FOR BUSINESS
111 E. 57th St. (Park & Lexington Aves.).
☎ *(212) 644-0670.*
Hours: *Mon-Fri 8:45am-3:30pm.*

Changing exhibitions every 6 to 7 weeks adorn the walls of this bank.

NEW YORK MARRIOTT MARQUIS 🍎
1535 Broadway (45th-46th Sts.).
☎ *(212) 398-1900.*

This striking and dramatic 50-story Marriott Hotel occupies prime real estate in Times Square's theater district. The 8th floor lobby ascends all the way to the top of the building; Marriott's trademark of the central column with exterior glass-enclosed elevators can be seen from every location in the lobby. Overhanging balconies are draped in ivy. The lobby is enhanced by black-and-white marble floors, an abundance of greenery (excellent fake trees and flowers!), tiny lights outlining balconies and trees, skylights, stylish bars and restaurants, and comfortable public seating.
Events: *Piano playing from 5:15pm-midnight.*

OLYMPIC TOWER
645 5th Ave. (51st & 52nd Sts.).
☎ *(212) 421-5980.*
Hours: *Mon-Sun 7am-midnight.*

This exclusive office and apartment skyscraper (1976, Skidmore, Owings & Merrill) was masterminded by a consortium including the famous Greek shipping magnate Aristotle Onassis. One of the first buildings with a public arcade, the Olympic Tower is a triumph of good taste—a combination of attractive rose/grey granite, mirrors reflecting the 2-story waterfall and abundant greenery. Classy shops line the arcade, evoking a wonderful European atmosphere. The waterfall creates a lulling backdrop for those who dine at the cafe or for those resting in the public seating areas.
Events: *Pianist Mon, Wed & Fri from noon-2pm.*

PARK AVENUE ATRIUM ♠
237 Park Ave. (46th St., entrance on Lexington Ave. also).
Hours: *Mon-Fri 8am-7pm.*
☎ *(212) 850-9786/9791.*

This building was renovated to include an attractive new atrium with a glass rooftop and terraced balconies housing flowers and cascading vines. Polished granite marble seats flank a central cafe dotted with lit trees; overhead hangs a 245-foot sunburst sculpture by Richard Lippold. Sponsored by the building owners, Olympic & York, 6 interesting exhibitions a year line the 2nd-floor balcony and the central atrium with everything from children's book illustrations, quilts, masks and animal art to computer graphics.

PARK AVENUE PLAZA
55 E. 52nd St. (Madison & Park Aves.).
Hours: *Mon-Fri 8am-10pm.*

This modern aquamarine-tinted glass skyscraper (1981, Skidmore, Owings & Merrill) finessed its way onto Park Avenue by buying up the air rights from and building over the landmark Racquet & Tennis Club (1881, McKim, Mead & White), all the while being "shoehorned" into a smaller plot in the middle of the block. A walk-through atrium reflects the overall modern design with greenish-black marble columns, chrome accents, greenery and a central waterfall, which stages a backdrop to the cafe area. Public seating flanks the cafe.

Take a few minutes to appreciate the Racquet & Tennis Club on Park Avenue. Modelled after a Florentine palazzo, this sports club for well-to-do members has a splendid terracotta frieze of tennis equipment under the top cornice of the building.
Events: *Live music in the arcade Mon-Sat noon-3pm.*

PARKER MERIDIEN HOTEL
Between 56th-57th Sts. and 6th-7th Aves.

A Neoclassical walk-through atrium with highly polished geometrically designed marble floors and mock pillars offers a pleasant seating area along the corridors of this luxury hotel. From 57th Street, a narrow neo-Romanesque arch gives the feeling of a sliver building, but there is considerable substance inside.

PLACE DES ANTIQUAIRES
125 E. 57th St. (Lexington & Park Aves.).
☎ *(212) 755-5377/758-2900.*
Hours: *Mon-Sat 11am-6pm.*

Billed as the International Center of Art and Antiques, this classy 2-tier atrium is lined with boutiques in the grand 19th C. European style. There's limited public seating, though a delightful central cafe offers a respite with piped-in classical music. For a view of the exterior of the building, walk down to the corner of Lexington Avenue and 57th Street to admire the curved white-granite facade and 2-story, circular marble sculpture.
Events: *Lectures on Wed at 2pm on antiques and arts in Gallery 53.*

PLAZA HOTEL
5th Ave. & Central Pk. S.

This splendid example of classical French and Flemish Renaissance styles came to life in 1907 thanks to architect Henry J. Hardenbergh. The interior lobby is indeed grand with the central Palm Court continuing the image. Be sure to drop in during the afternoon tea as sounds of violins are in the air.

SEAGRAM BUILDING ◀
375 Park Ave. (52nd-53rd Sts.).
☎ *(212) 572-7000.*
Gallery Hours: *Mon-Fri 9am-5pm. Closed Hols.*
Tours: *Tue at 3pm. Meet in the lobby or call for reservation, 572-7404.*

Be spirited and come see this famous skyscraper. Built in the International style in 1958 by Mies van der Rohe and Philip Johnson, this 38-story building held many innovations. It had no exterior walls in the traditional sense but, instead, floor-to-ceiling glass windows. It was one of the first modern buildings to forsake the "wedding cake" architecture (level setbacks), previously a zoning requirement. The first building to be set back from the street, its half-acre pink granite plaza with fountains and greenery was equipped with a subsurface snow-melting system.

Sponsored by the building's namesake, the tour also throws in a little plug by showing you their product line (no free samples, though), a schema of the distilling process and then some wonderful displays of European and American drinking implements. A small art gallery on the 4th floor offers exhibits of prints, photographs and drawings, which change every 3 months.

31 WEST 52ND STREET
The Lobby Gallery, 31 W. 52nd St. (5th-6th Aves., entrance also on 51st St.).
☎ *(212) 767-2666.*
Hours: *Mon-Sun 9:30am-6pm.*

Within the stunning rose-and-grey granite lobby of this building designed by Kevin Roche is an art gallery, which shows the works of art groups in all media (about 10 a year). Participants include the American Craft Museum, the Museum of Broadcasting, Deutsche Bank and Shearson Lehman Hutton.

TRUMP TOWER ◀ ◀
725 5th Ave. (56th-57th Sts.).
Hours: *Mon-Sat 10am-10pm.*

This controversial 68-story skyscraper (1983, Der Scutt & Swanke Cornell Partners) of bronzed glass with graduated stepped setbacks has been designed with distinctive and expensive (but good) taste both inside and out. The 6-story atrium provides the focal point with its 80-foot fountain (containing over 1,000 Italian rose marble pieces), bronze mirrors, gold chrome and greenery—a refuge from some of the most exclusive domestic and imported names in shopping. Orchids and

gardens abound all around; levels 4 and 5 are open to the public and feature concerts, fashion shows and exhibitions. The building reeks of exclusivity, from the English beefeater guards to the $10 million penthouse. And thanks to the building's namesake, it's no wonder this has been called the "world's most talked about address."

WALDORF-ASTORIA 🍎🍎
Park & Lexington Aves., 49th-50th Sts.

This famous Park Avenue hotel was originally 2 hotels at 34th Street and 5th Avenue, one built in 1893 by Henry J. Hardenbergh and named after John Jacob Astor's German village, Waldorf, and the other built in

1897 and named after his fur-trading post in Oregon, Astoria. The Waldorf-Astoria enjoyed great popularity well into the 1920s; it closed down and was demolished in 1929 (an office building took its spot). In 1931, the Waldorf-Astoria was rebuilt at its present location in the Art Deco style by Schultze and Weaver. The lobby off Park Avenue has a more classical feeling, with its mosaic floor medallion, gold-leaf decorative moldings, ceiling florets and floral medallions in the railings. Soft-colored murals line 3 sides of the lobby.

The main lobby off Lexington Avenue is lush with decorative carpeting, classical bas-reliefs, decorative grilles and marble columns. The pièce de résistance is the 1893 clock topped by a Statue of Liberty, supported by an 8-sided sculptural base depicting famous Presidents and Queen Victoria under which are plaques of sporting life and scenic vistas.

WARNER COMMUNICATIONS
75 Rockefeller Plaza (51st-52nd Sts.).
☎ *(212) 484-8000.*
Hours: *Mon-Fri 10am-6pm.*

For a short but sweet interlude, visit the Warner's lobby to see their art exhibitions featuring painting, photography or sculpture, which change every 4 to 6 weeks. They have "communicated" with us in the past with shows from DC Comics, the N.Y. Society of Women's Art, movie posters and the Stone Sculpture Society.

WOOLWORTH BUILDING ★★
233 Broadway (at Park Pl.).
☎ *(212) 553-2000.*
Hours: *Mon-Sun 24 hours.*

This absolutely magnificent 60-story example of eclectic Gothic architecture was built in 1913 by Cass Gilbert for Frank W. Woolworth. At 792 feet, it remained the world's tallest building until 1930. The official opening occurred when President Woodrow Wilson pressed a button from the White House, which illuminated 80,000 light bulbs. This was a glowing tribute to this "Cathedral of Commerce" with its fabulous spires, gargoyles, flying buttresses and lacy stone tracery.

The majestic 3-story lobby is a work of art. Seeing the walls of Skyros veined marble, delicate wrought-iron railings covered in pure gold leaf and a gorgeous jewel-like mosaic ceiling with a golden, luminous background, someone might think he or she had died and gone to heaven. But alas, there's more. A comical series of sculpted figures of the building's VIPs (including F.W. Woolworth counting his nickels and dimes) is discreetly perched in the arcade. And there are more tidbits to uncover; be sure to get a free brochure at the information desk to learn the whole story.

WORLD FINANCIAL CENTER ★★★★
West St. between Liberty & Vesey Sts.
☎ *(212) 945-0505 (events), 945-2600.*
Hours: *Buildings: Mon-Sun 7am-1am. Courtyard Gallery: Mon-Fri*

noon-7pm, Sat-Sun noon-6pm.
(See Battery Park City under "For the Birds.")

A part of the 92-acre Battery Park City on the Hudson River in lower Manhattan, this commercial and residential complex is staggering in its design, implementation and location. Architect Cesar Pelli (of Museum of Modern Art fame) created 4 different-sized, granite-and-glass towers (from 33 to 51 floors) with distinct rooflines and increasingly larger and larger windows the farther up you go. Two 9-story, matching domed "gatehouses" serve as entrance halls on Liberty Street into a world of polished marbles and sleek detailing. A total of 16 different marbles used throughout the center were apparently hand-picked in Italy by the architect. A series of walkways connect to the pièce de résistance, the Winter Garden, a stunning, 120-foot-high, vaulted glass-and-steel atrium set against the backdrop of the Hudson River (perfect for evening sunsets), and approximately the size of Grand Central's main waiting room. A sumptuous marble hourglass staircase flows down onto the grey-and-peach, diamond-patterned marble floor; the atrium is punctuated by sixteen 45-foot-high palm trees, benches and cafe dining. To the north of the Winter Garden is the 3-story, 45-foot-high European-style Courtyard with grey-and-peach checkerboard marble floor and glass roof. Flanking the walkways of the Winter Garden and Courtyard are an impressive roster of stores and restaurants.

On the waterfront is the Plaza, a 3.5-acre park considered a landmark in public space design; it's matchlessly placed in front of the Winter Garden and Courtyard, and surrounds the North Cove yachting marina. With marble-contoured benches, 2 twin 80-foot fountains, an understated iron fence containing a Walt Whitman quotation and some greenery, the Plaza is the northern part of Battery Park City's lovely esplanade, which runs along the Hudson River down to Battery Park.

Arts and entertainment flourishes at WFC. An exhibition space on the 2nd-floor balcony above the Courtyard presents ongoing shows, of everything from cartoon art to paintings. Photographic exhibitions line the north side of the Winter Garden. An amazing program of performances features well-known names in dance, theater, poetry and music, with about 75 yearly events in the Winter Garden. What an outstanding performance center! In just one recent month, the Arts & Events program presented American Ballroom Dancing, the Imperial Bells of China, and chamber music. The holiday decorations are not to be missed. Everything in this place is first rate!

Events: Weekday performances at either 12:15 or 6:30pm and Sun at 3pm, and summer entertainment at the Plaza.

WORLD TRADE CENTER ♦♦♦
Vesey, Liberty, West & Church Sts.
☎ *(212) 466-4170/7377/4233; observation tower: 466-7397.*
Hours: *Mon-Sun 9:30am-9:30pm (until 11:30pm Jun-Nov).*
Free Admission: *To the buildings' lobbies and the Observation Tower (Tower II) for Children under 6. Otherwise Adults $3.50, Seniors & Children 6-12 $1.75.*
2 WTC mezzanine houses "TKTS" booth (see "For the Matinee Idlers").

This world-famous center occupies 16 acres of prime real estate in lower Manhattan and houses businesses (including the Commodities Exchange; see "For the Exhibitionists") and governmental agencies (like the Customs House) involved in international trade. Built from 1962 to 1976 by Minoru Yamasaki & Associates and Emery Roth & Sons, the complex is made up of 6 buildings surrounding a 5-acre plaza with the twin towers as the focal point. The excavation of dirt and rock from this site was used for the 100-acre landfill called Battery Park City.

At 1,350 feet no longer the world's tallest building (surpassed by the Sears Tower in Chicago at 1,450 feet), the outdoor observation deck on top of 2 WTC (open weather permitting) is nevertheless the world's highest, at nearly a quarter-mile high. For faint-hearted souls, an enclosed observation deck on the 107th floor provides a spectacular panoramic view of N.Y.C., its majestic harbor, Long Island and New Jersey.

Outdoor sculpture monumentally decorates the wide-open concrete plaza area. The central fountain supports the slowly revolving bronze, 25-foot-high "Globe" by Fritz Koenig. Near the main entrance is Masayuki Nagare's highly polished black granite sculpture, believed to be the largest free-standing stone carving. Alexander Calder's 25-ton "World Trade Center Stabile" adds local color to the west side of the complex. Inside, "Sky Gate New York" by Louise Nevelson hangs on the mezzanine floor of 1 WTC; a large tapestry by Joan Miró adorns the mezzanine of 2 WTC.

Changing exhibitions are presented on 1 WTC mezzanine and 2 WTC lobby, including past shows on Japanese calligraphy and Hispanic heritage.

Events: *"Noontime on the Plaza" entertainment Mon-Fri (Jul-Sep) and special Hol programs, especially for children, 466-4170.*

For the Believers

Two myths surround our houses of worship. One is that you have to be a member (or even a believer) to set foot inside; if a nonbeliever does enter, there'll be the instant sell. The other is that they have strictly religious programs. Most churches and synagogues in fact gladly welcome all to their religious and cultural programs (especially active at holiday times). And as many are historical and architectural landmarks, they proudly offer guided tours at set times.

Most religious houses have heeded the call as do-gooders for our city's needy with shelters for the homeless, counseling programs and hot lunches for Seniors. If nothing else, these programs will transform you into a believer of sorts—that people in this city do care about the well-being of others.

As there are so many houses of worship throughout the 5 boroughs (many offering free cultural programs), this chapter had to be limited to Manhattan (except for the Church of St. Ann & the Holy Trinity in Brooklyn). Please consult neighborhood churches/synagogues for specific details.

> *"Remember that what you believe will depend very much upon what you are."*
>
> *– NOAH PORTER*

THE ABYSSINIAN BAPTIST CHURCH
132 Odell Clark Pl. (formerly W. 138th St.).
☎ *(212) 862-7474/7475.*
Hours: *Mon-Fri 9am-5pm, Sat by appt., Sun 1-6pm (Memorial Room); Sun services at 11am.*

Founded in 1808 as the first African-American Baptist Church, this was the congregation of Adam Clayton Powell, Sr. and Jr., the latter being the well-known and intrepid preacher-turned-politician. The present unassuming church was built in 1923 with an amphitheater-like sanctuary containing European stained-glass windows over the Italian marble pulpit and the organ. This acoustically sound sanctuary plays host to various musical groups, including the annual pilgrimage of the N.Y. Philharmonic (free dress rehearsal).

A special Memorial Room exhibits pictures, photos, documents and memorabilia relating to Adam Clayton Powell, Jr.'s stay in Congress.
Events: *A music program on most Sun at 3pm (Oct-Jun) featuring the church's choir or other choral groups; a tutorial program for children Wed from 1:30-3pm; and counseling.*

CATHEDRAL CHURCH OF ST. JOHN THE DIVINE ♥♥
1047 Amsterdam Ave. (at 112th St.).
☎ *(212) 316-7400.*
Hours: *Mon-Sun 7am-5pm, Mon-Sun sunrise to sunset (Biblical Garden).*
Guided Tours: *Tue-Sat at 11am & Sun at 12:45pm., 316-7540.*

This is the largest Gothic cathedral in the world, with a sanctuary over 600 feet long (the length of 2 American football fields) and vaulted ceilings soaring 124 feet high (a 12-story building). Begun in 1892 and not yet completed, the stone carving still goes on as does the centuries-old system of "setting out" a cathedral where master builder and mason design and plan each stone in the cathedral. Originally designed by Heins & LaFarge (responsible for the choir), the church was redesigned in the early 1910s by Ralph Adams Cram who employed Gothic principles at their highest.

The exterior main facade should particularly be noted for its central bronze doors depicting scenes from the Old and New Testaments and the splendid stone carvings on the portals. The interior is awe-inspiring. The nave with its 5 aisles and 14 bays (each representing the works of Man with altars, memorials and counseling areas) is a graceful blend of arches, vaults and stained-glass windows. The great rose window with its strong blues and yellows is beautiful. The 3 altars in the nave contain reredoses of superb craftsmanship. On the north and south walls of the crossing hang treasured tapestries woven on papal looms founded by Cardinal Barberini. Also hanging are the 17th C. English tapestries designed from Raphael cartoons of 1513.

The choir is a harmonious blend of different kinds of marble, stone and tile with vivid stained-glass windows behind the columns. The crowning glory of the choir and probably of the church are the 8 granite columns (6 feet in diameter, 55 feet high and weighing 130 tons each). Quarried in Maine and shipped to the Hudson River at 134th Street, the columns came in 2 pieces (one weighed 90 tons; it is alleged that during its transportation to the church, every manhole cover over which it passed was broken). Behind the choir are 7 chapels, signifying the 7 letters written by St. John the Divine and each representing a distinct ethnic group.

Besides the splendid religious artwork dotted around the cathedral, there are galleries for changing exhibitions at the Chapel of St. Boniface and St. Ansgar's Chapel. Also there's a photography wall opposite the Baptistry.

Outside you can visit the Biblical Garden with its 100 plants mentioned in the Bible and the occasional strutting peacock. A special Visitors Gallery in the stone yard offers a glimpse of stone cutting in progress. The Great Lawn is the site of "The Peace Fountain" by Greg Wyatt, considered one of the most important monumental free-standing religious sculpture in contemporary times.

Events: Boar's Head Festival (early Jan) with a mummer's play, parade, costumes, food displays; special weekly "Peace" programs (Sep-Jun) of music, dance or drama; Bach's St. John's Passion (spring); silent film series (Jul-Aug), 662-2133; Messiah performance at Christmas; St. Francis Day celebration (Oct) with animal parade; Senior drop-in center on Sat; and community programs.

CENTRAL SYNAGOGUE 🍎
652 Lexington Ave. (at 55th St.). Community Center: 123 E. 55th St. (Lexington & Park Aves.).
☎ *(212) 838-5122.*
Hours: Mon-Fri 9am-5pm (Fri til 4pm). Services on Fri at 5:30pm, Sat at 10:30am (10am in summer) & 1st Fri in month at 8pm, open to public except on High Holy Days.
Tours: By appt. only.

Imagine a 122-foot domed sanctuary punctuated in Moorish decor replete with colorful hand-stencilled walls, stained-glass windows, Spanish floor tiles, wooden pews with red silk cushions and a carved-wooden Torah ark (containing the holy scriptures) and you have a vision of this spectacular landmark synagogue. Built in 1872 by Henry Fernbach, one of the first Jewish architects in America, this is the oldest house for continued Jewish worship by a congregation in New York State. Even from Lexington Avenue, you will be impressed with the understated Moorish and Byzantine stone masonry and design.

A Judaica art collection of medieval through modern religious art objects is on display in the lobby of the Community Center. The Freedman Library offers books and periodicals in English on Jewish issues in a spacious and comfortable setting.
Events: Occasional lectures, concerts and community workshops.

CHRIST & ST. STEPHEN'S EPISCOPAL CHURCH
120 W. 69th St. (Columbus Ave. & Broadway).
☎ *(212) 787-2755.*

This quaint neighborhood church has an intimate sanctuary in which it offers many community events, with special consideration for Seniors.
Events: Classical concerts on Mon-Wed at 8pm & Sun at 3 & 7:30pm

(Sep-May) (donation).

CHRIST CHURCH UNITED METHODIST
520 Park Ave. (at 60th St.).
☎ *(212) 838-3036.*
Hours: *Mon-Fri 9am-5pm, Sun service at 9 & 11am.*
  Come visit this Byzantine and Romanesque church just to see the fabulous shimmering blue and gold mosaics in the vaulted ceiling and arched aisles.   Just as stained-glass windows in Gothic churches provide religious instruction, the mosaics in Byzantine ones also do so. A wonderful book explaining the symbolism can be obtained. Also, a stunning golden altar screen incorporates 16th C. holy paintings.
Events: *Film series on 1st Fri of month at 6:30pm with discussion to follow (fee) and free Game Day on 2nd Tue at 2pm.*

CHRISTIAN SCIENCE READING ROOMS
  Dotted around the city are many public reading rooms for the express purpose of spreading the word on Christian Science. In fact, the reading room is their mission. Their newspaper, *The Christian Science Monitor,*

CENTRAL SYNAGOGUE

is always available.

CHURCH OF JESUS CHRIST OF LATTER DAY SAINTS
2 Lincoln Center (Columbus Ave. & 65th St.).
☎ *(212) 595-1825.*
Hours: *Mon-Sun 10am-8pm.*
Show up any time and you will probably get your own personal tour. Learn the history of the Mormons from your guide, pictorial descriptions and movies. Go only if you are serious as they'll take you very seriously.

CHURCH OF ST. PETER'S
Barclay & Church Sts.
☎ *(212) 233-8355.*
Hours: *Mon-Fri 9am-4:30pm, Sun masses at 8, 9:30am & noon.*
Although this church has the distinction of being the oldest Catholic church in New York (dating back to 1838), the very first one was actually built in 1785 on this land bought from Trinity Church. Done in the Neoclassical style, this church is actually quite plain even with the obligatory stained-glass windows and ornate marble altar.

CHURCH OF THE ASCENSION
5th Ave. & 10th St.
☎ *(212) 254-8620.*
Hours: *Mon-Sat noon-2pm, 5-7pm. Sun service at 9, 11am & 6pm.*
Built in 1841 by Richard Upjohn (Trinity Church's architect), this fine example of Gothic Revival architecture is particularly known for John LaFarge's altar mural of "The Ascension" and Augustus Saint-Gaudens's marble altar relief of sculptured angels. Also, this church considers music to be an essential ingredient and boasts about its professional choir, which sings on Sun at 11am.
Events: *Sacred music on occasional Sun at 8pm, frequent organ recitals and music on Sun at 10:45pm before the service.*

CHURCH OF THE COVENANT
310 E. 42nd St. (1st-2nd Aves.).
☎ *(212) 697-3185.*
This small, intimate Presbyterian church (1871, J. Cleveland Cady) has a simple sanctuary accentuated by lovely wooden carved arches.
Events: *The Tudor City adult day program on Fri from 10am-3pm (except Hols) for Seniors with a full day of activities including a hot lunch, classes, games, movies, speakers, concerts and plays (fee).*

CHURCH OF THE HEAVENLY REST
5th Ave. & 90th St.
☎ *(212) 289-3400.*
Events: *"Heavenly Jazz" on Sun at 5pm (4 times a year, Oct-May, donation); the Canterbury Choral Society on Sun at 4pm (about 3 times in Nov, Feb & May, donation); and the York Theatre productions (fee).*

CHURCH OF THE INCARNATION
Madison Ave. at 35th St.

☎ *(212) 689-6350.*
Hours: *Mon-Fri 9am-5pm, Sun service at 8:30 & 11am.*
Tours: *Self-guided tour.*

This early Gothic Episcopal landmark church (1864, E.T. Littel) was rebuilt and enlarged in 1882 after a fire, but was renovated back to the original architect's plan in 1913. The interior sanctuary has an attractive altar with a chancel guarded by 2 carved oak angels by Daniel Chester French. The Caenstone reredos records the church's theme of the incarnation. Murals flanking the reredos are by John LaFarge, the famous American mural painter. His "Adoration of the Magi at the Nativity" is considered by some critics to be one of the best "new world" representations. There's a respectable collection of stained glass by Tiffany, Burne-Jones and LaFarge. A coffeehouse is extended to all after the 11am service.
Events: *Senior club on Tue from 1-4pm (tea provided).*

CHURCH OF THE INTERCESSION
Broadway & 155th St.
☎ *(212) 283-6200.*
Events: *Annual tribute to Clement Clark Moore, author of "Visit from St. Nicholas," on the Sun before Christmas at 4pm, including the recitation of the famous journey, caroling and a lighted procession to Moore's grave in Trinity Church in Washington Hts.*

CHURCH OF THE TRANSFIGURATION ♦
1 E. 29th St. (off 5th Ave.).
☎ *(212) 684-6770.*
Hours: *Mon-Sun 8am-6pm.*
Tours: *Sun at 12:30pm, except some Hols.*

Known as the "little church around the corner," this small Gothic Revival jewel (1849, Frederick Clarke Withers) approached through a lovely garden is probably best known for its chapel where thousands of Episcopal weddings have been performed.

The stained-glass windows in the sanctuary are clear favorites as they immortalize the famous actors who have worshiped here. The popularity with theater folk dates back to 1870 when Joseph Jefferson, in an attempt to arrange the funeral of his actor friend George Holland, was told to go to the little church around the corner as "they did those sorts of things." Both the nickname and endearment have endured. In fact, this church has always championed the cause of the deprived, beginning with its role in the underground railroad for slaves and then as a refuge for Eastern European immigrants. The church organized breadlines during the Depression and today offers Seniors a free hot lunch (5 days a week).

Upon entering the sanctuary, you will be bowled over by the gorgeous wooden carved screens with decorative Gothic arches, windows and sculpture. Also make a point of visiting the tiny but lovely Lady Chapel with its idyllic pastoral paintings and stained-glass doors and windows.

The tour on Sun at 12:30pm is well worth it as you gain further appreciation of the beauty of this "Gothic hodgepodge."

Events: A coffee hour after the Sun service at 12:30pm in the garden or parish house; occasional concerts and community services.

COMMUNITY CHURCH
30 E. 35th St. (Park & Madison Aves.).
☎ *(212) 683-4988.*
Events: *Group meetings with socializing and recreation on Wed from noon-2pm, brown bag lunch discussion group and adult discussion series (evenings).*

FIFTH AVENUE PRESBYTERIAN CHURCH
7 W. 55th St. (off 5th Ave.).
☎ *(212) 247-0490, 246-4200 (Prayer line), 246-4202 (Thought line).*
Hours: *Mon-Sat 8am-6pm, Sun service at 11am & 4pm.*

Beginning in 1809 as a congregation located downtown, this church moved to 5th Avenue in 1875. Thanks to the architect Carl Pfeiffer, this church proudly claims the largest Presbyterian sanctuary in Manhattan with seating capacity for 1,800. Its gently sloping floor affords excellent vantage points for all. The intricately hand-carved ash pews, pulpit and balcony are rich in Gothic ornamentation. The 6,000-pipe organ (Austin, 1961) is a sculptural masterpiece. Stained-glass windows by John Spence and "touched-up" by Tiffany add a light touch. Check to see if the lonesome tree is still growing out the 56th Street side of the roof (quite a miracle).
Events: *"Speaking English" tutorial on Tue at 1pm, counseling service, women's lunches at noon (fee) and Wed dinners at 6pm (fee), hiking and outing organization open to all ages.*

FIRST PRESBYTERIAN CHURCH
12 W. 12th St. (at 5th Ave.).
☎ *(212) 675-6150.*
Hours: *Mon-Fri 9am-5pm, Sun service at 11am.*

This church's roots date back to the first Presbyterian meeting in 1706, although this particular house of worship was not built until 1846 by Joseph C. Wells who was inspired by a church in Bath, England, and a tower at Oxford University's Magdalen College.
Events: *Adult study groups on Sun at 9:30am and occasional weekday evenings & Sun at 3pm vocal concerts.*

GRACE CHURCH
800 Broadway (at 10th St.).
☎ *(212) 254-2000.*
Hours: *Mon-Fri 10am-5:45pm (Sep-Jun), Sun service at 9 & 11am (10am Jul-Aug).*
Tours: *On most Sun at 12:30pm (Oct-Jun).*

This impressive 1846 example of Gothic Revival by James Renwick, Jr. (of St. Patrick's fame) sits poised on Broadway with all the Gothic trimmings including decorative white marble spires and columns, vaulted ceilings and arches, traceried windows, a lovely rose window and an attractive chapel house. Considered an important landmark in

N.Y.C., the rectory is one of the only (and earliest) Gothic residences to have survived.

Events: Organ recitals on Wed at 12:30pm (mid Sep-May) and choral works on occasional Fri at 8pm or Sun at 4pm.

HOLY TRINITY LUTHERAN CHURCH
Central Pk. W. & 65th St.
☎ *(212) 877-6815.*
Events: Bach Vespers on Sun at 5pm (late Oct-Easter), choral works performed at the Hols and a sung Eucharist on Sun at 11am.

THE INTERCHURCH CENTER
475 Riverside Dr. (at 120th St.).
☎ *(212) 870-3002.*
Hours: Mon-Fri 8:45am-4:30pm. Closed Sat, Sun & Hols.
Groups: By appt. only.

This multi-denominational center strives for Christian unity and cooperation. The main offering is 10 art exhibitions (lasting 4 weeks with 1-week breaks between) featuring paintings, photography or arts and crafts, not necessarily about religion. A simple, attractive sanctuary is also open to the public.

Events: An occasional musical performance at worship services (mid Sep-mid Jun).

JOHN STREET UNITED METHODIST CHURCH
44 John St. (Nassau & William Sts.).
☎ *(212) 269-0014.*
Hours: Mon-Fri 11:30am-3pm, Sun 11am service.

This oldest Methodist church in America stands amid the hustle and bustle of the Wall Street area. Built in 1841, this Italianate-style structure is the third on this site, although some floorboards, pews and the entrance were incorporated from the previous church. Its tastefully simple sanctuary proffers attractive stained-glass windows. The Wesley Chapel Museum contains memorabilia including paintings, furniture and books dating back to the 1760s.

Events: Occasional free concerts on Wed at 12:15-1pm.

JUDSON MEMORIAL CHURCH
55 Washington Sq. S. (at Thompson St.).
☎ *(212) 477-0351.*
Hours: Sun service at 11am.

This historic American Baptist (and United Church of Christ) church was erected in 1892 by McKim, Mead & White in the Italian Renaissance style. In the sanctuary, the stained-glass windows by John LaFarge are beautifully framed by coffered arches. The yellow brick tower is reminiscent of Italian campaniles, although today it serves as an N.Y.U. dormitory.

MADISON AVENUE PRESBYTERIAN CHURCH
73rd St. & Madison Ave.
☎ *(212) 288-8924.*

Hours: *Mon-Fri 9am-5pm, Sun service at 9:30 & 11:15am.*

Especially known for its musical programs, this church also has an inexpensive and good swimming pool open to adults on Tue-Thu 6-9pm and Sun 4-6pm.

Events: *The St. Andrews Music Society on most Sun at 4pm (Oct-May) presents chamber music (donation); Bible studies or church-related lectures on most Mon at 11am (Sep-May).*

MARBLE COLLEGIATE CHURCH
5th Ave. & 29th St.
☎ *(212) 686-2770.*
Hours: *Sun service at 11:15am. Or by appt.*

This Romanesque Revival church was built in 1854 by Samuel A. Warner on a farmer's plot (the city limits stopped at 23rd St.). Descended from the Dutch Protestant congregation of 1628, the church was named for its construction material (exterior marble came from Hastings-on-Hudson) and for the Dutch concept of having a rotating "college" of ministers serving several churches in the community (saves on sermon preparation). This church is probably best known for one of its ministers, Norman Vincent Peale, the author of *The Power of Positive Thinking.*

This is a church of firsts: the first to have overhanging balconies (before iron beams), the first to own an electrically operated pipe organ, the first to employ closed-circuit TV for service overflow and the first to have air conditioning. The sanctuary stands out for its elaborate hand-stencilled, gilded florid ceiling and walls. Also be sure to see the 2 Tiffany stained-glass windows of 1900 on the left. On the altar are some original 1850s carved wooden chairs employing the popular Romanesque arches.

Events: *A coffee hour after services on Sun at 12:15pm, counseling services, lunch for Seniors on Wed at 12:30pm for $1, Christian education hour on Sun at 10am and occasional seminars and meetings.*

MIDDLE COLLEGIATE CHURCH
50 E. 7th St. (at 2nd Ave.).
☎ *(212) 477-0666.*
Hours: *Mon-Fri 9am-5pm. Call for hours of art shows.*

This house of worship is part of the oldest Dutch Protestant congregation, dating back to 1628, along with the Marble Collegiate Church. This Victorian church's sanctuary contains some lovely Tiffany stained-glass windows as well as decorative hand-stencilled walls. Its photo gallery, 7th & 2nd, displays exhibits in a 50-foot-high meeting hall with domed ceiling and Tiffany skylights.

Events: *Occasional free concerts and performances by fledgling theater companies; Seniors' meetings on Tue at 1-4pm with refreshments, entertainment, lectures and bingo parties ($.50); an "Arts Enrichment" program for children 8-12 with 3 8-week sessions (donation); seasonal art exhibitions and dinner for AIDS patients on Mon at 6pm.*

RIVERSIDE CHURCH 🍎🍎
490 Riverside Dr. (at 120th St.).
☎ *(212) 222-5900.*
Hours: *Mon-Sun 9am-4:30pm, Sun service at 10:45am. Tower bells: Mon-Sat 11am-3pm, Sun 12:30-4pm ($1).*
Tours: *Sun at 12:15pm (Sep-Jun).*
Groups: *By appt. only.*

The multi-denominational Protestant congregation moved into this simple, elegant Gothic church in 1928 after a fire delayed the consecration. Modeled after Chartres Cathedral in France, Riverside upholds superbly the Gothic tradition of spaciousness and airiness with its marvelous ribbed, vaulted ceiling transcending 100 feet above the nave which, in itself, measures 215 by 89 feet. Vibrant stained-glass windows each represent a different facet of life (agriculture, music, the Bible, etc.), while the ones in the triforium depict the saints of the ancient church.

Moving on to the focal point, the chancel has a magnificent carved reredos of Indiana limestone, representing the 7 aspects of Christ's life interwoven with the 7 sides of the church's ministry, incorporating such notables as Lincoln, Leonardo da Vinci and Bach. The Italian marble floor maze, reminiscent of European churches, signifies a series of prayers or a crusade for those unable to go on the real ones. Try to see the Aeolian Skinner organ, which will cause you to stop for a moment. Faced with its 22,000 pipes, the organist certainly has to know what he's doing! In the lobby or narthex, you can appreciate the cross-groined Gothic arches and the 16th C. Flemish stained-glass windows.

Also, don't miss the Christ Chapel, a wonderful example of Romanesque architecture with barrel vaulting, rounded arches and a massive carved altarpiece of the life of Christ. Near the dining room, look for the clear-etched windows depicting the different church styles in America. If you have the chance, take the revealing tour on Sun at 12:15pm to learn more.

This church knows how to ring its own chimes as it has the distinction of having the world's largest tuned bell and the only 5-octave carillon. Donated by John D. Rockefeller, Jr., in memory of his mother, this set of 74 bells weighs over 100 tons and is played at a keyboard, with the heavier bells being electronically set into motion. The trip to the tower (392 feet high) offers a fascinating inspection of the bells as well as a great view over the Hudson River.

Events: *Carillon recitals on Sat at noon and Sun at 3pm (also on Hols), occasional Sun afternoon concerts and organ recitals on Tue at 7pm (summer) preceded by carillons at 6:30pm, classes (Sep-Jun, fee) and community programs.*

ST. BARTHOLOMEW'S CHURCH 🍎🍎
Park Ave. at 51st St.
☎ *(212) 751-1616.*
Hours: *Mon-Sat 8am-6pm, Sun services at 9 & 11am.*

Park Avenue wouldn't be the same without this dome-shaped landmark. Built in 1919 by Bertram G. Goodhue, this fabulous

Romanesque-Byzantine style Episcopalian church offers a colorful array of rich, salmon-colored bricks and white limestone bands, an exquisite geometric dome, striking arched and rose windows and an ornate entrance (the latter by McKim, Mead & White). Check out the impressive sculptural doors leading into the vestibule with its gold-leaf mosaics. Inside, stained-glass windows flank either side of the nave and transport you to the beautiful mosaic and marble altar. The geometric, hand-stencilled dome is outstanding.

Events: *Free breakfast and clothes program for the homeless and needy, community programs, counseling, guidance services, "Great Music" concerts on occasional Sun at 4pm (fall-spring, donation), infrequent theatrical readings by well-known actors sponsored by Free Theatrical Productions, noontime Messiah sing-alongs (Dec), musicals and dramas (fee) by St. Bart's Playhouse.*

ST. JOHN'S IN THE VILLAGE
224 Waverly Pl. (at 11th St.).
☎ *(212) 243-6192.*
Hours: *Mon-Fri 9am-5pm (Garden).*

This unassuming church possesses a delightful garden, which is maintained as a sanctuary and a place for peaceful reflection. It's best to visit in May when the flowers, trees and shrubs are blossoming.

ST. MARK'S-IN-THE-BOWERY
2nd Ave. at 10th St.
☎ *(323) 674-6377.*
Hours: *Mon-Fri 9am-4pm, Sun service at 10:30am.*

St. Mark's has certainly had its fair share of drama and transformation over the years. Completed in 1799 on the exact spot of Peter Stuyvesant's family chapel (Stuyvesant was an early Governor of New York, known for his intolerance), its first architectural face reflected the traditional box-like Georgian style. Its Greek Revival steeple and 2nd-story parish hall were added in 1828 and 1836, followed in 1854 by the weathervane and clock. Simple stained-glass windows were installed in 1885 and then replaced with more elaborate pictorial ones beginning in 1889. The rectory on 11th Street was completed in 1900 by architect Ernest Flagg. Bells and organs have been upgraded several times over the years. Then, tragically, fire struck in 1978, completely destroying the roof and inflicting heavy damage on the steeple and interior of the church.

Now the good news is that the reconstruction has progressed successfully and most of the church has reopened, with the highlight being the new stained-glass windows by Harold Edelman in the balcony. Set against the creamy white walls of the otherwise rather stark sanctuary, these new abstract colorful windows are a knockout. In the East Yard rests another reminder of the conflagration, an old bell cracked beyond repair. Pick up a brochure about the church and the windows.

Events: The Poetry Project with poetry performances on Mon at 8pm and readings on Wed at 8pm (Oct-Jun, donation); free workshops on poetry and writing, lectures and spring workshops on Sat mornings; outdoor summer concerts on Thu at noon (Jul) in the courtyard by 3rd Street Music School; and performances sponsored by the Danspace Project (contribution).

ST. MARTIN'S EPISCOPAL CHURCH
Lenox Ave. & 122nd St.
☎ *(212) 534-4531.*
Hours: *Mon-Fri 9am-4pm, Sat-Sun 10am-4pm, Sun service at 11am.*

Consecrated in 1944, this Romanesque landmark can be best appreciated for its wealth of mosaics replicating the famous paintings of the Renaissance, including such artists as Raphael, Michelangelo, Fra Filippo Lippi plus such Spanish masters as El Greco, Murillo and Ribera. A carillon of 42 bells (weighing over 18,000 lbs.) resides in the tower and is considered one of the finest in the U.S. Three of the heaviest and lowest bells were constructed to swing and are pulled by three bell-ringers.

Events: *A carillon recital on Sun at 10:30am before the service, played from a clavier, a Dutch and Belgian keyboard.*

ST. MICHAEL'S CHURCH
225 W. 99th St. (Broadway & Amsterdam Ave.).
☎ *(212) 222-2700.*
Events: *Occasional concerts and a festival of carols with all West Side churches on 2nd Sun of Dec (very popular).*

ST. PATRICK'S CATHEDRAL ♦♦
5th Ave. at 50th St.
☎ *(212) 753-2261.*
Hours: *Mon-Sun 7am-8pm with services throughout the day.*
Tours: *For schools and community groups by appt. only.*

Built between 1850 and 1888 (the Civil War curtailed construction

for a while) and now the seat of the Roman Catholic Archdiocese of New York, this famous Gothic landmark was designed by James Renwick, Jr., after the Cathedral of Cologne and is the largest Catholic cathedral in the U.S. The lovely Lady Chapel was a 1906 addition by Charles T. Mathews. The grandeur can be seen both inside and out. With gleaming white spires, 330-foot arched towers, flying buttresses, impressive sculpted bronze doors, French stained-glass windows, a world-class rose window (26 feet in diameter) and a 57-foot-high altar with a canopy, this cathedral is a must.

Pick up a brochure in the narthex and you can take a self-guided tour, learning about the cathedral including the great organ with 9,000 pipes ranging from 3 inches to 32 feet. What a wonderful place for finding your own peace in hectic midtown.

Events: *Organ recitals on Sun at 4:45pm.*

ST. PAUL'S CHAPEL ⁣⛪
Broadway & Fulton St.
☎ *(212) 602-0874.*
Hours: *Mon-Sun 8am-4pm, Weekday service at 1:05pm and Sun service at 9am.*
Tours: *By appt. only.*

Built in 1766 by Thomas McBean and designed to resemble St. Martin's-in-the-Field in London, this is the oldest public building still in use in Manhattan. The steeple was added in 1796.

This classic Georgian church in native stone has a simple elegance, especially inside. Soft blue and pink walls with white Corinthian columns offer a subdued backdrop for the ornate white and gold leaf pulpit (designed by Pierre L'Enfant, architect of Washington, D.C.). A fine example of 18th C. craftsmanship, the pulpit has a coronet and six feathers, the only emblem of British nobility in New York to survive in its original locale. George Washington attended an inaugural service here; a special box commemorates this. Display cabinets feature old drawings and photographs of the chapel and the surrounding area. Organ music plays for a considerable part of the day.

In the back a courtyard offers benches and trees, although it tends to be noisy because of the traffic. Eroded tombstones of revolutionary heroes can be barely deciphered. There is a good water fountain!
Events: *Free "Noonday Concerts" of classical music on Mon & Thu at 12:10pm.*

ST. PETER'S CHURCH ⛪⛪
619 Lexington Ave. (at 54th St.).
☎ *(212) 935-2200.*
Hours: *Mon-Fri 9am-6pm, Sun service at 8:45 & 11am.*

Dwarfed by the neighboring Citicorp Center, this Lutheran Church is in no way overshadowed as its modern architecture adds a refreshing vitality. Inspired by the biblical saying, "a shadow of a mighty rock within a weary land," this granite structure (1977, Hugh Stubbins & Associates) has one of the simplest and most beautiful sanctuaries ever seen. The natural wooden floors and pews punctuated by straight lines provide a neutral backdrop to the brightly colored needlepoint cushions, which were done by the congregation. The German Klais organ plays a major role as an important work of art. On the pulpit is the St. Peter's insignia (a cross with squares) representing a church within city blocks, and a 15th C. Belgian Iron Cross, the only old thing in the sanctuary.

Also don't miss the Chapel of the Good Shepherd, a small white side chapel, adorned with abstract wooden panels by Louise Nevelson, each with a special religious significance. The concourse level houses a 250-seat theater and space for changing exhibitions of photos or paintings.
Events: *Jazz vespers on Sun at 5pm; concerts on most Sun at 7pm; "All Night Soul," 12-hour celebration of jazz, on the second Sun in Oct; "Jazz at Noon" on most Wed at 12:30pm (Oct-Apr, donation); theater programs (fee); and community programs for the needy and elderly.*

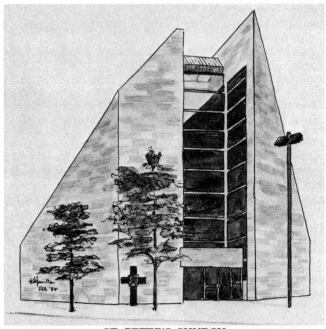

ST. PETER'S CHURCH

ST. THOMAS CHURCH &

5th Ave. at 53rd St.
☎ *(212) 757-7013.*
Hours: *Mon-Fri 7:30am-6pm, Sat 10am-5pm, Sun 7:30am-6pm (until 2pm, Jul-Sep), Sun services at 8, 9, 11am & 4pm.*
Tours: *Sun at 12:15pm (meet in rear of Chantry Chapel).*

This "Eclectic Gothic" Episcopal church (1914, Bertram Goodhue) can probably be best appreciated for its sculptural chancel reredos of religious and historical figures. This church has an impressive Gothic nave with vibrant blue stained-glass windows. Also check out the 5th Avenue facade as it is adorned with statues around a superb rose window. Two small books describing the history and architecture of the church are available upon request.

Events: *A sung evening prayer with full choir on Tue & Thu at 5:30pm and Sun at 4pm (Oct-May); a sung Eucharist on Wed at 12:10pm; an organ recital on Sun at 5:15pm (except Jun-Sep & Dec); and occasional Tue at 7:30pm concerts (donation).*

ST. VARTAN'S CHURCH

630 2nd Ave. (34th-35th Sts.).
☎ *(212) 686-0710.*
Hours: *Mon-Fri 9am-5pm, Sat 10am-3pm, Sun service at 10:30am. Museum: Mon-Fri 3-5pm, Sat-Sun noon-6pm (Museum).*

Consecrated in 1968, this church honors St. Vartan, an Armenian nobleman, who repelled the Persians' attempt to supplant Christianity with Zoroastrianism, the worship of fire. Designed in the traditional Armenian style with the distinctive dome and double intersecting arches, the spacious sanctuary has no columns to obstruct the view to the altar. The modern, brightly colored stained-glass windows depict biblical scenes; epoxy glue replaces conventional lead strips in these striking windows. Ask for a brochure describing the bas-reliefs and sculpture inside and out. The museum features exhibitions, usually of an Armenian artist or on an Armenian theme.

Events: Armenian Christmas (Jan 6th) and Martyrs' Day (Apr 24th) are both celebrated on the weekend closest to the date, Patron Saint Feast Day on Thu prior to Lent with special festivities during Easter, the One World Day Festival (Sep) and occasional concerts on Sun evenings.

THE SOCIETY FOR ETHICAL CULTURE
2 W. 64th St. (off Central Pk. W.).
☎ (212) 874-5210.

This society states its role to be "humanistic, religious and educational," inspired by the ideal that the supreme goal of life is to create a more humane society. Accordingly, the stress is on human needs, responsibilities and roles. At the 11am Sun meetings, the leader first shares his thoughts and then a panel featuring guest speakers addresses current and controversial issues with a humanistic accent.

Events: Concerts and workshops (some at a small fee), music performances and occasional organ programs on Sun at 10:45am.

TEMPLE EMANU-EL ◢
5th Ave. & 65th St. (weekday entrance at 1 E. 65th St.).
☎ (212) 744-1400.
Hours: Mon-Thu 10am-5pm, services on Fri at 5:15pm & Sat at 10:30am (not open to public on High Holy Days).
Tours and Groups: By appt. only.

This largest reform Jewish synagogue in the world (seating 2,500) was designed in 1929 in the neo-Romanesque style similar to the basilicas of Italy. The main sanctuary is striking for its sheer size and brilliantly colored stained-glass windows. The rose window depicts the 12 tribes of Israel and is flanked by menorah-shaped windows and the Hebrew symbol for life. The altar is stunning in its use of European marble and mosaic insets. The bronze grillework of the Ark's doors represents a simplified rendering of the 10 Commandments. The Great Organ has 7,600 pipes.

A side trip to the Byzantine Bethel Chapel reveals 2 domes supported by columns of granite and marble. Side walls incorporate stained-glass windows into an attractive Moorish design. The altar, predominantly in blue marble and mosaics, represents the 10 Commandments. Don't miss the Tiffany windows above the altar.

Events: An organ recital on Fri at 5pm before the service and a lecture series on 3 successive Sun at 11am (Mar & Nov).

TEMPLE EMANU-EL

TRINITY CHURCH ♥♥
74 Trinity Pl. (Broadway & Wall St.).
☎ *(212) 602-0847/0848.*
Tours: *Mon-Sun at 2pm.*

In the Gothic Revival tradition, this important church was rebuilt in 1846 by Richard Upjohn after the church had succumbed first to fire and then to poor construction. The congregation, chartered in 1697, was granted land by Queen Anne in 1705 which extended from Broadway west to the Hudson River and from Fulton St. north to Christopher St. in the Village. As a result it is one of the wealthiest institutions in the city (along with Columbia University) even though lawsuits about proper ownership continued into the 1950s (a whole other story).

The church's imposing spire symbolically looks down upon Wall Street. The 3 bronze doors by Richard Morris Hunt were modeled after the famous Baptistry ones by Ghiberti in Florence and depict the saying, "Thou didst open the kingdom of Heaven to all believers." With its vaulted ceilings, stained-glass windows, carved wooden choir stalls, a sculptural altarpiece, a beautiful organ, attractive smaller chapels and the magnificent exterior design, this church should be investigated. Visit its small museum and learn about its history (see "For the Culture Vultures"). The church also has a valuable archive on the history of N.Y.C. to the present.

Events: *"Noonday Concerts" on Tue at 12:45pm featuring chamber music, concerts or vocal recitals, lasting 30 minutes (a tradition dating back to their 19th C. organ recitals!) — call 602-0760; "Talks & Tours" lectures, community clinics and weekly courses on a full range of somewhat religious subjects.*

STEPHEN WISE FREE SYNAGOGUE
30 W. 68th St. (Central Pk. W.).
☎ *(212) 877-4050.*
Events: *Occasional free Fri evening guest speakers, weekday lectures featuring interesting speakers on social or political issues (thanks to the community-minded rabbi) and occasional special music services.*

Brooklyn

CHURCH OF ST ANN & THE HOLY TRINITY
Clinton & Montague Sts.
☎ *(718) 875-6960/834-8794.*
Hours: *Daily noon-2pm, Sun service at 11am.*

Designed by Minard Lafever in 1844, this is one of the earliest Gothic Revival structures in N.Y.C. Over 10 years ago, this landmark underwent an extensive and successful restoration as it had deteriorated badly while being closed for 10 years. Luckily for us, we can once again appreciate it, especially the renowned stained-glass windows created by William Jay Bolton. Considered some of America's first, the set of 60 windows with the most vibrant blues and greens (even on a rainy day) depict scenes from the New Testament and life of Christ. Also note the beautifully florid carved capitals on the columns, the ornated reredos and webbed ceiling.

Events: *The Incomparable Arts at St. Ann's program, which grew out of the impetus to save the church, offers a distinguished series of over 100 performances yearly in classical music, jazz, opera, dance and puppet shows (most at a fee).*

For the Society-Goers

New York has been called "the melting pot" of many nationalities. Nowhere else in the world can you see such a potpourri of faces or hear so many languages spoken. Throughout its brief history, America (especially N.Y.C.) was considered the "Land of Opportunity" by those seeking religious freedom or economic and social advancement, and immigrants came by the shipload to see if the streets were really paved with gold.

Today, golden opportunities do exist for those wanting to visit various cultures, all the while staying in N.Y.C. Thanks in part to the United Nations, cultural societies have sprung up all around (particularly in Manhattan), offering a phenomenal range of exhibitions, lectures, films, performances and library facilities. Their main goals are to act as a "home away from home," to provide cultural education and to engender a greater understanding between their people and Americans. And they love visitors.

> *"The ideal society would enable every man and woman to develop along their individual lines, and not attempt to force all into one mould, however admirable."*
>
> *— J.B.S. HALDANE*

AMERICAN IRISH HISTORICAL SOCIETY
991 5th Ave. (at 80th St.).
☎ *(212) 288-2263.*
Hours: *Tue-Sat 10:30am-5pm.*
  Founded in 1897 at the famous Revere House in Boston, the Society moved into this elegant 5th Avenue townhouse in 1940. The Society's collection of manuscripts, letters, books, memorabilia and photographs is incorporated into exhibitions. Upstairs on the 2nd floor reside busts of Theodore Roosevelt, John F. Kennedy and Commodore Barry (a naval officer during the Revolutionary War). An impressive library and archival collection is available by appt. only.
Events: *George Bernard Shaw plays occasionally and lectures.*

AMERICAN SCANDINAVIAN FOUNDATION
725 Park Ave. (at 70th St.).
Hours: *Wed-Sat noon-5pm.*
☎ *(212) 879-9779.*
Events: *Hans Christian Andersen storytelling hour in Central Park on Sat at 11am (May-Sep) at the statue of its namesake, and occasional concerts, readings, films and lectures.*

ASIAN ARTS INSTITUTE
26 Bowery (near Pell & Bayard Sts.).
☎ *(212) 233-2154.*
Hours: *Mon-Fri 11am-5pm. Call first.*
Events: *Infrequent art exhibitions.*

AUSTRIAN INSTITUTE
11 E. 52nd St. (5th & Madison Aves.).
☎ *(212) 759-5165.*
Hours: *Mon-Fri 9am-5pm (Sep-Jun). Library open year round.*
  The Institute's Library has over 6,000 books,
Events: *Art exhibitions, lectures, concerts and films.*

LEO BAECK INSTITUTE
129 E. 73rd St. (Park & Lexington Aves.).
☎ *(212) 744-6400.*
Hours: *Mon-Fri 9am-4pm (summer), Mon-Fri 9am-5pm (Fri until 3pm, winter).*
  Located in a fashionable and historic townhouse, this Institute was created primarily to preserve the history and culture of the German Jews over the centuries. A good place to trace ancestry, the computerized library contains over 60,000 books. The Institute's art collection consists of 90 paintings, and several thousand drawings and prints by leading German artists of the past 100 years.
Events: *Art exhibits and lectures.*

CARIBBEAN CULTURAL CENTER
408 W. 58th St. (9th-10th Aves.).
☎ *(212) 307-7420.*

Hours: *Tue-Fri 11am-6pm, Sat 1-5pm.*
Admission: *By contribution.*
Events: *About 5 exhibitions yearly, conferences, concerts, readings, lectures, folklore workshops, and the annual Caribbean Expressions Festival (Oct), a month-long celebration of Caribbean culture.*

CENTER FOR CUBAN STUDIES
124 W. 23rd St. (Lexington & 3rd Aves.).
☎ *(212) 242-0559.*
Hours: *Mon-Fri 9am-5pm.*
　　The Lourdes Casal Library emphasizes on the revolution and post-1959 period.
Events: *Lectures, films, seminars, exhibits, Spanish classes and symposia.*

CENTER FOR INTER-AMERICAN RELATIONS
680 Park Ave. (at 68th St.).
☎ *(212) 249-8950.*
Hours: *Tue-Sun noon-6pm.*
　　Housed in a neo-Georgian Park Avenue townhouse (1909, McKim, Mead & White), this Center has about 3 exhibitions each year, honoring and promulgating the works of lesser-known North American artists.
Events: *Occasional lectures and symposia (fee).*

CHINA INSTITUTE OF AMERICA
125 E. 65th St. (Park & Lexington Aves.).
☎ *(212) 744-8181.*
Hours: *Mon-Fri 10am-5pm. Closed Sat, Sun & Hols. Call first.*
　　This Institute, located in a fashionable East Side brownstone, presents good cultural exhibitions ranging from classical to folk or contemporary Chinese art.
Events: *Courses, lectures, demonstrations, symposia and workshops (not all free); Open House on Fri 8pm-midnight (Sep-Jun) for Chinese students and friends with films, dancing, choral singing, lectures and dumpling or wine tasting (fee).*

DEUTSCHES HAUS
42 Washington Mews (near 8th St. & University Pl.).
☎ *(212) 598-2217.*
　　Located on a charming cobblestone carriage street, this German cultural center operates in cooperation with the Goethe House.
Events: *Lectures, concerts and German courses through NYU (fee).*

DEUTSCHES HAUS, COLUMBIA UNIVERSITY
420 W. 116th St. (off Amsterdam Ave.).
☎ *(212) 280-3964.*
Hours: *Mon-Fri noon-6pm (Oct-May, gallery). Call first.*
Events: *Art shows, lectures, films and a coffeehouse hour on Wed from 3-5pm (German spoken).*

FRENCH CULTURAL SERVICES
972 5th Ave. (at 79th St.).
☎ *(212) 439-1400.*
Hours: Mon-Fri 9am-5:30pm (until 5pm in summer).
   On the 2nd floor of this magnificent townhouse (1902, McKim, Mead & White), built for Payne Whitney, is exhibition space for photos and paintings. Enjoy the Italian marble, circular lobby.

FRENCH INSTITUTE/ALLIANCE FRANÇAISE
22 E. 60th St. (Madison & Park Aves.).
☎ *(212) 355-6100.*
Hours: Mon-Thu 9:30am-8pm, Fri 9:30am-6pm, Sat 10am-1:30pm.
Events: Exhibitions in the lobby, first-rate French films with subtitles on weekdays (nominal fee); and lectures and courses (fee).

GALLERIA VENEZUELA
7 E. 51st St. (5th & Madison Aves.).
☎ *(212) 826-1660.*
Hours: Mon-Fri 9am-2pm.
Events: Exhibitions of art or photos of South America or by native artists.

GOETHE HOUSE
1014 5th Ave. (82nd-83rd Sts.).
☎ *(212) 972-3960 (subject to change).*
Hours: Tue & Thu noon-6pm, Wed, Fri-Sat noon-5pm. Call first.
   This New York branch of the German Cultural Center is conveniently located in a charming townhouse across from the Metropolitan Museum of Art. A delightful courtyard outside the Library (containing over 16,000 books) offers an escape from the antics of 5th Avenue.
Events (call for mailing list): About 5 art exhibits yearly, German films with English subtitles, film festivals, puppet shows for kids, lectures and the German Book Fair (Mar).

INTERNATIONAL HOUSE
500 Riverside Dr. (at 123rd St.).
☎ *(212) 316-8400.*
   Since 1924, this residence house has opened its doors to international students, giving them an opportunity to share in a truly international experience. A varied cultural program allows for mingling and social interaction; many activities are open to the public. Enjoy the neighboring Sakura Park.
Events (call for mailing list): Occasional lectures at 8pm; a cultural hour on Thu at 10pm with song, dance, food and films of a different country (twice a month); art shows; Annual Night of Nations Festival in early Apr (fee).

ITALIAN CULTURAL INSTITUTE
686 Park Ave. (68th-69th Sts.).
☎ *(212) 879-4242.*

Hours: *Mon-Fri 9am-12:30pm, 1:30-4:30pm.*

Housed in a gorgeous neo-Georgian and neo-Federal townhouse (1918, Delano & Aldrich), this Institute's strong suit is its library of Italian books, periodicals and films (available for schools).

JAPAN HOUSE ♦
333 E. 47th St. (1st-2nd Aves.).
☎ *(212) 832-1155/752-0825.*
Hours: *Tue-Sun 11am-5pm, Tue-Thu 10am-4pm (Library, by appt.). Call first, monthly breaks between shows.*
Admission: *By contribution.*

In addition to being a top-notch art gallery, the Japan House (home of the Japan Society) is also noted for its classic Japanese building design. The Japanese belief that your home should incorporate the beauty of nature is achieved here par excellence. A small, well-lit atrium contains an indoor lily pond surrounded by bamboo trees. Shoji screens add to the simple but elegant atmosphere. You can also appreciate the outdoor garden in nice weather.

The exhibitions (about 3 a year) feature outstanding Japanese art. A library contains over 6,000 books in Japanese and English.
Events: *Films, courses, lectures, symposia and cultural performances, usually at a fee.*

KOREAN CULTURAL SERVICE
460 Park Ave. (57th-58th Sts.).
☎ *(212) 759-9550.*
Hours: *Mon-Fri 9am-5pm.*
Events: *Library with over 10,000 books, art exhibitions every 2 to 3 months, dance performances, concerts, lectures, symposia and seminars (fee).*

MAISON FRANÇAISE
16 Washington Mews (near 8th St. & University Pl.).
☎ *(212) 998-8750.*
Hours: *Mon-Fri 9am-6pm.*

Affiliated with NYU, this French cultural society is located on a very charming carriage street, which is worth a trip in itself.
Events: *Occasional exhibitions, symposia, lectures on Mon-Thu at 8:15pm and French films with subtitles on Fri at 7pm (donation).*

MAISON FRANÇAISE, COLUMBIA UNIVERSITY
Buell Hall (near Low Library), near the 116th St. & Amsterdam Ave. entrance.
☎ *(212) 854-4482.*
Hours: *Mon-Fri 10am-5pm (Oct-May). Call first.*
Events: Lectures, French documentary films (on alternate Thu at noon & 1pm, bring lunch), art shows, concerts (about 1 per month) and receptions.

NIPPON CLUB
115 E. 57th St. (Lexington & 3rd Aves.).
☎ *(212) 753-9090.*
Hours: *Mon-Fri 11am-7pm. Closed Hols & Nov.*
Events: *Art shows, occasional lectures, demos, performances and classes (fee).*

RUMANIAN SOCIETY
200 E. 38th St. (at 3rd Ave.).
☎ *(212) 687-0180.*
Hours: *Mon-Thu 9am-1pm, 2-5pm, Fri 9am-2pm.*
Events: *Library of over 14,000 books, occasional subtitled movies, concerts and exhibitions.*

THE SPANISH INSTITUTE
684 Park Ave. (68th-69th Sts.).
☎ *(212) 628-0420.*
Hours: *Mon-Fri 9:30am-5:30pm.*

Housed in a stunning neo-Georgian and neo-Federal townhouse (1926, McKim, Mead & White), the Hastings Gallery sponsors about 12 exhibitions a year, mainly of the art of young Spaniards.
Events: *Library, films at the Cine Club, lectures, seminars, symposia, concerts and language courses (fee).*

SWISS INSTITUTE
35 W. 67th St. (Central Pk W. & Columbus Ave.).
☎ *(212) 496-1759.*
Hours: *Thu-Tue 2-7pm. Closed Wed.*

In this Gothic townhouse, attractive gallery space provides a backdrop for monthly shows by contemporary Swiss artists in all media.
Events: *Free concerts, lectures, film screenings, dance festival (fee) and seminars (some fee).*

TURKISH CENTER
821 U.N. Plaza (at 46th St.).
☎ *(212) 682-8395.*
Events: *Photography exhibitions.*

UKRAINIAN INSTITUTE OF AMERICA
2 E. 79th St. (off 5th Ave.).
☎ *(212) 288-8660.*
Hours: *Tue & Sat 2-6pm, or every day by appt.*
Events: *Occasional art exhibits, concerts, lectures and workshops.*

YIVO INSTITUTE FOR JEWISH RESEARCH
1048 5th Ave. (at 86th St.).
☎ *(212) 535-6700.*
Hours: *Mon-Fri 9:30am-5:30pm. Library & Archives closed on Wed.*

An elegant 1919 French Renaissance landmark in the Louis XIII style with an impressive 2-story marble lobby and decorative dome houses exhibitions dedicated to the study of Eastern European Jewry. A library of 300,000 volumes and archives are open to the public.

Events: *Seminars and lectures on occasional Wed from 6-9pm, walking tours (fee), the annual Yiddish Book Fair at the Armory (May) and the Max Weinreich Center for Advanced Jewish Studies (fee).*

YUGOSLAV PRESS AND CULTURAL CENTER

767 3rd Ave. (at 48th St.).

☎ *(212) 838-2306.*

Hours: *Mon-Fri 10am-5pm.*

Events: *Library, art exhibits, occasional concerts, films and lectures with refreshments.*

For the Tourists

Sometimes there's nothing like a good tour to help you appreciate fully an art collection, a historical house, a famous building or a behind-the-scenes look at how certain things work (like the courts, the police department or the post office). Many places offer scheduled tours on certain days and times or special group tours by appointment. Of course, a tour can be much affected by the guide, who can enliven the subject matter or put you to sleep. What follows is a listing of where you can find tours. In cases where various tour guides were reliably good, these are especially recommended.

"Nothing is so unbelievable that oratory cannot make acceptable."

— *CICERO*

AMERICAN MUSEUM OF NATURAL HISTORY ♦♦♦♦
(See "For the Culture Vultures.")
Highlight Tours: *Mon-Sun from 10:15am to 2:30pm & Wed at 6:30pm (Jul-Aug). Meet at the Info Desk on the 1st fl., 769-5566.*
Student Tours: *Before 1pm weekdays by appt. only.*
For a comprehensive overview of the museum's finest, this highlight tour should not be missed. Conducted by extremely knowledgeable guides (who study for 6 months), the tour lasts about 1 hour. Meet at the Info Desk on the 1st floor.

BRYANT PARK
(See "For the Birds.")
Tours: *When Park re-opens on Thu 12:30pm (May-Sep). Check first.*
The "Once Around the Park" tour gives you in-depth background on the park's history, the neighboring skyscrapers and the present-day park attractions.

CATHEDRAL CHURCH OF ST. JOHN THE DIVINE ♦♦
(See "For the Believers.")
Tours: *Tue-Sat at 11am & Sun at 12:45pm, 316-7540.*

CENTRAL PARK, THE DAIRY
. S. of 65th St. transverse between the Zoo and Carousel.
☎ *(212) 397-3165.*
(See Central Park under "For the Birds.")
Tours: *Occasionally on Sun at 2pm by Urban Park Rangers.*

CENTRAL SYNAGOGUE ♦♦
(See "For the Believers.")
Tours: *By appt. only.*

CHURCH OF JESUS CHRIST OF LATTER DAY SAINTS
(See "For the Believers.")
Tours: *Throughout the day, upon request.*

CHURCH OF THE TRANSFIGURATION ♦
(See "For the Believers.")
Tours: *Sun at 12:30pm, except some Hols.*
This charming and cozy "little church around the corner" offers a very good tour after the Sun morning service. It lasts about 30 minutes with refreshments afterwards.

CITY HALL ♦♦
(See "For the Culture Vultures.")
Tours: *Mon-Fri between 10am-3:30pm by appt. only (2 weeks in advance).*
Reservations only by mail, send to: City Hall Tours, 250 Broadway, N.Y., N.Y. 10007 and include name, affiliation/organization, address, daytime telephone #, preferred date & time and number in group.
To learn about our city government, both past and present (with juicy tidbits thrown in), come on this thoroughly enjoyable tour, lasting about

45 minutes. You will learn why the original building had marble only on the south-facing facade, why people were originally fearful of the hanging staircase in the stunning rotunda and why the dates on 2 different city crests are not the same. In addition to the history and architecture of City Hall, the workings of city government are also revealed. A visit to the Blue Room, the site of the Mayor's press conferences (not otherwise open to the public) is also included. The Governor's Room, now the Museum, is the last port-of-call where you are presented with several brochures. Thank you, Mayor Dinkins, for this civic-minded gesture.

THE CLOISTERS 🍎🍎🍎
(See "For the Culture Vultures.")
Tours: *Tue-Fri at 3pm, Sun at noon. Garden tours on Tue-Sun at 1pm (May-Jun, Sep-Oct)..*
Groups: *By appt. only (fee).*

COLUMBIA UNIVERSITY 🍎🍎
(See "For the Knowledge Seekers.")
Tours: *Mon-Fri at 3pm (Sep-mid May), Mon-Fri 10am & 2pm (mid May-Aug), weather permitting. Tours are suspended during final exams.*

COMMODITIES EXCHANGE (COMEX) 🍎
(See "For the Exhibitionists.")
   A prearranged tour and slide show for 5 or more people can be set up during the week. Definitely worthwhile and informative since the exhibits themselves are not too helpful.

THE COOPER-HEWITT MUSEUM 🍎🍎🍎
(See "For the Culture Vultures.")
Tours: *Occasional Tue at 6:15pm.*

THE COURTS
(See Supreme Court of N.Y. and the U.S. Courthouse, below.)

FEDERAL RESERVE BANK OF NEW YORK 🍎
33 Liberty St. (Nassau & William Sts.).
☎ *(212) 720-6130.*
Tours: *By appt. only with 7 days' notice.*
   Housed in a massive 1924 Italian palazzo structure, the Federal Reserve is crucial to our banking system. Come learn a little about its role in controlling the money supply and the economy and what is required of member banks. The highlight is seeing the machines that clean and count money and detect counterfeit bills. The trip to the gold supply in the basement is also impressive; a vault with a 100 compartments houses more gold bars than Fort Knox, representing 80 foreign countries, with one-quarter of the world's known gold reserves. When countries' balances shift, gold is simply transferred here.
   Brochures, some in comic book format, on the story of money, inflation, banks and consumer credit are available for the taking. The guides can be sketchy and not always as knowledgeable as they should

be. But you get a cash reward (somewhat shredded) for going! If you arrive a little early, be sure to check out the art exhibition and electronic displays on the 1st floor.

GRACE CHURCH ¢
(See "For the Believers.")
Tours: *On most Sun at 12:30pm (Oct-Jun).*

GRACIE MANSION ¢¢
East End Ave. at 88th St.
☎ *(212) 570-4751.*
Tours: *By appt. only on Wed (Apr-Nov 15). Subject to change.*
Suggested Donation: *Adults $3, Seniors & Children $1.*

For an absolutely delightful 1-hour tour, come and learn about the checkered history of Gracie Mansion and see much of the 14-room official residence of the Mayor. The tour inspects the two wings that comprise the mansion (though no bedrooms are on the tour): the original

1799 house and the 1966 Susan B. Wagner wing, which is used primarily for official duties. Federal period furniture and decor provide the main architectural theme with many original antiques, furniture, chandeliers, mirrors and paintings.

Of particular beauty are the original mantelpieces and garnitures, chandeliers and bull's-eye mirrors in the Wagner wing. The 1799 wing serves as the Mayor's living quarters and tends to be dotted with many presents amassed by the Mayor's office over the years and with paintings pleasing to the current chief. On clement days, the tour includes a trip around the lovely grounds.

A big thanks go to former Mayor Koch for opening up the Mansion and waiving his stipend for interior decoration and establishing instead the Gracie Mansion Conservancy. This group, which is responsible for ongoing renovations of the entire property including the 2.5-acre grounds and gardens, runs the tours. Rarely do you find volunteer guides as knowledgeable and gracious as those found here.

GRAND CENTRAL DISTRICT TOURS
Philip Morris Bldg. at 42nd St. & Park Ave.
☎ *(212) 986-9217.*
Tours: *Fri at 12:30pm (weather permitting).*
  Billed as an "urban detective and historian," Justin Ferate takes you on an excellent free walking tour of the courtyard of Philip Morris, the Bowery Savings Bank, the Art Deco delights of the Chanin and Chrysler Buildings, Grand Central Terminal and the Lincoln and Helmsley Buildings.

GRAND CENTRAL TERMINAL ⚫
(See "For the Lobbyists.")
Tours: *Wed at 12:30pm, meet at Chemical Bank.*
  The Municipal Art Society offers an excellent free behind-the-scenes tour of this Beaux-Arts beauty, exploring the Whispering Gallery and the glass catwalks overlooking the main concourse, all the while teaching about the design innovations, the celestial ceiling and the landmark battle. The tour lasts about 1 hour; tour guides are extremely knowledgeable and interesting.

GREENWALD FOUNDATION
Lenox Hill, P.O. Box 610.
☎ *(212) 473-6263.*
  As the organization of "Friends of" various city parks, they publicize the tours of city parks (contribution $1).

HEBREW UNION COLLEGE—JEWISH INSTITUTE OF RELIGION
(See "For the Knowledge Seekers.")
Tours: *For groups by appt. only, Mon-Fri 9am-5pm.*
  All denominations are welcome; the tour includes a short history of Reform Judaism, the architecture of the new building and a chat about the exhibits.

IBM GALLERY OF SCIENCE AND ART ⚫⚫⚫
(See "For the Culture Vultures.")
Gallery Talks: *During the day and vary by exhibit. Tours for groups by appt., 745-5214.*

INTERNATIONAL LADIES' GARMENT WORKERS UNION (ILGWU)
1710 Broadway (at 54th St.).
☎ *(212) 265-7000 ext. 330.*
Groups: *High school students and older (interested in fashion), maximum of 25 per group.*
Tours: *Mon-Thu at 10am by appt. only (tour lasts about 3 hours).*
  You will certainly leave this tour knowing very clearly what the ILGWU is. In fact, at every opportunity you are made aware of this, either in

the 17-minute "We are the ILGWU" filmstrip or during the Q&A period that follows or in the free brochures that you are given. A tour of a factory is quite interesting as you can see how one of the most labor-intensive industries actually works. And by all means, "Look for the union label...."

METROPOLITAN MUSEUM OF ART (MMA) 💰💰💰💰
(See "For the Culture Vultures.")
Groups: *By appt. only.*
Tours: *Various tours of different collections and wings take place throughout the day; consult the kiosk in the Great Hall or call 879-5500 ext. 3791.*
Museum Highlights Tours: *Tue-Fri 10:15am 1:15 & 3:15pm.*
Gallery Talks: *Throughout the day; consult kiosk.*
There always seems to be some specialized tour or gallery talk going on here; make a point to visit the Great Hall Information Desk to be kept informed. Consult the monthly calendar which is sent to members.

MID-MANHATTAN LIBRARY (NYPL)
(See "For the Bookworms.")
Tours: *Mon, Wed & Fri at 2:30pm.*
The tour reveals what's on each floor with a Q&A session afterwards.

EL MUSEO DEL BARRIO 💰
(See "For the Culture Vultures.")
Tours: *Wed-Fri 11am-2pm for groups by appt. only (bilingual).*

MUSEUM OF THE CITY OF NEW YORK 💰💰💰
(See "For the Culture Vultures.")
Tours: *Guided tours for school grades K-12 on Tue-Fri am, appt. only (contribution appreciated). Guided tours for adult groups of 15+ on Tue-Fri pms, appt. only ($4 per person). Self-guided tours on Tue-Fri afternoons for children and adults.*

NEW YORK CITY MOUNTED POLICE STABLES
(See "For the Kiddies.")
Tours: *Arranged of the stables by appt. only.*

NEW YORK POLICE DEPARTMENT MUSEUM 💰
(See "For the Culture Vultures.")
Tours: *For all ages by appt. only.*
N.Y.C.'s finest really display a fascinating and very human side to their force thanks to an excellent tour of their museum. A 30-minute Q&A session on the police department is followed by a visit to the museum.

NEW YORK PUBLIC LIBRARY, 42ND STREET CENTRAL RESEARCH LIBRARY 💰💰💰
(See "For the Bookworms.")
Tours: *Mon-Sat at 11am & 2pm. Group tours by appt. only, 930-0501.*
For an interesting in-depth view of this superb Beaux-Arts triumph,

stick with this rather long and sometimes rambling tour. Some guides are more interesting than others.

NEW YORK PUBLIC LIBRARY FOR THE PERFORMING ARTS (NYPL) 🍎🍎
(See "For the Bookworms.")
Tours: *Wed at 2pm.*
Tours of this excellent specialized library include a visit to the galleries and the various performing arts collection rooms.

NEW YORK STOCK EXCHANGE 🍎🍎
(See "For the Exhibitionists.")
Tours: *Self-guided. Temporarily closed, call for reopening.*

OLD MERCHANT'S HOUSE 🍎
(See "For the Culture Vultures.")
Tours: *Continually on Sun 1-4pm (closed Aug) or weekday tours by appt. only for groups of 20-50.*

THE PLAYERS CLUB 🍎
16 Gramercy Pk. S. (on 20th St. near Irving Pl.).
☎ *(212) 228-7610.*
Tours: *By appt. only Mon-Fri 9am-noon for academic groups, maximum of 20.*
Library upon appt. only for research, Mon-Fri 10am-5pm.
Intent on elevating the actor's place in society, Edwin Booth (considered by some the best American Shakespearean actor) founded the Players Club in 1888 in this charming Gramercy Park brownstone, renovated by Stanford White. Perhaps today best known because of his infamous brother (John Wilkes Booth, who assassinated President Lincoln in 1865), Edwin has nonetheless left his mark by establishing this museum-like private club for artists, writers, musicians, patrons of the arts and, of course, actors.

The librarian takes you on the tour, recounting juicy tidbits about the present members as well as the life and times of Edwin Booth. Display cases of props and costumes recreate Booth's *Hamlet, Macbeth* and *Richard II.* And the walls are a never-ending picture gallery of who's who in the theater, including paintings, photos, caricatures, playbills, notices and lithographs of faces from the past 100 years. Each room is rich in memorabilia, Shakespearean quotations and theatrical inspiration (all those famous faces peering down!). The highlight is the untouched, unrenovated 19th C. Booth bedroom with many of his personal objects, including a picture of his brother.

Also of special interest is the library, which began with Booth's collection of 1,000 books and today has grown into an important theatrical research library. A round of applause to this club for allowing us to share in its history.

RIVERSIDE CHURCH 🍎🍎
(See "For the Believers.")

Tours: *Sun at 12:15pm (Sep-Jun).*

For an excellent introduction to this beautiful and much undiscovered landmark, make a pilgrimage to this superb church. You won't be disappointed.

ROCKEFELLER CENTER TOUR 🍎🍎🍎
(See "For the Exhibitionists.")
Tours: *Mon-Sun 9:45am-4:45pm, every half hour. Reservation needed for groups of 18 or more (fee).*

Although Rockefeller Center is a mandatory free attraction, you may want to consider an expenditure for this excellent 1-hour walking tour. A knowledgeable, fast-paced guide whisks you all around, including the NBC studios, RCA Observation Roof and Radio City Music Hall (most of which are never free).

ST. PAUL'S CHAPEL 🍎
(See "For the Believers.")
Tours: *By appt. only.*

ST. THOMAS CHURCH 🍎
(See "For the Believers.")
Tours: *Sun at 12:15pm.*

SEAGRAM BUILDING
(See "For the Lobbyists.")
Tours: *Tue at 3pm. Meet in the lobby, call for reservations, 572-7404.*

SEVENTH REGIMENT ARMORY

SEVENTH REGIMENT ARMORY ♦♦♦
643 Park Ave. (66th-67th Sts.).
☎ *(212) 439-0300/744-2968.*
Tours: *Call in advance.*

This place is a must regardless of your military views, for this impressive landmark of the 7th Regiment offers occasional tours. Of interest are rooms designed by many decorators such as Louis Comfort Tiffany and Stanford White, containing much of the original 1880 furniture and decor. The Veterans Room is absolutely the highlight and completely beyond description; it must be seen. But each room offers something special. In addition, flags, uniforms and weapons of the 7th Regiment are displayed. Artwork mainly featuring native sons adorns the walls. Give yourself at least an hour to do the Armory justice. Special events, such as exhibitions, are held year round, but in most cases carry an admission fee.

The Armory still serves the 7th Regiment during the day and then opens its doors to the homeless at night. A Park Avenue address, not bad!

SHAPIRO'S WINERY
126 Rivington St. (Norfolk & Essex Sts.).
☎ *(212) 674-4404.*
Groups: *By appt. during the week.*
Tours: *Sun 11am-4pm, except Hols and cold weather.*

Founded in 1899, this is Manhattan's only extant winery. Come and see the process of making kosher wines (in fact, 26 different-flavored wines: cream honey, cherry, blackberry, plum, pina cocatina as well as the more traditional kinds). Shapiro's receives the grapes from upstate New York and begins the fermentation process in 1,400-2,000 gallon oak casks (and they're big), later transporting the wine to 4,000-5,000 gallon barrels (even bigger). When the time is ripe, Shapiro's bottles around 500,000 gallons a year. The grand and romantic concept of chateau or vineyard bottled wine will be completely shattered for you when you see the rather shabby facilities at Shapiro's. However, if you're into sweet wines, you do get to taste a selection of the various flavors, so it shouldn't be a total loss!

THE ABIGAIL ADAMS SMITH MUSEUM ♦
(See "For the Culture Vultures.")

A visit to this late 1700s coach house will automatically hook you up with the next available tour, run by the Colonial Dames of America and lasting about 30 minutes. Guides are very interesting and well informed.

STUDIO MUSEUM OF HARLEM ♦
(See "For the Culture Vultures.")
Group Tours: *By appt. only on Wed-Fri 10:30am-3pm, Sat 1-5pm.*

SUPREME COURT OF NEW YORK ♦
(See "For the Exhibitionists.")

Tours: *Mon-Fri 10:15am for groups (4th graders and up) or individuals by appt. only.*

Want to learn more about our legal system? The difference between a criminal and civil case? Who's who in the courtroom? For an informative and interesting morning at the N.Y. Civil and Criminal Supreme Courts, call and arrange a tour for your group or yourself.

The first part consists of a 30-45 minute discussion in an empty courtroom where you become involved in a Q&A session and then a mock trial. Afterwards you're off to see an actual ongoing trial on which you've already been briefed. This is excellent for any age group as the coordinator and guide custom design this program accordingly. There's also a worthwhile exhibit in the rotunda.

TEMPLE EMANU-EL 🍎
(See "For the Believers.")
Tours: *By appt. only.*

TRINITY CHURCH 🍎🍎
(See "For the Believers.")
Tours: *Mon-Sun at 2pm.*

UNITED NATIONS 🍎🍎🍎
(See "For the Exhibitionists.")
Tours: *Daily 9:15am-4:45pm, every 15 minutes (fee).*

This 1-hour tour provides an excellent glimpse behind the scenes of this world-famous institution. The tour is given in 25 different languages, and it is recommended that reservations be made for a tour other than in English.

U.S. COURTHOUSE
(See "For the Exhibitionists.")
Tours: *For groups of 20 or fewer, by appt. only.*

Tours for adults usually include a summary briefing and then sitting in on a Court of Appeals case in the morning and/or District court session in the afternoon. You will receive the pamphlet "A Citizen's Guide to the Federal Courts." Tours for schoolchildren are more comprehensive.

URBAN PARK RANGERS
(See N.Y.C. Department of Parks & Recreation under "For the Birds.")
Tours: *Throughout the year of N.Y.C. parks for children and adults.*

WALKING TOUR GUIDES
"Where They Lit Up New York," Con Edison Consumer Education, 4 Irving Pl., N.Y., N.Y. 10003.

This walking tour through Thomas Edison's "First District" in lower Manhattan (the first area to receive electricity) is very interesting and well done.

Adventures on a Shoestring, 300 W. 53rd St., N.Y., N.Y. 10019, 265-2663.

Inexpensive tours of New York City are of interest.

"42nd Street, River to River," J.M. Kaplan Fund & Department of Cultural

Affairs.

This fascinating in-depth account of that wonderful, often maligned thoroughfare, 42nd Street, is available at most locations on 42nd St.

"Jurors' Guide to Lower Manhattan," 5 Walking Tours, Municipal Art Society, 935-3960.

Given out free to those lucky souls on jury duty, this is an excellent walking guide of historic buildings and sites as well as ethnic communities like Chinatown, Little Italy, the Lower East Side or the artists' world of Soho and Tribeca and the Financial District. Exceptionally well written and interesting, copies can be obtained at the Urban Center, 457 Madison Ave. (at 51st St.) for a nominal fee.

"Heritage Trail," N.Y. Convention & Visitors Bureau, 2 Columbus Circle, 397-8222.

A 3-mile self-guided tour of Civic Center to South Street Seaport.

WESTSIDE PIERS AND CRUISE LINES
Check the newspapers for ship departures as that is always a fun thing to see. Call about visiting policies as some don't allow spectators.

WHITNEY MUSEUM OF AMERICAN ART 🍎🍎🍎
(See "For the Culture Vultures.")
Gallery Talks: *Tue-Thu at 1:30, 2:30, 3:30pm (Tue at 6:15pm), Fri at 12:30 & 2:30pm, Sat-Sun 2 & 3:30pm..*

WHITNEY MUSEUM OF AMERICAN ART AT EQUITABLE CENTER 🍎
(See "For the Culture Vultures.")
Gallery Talks: *Tue-Fri at 12:30 & 2:30pm, Sat at 1pm.*

WHITNEY MUSEUM OF AMERICAN ART AT PHILIP MORRIS 🍎🍎
(See "For the Culture Vultures.")
Gallery Talks: *Mon, Wed & Fri 12:30pm.*

WHITNEY MUSEUM OF AMERICAN ART DOWNTOWN AT FEDERAL RESERVE PLAZA 🍎
(See "For the Culture Vultures.")
Gallery Talks: *Mon, Wed & Fri at 12:30pm.*

WORLD TRADE CENTER 🍎🍎🍎
(See "For the Lobbyists.")
Pick up free brochure with walking tours of the area at the Info Desk.

The Bronx

BRONX HERITAGE TRAIL
☎ *(212) 881-8900.*
Sponsored by the Bronx County Historical Society, a free self-guided

tour brochure of the 3 historic houses includes the Valentine-Varian House, Edgar Allan Poe Cottage and Van Cortlandt Mansion.

THE NEW YORK BOTANICAL GARDENS 🍎🍎🍎
(See "For the Birds.")
Tours: *Conservatory: weekends 11am-4pm, meet at Palm Court. Garden grounds: Sat-Sun 1 & 3pm (Apr-Oct), meet at Visitors Center. Groups by appt.*

NEW YORK MARITIME COLLEGE
(See "For the Knowledge Seekers.")
Tours: *On weekends, usually Sat.*
For a tour of the landmark Fort Schuyler, write to Office of Community Relations at SUNY, Fort Schuyler, N.Y. 10456 and include desired date, time and number in group (including children 6 and over).

URBAN PARK RANGERS
(See individual parks in "For the Birds" for their tours.)

WAVE HILL 🍎🍎
(See "For the Birds.")
Tours: *Sun at 2:15pm and occasionally on Sat at 3pm.*

Brooklyn

BROOKLYN ACADEMY OF MUSIC 🍎
(See "For the Music Lovers.")
Tours: *For school groups or community centers, by appt. only.*
Guided tours backstage reveal how concerts and performances are put on, including stage sets and props. Occasional free concerts include Children's Free Opera (718-636-4130).

BROOKLYN BOROUGH HALL
209 Joralemon St. entrance (at Court St.).
☎ *(718) 855-7882.*
Tours: *Wed at 12:30pm.*
This tour sponsored by The Fund, consists of the architectural masterpiece of Brooklyn Borough Hall and the history of Brooklyn.

BROOKLYN BOTANIC GARDENS 🍎🍎🍎🍎
(See "For the Birds.")
Tours: *Sun at 1pm (Mar-mid Nov).*
Tours of these wonderful gardens shouldn't be missed.

BROOKLYN HISTORIC DISTRICTS & LANDMARKS GUIDE
Free at Borough Hall, 209 Joralemon St. or send $5 to The Fund for Borough of Brooklyn, 16 Court St., Suite 1400W, Brooklyn, N.Y. 11241.
☎ *(718) 855-7882.*

This 74-page book and calendar reveals the history, descriptions and tours of the various historical districts and architectural wonders.

BROOKLYN HISTORICAL SOCIETY & MUSEUM 🍎
(See "For the Culture Vultures.")
A noonday program in fall and spring features guided tours of the neighborhood as well as lectures or films (some offered in conjunction with St. Ann's).

BROOKLYN MUSEUM 🍎🍎🍎🍎
(See "For the Culture Vultures.")
Tours: *By appt. only.*

GREEN-WOOD CEMETERY
(See "For the Birds.")
Tours: *Sat or Sun (May-Nov), reservation required.*

LEFFERTS HOMESTEAD
(See "For the Culture Vultures.")
Tours: *By appt. only.*

PROSPECT PARK 🍎🍎🍎
(See "For the Birds.")
Tours: *Sun at 1pm, sponsored by the Urban Park Rangers.*

URBAN PARK RANGERS
☎ *(718) 287-3400.*
Tours: *For walking tours throughout the borough.*

Queens

ALLEY POND ENVIRONMENTAL CENTER 🍎
(See "For the Birds.")
Tours: *Park's wetlands and woodlands all year round; call for day and time.*

CHUNG-CHENG GALLERY 🍎
(See "For the Artists.")
Tours: *For groups by appt. only.*

FLUSHING "FREEDOM MILE" TOUR
Along Northern Blvd.
☎ *(718) 939-0647.*
Visit 19 historic homes and landmarks along Northern Blvd. from Parsons Blvd. to Lawrence St. Obtain the 1-page tour from the Friends Meeting House or Queens Historical Society, 143-35 37th Ave., Flushing.

FORT TILDEN AREA
(See "For the Birds.")
Tours: *Sun at 1pm (Jul-Aug) or groups by appt.*

JAMAICA BAY WILDLIFE REFUGE 🍎🍎
(See "For the Birds.")
Tours: *Nature walks on weekends (spring-fall) and weekday eve "Moon Prowls." Call for times.*

QUEENS HISTORICAL SOCIETY
143-35 37th St., Flushing.
☎ *(718) 939-0647.*

For a listing of organized tours of landmarks and historic communities by competent leaders (for fee), obtain the free *Guided Tours of Queens Booklet*, which can give you good ideas even if you don't actually take the tours.

URBAN PARK RANGERS
☎ *(718) 699-4204.*

For walking tours during the year throughout the borough.

Staten Island

CLAY PIT PONDS STATE PARK RESERVE 🍎
(See "For the Birds.")
Tours: *Walking tours on many Sun at 11am. Groups by appt. or self-guided tours available.*

GREAT KILLS PARK
(See "For the Birds.")
Tours: *Nature walks on Sun at 10am (Jul-Aug), groups on weekdays at 10am & 1pm by appt. only. Occasional Urban Park Rangers tours.*

RICHMONDTOWN RESTORATION VILLAGE 🍎🍎🍎
(See "For the Culture Vultures.")
Tours: *Guided tours by appt. only ($1.75 per person). Self-guided tours last about 2 hours.*

SNUG HARBOR CULTURAL CENTER 🍎🍎🍎
(See "For the Culture Vultures.")
Tours: *Sat & Sun at 2pm from Visitors Center. Tree tours on Sun at 1pm (Jun-Aug) by S.I. Botanical Society. Groups by appt. only.*

URBAN PARK RANGERS
☎ *(718) 667-6042.*

For walking tours during the year throughout the borough.

For the Birds

In this city of skyscrapers and sidewalks, parks (big and small) become meccas. Offering trees and grass for peaceful relaxation, many are also recreational playgrounds for active and passive sports, everything from football to frisbee. In nice weather, our parks are transformed into outdoor entertainment centers offering concerts, plays and festivals for all. Also, N.Y.C.'s parkland includes miles of wonderful beaches and nature refuges of all kinds.

> *"It is the marriage of the soul with Nature that makes the intellect fruitful, and gives birth to imagination."*
>
> *— HENRY DAVID THOREAU*

BATTERY PARK
State St. & Battery Pl., lower Manhattan on Hudson River.
☎ *(212) 397-3101.*
Ferries for Statue of Liberty & Ellis Island leave from here.

This 22-acre landfill park derives its name from the line of guns along State Street, the original shoreline. Situated on the Hudson River, the promenade affords excellent views of New York harbor, the Statue of Liberty, Ellis Island and New Jersey. With its spacious lawns, plentiful trees and benches, this park offers a welcome retreat from the towering skyscrapers in the Financial District. Lovely cherry trees are always gorgeous in the spring. Modern sculpture abounds with tributes to Giovanni da Verrazano (who discovered New York Harbor), Emma Lazarus (who wrote the poem inscribed on the Statue of Liberty) and those WWII sailors lost at sea. Castle Clinton, once jutting out 300 feet offshore, now stands fortified in this highly charged park (see "For the Exhibitionists").

Events: *Folk dancing on Sat & Sun from 2-6pm, occasional festivals and Hol programs for Memorial Day, July 4th, Labor & Columbus Days.*

BATTERY PARK CITY (BPC) ♦♦♦
Along Hudson River from Chambers St. to Battery Pk.
☎ *(212) 416-5300.*

One of N.Y.C.'s latest and most successful commercial, residential and park complexes, Battery Park City encompasses 92 acres in lower Manhattan; much of the landfill for its construction came from the excavation of the World Trade Center. With the World Financial Center as its shining star, BPC has apartment buildings, parks, esplanades, marinas and public art lining premiere property on the Hudson River. Plan to visit during clement weather, so you can appreciate the incomparable views and tasteful design of this complex.

If you begin at the World Financial Center and Plaza (see "For the Lobbyists"), take a delightful stroll southward down the esplanade, made from attractive hexagonal stones. At Albany Street, Ned Smyth's "Upper Room" is a stone-studded, colonnade court housing a long table inlaid with mosaics and six chessboards (seats 12 — references have been made to a modern-day Last Supper) and a palm-crowned center column of gold and mosaic inlays. R.M. Fischer's "Rector Gate" embraces Rector Street with a stainless-steel, 45-foot-high arch topped off with a lightning rod and "torchere" that is lit up at night. Farther along at West Thames Street is "Sitting/Stance" by Richard Artschwager, a triangular outdoor room decorated with 2 purple-wood lounge chairs, 2 9-foot granite Egyptian chairs and 2 stainless-steel picnic tables with a lighting fixture and honey locust tree.

At the bottom of the esplanade is the 3-acre South Cove Park, lining a quarter-mile rectangular inlet of the Hudson River. A lower-level walkway, punctuated with rocky outcroppings (to simulate the shoreline), lampposts with nautical blue fixtures and wooden railings, and an upper boardwalk-style path lead you to a lookout tower, a tiny island, a wooden-bowed footbridge and a striking semi-circular jetty framed by a canopy of wooden Japanese-style arches. Eventually South

Park will be completed and will connect Battery Park City with Battery Park, making the lower Hudson River area an even more extraordinary place to live, work or visit.

Events: Indoor arts and entertainment at the World Financial Center and outdoor summer entertainment, especially at The Plaza.

BOWLING GREEN PARK
Broadway & State St., across from the Old Customs House.
☎ *(212) 397-3101.*

This small triangular park in lower Manhattan was actually the first park in N.Y.C., although it started out as a bowling green. A simple iron fence, now a landmark, was added in 1771 to enclose the green and to protect the equestrian statue of George III, which was melted down for ammunition during the Revolutionary War. Look for the bull at the tip of the park, ready to charge on the financial district.

Benches encircling the central fountain now provide an excellent vantage point for admiring the glorious **Old Customs House** (to house the National Museum of the American Indian in 1992), on the site where Peter Minuit bought Manhattan from the Indians for $24 in 1626. Built in 1907, this regal Beaux-Arts edifice by Cass Gilbert features extraordinary symbolic decoration. At the base, four heroic sculptures by Daniel Chester French depict Asia, America, Europe and Africa. Statues above the columns represent 12 ancient and modern commercial centers. The capitals of the columns are each decorated with the head of Mercury, the Roman God of Commerce. The main window arches contain heads representing the eight "races" of mankind: Caucasian, Hindu, Latin, Celtic, Mongolian, Eskimo, Slavic and African. The crowning glory is a cartouche with the arms of the United States.

BRYANT PARK
40th-42nd Sts., E. of 6th Ave. (closed, under renovation).
☎ *(212) 408-0100 (Parks).*

Originally called Reservoir Square, as the Croton Reservoir occupied the current library site, this park was also the home of the Crystal Palace, America's first World's Fair in 1853-54. Unfortunately, this dazzling glass and iron pavilion suffered a fate similar to that of its English namesake, and was destroyed by fire in 1858. During the Civil War, the land served as a drill ground for the Union Army. Set aside as a park in 1884 and named for poet and journalist William Cullen Bryant (one of the first to address the needs for public parks), it was not landscaped until 1934.

After its major renovation, this 10-acre park will be restored to its previous beauty, surrounded by the Public Library and impressive skyscrapers (especially the Grace and American Radiator Buildings).
Events: *Call for events as previous tours and performances may be continued when re-opened.*

CATHEDRAL CHURCH OF ST. JOHN THE DIVINE 🍎🍎
(See "For the Believers.")

A Biblical Garden, with the occasional strutting peacock, contains over 100 plants mentioned in the Bible.

CENTRAL PARK 🍎🍎🍎🍎
59th-110th Sts., between 5th Ave & Central Pk. W.
☎ *(212) 397-3156/755-4100.*

The escape valve for most Manhattanites, Central Park offers 840 acres of landscape and recreational attractions all year round. Its history began in 1844 when William Cullen Bryant urged in his *N.Y. Evening Post* that a "central part of the island" be set aside for a park before urban expansion made it too expensive. Andrew Jackson Downing was the first landscape designer of the park, but his death in 1852 led the way for his partner, Calvert Vaux, to team up with Frederick Law Olmsted. From 1859 to 1867, the creative genius of Olmsted and Vaux (with major support from Jacob Wrey Mould and Ignatz Pilat) designed and managed this mammoth undertaking. They had to negotiate difficult terrain and swamps in order to plan for public access facilities, plants, trees, flowers, lakes and recreational areas. Although much of the original design has been altered due to the intrusion of concrete and asphalt, ballfields, overgrown plantings and vandalism, their efforts have remained central to this vertical city.

Places of Interest
Hans Christian Andersen Statue, 74th St. & Conservatory Pond (east side). Storytelling on Sat at 11am for children 4+ (May-Sep).
The Arsenal Gallery, at 64th & 5th Ave. (See "For the Exhibitionists.")
Bandshell. See Naumberg Bandshell below.
Belvedere Castle, 79th St., S. of the Great Lawn. This Victorian

castle has recently been restored to live up to its name, which means "beautiful view" in Italian. As a Learning Center for children and adults, it offers comprehensive educational programs with audience participation, self-guided tours, exhibits on the history of the castle (Tue-Sun 11am-5pm, except Fri 1-5pm), children's activities on Sat at 1-2:30pm (reservation required, 772-0210) and family programs on some Sun at 2 & 3pm.

Carousel, near 65th St. & mid-park. Weather permitting, Mon-Fri 10:30am-4:30pm, Sat-Sun 10:30am-5:30pm (winter closing 1 hour earlier), $.75 a ride, 879-0244.

Chess & Checkers House, near 65th St. & mid-park, across from the Dairy. Built-in chess tables and benches available for those wanting to play or watch; many serious games with timers! Bring game pieces, Mon-Sun 11:30am-4:30pm.

Children's Zoo, 5th Ave. & 65th St. Open Mon-Sun 10am-4:30pm. Admission $.10. Small barnyard animals, birds and reptiles on display, 408-0271.

Conservatory Garden, 5th Ave. & 105th St. The North Garden is abloom with flowering plants, fountains and trellises; the South Garden features large perennial beds interspersed with 3,000 different annuals (roses in Jun & Sep), 397-3137/373-8810.

Conservatory Pond, 74th St. & 5th Ave. Favorite spot for enthusiasts of model sailboats. Permits are needed, 360-8133.

The Dairy, S. of 65th St. transverse between the Zoo & Carousel. Open Tue-Sun 11am-5pm (Fri 1-5pm) for viewing the video and exhibits or dropping in on the Visitors Center (see "For the Exhibitionists"), occasional free guided park tours by the Urban Park Rangers usually on Sun at 2pm (Apr-Sep), concerts on Sat-Sun (occasional weekdays) at 1pm (Jun-Aug), family workshops, performances and self-guided walking tour of Central Park (fee), 397-3156.

Delacorte Musical Clock, 5th Ave. & 65th St., between Children's Zoo and main Zoo. A charming animated bronze clock with animal figures in an architectural setting by Andrea Spadini (sculptor) and Edward C. Embury (architect), completed in 1965. Every half hour, there's a delightful performance.

Delacorte Theatre, 81st St., S. of the Great Lawn. Joseph Papp's N.Y. Shakespeare Festival offers 2 fully staged theatrical productions on Tue-Sun at 8pm (Jul-Labor Day) in the amphitheater. Tickets are given out at 6pm *only* to those in line around the Great Lawn. Always worthwhile, 861-PAPP/7277.

Doris C. Freedman Plaza, 5th Ave. & 60th St. An entrance to the park is eye-catching with modern sculpture (such as Moore, Noguchi, Dubuffet, Nevelson), selected by the Public Art Fund and changing every 6 months.

Great Lawn, 80th-84th Sts. & mid-park. The site of many wonderful summer evening concerts performed by the Metropolitan Opera and the N.Y. Philharmonic (see "For the Music Lovers"), 408-0209 (ball permits).

Heckscher Playground, 61st-65th Sts. & mid-park. For permits, 397-3114.

Heckscher Puppet House, 62nd St. (enter at 59th St. & 7th Ave.). Shows on Mon-Fri at 10:30am & noon. Admission $2; reservation needed, 397-3162.

Lasker Pool & Rink, 106th St. & mid-park. Open daily 11am-8pm for swimming (May-early Sep) or ice skating and hockey (Oct-Apr), 722-9781/397-3142.

Loeb Boathouse, 74th St. & N.E. corner of lake. Boat rentals and bike center. Occasional free workshops on bikes, 288-7281.

Naumberg Bandshell, 72nd St. & mid-park. Occasional outdoor entertainment includes the N.Y. Grand Opera on Thu at 8pm (Jul), dance and music on Wed at 7:30pm (Aug), plus more sponsored by the Department of Cultural Affairs, 360-8196/755-4100.

North Meadow Center, 97th-102nd Sts. & mid-park. Sports fields for organized games with permits (397-3114), men's and women's locker rooms, open daily 7am-dusk, 360-8200.

Rambles, N. of 72nd St. A wooded hilly area, good for bird watching.

Recreation House, 98th St. & mid-park. Checkers, chess, handball, modified paddle tennis, pool, shuffleboard and Zimm Zamm (whatever that may be).

Shakespeare Garden, 80th St. E. of West Dr. Volunteers needed for fertilizing, planting and maintaining the garden on weekends, 360-8111.

Sheep Meadow, 66-69th Sts. west side, across from Tavern on the Green. Open field for passive play; no organized sports, 360-8200.

Strawberry Fields, 72nd St. & Central Pk. W. In memory of John Lennon, 2.5 acres including a variety of shrubs, vines, perennials and, of course, strawberry plants. On the main walk, look for the mosaic medallion with the word "imagine."

Swedish Cottage Marionette Theater, 81st St. & west side. Shows

($3), reservation required, 988-9093.

Woolman Rink, 63rd St. & mid-park. Ice skating (Oct-Apr), 517-4800.

Zoo, see below.

Activities

(Call Special Events, 360-8166, or for list of annual events, 360-8126. Obtain a copy of *Green Pages* for a comprehensive park listing.)

Art Exhibits, along the north sidewalk of Central Pk. S. and 6th Ave. 150 participants show paintings, drawings, sculpture, prints, etchings, silkscreens, photos and crafts on several weekends (May-Oct) from 11am-6pm.

Ballfields. For softball teams spring-mid Sep and football teams mid Sep-winter obtain permits, 408-0209.

Bicycle Racing, 79th St. & East Dr. Sat at 7am (Mar-Nov) for members of the Century Road Club Assn. only, (718) 343-8888.

Bicycle Riding. Over 6 miles of park roads with special lane; rentals at the Loeb Boathouse, 861-4137 (fee).

Boating. See Loeb Boathouse under "Places of Interest."

Folk Dancing, at the King Jagiello Statue at 88th St. E. of Belvedere Lake on Sat-Sun at 2pm-dusk (Apr-fall), weather permitting.

Horseback Riding. Over 6 miles of bridle paths; rent horses at Claremont Stable, 175 W. 89th St., 724-5100.

Horse-drawn Carriage Rides, at Central Pk. S. & 5th or 6th Aves. A wonderful and romantic way to explore the park, but expensive, 246-0520.

Horseshoe Pitching, 97th St. & Central Pk S. Bring horseshoes.

Ice Skating, at Lasker and Woolman Rinks; see "Places Of Interest" above.

Jogging Trails, around the reservoir (1.58 miles) at 84th-96th Sts. and around park roads.

Lawn Bowling Area, N.W. corner of Sheep Meadow. Enclosed manicured greens for lawn bowling (bocci ball), permits, 360-8133.

Model Yacht Races, at Conservatory Pond (see "Places of Interest" above).

Roller Skating, N.W. corner of Sheeps Meadow at 69th St., 360-8157.

Running. The 1.58-mile path around the reservoir is especially popular. For group runs, meet at Engineer's Gate (90th St. & 5th Ave.) on Mon-Fri 6:30-7:30pm and Sat at 10am, organized by the N.Y. Road Runners Club, 860-4455.

Sledding, Burn's Lawn at 79th St. & 5th Ave. (small children), Pilgrim Hill at 72nd St. & 5th Ave. and Cedar Hill at 78th St. & mid-park.

Special Events. For info, 360-8166.

Storytelling, at Hans Christian Andersen Statue, E. 74th St. near Conservatory Pond on Sat at 11am (May-Sep).

Swimming, at Lasker Pool (see "Places of Interest" above).

Tennis, courts at 95th St. & mid-park. Permits and sign-up required, 360-8133/397-3194.

Tours by the Urban Park Rangers. Throughout the park for adults and children, all year round, 427-4040.

Volunteer Work. Those interested in pruning, weeding and other park clean-up activities may sign up for 8-week programs. Included each week is a 1-hour lecture on a related park subject, L.I.V.E. in calendar, 535-1166.

Walking/Health Walking and Race Walking, Engineer's Gate, 5th Ave. & 90th St. For clinics every Sat at 9am and group "walk-outs" on Sun.

CENTRAL PARK ZOO ☀ ☀ ☀
Central Park, 64th St. & east side.
☎ *(212) 439-6500.*
Hours: *Mon-Fri 10am-5pm, Sat-Sun 10am-5:30pm (closes 4:30pm Nov-Apr, Tue til 8pm May-Sep).*
Free Admission: *Children under 3. Otherwise Adults $2.50, Children 3-12 $.50.*

This beautifully designed zoo with indoor pavilions and outdoor environments for exotic and favorite animals is a wonderful experience. Tasteful landscaping and varied terrain add to the visual excitement; animals are arranged according to temperate zones. What's so nice about this small zoo is that they concentrate on just a few animals and do them justice.

In the Central Garden are the playful seals; feeding time is always lively. A visit to the penguin cove brings you into their diving and frolicking world. Climb past the rocky cliffs of the polar bears and arctic foxes. A monkey colony lives amid the rocks of the man-made pond of the temperate territory where swans swim underfoot. The Rain Forest pavilion re-creates the steamy life of the tropics with its rich vegetation and animal life in riverbank, cave, treetop and jungle habitats. A zoo gallery features animals in art.

CITY HALL PARK
At Centre St. & Broadway, Chambers St.& Park Row.
☎ *(212) 397-3090.*

Originally a Dutch bowling green and then a hotbed for unfair-taxation demonstrations in the 1770s, this small, attractive village green or "common" was once a hub of activity with City Hall, the main post office, the city's first art museum, a public school and printer's row.

Today, with only City Hall and the Tweed Courthouse, it still offers a respite from city government with reminders of our past through statues of Horace Greeley (founder of *The N.Y. Tribune*) and Nathan Hale (hanged as a spy by the British in 1776 and famous for saying, "I regret I have but one life to lose for my country"). Visits to City Hall and the Woolworth Building are worthwhile (see "For the Culture Vultures" and "For the Lobbyists").
Events: *Occasional outdoor lunchtime concerts, tours by the Urban Park Rangers and Christmas tree lighting ceremony in Dec.*

COLUMBUS PARK
At Worth, Mulberry & Baxter Sts.

☎ *(212) 397-3109.*

Chinatown and the surrounding Lower East Side were home to thousands of immigrant slumdwellers at the turn of the century. Thanks to Jacob Riis's photographs of the area, the public conscience was raised and this park was created in 1892. Today it serves as a playground for Chinatown.

Events: *Summer camps, play groups, arts & crafts and team sports.*

EXXON MINI-PARK
Between 6th-7th Aves. at 49th-50th Sts.

Under new construction, this park plans to re-open in 1993.

FIRST BOSTON PLAZA
77 W. 45th St. (at 6th Ave.).
☎ *(212) 536-5968.*
Hours: *Mon-Sun 7am-8:30pm (May 15th-Sep 15th), and Mon-Sun 7:30am-7:30pm (Sep 16th-May 14th).*

This brown brick esplanade with trees and greenery offers a delightful respite for open-air seekers. The plaza occupies an entire block and provides tables (some with umbrellas) and chairs. Additional seating is available around the 2 central brick fountains; moats surround and connect the fountains. Sculpture enhances the plaza's design. Occasional summer events.

FORT TRYON PARK
Northern Manhattan, S. of Dyckman, W. of Broadway, E. of Henry Hudson Pkwy.

For absolutely splendid views of the Hudson River and the N.J. Palisades, enjoy the 62 acres of this peaceful park, an outpost in the Revolutionary War. The central plaza was named in honor of Margaret Corbin, a Revolutionary War heroine, who fought in her husband's place after his death until she herself was badly injured. There are informal garden areas. Don't miss The Cloisters (see "For the Culture Vultures"), especially the flower and herb gardens with 200 species of plants of the Middle Ages.

Events: *The Annual Medieval Festival (Sep), classical music and dance on Tue at 7pm (Jul-Aug) and occasional walking tours.*

MARCUS GARVEY PARK
120-124th Sts., Lenox & Madison Aves.
☎ *(212) 397-3118.*

This park boasts the last remaining city firetower, Mt. Morris Watchtower, built in 1856 of cast iron. The Mt. Morris Garvey Recreation Center at E. 122nd St. & Mt. Morris Rd. offers programs for Girl Scouts, the handicapped, seniors and community groups. Free summer concerts.

GRACE BUILDING PLAZA
43rd St. & 6th Ave.
☎ *(212) 869-9700.*

Located behind this graceful 1974 building by Skidmore, Owings &

Merrill, a small plaza with limited seating offers concerts on Tue from 12:15-1:15pm (late Jun-Labor Day).

GRAMERCY PARK
20th-21st Sts. between Park Ave. S. & 3rd Ave.
This lovely park, reminiscent of classy London residential squares, is not open to the public. Its history started in the early 19th C. when Samuel Ruggles bought up this wooded area in hopes of transforming it into upper-class residential townhouses. He lured the city's elite by promising them that only they would have a golden key to the square's park. This offer proved enormously successful and remains in practice; today this is still a very desirable neighborhood. Many famous people have lived here, including Stanford White (the architect who was shot by Harry K. Thaw for having "flirted" with Thaw's wife, Evelyn Nesbit), Peter Cooper (philanthropist), Edwin Booth (actor who lived at #16, now the Players Club) and Samuel Tilden (politician who lived at #15, now the National Arts Club). Both the Players Club and the National Arts Club are worthy of visits (see "For the Tourists" and "For the Artists").

GRAND ARMY PLAZA
5th Ave. between 58th-60th Sts.
A popular movie set location, this famous square was designed by Thomas Hastings (N.Y. Public Library architect) in 1912 in an attempt to unite this area with Central Park's entrance at 60th St. The Pulitzer Fountain with sculpture by Karl Bitter and the equestrian statue of General Sherman (of Civil War fame) by Augustus Saint-Gaudens give the plaza monumentality. Outdoor entertainment abounds in good weather.

HANOVER SQUARE
Pearl & Hanover Sts.
Named for the English royal family of the King Georges, this was originally a public common for a ritzy residential area. In the late 1600s, it became the location of the city's first printing house (see plaque at 3 Hanover Sq.). Then the first newspaper, *The New-York Gazette*, began weekly publication here in 1725 under William Bradford. Tragically, this was the center of the Great Fire of 1835. Today this small square offers benches and trees with reminders of days past.

THE HORTICULTURAL SOCIETY OF NEW YORK
128 W. 58th St. (6th-7th Aves.).
☎ *(212) 757-0915.*
Hours: *Mon-Fri 10am-6pm.*
This nonprofit organization has been dedicated to the love of flora since 1900. It offers exhibits featuring flowers and plants portrayed in various artistic media. A 23-foot greenhouse displays some unusual and new plants for viewing as well as for sale. The library with its pleasant reading room houses books and periodicals for gardeners and plant lovers.
Events: *Free flower shows, lectures and workshops; courses (fee) on*

*everything from Japanese flower arrangement to cooking with flowers;
garden tours (fee); community service programs: maintains 25-30
community gardens in the city with expertise on tools, seeds and plants;
and the N.Y. Flower Show (Mar) on the Hudson River Pier at 52nd St. (fee).*

INWOOD HILL
*207th & Seamen Aves., E. of Hudson River, S. of Harlem River, N. of
Dyckman St.*
☎ *(212) 397-3185.*

With 196 acres of undeveloped wooded land and steep rocky sides,
this park offers good terrain for hiking. A good variety of trees and
wildflowers can be found. This park can be fairly deserted during the
week, so it's best to frequent it on the weekends.

*Events: Special programs for sports (basketball and track) and
afterschool activities.*

ASSER LEVY PLACE
E. 23rd-25th Sts., between 1st Ave. & East River Dr.
*Hours: Mon-Fri noon-8pm, Sat-Sun 11am-7pm (Memorial Day-Labor
Day).*

Modelled on the Neoclassical baths of Rome, these public baths were
built in 1906 to benefit the neighborhood slumdwellers; today there is
a public swimming pool.

McGRAW-HILL MINI-PARK
Between 6th-7th Aves. & 48th-49th Sts. Closed in winter.

This walk-through park with cascading waterfall (which you also can
walk through) offers a delightful setting with benches and a refreshment
kiosk.

MADISON SQUARE PARK
Between Madison & 5th Aves. & 23rd-26th Sts.

In honor of President James Madison, this park was formally created
in 1844. Its early claim to fame was as the birthplace of the first
organized baseball team, the Knickerbocker Baseball Club in 1845.
From 1853 to 1856, the Hippodrome, an entertainment center/circus,
attracted thousands of visitors to the park. During the second half of
the 19th C., this became a fashionable residential area.

In 1879, Madison Square Garden (the first and original sports arena)
was built at 26th Street and Madison Avenue; it sadly no longer stands.
It was an ornate Italian palazzo with a bell tower, which caused quite a
stir, thanks to its gilded statue of nude "Diana" by Augustus Saint-
Gaudens perched 332 feet above. The Garden served as the site of
Stanford White's death; he was shot in the roof garden by Harry K. Thaw,
the millionaire with whose wife, Evelyn Nesbit, White had "flirted." By
the early 20th C., the social elite continued their flight uptown, ending
the park's heyday.

Take a few moments to admire some of the fine statues in this park;
"Admiral David G. Farragut" (of Civil War fame) by Augustus Saint-
Gaudens and "William Henry Seward" (Secretary of State under Lincoln

and the man who purchased Alaska for the U.S.) by Randolph Rogers. Located at 5th Avenue and 23rd Street is the famous **Flatiron Building** (1902, D.H. Burnham), one of the first steel-caged buildings in the city. Cleverly built into a triangular piece of land, this heavy limestone and terracotta building in the French Renaissance style was also the tallest (300 feet) for many years.

MORNINGSIDE PARK
W. 110th-120th Sts., E. of Columbia University.
☎ *(212) 397-3117.*

Designed by Olmsted and Vaux (the architects of Central and Prospect Parks), this park has its own natural beauty with hilly terrain and steep cliffs. At Manhattan Avenue & W. 144th Street, bronze statues of Washington and Lafayette by Bartholdi (Statue of Liberty sculptor) were erected in 1900. It is unfortunately not a safe place to stroll around now.

Events: *Preschool programs on Mon-Fri 9am-1pm.*

LOUISE NEVELSON PLAZA
At William St. & Maiden La.

A small triangular park wedged between the narrow streets and skyscrapers of the Financial District, the Plaza offers trees, benches and 5 wonderful sculptures by Louise Nevelson (donated by her to the city in 1977).

N.Y.C. DEPARTMENT OF PARKS & RECREATION
830 5th Ave. (at 65th St.), Room 311.
☎ *(212) 360-8111/360-1333.*
Obtain a copy of the "Green Pages" for a listing of all park services and numbers.

The city's Department of Parks & Recreation maintains 26,175 acres in 572 parks, 775 playgrounds, 350 malls and squares, 38 swimming pools, 535 tennis courts, 890 playing fields, numerous historic houses and about 15 miles of beaches (and that spells phenomenal activity in the 5 boroughs). Each month the department publishes a pamphlet on special events in the city. By sending a self-addressed, stamped business envelope, you can discover what's going on. Most events are free. You can send several envelopes at a time and they will use them for subsequent mailings. This is a must for anyone who wants to know some of the not-so-well-known happenings in the city, especially the excellent walking tours by the Urban Park Rangers.

OUTDOOR PLAZAS
Thanks to city legislation, many modern buildings are now equipped with wonderful public plazas (indoor or outdoor), inclusion of which allowed builders to increase the number of floors of their skyscrapers. All provide public seating and an opportunity for dining al fresco with your own snacks. Some get fancy and offer trees, fountains and modern sculpture, which adds to the general ambiance. Many of the buildings attract food vendors and street entertainers. Listed below is a small

sampling of some favorite plazas in Wall Street, Civic Center and Midtown, areas where many working people or tourists are in need of a restful diversion. In addition, 6th Avenue (a.k.a. Avenue of the Americas), Park Avenue and 3rd Avenue (40th-57th Sts.) are liberally strewn with these public plazas.

Wall Street Area

1 Chase Manhattan Plaza, at Nassau St. between Cedar & Liberty Sts. The highlight of this wide open esplanade for the Chase Manhattan Bank (built by Skidmore, Owings & Merrill in 1960) is the fabulous black & white Dubuffet sculpture entitled "Group of 4 Trees." Attractions include lunchtime concerts in good weather, the Downtown Dance Festival performances on weekdays at noon (Sep) and art installations in lobby.

125 John Street, at Fulton and Water Sts. This flashy, multi-colored, multi-leveled plaza with modern seats features an unusual modular clock, which is always fun to watch. In the lobby, there are futuristic tunnels surrounded by neon lights leading to the elevators. All of this attempts to create "an atmosphere of pleasure, humor and excitement for people."

1 Liberty Plaza, 165 Broadway between Trinity & Broadway and Liberty & Cortlandt Sts. (across from the World Trade Center). Stone steps for sitting and listening to the street music offer a good vantage spot for viewing Noguchi's delicately balanced, brightly colored red cube at 140 Broadway.

Nassau Street Mall, Maiden La. & Nassau St. This pedestrian walkway is lined with wonderful smells and bargains galore.

Vietnam Veterans Plaza, 55 Water St. Plaza. This expansive elevated brick esplanade with a river view is an excellent place for sunbathing and listening to concerts in the summer. The Vietnam War Memorial is a wall of translucent green glass inscribed with writings by or about Vietnam vets.

Wall Street Plaza, at Water & Pine Sts. A polished stainless sculpture by Yu Yu Yang (a tribute to the *Queen Elizabeth II*, which burned in Hong Kong harbor) is a highlight of this small concrete plaza.

World Trade Center, at Vesey, Liberty, West & Church Sts. One of the most expansive concrete plazas, dwarfed by the overwhelming towers, is dotted with sculpture and occasional flowerbeds; an excellent spot for summer outdoor concerts presents "Noontime on the Plaza" on Mon-Fri (Jul-Sep).

Civic Center

Family Court, Centre & Lafayette Sts. at Hogan St. A wide-open city block with benches offers great suntanning opportunities.

Jacob Javits Building, 26 Federal Plaza. Elevated plaza with benches and trees provides a respite for government employees.

Police Plaza, Ave. of the Finest, behind Municipal Building and in front of the police headquarters. An attractive brickwork plaza with feathery honey locust trees and benches features an enormous 5-leaf sculpture. Wonderful smells from food vendors are tempting; tables with umbrellas and chairs are set up for dining al fresco. And this place should be safe enough!

Midtown

Bell Plaza, 41st-42nd Sts. at 6th Ave. Behind the AT&T Building is an attractive area with low brick waterfalls and some seating; concerts in the summer.

1 Dag Hammarskjold Plaza, 2nd Ave. & 47th St. This brick multi-level esplanade has limited seating from which to enjoy the brick, arched waterfall and lunchtime music (summer).

2 Dag Hammarskjold Plaza, 866 2nd Ave. (46th-47th Sts.). This open esplanade with limited seating offers monumental outdoor sculpture shows, changing every 4 months.

Exxon Building, 1251 6th Ave. A 2-tier expansive fountain with a little park area on either side is a few steps up from the street level. Some nice shady areas are available; look for summer concerts on Tue & Thu at 12:30pm.

Fisher Park, between 54th-55th Sts. off 6th Ave. behind the Burlington Building. Permanent wooden tables, chairs and benches provide a great spot for dining outdoors. An attractive waterfall and kite sculpture perk it up.

40th-41st Sts. between 1st-2nd Aves. Go up the stairs to the 2nd-floor mezzanine for comfortable seating and a respite from street level.

Paley Park, 53rd St., E. of 5th Ave. This "pocket park" with its 2-story waterfall offers a soothing counterpoint to 5th Avenue traffic. A wonderful setting with lots of seating and feathery trees.

One Penn Plaza, 8th Ave. between 33rd-34th Sts. A small concrete esplanade with some trees, plants and minimal seating faces one of the largest color ads painted on the full length of a building on 34th St. and to the west is the classical post office inscribed with the famous "Neither rain, nor sleet...." Look for occasional concerts on Wed from noon-1pm (Jun-mid Sep).

J.C. Penney Building, 1301 6th Ave. A plaza below street level reveals sculpture, greenery and some benches.

St. Bartholomew's Church, Park Ave. & 50th St. This well-manicured flowering garden sprouts fountains and benches.

Sculpture Terrace, 57th St. near S.W. corner of Park Ave. next to the Venezuelan House. This park houses sculpture interspersed with benches and trees.

Time-Life Building, 6th Ave. between 50th-51st Sts. This is an excellent spot for people-watching and sunbathing.

RIVERSIDE PARK

West side along Hudson River from 72nd-145th Sts.

This hilly narrow strip of parkland, majestically overlooking the Hudson River, was the creation of Frederick Law Olmsted, the architect for Central and Prospect Parks. Generally inspired by Andrew Haswell Green in the 1870s for a reasonable budget, the park ended up costing over $6 million thanks to Boss Tweed's finagling. There's a boat marina at 79th Street and Grant's Tomb at 110th Street. Concerts and theatrical productions run in the summer at the Riverside Park Rotunda.

ST. JOHN'S IN THE VILLAGE
224 Waverly Pl. (at 11th St.).
☎ *(212) 243-6192.*
Hours: *Mon-Fri 9am-5pm.*
A delightful Church Garden (not visible from the street) is an ideal refuge and spot for peaceful reflection, especially in May with its spring blossoms.

ST. MARK'S PARK
2nd Ave. & 10th St.
☎ *(212) 397-3192/674-6377.*
This small rectangular park at St. Mark's-in-the-Bowery, the burial ground for Peter Stuyvesant and his family, now offers "A Little Noon Music" on Thu at noon (Jul).

ST. VARTAN'S PARK
2nd Ave. between 35th-36th Sts.
Named for the cathedral across the way, which sponsors festivals, this park provides a wide range of sporting facilities and seating areas.

CARL SCHURZ PARK
82nd-90th Sts. & East End Ave.
Walk along the park's riverside promenade and enjoy the East River view of Queens and several of the city's bridges; watch out for joggers as this is a favorite venue. It also serves as a pleasant place to picnic and sunbathe. Gracie Mansion, the Mayor's residence, is situated in the northern part of the park.
Events: *Walking tours including the history of Gracie Mansion, concerts on Wed at 7:30pm (Jun-early Aug) and National Chorale concerts during the summer, 333-5333.*

STUYVESANT SQUARE
E. 15th-17th Sts. & 2nd Ave.
Thanks to Peter Stuyvesant's generous land donation, we have this square, which was formally laid out in 1846 in the French symmetrical design style. The statue of Peter Stuyvesant was installed in 1941 by Gertrude Vanderbilt Whitney, founder of the Whitney Museum.

TOMPKINS SQUARE PARK
7th-10th Sts. between Aves. A & B.
☎ *(212) 397-3109.*
This East Village park offers numerous recreational facilities for the neighborhood; a bandshell houses many concerts during the summer.
Events: *Occasional summer concerts; and an annual art festival (mid Jun) with painting, sculpture, crafts, poetry, music, dance, children's activities and ethnic food.*

TUDOR CITY PARK
Between 41st-43rd Sts. and 1st-2nd Aves.
Peaceful gardens and a playground for children can be enjoyed in view of the United Nations.

UNION SQUARE PARK
Between 14th-17th Sts. and Broadway & Park Ave. S.
☎ *(212) 397-3115.*
Although this was designated as a city park in 1815, formal landscaping was not done until 1839 with the area's rise to social prominence. During the second half of the 19th C., 14th Street was labelled "Ladies Mile," the midpoint for ritzy stores that lined Broadway from 8th-23rd Streets. By 1900, the elite had moved uptown with businesses following, leaving this area to immigrants and industry. Many homes became tenements packing cheap labor into the area. Before WWI, the park became the hub for radical politics, such as anarchism, socialism and communism. Though 14th Street is today loaded with discount stores, Union Square still manages to attract offbeat characters and drug dealers.

The park, however, contains some splendid outdoor statues. Highlights are "Equestrian Statue of George Washington" and "Abraham Lincoln," both by H.K. Brown; and "Marquis de Lafayette" by Frédéric Auguste Bartholdi (Statue of Liberty sculptor) in appreciation of American assistance during the Franco-Prussian War.
Events: *Greenmarket on Wed, Fri & Sat 9am-4pm (May-Nov), occasional summer music and the city's mobile entertainment in the summer.*

UN PEACE GARDEN
United Nations, 1st Ave. & 45th St.
Hours: *Mon-Sun 9:30am-5pm.*
This 12-acre park overlooking the East River has a fabulous rose garden with over 1,000 bushes and 44 varieties.

WASHINGTON MARKET COMMUNITY PARK
Chambers & Greenwich Sts.
☎ *(212) 306-3322.*
Named for the wholesale markets that once thrived in the area, this small (only 1.5 acres) park of splendid trees, roses, azaleas and rhododendrons with an old-fashioned Victorian gazebo is laid out in the tradition of curvilinear pathways. A jungle gym for kiddies is an active place.

WASHINGTON SQUARE PARK
Waverly Pl., University Pl., W. 4th & MacDougal Sts.
The impressive arch, a landmark designed by Stanford White in 1893 for Washington's centennial inauguration, is reminiscent of the Arc de Triomphe in Paris and triumphantly serves as the gateway to 5th Avenue. Originally a potter's field for plague victims in the late 1700s and then a military drill area, this park today is a haven for free entertainment of all kinds, with a playground for kids. History abounds

all around. Be sure to investigate the elegant 1830s Federal townhouses of red brick and white trim on the north side. The northeast corner housed at one time the literary set, including Henry James, Edith Wharton and John Dos Passos.

Events: *Folk dancing on Fri 7:30-10:30pm (mid Jun-Labor Day), summer concerts (see "For the Music Lovers"), Washington Square art show in May & Sep, Halloween Day parade and cooperative programs for kids of all ages, 408-0204.*

The Bronx

THE BRONX ZOO ♦♦♦♦
Fordham Rd. at Bronx River Pkwy.
☎ *(212) 367-1010.*
Hours: *Mon-Fri 10am-5pm, Sat, Sun & Hols 10am-5:30pm (Mar-Oct); and Mon-Sun 10am-4:30pm (Nov-Feb). Children's Zoo open in Apr-Oct and closes one-half hour earlier.*
Admission: *Free on Tue, Wed & Thu for all and always for Seniors and Children under 2. Otherwise suggested contribution, Adults $4.75 & Children $2 (summer) or Adults $2.50 & Children $1 (winter). Children's Zoo $1 (Adults $1.50). Children under 16 must be accompanied by an Adult.*

One of the largest zoos in the world, with 265 acres containing over 3,850 animals, this is a treat for all. Wherever possible, animals are in outdoor environments usually arranged by continent, such as the North American trail, the African Plains and Wild Asia (seen from the monorail Bengali Express in Apr-Oct for a fee). You walk past cheetahs, lions, giraffes, camels, tigers, ostriches, flamingos, boat-billed herons, scarlet ibises, penguins, vultures and eagles. The zoo's collection of reptiles and amphibians is considered one of the finest in the world. The Zoo Court, comprised of handsome Beaux-Arts buildings, features monkeys, gorillas, elephants, sea lions and big cats. Indoor pavilions include Jungleworld (tropical Asian wildlife), World of Darkness (nocturnal animals), the Reptile House, the Aquatic Bird House, the Houses of Apes, and the Mouse House.

The Children's Zoo offers over 40 species of animals in their natural habitat with 13 participatory exhibits, an animal nursery and picture taking with the animals.

Events: *Feeding times: crocodiles at 2pm (Mon & Thu), sea lions at 3pm, penguins at 11am & 3:45pm; thunderstorms in South American rain forest at the World of Birds at 2pm; rainstorms for reptiles and amphibians at the World of Reptiles at 11:30am & 3pm; and pelicans at 11:30am.*

ROBERTO CLEMENTE STATE PARK
W. Tremont Ave. & Mathewson Rd.
☎ *(212) 299-8750.*
Hours: *For Pool, daily noon-8pm (summer), otherwise Mon-Fri 3-5:30pm (ages 7-14), Mon-Fri 6-10pm (ages 15 and over).*

With an Olympic-sized swimming pool, playgrounds, courts, ballfields, a waterfront promenade, sitting areas and a variety of programs for children, youth, senior citizens and the disabled, this state park is an important part of recreational life in the Bronx.

Events *(for brochure, write to: N.Y.S. Office of Parks, Recreation & Historic Preservation, N.Y.C. Region, 1700 Broadway, N.Y., N.Y. 10019): Gazebo concerts on Wed at 6pm and Sun at 2pm (summer) and dance performances.*

CROTONA PARK
Crotona Pk. N. & S., Fulton Aves. & Claremont Pkwy.
☎ *(212) 822-4115/598-0096.*

This 147-acre park offers 1 Olympic-sized swimming pool, a recreational center, ballfields, courts for basketball, handball, volleyball and tennis, picnic areas and Indian Lake.

Events: *At the boathouse (Crotona Pk. E. at Charlotte St. & Suburban Pl.), Urban Park Ranger tours on most Sun at 1pm; Junior Ranger Program (ages 8-13) in the summer; occasional summer concerts and Hol festivities, 822-4115.*

THE NEW YORK BOTANICAL GARDENS ✦✦✦
Southern Blvd. at 200th St., South of Mosholu Pkwy.
☎ *(212) 220-8777/8700/8747.*
Hours: *Tue-Sun 10am-6pm (Nov-Mar) and 10am-7pm (Apr-Oct) for grounds. Conservatory: Tue-Sun 10am-5pm (Sat & Sun til 6pm in summer). Rock and native plant gardens: Tue-Sun 10am-6pm (Apr-Oct). Rose Garden: Tue-Sun 10am-6pm (mid May-Nov). Buildings closed Mon (exc. N.Y.C. Hols), Thanksgiving, Christmas and New Year's Day (grounds always open).*
Admission: *Conservatory free on Sat 10am-noon and free always for Children under 6. Suggested contribution $3. For Conservatory, Adults $3.50, Children, Seniors & Students $1.25. Parking fee $4 including one free admission to Conservatory.*
Groups: *By appt., 220-6775.*
Tours: *Garden grounds: Sat-Sun 1 & 3pm (Apr-Oct), meet at Visitors Center. Conservatory: weekends about every hour (11am-4pm, free with admission fee), meet at Palm Court.*
Telephone Plant Service: *Tue-Fri 1-4pm, (212) 220-8634/8681.*

Come spend the day meandering around this 250-acre paradise of woods, formal and informal gardens, enclosed gardens (the Conservatory) and exhibits in the Museum Building. Paths wind their way through acres and acres of dogwoods, magnolias, cherry trees, willows, hemlocks, pines and crabapples. Be sure to find Daffodil hill in early spring, Rhododendron valley and Azalea way in late May/early Jun. The Twin Lake area is great for picnics as you are surrounded by legume, magnolia and beech trees. The Lorillard Snuff Mill, a landmark 1840s limestone and brick mill, which harnessed the Bronx River to grind tobacco leaves into snuff until 1870, offers a serene picnic area alongside a babbling brook. There's an attractive rock garden with an Oriental flavor of bonsais.

The inviting central mall lined with tulip trees leads you to the Conservatory, a turn-of-the-century glass pavilion. With "an acre of gardens under glass," there are 11 interconnecting galleries and pavilions of distinct environments including a palm court, a fern forest, tropical and desert plants and ever-changing floral displays. Inspired by the 1851 Crystal Palace in London, this cast-iron and glass landmark is shattering! Check out the Peggy Rockefeller rose garden containing over 2,700 varieties arranged in typical strict French-style symmetry. The Demonstration Gardens take you down the garden paths where you can get landscaping and gardening ideas, learn about vegetable and herb gardens, and soak in the smells of Helen's Fragrance Garden.

The Museum Building contains the herbarium with over 4 million dried plants, exhibits, the library (220-8751) and a gift shop. Pick up a brochure and a map there.

Events *(for recorded message, (212) 220-8777): 6 to 8 major flower shows a year, such as the fall harvest, a Christmas show and a spring blossom; concerts, lectures and classes, (212) 220-8747.*

PELHAM BAY PARK &

N.W. part of the Bronx, at Hutchinson Pkwy., Pelham Bay Pkwy. & City Island Rd.
☎ *(212) 430-1890.*
Tours: *By Urban Park Rangers, (212) 885-3346.*

This is the largest city park, with 2,118 acres of "salt marshes, estuaries, forests, creeks, lagoons, coves, inlets, bogs, meadows, islands and beaches." With miles and miles of hiking trails and bridle paths, 2 golf courses (at Pelham Split Rock Golf Club) and facilities for boating, tennis, bicycling and running, this park is for the sports enthusiast. With 13 miles of saltwater coastline, there are fishing, swimming and bird-watching opportunities galore.

Places of Interest

Bartow-Pell Mansion. See for "For the Culture Vultures."

Environmental Center, across from Section 11 of Orchard Beach. Occasional workshops on nature and the environment are offered, (212) 548-7880.

Hunter Island. It features nature trails for hiking; a good spot for bird watching.

Orchard Beach. A 1.6-mile crescent-shaped sandy beach has been restored to its previous glory as the "Riviera of The Bronx." Each of the 12 distinct sections seems to have its own following. For instance, Section 1 attracts those wanting solitude, #5 is called "little Puerto Rico," #8 is for young divorced women, #9 is called "Hollywood" and the elderly visit # 12. Urban Park Rangers lead tours, 885-1828/3346. This is a good spot for bird watching of all kinds!

Thomas Pell Wildlife Refuge. This refuge offers 50 acres of salt marshes.

Twin Islands. This is a good place for bird watching and views of Long Island Sound.

POE PARK
Grand Concourse & E. Kingsbridge Rd.

A small tribute to Edgar Allan Poe, this park with its bandshell offers occasional concerts on Tue eve (summer). While you're here, visit the Poe Cottage Museum (see "For the Culture Vultures").

VAN CORTLANDT PARK
242nd St. & Broadway
☎ *(212) 430-1890.*
Tours: *By Urban Park Rangers, 548-7070.*

The 3rd largest in N.Y.C., this park has 1,146 acres of varied terrain including wetlands, hilly wooded areas with wildlife and flat meadows containing athletic fields. Miles for hiking, jogging, cross-country skiing, horseback riding and 2 public golf courses (Mosholu and Van Cortlandt, the first municipal one in the country) make this park a recreational haven. For a copy of the park's newsletter, write to: Bronx Urban Park Rangers, Ranaqua, Bronx Park, Bronx, N.Y. 10462.

Places of Interest
Northeast Section. Here's the start of the nationally registered Old Croton Aqueduct hiking trail, which runs north to south of the entire park.

Northwest Woods. A ramble with wildlife includes the Cass Callagher nature trail at Mosholu and Broadway.

The Parade Grounds, along Broadway. Recreational facilities are located on 150 acres; occasional summer entertainment is offered.

Van Cortlandt Lake. The largest freshwater body in the Bronx.

Van Cortlandt Mansion. See "For the Culture Vultures."

Vault Hill, located above the Parade Grounds. A 110-foot-high burial ground for the Van Cortlandt family during the 18th & 19th C. was used to hide city records during the Revolutionary War.

WAVE HILL ♣♣
675 W. 252nd St. (249th St. & Independence Ave.).
☎ *(212) 549-3200.*
Hours: *Mon-Sun 10am-4:30pm (Labor Day-Memorial Day), Mon-Sun 10am-5:30pm (Wed til sunset), Sun til 7pm (Memorial Day-Labor Day) . Learning Center Sat & Sun noon-4:30pm. Greenhouse Mon-Sun 10am-noon, 2-4pm.*

Admission: *Free weekdays to all and always for Children under 6; weekends Adults $2, Children & Seniors $1.*
Tours: *Orientation walk on Sun at 1:15pm; garden and greenhouse tour on Sun at 2:15pm and occasionally on Sat at 3pm.*
With a commanding position overlooking the Hudson River, this 28-acre estate has some breathtaking vistas. The only preserved Hudson River estate in N.Y.C., Wave Hill offers beautiful rolling lawns with grand old trees, formal and informal gardens, greenhouses and 2 mansions. With a checkered background, this estate has seen many lords of the manor. It began in 1836 with William Morris, a N.Y. lawyer, who bought 15 acres for his summer house. Then William Appleton, a prominent N.Y. publisher, created quite a social center for writers and philosophers.

In 1893, the financier George Perkins bought 20 more acres and went to town landscaping it with stunning gardens, exotic trees and greenhouses. Concerned with maintaining his fabulous view of the Palisades, he bought up the corresponding section across the river. In 1912, he encouraged the Rockefellers and Harrimans to join in and create N.J.'s Palisades State Park. Other famous dwellers were the young Teddy Roosevelt, Samuel Clemens (Mark Twain) and Arturo Toscanini. In 1960, the Perkins-Freeman family gave the estate to the city.

Today there's a lot to enjoy. Outdoors you will find enormous elms, Norway maples, hemlocks, copper beeches and conifers. A wild garden built on a natural incline overlooks the 2 mansions. More formal gardens include herbs, roses and flowerbeds. A small but lovely greenhouse has a constant array of flowering plants, cacti and tropical plants. In early Jun don't miss the blossoming wisteria overhanging the Glyndor House.

The Wave Hill House Gallery offers several changing natural history exhibits and art shows. The Toscanini Archives, containing rare moments from the maestro's NBC symphony concerts never commercially recorded, are available for listening by appointment.
Events: *Lectures, workshops, bird and garden walks, concerts, seasonal plantings, demonstrations, outdoor dance and art shows. The Learning Center offers a wonderful program for children, including changing exhibitions on the natural history of the area; aquariums; a touch table with bones, barks, stones, etc.; slide shows, workshops, demonstrations (like maple syrup making) and nature walks.*

WOODLAWN CEMETERY 🐦
Webster Ave. at E. 233rd St.
☎ *(914) 920-0500.*
Hours: *Mon-Sun 9am-4:30pm.*
Groups: *By appt. only. Maps available at the Admin. Office gate.*

This attractively landscaped cemetery with its natural bird sanctuary and superb mausoleums epitomizes the 19th-C. Romantic ideal of death. In 1863, Rev. Absalom Peters bought up 313 rural acres to develop a beautiful country cemetery. Thanks to the new Harlem railroad line, all of New York City's ritziest could be easily transported to this final resting spot.

Today it remains an idyllic setting for a drive (or walk), while you admire the grand mausoleums of the honor roll, including Fiorello La Guardia (a simple fiorello flower decorates his tomb), Admiral Farragut, Joseph Pulitzer, William "Bat" Masterson (frontier peace enforcer), Herman Melville, Duke Ellington, George M. Cohan, F.W. Woolworth, J.C. Penney, Jay Gould (railroads), John "Bet a Million" Gates (entrepreneur who made his fortune from barbed wire in Texas), Herman Armour (meat-packing millionaire), Roland H. Macy (as in the world's largest department store) and Elizabeth Cady Stanton (suffragette).

Look at the 1905 mausoleum of Oliver Hazard Perry Belmont (a financier, horse lover and race track developer), as it was fashioned after the chapel at Château d'Ambroise in France. The most elaborate and expensive tribute is John Harbeck's miniature Gothic cathedral with its hand-laid mosaic dome and bronze gates with bas-reliefs. The most bizarre epitaph, belonging to George Spenser (d. 1904), states, "Lost life by stab in falling on ink eraser, evading 6 young women trying to give him birthday kisses in the office of Metropolitan Life Building." Let that be a lesson to us all!

Events: A monthly concert or walking tour.

Brooklyn

FLOYD BENNETT FIELD

Off Exit 11S of the Belt Pkwy., Gateway National Recreational Area, Jamaica Bay Unit.

☎ *(718) 338-3338.*

As N.Y.C.'s first municipal airport, Floyd Bennett Field saw the flying skills of such pilots as John Glenn, Wrongway Corrigan, Wiley Post and Howard Hughes. Today it serves as the administrative headquarters for Gateway National Recreational Area. The William F. Ryan Visitor's Center houses exhibits on aviation.

Events: African-American festival (mid Jul), (718) 338-3703; Harvest Fair (Aug) with gardeners' delights and music and dancing; and Hispanic Fair (Aug).

BRIGHTON AND MANHATTAN BEACHES ♣

East of Coney Island, Coney Island & Brighton Aves. and Oriental Blvd. & Irving St.

☎ *(718) 946-1373.*

Hours: Sunrise to sunset with swimming from 10am-6:30pm (in season).

Brighton Beach is a lively spot where people congregate on the Boardwalk all year round. The neighboring community is home to hundreds of thousands of Russian emigrés, so those interested in snacking on some Russian delicacies are in luck. One of the cleanest of the city beaches, Manhattan Beach offers a nice beach, boardwalk and changing rooms at Oriental Blvd. (though parking is limited).

BROOKLYN BOTANIC GARDENS 🍎🍎🍎🍎
1000 Washington Ave., N. of Prospect Pk.
☎ *(718) 622-4433.*
Hours: *Tue-Fri 8am-6pm, Sat, Sun & Hols 10am-6pm (Apr-Sep), Tue-Fri 8am-4:30pm, Sat, Sun & Hols 10am-4:30pm (Oct-Mar). Closed Mon (exc. Hols).*
Free Admission: *To the grounds and for Children under 3 to Conservatory. Contributions to the gardens. Conservatory: Adults $2, Seniors & Children $1.*
Tours: *Sun at 1pm (Mar-mid Nov).*

For an absolutely splendid outing, come visit this 52-acre floral paradise with over 12,000 different kinds of plants representing almost every country. Of course there's always a different visual experience, thanks to nature's varied blooming schedule. Take cherry blossom lane in late Apr/early May or the rose garden with 5,000 bushes and 900 varieties in early Jun/late Sep. The glacial rock is also surrounded by a splendid array of bloomers. The Shakespearean herb garden in a 16th C. Elizabethan knot design has 200 different varieties, many mentioned in the plays. There's a fragrance garden for the blind containing scented flowers, textured leaves and braille plaques.

Don't miss the Japanese Hill & Pond Garden with sculptured trees, a waterfall, an Oriental shrine and ornaments overlooking a pond with a pagoda. Another Japanese attraction is the enclosed replica of a 15th C. Buddhist Temple of Kyoto with abstract but simple gardens.

Another must is the Steinhardt Conservatory, a glass-enclosed botanical museum with tropical, desert, aquatic and bonsai environments. An incredible variety of lilies grace the pond in front of the Conservatory. A Local Flora Section offers plants native to New York in various landscapes. A Children's garden offers gardening classes and plots for kids in the summer at a small fee. Also, visit the Chase Manhattan Discovery Center (see "For the Kiddies"). The Administration Building (1917, McKim, Mead & White) houses a Herbarium and a research and reference library.

Events: Classical concerts on Sun at 3pm (Jul-Aug), lectures and courses, exhibitions, occasional films and plant sales and the Cherry Blossom Festival in late Apr or early May.

BROOKLYN CENTER FOR URBAN ENVIRONMENT
Prospect Pk., Tennis House.
☎ *(718) 788-8500.*

This nonprofit center offers a wide range of nature and environmental programs for people of all ages. An emphasis on urban environment in relationship to the total environment is particularly important; many tours examine the city's infrastructure, architecture and industry.
Events: Walking, bus and boat tours throughout the year (some free); and programs for children in schools and after school.

BROOKLYN ZOO
Prospect Pk., Empire Blvd. & Flatbush Ave.
☎ *(718) 965-8900.*

The Brooklyn Zoo is undergoing renovation and plans to re-open in 1992-93.

CONEY ISLAND
S. Brooklyn (Ocean Pkwy.).

With its famous 2.5-mile boardwalk and amusement park, Coney Island was labeled the "world's largest playground" during its heyday from the turn of the century to WWII. It proudly boasted the thrill of the Cyclone and the delights of Luna Park, Dreamland and Steeplechase Pier. Today much of the glitter has faded, although Astroland and Wonderwheel still remain. The miles of sandy beaches are still very popular, but unfortunately the image of Coney Island has become less favorable. A trip to the New York Aquarium is worthwhile, especially for the young ones.
Events: Easter Sun bathing suit and fashion show on boardwalk, and "Dancing in the Streets" festival featuring folk dancing adjacent to the boardwalk (Jun-Aug).

EMPIRE-FULTON FERRY STATE PARK ♿
New Dock St. (under Brooklyn Bridge).
☎ *(718) 858-4708.*
Hours: *Mon-Sun 10am-8pm (mid May-Sep), Mon-Sun noon-6pm (Oct-mid May).*

As the most accessible waterfront in Brooklyn, this state park dotted with sculpture on its open lawn has become a popular location for shooting commercials and movies thanks to its spectacular view of Manhattan.
Events: Lunchtime concerts or theater on Tue 12-12:30pm (summer), dance performances and annual sculpture show.

GATEWAY ENVIRONMENTAL STUDY CENTER
Floyd Bennett Field, Jamaica Bay.
☎ *(718) 252-8285.*

School Groups: *By appt. only.*

This environmental center develops programs for teachers and students (run cooperatively with the N.Y.C. Board of Education) as well as for community groups.

Events: *A wide range of public programs throughout spring, summer & fall.*

GATEWAY NATIONAL RECREATIONAL AREA

Administrative Headquarters, Floyd Bennett Field, Brooklyn, N.Y. 11234.
☎ *(718) 338-3338.*

Encompassing more than 26,000 acres of beach, forest, dune and marshland, located at the entrance to the N.Y./N.J. estuary, this valuable national park land consists of 4 units: Jamaica Bay (Brooklyn), including Jamaica Bay Wildlife Refuge (Queens), Floyd Bennett Field, Canarsie Pier and Gateway Environmental Study Center; Breezy Point (Queens) with Fort Tilden Area & Jacob Riis Park; Great Kills Park & Miller Field (S.I.); and Sandy Hook (N.J.). See individual unit for listing (except Sandy Hook, which is not covered); see "For the Music Lovers" for Canarsie Pier.

GREEN-WOOD CEMETERY

5th Ave. to Ft. Hamilton Pk., 20th-37th Sts.
☎ *(718) 768-7300.*
Hours: *By appt. only.*
Groups: *Sat or Sun (May-Nov), (718) 788-8549.*

Originally consecrated with the bodies of Revolutionary War soldiers, it was chartered in 1839 as a nonsectarian, nonprofit cemetery. With 478 acres of beautiful shrubs, trees and flowers strewn with 20 miles of paths throughout its hilly terrain, this cemetery reflects the prevailing Romantic attitude of the 19th C. that cemeteries should be for the living as well as the dead.

The "In Crowd" was buried here, including Peter Cooper (inventor, entrepreneur and philanthropist), Horace Greeley (publisher of *The N.Y. Tribune*), DeWitt Clinton (Governor of N.Y. and father of the Erie Canal), Samuel F.B. Morse (telegraph inventor and painter) and Henry Ward Beecher (clergyman and abolitionist). Today, since it is still maintained as a cemetery, it's not open to the public (except for tours or prearranged appts.), but it is possible to admire the grounds by walking around it. Check out the superb brownstone Main Gate (built by Richard Upjohn in 1861) at 5th Avenue & 25th Street, with its fine examples of Gothic Revival spires and turrets.

JAMAICA BAY UNIT

(See Floyd Bennett Field, Gateway Environmental Study Center and Jamaica Bay Wildlife (Queens).)

ASSER LEVY/SEASIDE PARK

Seabreeze Ave. & W. 5th St.
☎ *(718) 783-3077.*

Many concerts take place at the Bandshell during the summer.

NEW YORK AQUARIUM ⚫⚫
W. 8th St. at Surf Ave., E. of Coney Island amusement area.
☎ *(718) 265-FISH/265-3454.*
Hours: *Mon-Sun 10am-4:45pm, summer hours Mon-Fri 10am-4:45pm, Sat, Sun & Hols 10am-5:45pm.*
Free Admission: *Adults 65+ on Mon-Fri after 2pm (except Hols). Otherwise Adults $4.75, Children 2-12 $2. Special group rates available, reservation required.*

For a memorable voyage in undersea life, visit the aquarium. Thanks to special viewing panels in all tanks, you can be dazzled by colorful and bizarre creatures, nearly 10,000 in all (300 different species).

In the main exhibition pavilion are beluga whales and a highly charged electric eel, which lights up with its own 600-volt jolt. Native fish from around the world, such as piranhas, butterfly fish, clownfish, lionfish, poisonous stonefish and octopi, can be admired in their native habitat. An 85,000-gallon shark tank safely affords us a glimpse of sharks on the prowl. Creatures from the famous Bermuda Triangle can be easily viewed, with the huge turtles stealing the show.

Outside, sea lions, seals and dolphins put on their own shows daily (weather permitting), while a nearby colony of penguins is irresistible. The Discovery Cove takes you past coastal sea life, including live animals, dioramas, interactive video terminals and demonstrations. The 300-foot-long Sea Cliffs will reveal a rocky coast habitat in 1992.

A Children's Cove houses goldfish and turtle ponds, a "touch-it" tank with sea stars and urchins, and display cases of sponges and conchshells. Thanks to color pictures for identification, maps and informative descriptions, you will find this an educational and enjoyable journey.
Events: *Feeding hours for whales, seals, penguins and sharks; and special educational programs, classes and tours (fee).*

PROSPECT PARK ⚫⚫⚫
Prospect Pk. W., S.W., Flatbush, Ocean & Parkside Aves.
☎ *(718) 788-0055/965-8951.*
Hours: *Mon-Sun sunrise to sunset.*
Tours: *Sun at 1pm, sponsored by the Urban Park Rangers.*
☎ *(718) 856-4210.*

Conceived, planned and implemented from 1866 to 1873 by the Central Park duo, Frederick Law Olmsted and Calvert Vaux, this 526-acre park grew out of the need for more recreational parkland and the ongoing rivalry between Manhattan and Brooklyn (as Manhattan already had Central Park). Prospect Park is considered by some to be Olmsted and Vaux's finest achievement!

The architects successfully worked the park into the surrounding terrain by blending in the wide-open meadow lands, rugged wooded areas and the lovely lakes. They cleverly separated the pedestrian, vehicular and equestrian traffic and threaded "green parkways" leading out from the park to other parts of Brooklyn, making the journey to and from the park all the more pleasant. The use of effective landscaping on the park's perimeter succeeded in blocking out the city streets.

Today, while many renovated projects are under way, Prospect Park remains a special beauty of Brooklyn. However, be advised not to walk around alone or at night.

Events: Children's & adult programs, everything from volunteering, tours, workshops, concerts, theater and dance; "Welcome Back to Brooklyn" festival on the 2nd Sun (Jun) featuring the coronation of King or Queen of Brooklyn, children's parade and day-long entertainment.

Places of Interest

Bandshell, at 10th-11th Sts., entrance at 9th St. & Prospect Pk. W. This stages a wide range of entertainment in the summer (see "For the Music Lovers").

Boathouse on the Lullwater, across the inner road from Lefferts House, entrance at Ocean Ave. & Lincoln Rd. Built by Helmle & Huberty in 1905 in the Italian Renaissance style, today it houses the Visitors Center with free info, maps, bathrooms, special children's events and art exhibitions on park themes by contemporary artists.

Carousel, inside Empire Blvd. entrance near the Zoo. This newly restored merry-go-round offers rides Mon-Sun noon-5pm for 50¢.

Children's Farm, Flatbush Ave. near Empire Blvd., near the Zoo. This working farm has many domesticated animals, good for small children, Wed-Sun 10am-4pm (Apr-Labor Day), (718) 965-6560/6587.

Grand Army Plaza, N.E. corner of Park, Flatbush & Eastern Pkwys. A grand entrance to the Park with the Soldiers' & Sailors' Memorial Arch (1892, John H. Duncan) honoring the Union men in the Civil War. It is topped by "Quadriga," a heroic horsedrawn chariot by Frederick Mac-

Monnies. A 6-story spiral staircase takes you to the top-floor gallery, an alternative space for sculpture shows (8 weeks in both the sring & fall, Sun 12:30-4pm, hours may expand). The public is invited to the art openings. Group tours can be arranged with the excellent curator. If the roof is open, you can climb to the top of "Quadriga" for a great view of the city's skyline.

Long Meadow. This 90-acre meadow area has 7 ballfields and spots for passive recreation.

Picnic House, 3rd St., follow Park Dr., 1st building on left. The Prospect Park Alliance sponsors New Prospects programs for adults, performances on Sun at 3pm, children's programs especially on Sat-Sun (Jul-Aug), theater and readings.

Prospect Lake. Pedal boat rentals available.

Tennis House. Hot Prospects held here on Sat at 3pm (summer), 438-1200; and the Brooklyn Center for Urban Environment holds classes, workshops and tours (fee).

Wollman Rink, East Dr. between Lincoln Rd. & Parkside Ave. This is Brooklyn's only ice skating rink, call for hours and fees, 965-6561.

Queens

ALLEY POND ENVIRONMENTAL CENTER &
228-06 Northern Blvd., Douglaston.
☎ *(718) 229-4000.*
Hours: *Mon-Sat 9am-5pm, Sun 9am-4pm.*
Groups: *By appt. only (possible fee).*

An oasis among urban sprawl with highways bordering it, this nonprofit environmental center encompasses 750 acres of woodlands, ponds, salt & freshwater marshes, gardens, nature trails and picnic areas. At the center, there's a permanent collection of marine life and indigenous animals, such as live snakes, turtles, frogs, fish, insects and rabbits as well as stuffed pheasants, egrets, flying squirrels, raccoons and muskrats. Changing natural science exhibitions have featured photos and artifacts of Long Island. Trails throughout the grounds provide pleasant perambulations for one and all.

Events *(call for program guide): A program of courses, seminars, lectures on natural science, guided tours and hikes (some with fees), craft and nature programs (emphasis on children), astronomy and stargazing sessions on 2nd Fri of month at 7:30pm (fee), summer internships for ages 16-25, summer nature workshops for kids (fee) and for handicapped groups (free), and special Hol events (like Arbor Day).*

BREEZY POINT DISTRICT
Gateway National Recreational Area.
☎ *(718) 474-4600.*
(Includes Fort Tilden Area, Jacob Riis Park and Breezy Point Tip, the western portion of Breezy Point peninsula, site for bird nesting colonies

and endangered species.)

FLUSHING MEADOW, CORONA PARK 🍎🍎
Across from Shea Stadium, Roosevelt Ave., L.I.E. and Grand Central Pkwy.
☎ *(718) 507-3000.*

Encompassing part of the 1964 World's Fair grounds, this 1,275-acre city park with 2 lakes and a nature preserve has retained several mementos, like the awe-inspiring Unisphere, the New York State Building (Queens Museum) and "Exedra," a marble bench marking the site of the Vatican Pavilion (located between the Unisphere and the pedestrian bridge to Meadow Lake). With a wide and varied roster of programs, there's something happening almost every weekend, at least during the summer. Sports enthusiasts will enjoy Shea Stadium and the National Tennis Center (sorry, no free events).

Events: *Various summer festivals with cultural and recreational activities: Queens Day, Colombian, Ecuadorian and Korean Festivals annually; Children's Safari Run (Apr); ice skating at the N.Y. State Bldg.; outdoor exhibitions; a Winter Festival with cross-country skiing at Shea Stadium; and outdoor summer music.*

Places of Interest
Ballfields. Many fields are located throughout the park for football, softball, cricket and model airplane flying; by permit only, (718) 520-5932.

Carousel, 111th St. & 54th Ave. A restored 1910 carousel, the biggest in N.Y.C., (718) 592-6539.

Children's Zoo, across from the main Zoo. Under construction until summer 1991; see Queen's Zoo.

Hall of Science, near the Zoo. See "For the Kiddies."

Meadow Lake. Around the 2.5-mile perimeter, bicyclists and joggers take exercise.

New York State Building. This houses the Queens Museum; see "For the Culture Vultures."

Pitch 'N' Putt, S.E. of Passerelle Ramp, N. end of park.

"Playground for All Children," Corona Ave. & 111th St. A 3.5-acre playground for disabled and able-bodied children offers apparatus that can be hand-operated, crawled over or otherwise negotiated (Mon-Fri 1:30-5pm, Sat-Sun 10am-5pm, (718) 699-8283). Interpretive nature trails are lined with "hands-on" objects with plaques in English and in braille.

Queens Museum, located in the N.Y. State Building. See "For the Culture Vultures."

Queens Theater-in-the-Park, across from the N.Y. State Building. See "For the Music Lovers."

Queens Zoo. See listing on following pages.

Swedish Playground, next to Pitch'N'Putt. Adventure-type playground.

Urban Park Rangers, located in the Passerelle Building. They sponsor lectures and tours of the park, (718) 669-4204.

Willow Lake, southern border of park. This serves as the nature area with wetlands.

World's Fair Marina, Flushing Bay, off Northern Blvd. This is a haven for yacht yearners, (718) 478-0480.

FOREST PARK ♣
Woodhaven Blvd. & Forest Park Dr.
☎ *(718) 441-7213.*

This park offers recreational facilities, a golf course, tennis, a Carousel (Apr-Oct) and a Bandshell for summer music, dancing and children's activities.

FORT TILDEN AREA
Gateway National Recreational Area, Breezy Point Unit, Rockaway Peninsula.
☎ *(718) 474-4600.*
Tours: *Sun at 1pm (Jul-Aug), call for reservation.*

For exploration of marine life along the ocean and bay beaches, this national park offers an enormous range of activities. An old fort with gun batteries and nike installations used to protect N.Y. and N.J. can also be visited.

Events *(call to confirm and make reservations): Nature walks on weekends or on weekday eves (summer), workshops, surfcasting on Sat am (Jul-Labor Day), astronomy night on some Sun at 7:30pm (Jul-Aug), arts & crafts workshops on Sat afternoon (Jul-Aug), biking and hiking excursions (Jun-Aug), Senior Citizen Center activities, picnicking, and clinic for children with disabilities (Jul-Labor Day).*

JAMAICA BAY WILDLIFE REFUGE ♣♣
Gateway National Recreational Area, Jamaica Bay Unit, Cross Bay Blvd., Howard Beach.
☎ *(718) 474-0613.*
Hours: *Mon-Sun sunrise to sunset, except Christmas & New Year's Day. Visitors Center Mon-Fri 8:30am-5pm, Sat-Sun 8:30am-6pm.*
Groups: *By appt. only.*

With its 9,155 acres of tidal marsh and open water land under the Atlantic Flyway (a migratory sky route), it's not surprising that over 320 different bird species have been sighted, making this a popular bird-watching spot. A 2-mile trail threads its way through trees, brambles, shrubs, reeds and wildflowers along a freshwater pond and the saltwater marshes of Jamaica Bay. Bring your binoculars and bird book as you will have a visual feast; it's a true refuge for city dwellers.

Events *(call to confirm and make reservations): Nature walks on most weekends (spring-fall) and weekday eve "moon prowls," workshops in nature skills, astronomy nights, lectures, guided tours, summer craftsmobile, natural science exhibits at center, and environmental programs for school groups (spring & fall).*

QUEENS BOTANICAL GARDENS
43-50 Main St., Flushing.
☎ *(718) 886-3800.*
Hours: *Tue-Sun 10am-7pm.*

This intimate 30-acre garden (once a garbage site) now offers a gentle perambulation among crabapple and cherry trees, weeping willows, shrubs and flowers. Special gardens of roses, herbs and an apiary add interest; the blossoming highlights are the roses in summer and the chrysanthemums in fall. A Wedding Garden and Patio offer a romantic setting for party-goers or for those taking their nuptials.
Events: *Occasional exhibits, lectures, workshops, concerts and films.*

QUEENS ZOO
Flushing Meadow, Corona Park, 111th St. at 54th Ave., Flushing.
Under construction, plans to re-open summer of 1991.

JACOB RIIS PARK 🍎
Gateway National Recreational Area, Breezy Point Unit, Rockaway Peninsula.
☎ *(718) 474-4600.*

The focal point of the Breezy Point unit, this park was named for the journalist (1849-1913) who crusaded for improved housing and recreational facilities. One of the cleanest and finest in the metropolitan area, this mile-long sandy beach with boardwalk on the Rockaway Peninsula attracts people by the droves in the summer. Athletic facilities, handball courts and surf fishing (in designated areas) plus an 18-hole pitch'n'putt add to the outdoor fun. Call for information on events.

ROCKAWAY BEACH 🍎🍎
Rockaway Peninsula, at Beach 9th-Beach 149th Sts.
☎ *(718) 318-4000.*
Hours: *Dawn to dusk. Swimming only from Memorial Day-Labor Day when lifeguards are on duty.*

Stretching along the Atlantic Ocean for 10 miles, this is the longest municipal beach in the U.S., with a boardwalk running almost the entire length. Its sandy beaches are excellent for sunbathing. For amusement lovers, Rockaway Playland at Beach 98th St. will add thrill (not free). Picnic areas and playgrounds (especially from Beach 77th-106th Sts.) are also available.

SOCRATES SCULPTURE PARK 🍎
32-00 Vernon Blvd., Long Island City.
☎ *(718) 956-1819.*

Outdoor installations of monumental size and environmental works overlook the Manhattan skyline.
Events: Summer entertainment.

Staten Island

CLAY PIT PONDS STATE PARK RESERVE ⚫
83 Nielsen Ave., Charleston.
☎ *(718) 967-1976.*
Hours: *Grounds: Mon-Sun dawn to dusk.   Park Preserve Building: Mon-Sun 9am-5pm.*
Groups: *By appt. only.*
Tours: *By appt. or self-guided tours; walking tours on many Sun at 11am.*
   With 250 acres on undeveloped, ecologically important land, this state park offers varied activities for the whole family. Clay (for pottery making) was an important natural resource, first used by the Indians and then by S.I. companies until 1929. The abandoned claypits filled with water and today they, along with ponds, bogs, swamps, sand barrens, woodlands and spring-fed waters, support interesting vegetation and wildlife all year round. Hikers' delights include Abraham's Pond and Ellis Swamp Foot Trails.
Events: *Historical field trips, lectures, films, horseback riding, walking tours on many Sun at 11am, workshops and recreational activities (usually Sat-Sun).*

CLOVE LAKES PARK ⚫
1150 Clove Lake, off Victory Blvd., Sunnyside.
☎ *(718) 390-8000.*
Tours: *Occasionally by Urban Park Rangers, (718) 667-6042.*
   This 191-acre park is a popular place for fishing, boating, hiking, horseback riding and running. Special facilities include 4 lakes, picnic areas, nature trails, ballfields, a children's wading pool, an outdoor ice skating rink (720-1010) and a boathouse.

WILLIAM T. DAVIS WILDLIFE REFUGE
Off Travis Ave. on western shore, New Springville.
☎ *(718) 727-1135.*
Hours: *Sunrise to sunset.*
Tours: *By appt. only in the spring & fall.*
   The city's first wildlife refuge offers 260 acres of mature woodlands, open fields, tidal marshes and freshwater wetlands. Two major trails reveal distinctive communities of plants, mammals, amphibians and birds, all living in a natural environment.

GREAT KILLS PARK & MILLER FIELD
Gateway National Recreational Area, off Hylan Blvd. & Buffalo Ave. (Great Kills) and New Dorp La. & Hylan Blvd. (Miller Field).
☎ *(718) 351-8700/0473.*
   Thanks to the calm waters of lower New York and Raritan Bays, this national park offers particularly good swimming and fishing. Crooke's Point is an excellent wildlife preserve, in particular a migration stopping point for monarch butterflies to and from Mexico. Miller Field, an old hangar, is a sports complex with ballfields and a roller hockey rink. An

environmental education center sponsors field trips for schools and organized groups.

Events *(call to confirm and make reservations): A 28-minute film at the Visitors Center on weekends (Jul-Aug), nature walks on Sun at 10am (Jul-Aug), ranger tours, astronomy nights on some Sat at 7:30pm, occasional concerts on Wed or Fri at 8pm (Jul-Aug), Seniors' programs, and special Hol events.*

THE GREENBELT
Administration Office, 200 Nevada Ave.
☎ *(718) 987-6233.*

This organization is the caretaker for 2,500 acres of parklands and 2 major trails: the 8.5-mile Blue Trail, starting at the College of S.I. and stretching E-W to High Rock to Latourette Parks; and the White Trail, running N-S from Willowbrook to Great Kills Park.

HIGH ROCK ENVIRONMENTAL CENTER ♦
The Greenbelt, 200 Nevada Ave. (near Richmondtown).
☎ *(718) 667-2165.*
Hours: *Mon-Sun 9am-5pm (Visitors Center).*
Tours: *Self-guided and guided available.*

This National Environmental Landmark is a real forest of 94 acres of woodlands, swamps and freshwater ponds with 5 wilderness trails. Printed trail maps and natural science exhibits are available at the Visitors Center. Other attractions include the Sensory Garden for the visually impaired and a Centennial Garden of once-endangered S.I. flora moved from construction sites.

Events: *Workshops and lectures in classrooms by appt. only, concerts and special events.*

LATOURETTE PARK & GOLF COURSE
The Greenbelt, Richmond Hill Rd. near Richmondtown.
☎ *(718) 351-1840.*

With 455 acres of woodlands, trails and wetlands, this park features a golf course, clubhouse and restaurant (not visited).
Events: *Skiing and sledding.*

SILVER LAKE PARK
Victory Blvd., Clove Rd. & Forest Ave., Sunnyside.
☎ *(718) 816-5466.*
Tours: *By Urban Park Rangers, (718) 667-6042.*

Comprised of 209 acres of grassy fields for passive recreation, this park features tennis courts and a golf course, (718) 447-5686. Call (718) 390-8000 for special events.

SOUTH & MIDLAND BEACHES & FDR BOARDWALK ♦
Lower N.Y. Bay from Ft. Wadsworth to Miller Field, New Dorp.
☎ *(718) 816-6804.*

With a commanding view of the Verrazano Bridge and lower New York Bay, this long sandy beach is popular especially in the summer; a 2.5-mile boardwalk (4th largest in the world) allows bicycling before 1pm (except during the summer) and fishing by permit (Oct-May).

STATEN ISLAND BOTANICAL GARDENS
1000 Richmond Terr., Snug Harbor.
☎ *(718) 273-8200. Horticulture hot line on Mon-Fri 9am-noon.*
Hours: *Mon-Sun 9am-dusk.*
Tours: *Tree tours on Sun at 1pm (Jun-Aug).*
Interspersed among the classical buildings of Snug Harbor are special rose, floral, Victorian, herb and tree gardens, all adding to the overall splendor of the grounds. The Lion's Garden, a sensory garden for the visually impaired and a bonsai collection in the greenhouse are the special attractions. The Duck Pond is a favorite for the kids. Plans include the building of a Chinese Garden, which would serve as a reminder of the sailors' China Trade trips, and a Children's Garden with a display of perennials and flowers where storytelling will be held. A reference library of 2,000 books is available upon request. A trip here should include other Snug Harbor activities (see "For the Culture Vultures").
Events: *Plant and birdseed sales, classes (fee), Annual Flower Show & Harvest (Oct), and Christmas greenhouse display.*

STATEN ISLAND ZOO ♨
614 Broadway, West Brighton.
☎ *(718) 442-3100/3101/3174.*
Hours: *Mon-Sun 10am-4:45pm. Closed New Year's Day, Thanksgiving & Christmas.*
Free Admission: *Wed for all, Children under 3 & Seniors always. Otherwise Adults & Children $1.*
School Groups: *By appt. only. Supplemental class material available (small fee).*
This small (only 8 acres) but interesting zoo will offer you a satisfying few hours. Because it is small it concentrates on small, socially interactive animals like prairie dogs, raccoons, otters and birds, with an emphasis on a learning experience for the whole family.
The zoo has a famous reptile collection, particularly strong in rattle-snakes and pythons. The Children's Center and Farm are great for kids as they are allowed to touch, pet and feed the animals. Free brochures on some of the animals are available at the educational center. An aquarium and animal hospital are the most recent additions; a South American tropical forest is under construction and will offer a boardwalk jaunt through an exotic tropical forest.
Events: *Feeding times for animals, natural history films and lecture series (fall & winter), puppet shows, zoo Olympics and zoo safari day camp for ages 5-12 for one week (summer).*

WALKER PARK & TENNIS CLUB
Between Davis and Bard Aves. (1 block from Richmond Terr.).
☎ *(718) 442-9696.*
In 1872, the S.I. Baseball & Lawn Tennis Club held the first tennis match in America at Walker Park; today it offers a playground, club-

house, ballfields, tennis courts and cricket lawns.

WILLOWBROOK PARK
Victory Blvd. near Richmond Ave.
☎ *(718) 698-2186.*
    This N.Y.C. park features a pond for feeding wild ducks and geese, a lake for ice skating, rowboat rentals, picnic areas and ballfields.
Events: *Model airplane flying, horseshoe and archery events.*

WOLFE'S POND PARK & BEACH
Hylan Blvd. & Cornelia Ave.
☎ *(718) 984-8266.*
    This N.Y.C. park consists of 170 acres of wooded parklands of which 20 acres are for picnicking, bathing, rowboating and freshwater fishing. There's a 0.4-mile beach on Raritan and Prince's Bay (Holton to Cornelia Sts.).

For the Health Nuts

Here are some tips for free medical advice and exercise to promote good health. Consult "For the Birds" for additional sporting news.

"The first wealth is health."

— RALPH WALDO EMERSON

AMERICAN YOUTH HOSTELS (AYH)
75 Spring St. (Crosby & Lafayette Sts.).
☎ *(212) 932-2300.*
Throughout the year, AYH sponsors free clinics in cross-country skiing and waxing, downhill skiing and equipment seminars in bicycling and backpacking. They also organize bike trips throughout the boroughs (fee).

BLUE CROSS/BLUE SHIELD OF GREATER NEW YORK
Health Education Center, 3 Park Ave. (at 34th St.).
☎ *(212) 251-2323.*
Hours: *Mon-Fri 9:30am-4:30pm. Some evening events. Closed Hols.*
Groups: *Advance registration for groups of 10 or more.*
A gold mine of tips await the health conscious. Besides brochures there are an unbelievable number of free workshops on all sorts of topics, such as nutrition, mind over matter (assertiveness), heart attacks and physical fitness. This is a great service to all.

DEPARTMENT FOR THE AGING
(See "For the Golden Agers.")

LENOX HILL HOSPITAL HEALTH EDUCATION CENTER
1080 Lexington Ave. (at 76th St.).
☎ *(212) 439-2345.*
Hours: *Mon-Fri 9:30am-4:30pm.*
Want to get some free medical advice without having to wait weeks for an appointment? This service arm of Lenox Hill Hospital offers pamphlets, lectures, screenings and films on a wide range of medical topics. Lectures for groups can be arranged. Free nutrition counseling is available every Tue at 2pm. Blood pressure, hearing and visual acuity tests are given on some Thu. The best service is Tel-Med, a free telephone library for the public (see below).

MOUNT SINAI MEDICAL CENTER
(See "For the Knowledge Seekers.")
Occasional panel discussions on a broad range of medical and societal issues and courses on health promotion are held throughout the city (some at a fee).

N.Y.C. DEPARTMENT OF PARKS & RECREATION SPORTS DIVISION
☎ *(718) 507-3072/3118.*
(See "For the Birds.")
As caretakers of the city's parks and recreational facilities, this department organizes and sponsors an incredible number of athletic events annually throughout the 5 boroughs. To receive the free monthly calendar, send self-addressed envelopes (more than 1 at a time for successive months) to 830 5th Ave., Room 311, N.Y., N.Y. 10021.

N.Y.C. TECHNICAL COLLEGE (CUNY)
(See "For the Knowledge Seekers" under Brooklyn.)

Free dental hygiene clinics and ophthalmic services at a low cost.

NEW YORK ROAD RUNNERS
9 E. 89th St. (off 5th Ave.).
☎ *(212) 860-4455.*
Those wonderful people who bring you the N.Y.C. Marathon (26 miles through the 5 boroughs on the 1st Sun in Nov) sponsor running clinics and group runs; meet at Engineer's Gate, Central Park, 5th Ave. at 90th St., on Mon-Fri 6:30-7:30pm and Sat at 10am.

PLANNED PARENTHOOD
☎ *(212) 777-2002.*
For general information on reproductive health care including abortions, contraceptives and prenatal care, Planned Parenthood can provide free brochures. However, their workshops do carry a nominal fee. A free Parent Educational program is available at their 161-10 Jamaica Avenue office.

ST. VINCENT'S HOSPITAL AND MEDICAL CENTER
Health Action Center, 36 7th Ave. (12th-13th Sts.). Programs held at 205 W. 12th St.
☎ *(212) 790-7572.*
Hours: *Mon-Fri 10am-5pm.*
Monthly programs offer free blood-pressure screening on Wed from 10:30am-12:30pm, Stop Smoking and FoodSMARTS classes (modest fee) and free pamphlets.

TEL-MED
Lenox Hill Hospital Health Education Center, 1080 Lexington Ave. (at 76th St.).
☎ *(212) 439-3200.*
Hours: *Mon-Sun 24 hours.*
This free telephone health library for the public offers tapes on medical or health subjects approved by Lenox Hill Hospital doctors. Through touch tone phones, you plug in the number corresponding to your desired topic; each tape runs 3 to 5 minutes. Tel-Med tapes are great for providing basic health information, but are not to be construed as an individual diagnosis. Tape reference numbers can be obtained at the above address.

URBAN PARK RANGERS
☎ *(212) 427-4040.*
Sponsored by the N.Y.C. Department of Parks & Recreation, the Rangers organize walks throughout the year. Call each borough: Bronx (212) 430-1832, Brooklyn (718) 287-3400, Queens (718) 699-4204 and Staten Island (718) 667-6042. The guides are on the whole quite knowledgeable.

YORK COLLEGE (CUNY)
(See "For the Knowledge Seekers" under Queens.)
Consult its Health Promotion Center, (718) 262-5205.

For the Knowledge Seekers

Most people think that you have to be a student to enjoy the activities of a school. Nothing could be further from the truth. Most colleges and universities clamor for the public to attend their concerts, theater performances and art shows, many of which are free and important showcases for their students' works.

In the case of music schools, where performance is an integral part of the curriculum, nothing is more demoralizing for students than performing to a half-filled auditorium. Some of tomorrow's famous musicians and opera stars can be seen today for free. Most colleges and schools operate on a Sep-May (possibly Jun) school year, and quite frequently things change from year to year. It's always best to call first. (Please note that the rating system does not evaluate the academic achievements of the colleges and universities, just the cultural and educational programs for the public.)

> *"If a man empties his purse into his head, no man can take it away from him. An investment in knowledge always pays the best interest."*
>
> — *BENJAMIN FRANKLIN*

ART STUDENTS LEAGUE OF NEW YORK
215 W. 57th St. (7th Ave. & Broadway), 2nd fl.
☎ *(212) 247-4510.*
Hours: *Mon-Fri 10am-8pm, Sat 10am-3pm.*

Since breaking away from the National Academy of Design over 100 years ago, this League has been offering instruction to aspiring artists (with no arduous membership requirements). Although this building is somewhat unimpressive (even though it's an 1892 French Renaissance landmark by Henry J. Hardenburgh), the gallery shows top-notch students' and instructors' works (summer show). Relatively inexpensive drawing classes with live models are available.

BARNARD COLLEGE
3009 Broadway (at 117th St.)
☎ *(212) 854-2096/5262.*

This excellent all-women's college was founded begrudgingly in 1887 by Columbia College, which did not admit women. Today it is particularly known for its science and foreign-language departments. All buildings can be reached from the main address; ask the guard at the gate for directions.

Events

Concerts. Chamber music on most Tue-Thu noon-1pm (Sep-early May) at McIntosh Student Center.

Films. "Zooprax" Film Society films on occasional Tue, Fri & Sun at 7, 9 & 11pm at Altschul Aud. ($2); and Columbia's Deutsches Haus features German films (subtitles) on occasional weekdays at 8pm at Altschul Aud.

Special Events. Winter and Spring Festivals (Feb & Apr) of student art exhibits, dance celebrations, poetry readings, chamber music and demonstrations.

Theater. Gilbert & Sullivan Society productions at Minor Latham Playhouse, 854-2079, or Horace Mann Aud. at CU's Teacher's College (fee), 854-7460.

BARUCH COLLEGE (CUNY)
17 Lexington Ave. (at 23rd St.).
☎ *(212) 725-3000.*

The largest business school in the country, this arm of CUNY offers undergraduate and graduate degrees in business.

Events

Art Exhibits. At Baruch College Gallery (135 E. 22nd St., ground floor), 5 professional shows per year accompanied by symposia and gallery talks (Mon-Fri noon-5pm, Thu til 7pm), 387-1006.

Concerts. Recitals by music students (Dec & May), 725-3291.

Lectures. The "Globus Lecture Series" featuring top names (like Beverly Sills) several times a year, and weekly lectures on business, art and science, 505-5891.

Sporting Events. Basketball games at the Lexington Avenue Armory between 25th & 26th Sts., 725-3242.

Theater. Student performances twice a year.

BLOOMINGDALE HOUSE OF MUSIC
323 W. 108th St. (Broadway & Riverside Dr.).
☎ *(212) 663-6021.*
Since 1964 this nonprofit community music school has offered low-cost music instruction as well as free music lessons to public school students. A valuable experience for both students and the community is the concert series, with free concerts on Fri at 8pm and Sun at 3pm. Receptions usually follow the concerts; no tickets are necessary.

BOROUGH OF MANHATTAN COMMUNITY COLLEGE (CUNY)
199 Chambers St. (Greenwich & West Sts.).
☎ *(212) 618-1000.*
Six blocks north of the World Trade Center, this community college is the first one in N.Y.C. to offer degrees in cable and corporate communications. A strong emphasis is also placed on business management and data processing.
Events
Lectures. Special series scheduled for each semester, 618-1605 for mailing list.
Performances. The Performing Arts Center offers a wide variety of theater, opera and dance performances (some at a fee) with occasional student ones in its 3 theaters (with 99, 299 and 1,000 seats), 618-1900 for box office or 618-1443 for information about performances.

CENTER FOR THE MEDIA ARTS
226 W. 26th St. (7th-8th Aves.).
☎ *(212) 807-6670.*
Hours: *Mon-Fri 9am-9pm (Gallery on 1st lower level). Closed Christmas & July 4th.*
Tours: *Of facilities by appt. only.*
A 10-story converted warehouse embraces this boldly decorated media center dedicated to providing "hands-on" practical experience in the professional fields of TV production, broadcast engineering, audio-arts, graphic technology (desktop publishing and advertising art) and photography.
Events
Art Shows. The Germain School of Photography Gallery, 1st lower level, features students' and faculty works every 2 weeks.
Seminars. Introductory media arts seminar (3-4 times a month) on weekday evenings features guest speakers and faculty members.

CITY COLLEGE OF NEW YORK (CUNY)
W. 130th-140th Sts. between Amsterdam Ave. & St. Nicholas Terr.
☎ *(212) 650-7000/6754.*
Information: *At Finley Student Center in the North Academic Center, 650-5338.*
This city college was founded in 1849 when the state legislature voted to begin a free institution of higher education for those attending city schools and capable of passing an entrance exam. Today it's comprised

of the South Campus (originally the Academy & Convent of the Sacred Heart) and the North Campus (the neo-Gothic buildings from 138th-149th Streets designed by George B. Post in 1905 and embraced by delicate wrought-iron archways). With a reputation for educating city notables, like Ed Koch, Henry J. Stern and Herman Badillo, this college excels in engineering, psychology, chemistry, economics and literature (certainly the right ingredients for making a good politician!).

Places of Interest

Aaron Davis Hall, 134th St. & Convent Ave. Built by Abraham Geller in 1978, this center houses 3 indoor and 1 outdoor theaters, 650-6900 or box office, 650-5979.

North Academic Center, 138th St. between Convent & Amsterdam Aves., 650-4292. This is where the Info Center, 650-5338, and Cohen Library, 650-7271, can be found.

Shepard Hall, 139th St. at Convent Ave.

Events: *Consult "The Campus," "The Paper" or "Nightwatch."*

Art Shows. At Compton-Goethals Hall Gallery (1st fl.), student shows (Mon-Fri 9am-4pm); and at Aaron Davis Hall, lobby area (Mon-Fri 9am-5pm and Sat noon-5pm), exhibitions featuring work by graduate students, alumni (Apr) and occasional visiting shows from the Metropolitan Museum of Art.

Concerts. Faculty, student and professional recitals on most Thu at 12:15pm and some Tue at 2pm at either Shepard Hall (Room 200) or at Aaron Davis Theater A or B (Oct-Dec, Feb-May, except Hols), 650-5411; evening performances featuring orchestral or choral works at Aaron Davis Hall on Thu or Fri at 7pm; and concerts featuring such groups as Opera Ebony, Orpheus Ensemble and Boys Choir of Harlem.

Exhibits. At Cohen Library, atrium lobby & 5th fl. (gallery space and archives) during regular library hours, featuring a potpourri of archival material and artwork, 650-7611.

Lectures/Workshops. A wide range of topics, sponsored by the individual departments, 650-5310 for calendar info.

Special Events. Spring Arts Festival; and monthly children's festivals (Sat & weekdays) featuring films, puppet shows and mimes.

Theater/Dance. Performances by students in the Theater Department and Teatro Latino at Aaron Davis Hall, 650-6900, and by the in-residence groups, Negro Ensemble Company & the Dance Theater of Harlem; the Leonard Davis Center for the Performing Arts also sponsors a full complement of events (fee mainly), 650-8151.

CITY UNIVERSITY OF NEW YORK (CUNY)
☎ *(212) 794-5555.*

The freebie days at CUNY disappeared in 1976, at which time anyone with a H.S. diploma (or equivalency) who lived in New York could attend one of the colleges in the CUNY network. By private school standards, however, tuition today is cheap. The 18 CUNY colleges (9 senior, 7 community, 1 technical and 1 medical) include Baruch, Bronx Comm., Brooklyn, City, Medgar Evers, Hostos Comm., Hunter, John Jay, Kingsborough Comm., La Guardia Comm., Herbert H. Lehman, Manhattan Comm., Mount Sinai School of Medicine, N.Y.C. Technical,

Queens, Queensborough Comm., Staten Island and York.

COLUMBIA UNIVERSITY ♠♠
114th-120th Sts. between Broadway & Amsterdam Ave.
☎ *(212) 854-1754/2845/5573.*
Info Center: *201 Dodge Hall at 116th St. & Broadway, left of entrance gates (map and guided tour).*
Tours: *Mon-Fri at 3pm (Sep-mid May), Mon-Fri 10am & 2pm (mid May-Aug), weather permitting; tours suspended during final exams, 854-2845 (visitors) or 854-2521 (prospective students).*

One of the nation's oldest and wealthiest institutions, Columbia was chartered in 1754 by King George II of England and named King's College. The first classes were held at Trinity Church; shortly thereafter the church donated 5 acres of its vast holdings of what is now Church, Barclay and Murray Streets to the new college. After the Revolutionary War, King's College changed its name to Columbia.

In 1814, in need of financial aid, Columbia received a plot of land (but no money) on 5th Avenue between 47th-51st Streets (way above the city limits and of very little use) from New York State. (This rocky weed patch, once the site of the Elgin Botanic Gardens, later became the valuable real estate for Rockefeller Center; today it is owned by Mitsubishi, a Japanese corporation.) However, it wasn't until 1857 that Columbia moved to the midtown area to occupy the old asylum for the deaf and dumb on Park Avenue & 50th Street. Then, in 1897, another move took Columbia to the current Morningside Heights campus, where the college bought parcels of land from the Bloomingdale Insane Asylum. The focal point then and now remains the Low Memorial in the Quad, built by McKim, Mead & White in 1897.

Today Columbia is the smallest of the Ivy League colleges and is particularly known for its professional schools in architecture, business, education, journalism, law and medicine.

Places of Interest
Avery Hall, near Low Library. The School of Architecture, special library and exhibitions in Gallery Space level 100.

Butler Library, 115th & Broadway. The main library, housing exhibitions and offering lectures, 854-2271.

Casa Italiana, 1161 Amsterdam Ave. (at 117th St.). A landmark Italian Renaissance palazzo (1927, McKim, Mead & White) houses the Italian Studies Department; films, lectures and symposia, 854-2306.

Deutsches Haus, 420 W. 116th St. The German cultural society presents art shows, lectures, films and coffeehouse hour on Wed from 3-5pm, 280-3964.

Dodge Hall, 116th St. & Broadway. The School of Arts offers exhibits and houses the Info Center, 854-2845.

Earl Hall, 117th St. & Broadway. Lectures, concerts and folk dancing, 854-3574/3576/6242.

Ferris Booth Hall, 115 St. & Broadway. Films and lectures, 854-3611.

Gallery Space, at Avery Hall level 100, 116th St. & Broadway.

Hamilton Hall, 1130 Amsterdam Ave. at 116th St. Tours for prospective Columbia College students only, 854-2521.

Low Library, 116th St. & Broadway. Modeled after the Greek Pantheon, this domed structure was a gift from Seth Low, former Mayor of Brooklyn and Columbia president from 1890 to 1901, who donated this in tribute to his father, A.A. Low, a wealthy China trade merchant. Daniel Chester French's "Alma Mater" graces the stairway. Exhibitions can be found in the Rotunda and Columbiana Room, which houses the original King's College library, 854-6800.

Maison Française, at Buell Hall (near Low Library). This French cultural society offers lectures, films, art shows (Mon-Fri 10am-5pm) and receptions, concerts, a library and French "Cafe Conservation" on Wed from 4-5:30pm, 854-4482.

Horace Mann Theater, Teacher's College, Broadway & 120th St. Theater, dance and music productions, 678-3490 for reservations.

McMillin Theater, 116th St. & Broadway at Dodge Hall. Panel discussions, lectures and concerts, 854-1633.

St. Paul's Chapel, 117th St. & Amsterdam Ave. (near Low Library). Worth a detour to admire this grand Byzantine-style brick and limestone landmark church (1907, Howells & Stokes). Designed after a Greek-cross plan with a Byzantine dome of richly colored Guastavino tiles, this church also combines classical Romanesque and Renaissance styles. Concerts, 854-6625/6242.

Teacher's College, 525 W. 120th St., 678-3000.

Events: *Consult "The Record" (854-2845) or "Columbia Spectator" (854-4771).*

Art Shows & Exhibits. At Low Memorial Library Rotunda, Mon-Fri 9am-5pm and in the Columbiana Room, Mon-Fri 1-5pm, which houses books and memorabilia on Columbia and N.Y.C. plus the interesting King's College room restoration circa 1750s; at Butler Library, 6th fl., Mon-Fri 9am-5pm, 854-2231; at Maison Française, Mon-Fri 9am-5pm, 1 per month on a French theme; at the Deutsches Haus, Mon-Fri 1-4pm; at Gallery Space, Avery Hall level 100, Mon-Fri 9am-5pm, 854-3314; at the Wallach Art Gallery in Schermerhorn Hall, 8th fl., Wed-Sat 1-5pm, 854-7288; at the Dodge Hall lobby, the Brander Matthews collection of stage set replicas spanning the centuries; at Lehman Library, Int'l Affairs, 420 W. 118th St., Room 406, the Herbert H. Lehman Papers, 854-3060; at Macy Gallery at Teacher's College, 4th fl., Mon-Fri noon-5pm for doctoral students' work as well as occasional professional artists, 678-3360; at Architecture Gallery at Buell Hall, Tue-Sat noon-6pm, 854-3414; and at the Post-Crypt Art Gallery, St. Paul's Chapel, lower level, Tue-Fri 2-6pm, Fri-Sat 9pm-12:30am, 854-1953.

Concerts. Organ recitals at St. Paul's Chapel on Thu at 12:05pm (Oct-Nov & Feb-Apr), the Bach series on Thu at 8pm (end May-Jun) and "Post-Crypt" coffeehouse on Fri & Sat at 9pm (Oct-Dec, Feb-early May); and at Maison Française, concerts once a month featuring French chamber music or French artists.

Films. At Ferris Booth Hall on occasional Tue or Thu & Sun at 8 & 10pm (fee); at Earl Hall (donation); at Maison Française, French documentaries on alternate Thu at 8pm (Oct-Dec, Feb-May); at Casa Italiana, Italian movies with subtitles, Piccolo Theater, 2nd fl., on Fri at 8pm (contribution), 854-2306; at Barnard's Altschul Aud. for German films sponsored by Deutsches Haus, 280-3964; and free films on Wed at 9pm (summer) at Furnald Lawn.

Lectures. At Low Memorial Library, the "Brampton Series"; at Earl Hall; at the School of Architecture's Avery Hall on some Wed at 6pm; at the School of Int'l Affairs for "Brown Bag lunch & lecture" (suspended during exams), 854-2845; at the Business School; at Deutsches Haus on occasional Thu at 8pm (sometimes in German); and at Maison Française.

Special Events. WBAI Christmas crafts fair and block party (Mar or Apr).

Theater. The Center for Theater Studies' occasional performances at Horace Mann Theater and Bache Miller Theater, 116th St. & Broadway, 854-1633; professional music productions at Dodge Hall, 2nd fl.; at Shapiro Theater, undergraduate openings, 854-6960; and Theater Department one-act plays.

COOPER UNION 🍎
Cooper Square, 7th St. & 3rd Ave.
☎ *(212) 254-6300.*

Since 1859, Cooper Union has been offering tuition-free education (primarily in art, architecture and engineering) to those demonstrating superior capabilities, thanks to the genius and generosity of Peter Cooper. Cooper was a philanthropist, inventor, humanitarian and self-made millionaire (from glue manufacturing, iron smelting and railroads). However, he always felt a bit inadequate due to his lack of education and always had a dream to bring free education to the masses. Cooper Union was the realization of that dream, which he was able to enjoy during his lifetime.

The Great Hall, built by Frederick Peterson in the Italianate style, with new steel railroad beams from Cooper's New Jersey rolling mill, has the distinction of offering the longest-running free public lecture series in the U.S. It opened unofficially back on Feb. 27, 1860, with Lincoln's "Right Makes Might" speech against slavery, which some consider helped him to win the presidency. Cooper had a dream to offer free lectures to the public (not only the students) to help make them more socially and politically aware. Many famous people, including 4 other Presidents—Theodore Roosevelt, Woodrow Wilson, Grover Cleveland and U.S. Grant—and a wide range of other personalities—Mark Twain, Susan B. Anthony, Benjamin Spock and Emma Goldman—have spoken here.

Events: Call for free calendar, 353-4196.

Art shows. At Houghton Gallery, 7 E. 7th St., 2nd fl., Mon-Sat 11am-7pm for student and professional shows. Call first.

Lectures. A critique series with well-known artists and scholars sponsored by the Humanities & Social Science Department, 353-4196.

Performances. An excellent program offering lectures, readings, dance, jazz and classical music on weekdays & Fri at 8pm (mid Sep-May, mostly free).

CUNY GRADUATE SCHOOL AND UNIVERSITY CENTER
33 W. 42nd St. (5th-6th Aves.).
☎ *(212) 642-1600.*

In pursuit of higher education, this graduate center offers a wide variety of masters and doctoral programs in liberal arts and sciences as well as the baccalaureate program for CUNY. Housed in the Aeolian Hall (originally built in 1912 but renovated in 1966 by Carl J. Petrilli to include the walk-through mall and gallery area) and continuing in its musical footsteps, CUNY sponsors good chamber music in the 3rd-floor concert hall, which hosted the premiere of George Gershwin's "Rhapsody in Blue" in 1924.

Events: Consult calendar of events in lobby.

Art shows. In the Mall, a wide range of professional artwork, primarily sculpture and painting, Mon-Fri 9am-6pm; at the Library, concourse level, Mon-Fri 9am-6pm; and in the Dining Commons, 18th fl., Mon-Fri 10am-7pm.

Concerts. Occasional chamber music or recitals on weekdays at 8pm on 3rd fl.; and occasional outdoor concerts in the Mall (summer).

Lectures. Scheduled by individual departments.

Theater. Occasional play readings.

DOWNTOWN COMMUNITY TV CENTER (DCTV)
87 Lafayette St. (Walker & White Sts.), 2 blocks below Canal.
☎ *(212) 966-4510.*

Located on the fringes of Chinatown, this center was founded in 1972 to offer free media opportunities to the depressed neighboring communities. Built in 1895 by Napoleon LeBrun & Sons appropriately in the early French Renaissance style (epitomized by the French chateaus of the Loire Valley), this landmark firehouse inflames many with the fervor to make video programs that depict and enrich the lives of the community at a nominal fee. A truly remarkable and invaluable service to the community (P.S. You don't have to live in the community to join in).

Events

Special Programs. Internships for residents and college students as well as employment for high school students on summer videoteams; exhibit space for musicians, dancers and filmmakers; and Outreach programs for city high school students.

Workshops. Introductory 3-week workshops on Thu evenings are given in English, Chinese and Spanish.

THE EDUCATIONAL ALLIANCE
197 E. Broadway (Jefferson & Clinton Sts.).
☎ *(212) 475-6200.*

This fine arts school offers a varied palette of inexpensive drawing, painting and photography classes with scholarships for gifted and needy young artists (ages 11-20). Welding and metal working in the fine arts are offered at only a few schools in the city, this being one.

Events

Art Shows. Solo or group shows in all media, call for hours.

Classes. In photography for Seniors on Tue at 1:30pm including 8 sessions (fee).

Lectures. The Alliance of Figurative Artists meets on Fri at 9pm (Oct-mid May) at the coffeehouse ($1 but free coffee) with a lecture or performance.

Performances. At the Mazer Theater and sponsored by the Lee Kohns Cultural Arts Center, chamber music, films, children's theater, lectures and jazz.

EMPIRE STATE COLLEGE
State University of New York, 666 Broadway (Bleecker & Bond Sts.), 3rd fl.
☎ *(212) 598-0640.*

This innovative "school without walls" believes in the value of bringing life experience into the curriculum. With a strong emphasis on liberal arts, business and computer science, this SUNY college is heavily based in tutorials.

Events
Art Shows. Photography exhibitions of either documentaries or photojournalism, Mon-Thu 10am-6pm, Fri noon-5pm.

FASHION INSTITUTE OF TECHNOLOGY (F.I.T.) ♦
227 W. 27th St. (7th-8th Aves.).
☎ *(212) 760-7760/7848.*

Started in 1944 by the Educational Foundation for the Fashion Industries, F.I.T. still continues to train illustrators, designers, pattern-makers, buyers and advertising managers, tailoring them to fit key fashion positions.

Events
Art Shows. In the Newhouse Galleries, excellent professional and student exhibitions on Tue-Fri noon-8pm, Sat 10am-5pm; and at Buildings "C" and "D," display cases highlight top students' works.

FORDHAM UNIVERSITY
Lincoln Center Campus, 113 W. 60th St. (Amsterdam & 9th Aves.).
☎ *(212) 841-5100/5360.*

Built in 1968, this Manhattan campus is nestled in the Lincoln Center complex and specializes in art, humanities, social and natural sciences. See Fordham University listing in the Bronx.

Events: Consult "The Observer" or call student government, 841-5152.

Art Shows. At the Lowenstein Library Gallery, Mon-Fri 8:30am-10pm, Sat 10am-6pm and at the Robert Moses outdoor sculpture center, 841-5133.

Concerts. Jazz concerts sponsored by the Office of Campus Ministries; the "Falcon Series" of 20th C. chamber music (nominal fee) 5 times a year; and student concerts by the Division of the Arts.

Films. Occasional series; consult student government.

Lectures. A wide range of lectures.

Special Events. African Harvest Festival (early Dec); jazz performances and lectures for Black History Month.

Theater. Good yearly productions by Drama Department in Pope Aud. (seats 500).

HENRY GEORGE SCHOOL
121 E. 30th St. (Park Ave. S. & Lexington Ave.).
☎ *(212) 889-8020.*

For over 50 years, this economics institute has been offering *free* courses and lectures. A reference library is available by appt. only.

Events

Courses. 10-week courses on contemporary economic and social issues in winter and fall on Mon-Fri 5:30-8:30pm.

Films. Lunch-time films and discussions (Sep-early Dec).

Seminars. Spring seminar series on Wed at 5:30-7pm (May) and Sat at 1-3pm on basic economic issues.

THE GREENWICH HOUSE MUSIC SCHOOL
46 Barrow St. (7th Ave. S. & Bleecker St.).
☎ *(212) 242-4770.*

Since 1914 music students have come here to make music in these 2 adjoining brownstones located on a quiet Greenwich Village residential street. Although most concerts and master classes are not free, the student and faculty concerts are (usually on weekdays at 8pm). Ask to be put on the "Culture Calendar" mailing list for events at the school and in the community.

HARLEM SCHOOL OF THE ARTS
645 St. Nicholas Ave. (at 141st St.).
☎ *(212) 926-1400.*

This nonprofit arts school offers pre-professional instruction in music, drama and graphic arts. Housed in an architectural award-winning building, the school stages a variety of performances during the year, usually on weekdays or Sat afternoons. A year-end requirement is for students to perform under the guidance of the faculty.

Events: *An art and humanities program of concerts, literature and art exhibitions throughout the year.*

HEBREW ARTS SCHOOL
129 W. 67th St. (Broadway & Amsterdam Ave.).
☎ *(212) 362-8060.*

This nonsectarian institution is dedicated to teaching excellence in art, dance, music and theater for children and adults. Music students perform at the Ann Goodman Recital Hall, dance students kick up their heels at Merkin Hall, and art students have shows of their work (Sep-Jun).

Events

Art Shows. At the Art Gallery in Abraham Goodman House, student and professional exhibitions, Sun-Thu noon-6pm.

Concerts. Adult student concerts (2 times a year), the Young People's monthly concerts performed by gifted students on some Sun at 2pm (Sep-Jun) and faculty concerts on Sun at 3pm (3 times a year).

HEBREW UNION COLLEGE—JEWISH INSTITUTE OF RELIGION

1 W. 4th St. (Broadway & Mercer St.).
☎ *(212) 674-5300.*
Hours: *Tue-Fri 10am-4pm, Sun with lecture or concert (Joseph Exhibition Room).*
Groups: *By appt. only on Mon-Fri 9am-5pm, contact Office of Community Relations.*

This college trains rabbis and cantors in the new progressive move-ment of Judaism and has the only school of sacred music in America. Although most courses are for the students, some free public ones are offered from time to time. The new modern building (don't take the institutional-looking facade too seriously) provides attractive lounge areas on all floors with the archaeological exhibits. The library contains 110,000 volumes and is noted for its modern Hebrew literature.

Events

Art Exhibits. At the Joseph Exhibition Room, wonderful shows (about 3-4 a year with a 1-week break between) on Judaica, Jewish artists, Jewish themes or archaeology.

Lectures. "Add Life to Years" series with occasional guest speakers.

Special Programs. The "Sunday Afternoon at the College" program on some Sun at 3pm (Oct-Jun, except Hols) of music or lectures; and services for young adults on Fri at 6pm, open to the public.

Tours. A tour of the college includes a history of Reform Judaism, the architecture of the building and a chat about the exhibits (all denominations welcome).

HIGH SCHOOL OF FASHION INDUSTRIES

225 W. 24th St. (7th-8th Aves.).
☎ *(212) 255-1235.*

This specialized city high school offers free evening classes (Tue & Thu at 6:30pm) in fashion for those in the industry wishing to upgrade their skills.

Events: *Fashion shows of students' works in May (nominal fee).*

HUNTER COLLEGE (CUNY)

68th St. between Lexington & Park Aves.
☎ *(212) 772-4000/4068.*

Founded in 1870, this is one of the oldest CUNY colleges. Today it boasts a strong liberal arts curriculum. Nationally, this coed college ranks number one in the number of its women graduates who have earned Ph.D. degrees. Two modern skyscrapers (Hunter East & West) at Lexington Avenue & 68th Street give Hunter a new architectural image as well as additional space. The Center for Puerto Rican Studies independently offers a wide range of activities and facilities, including a library.

Events: *Consult "The Hunter Envoy" or "Renazette."*

Art Exhibits. At Bertha & Karl Leubsdorf Gallery, S.W. corner of Hunter West lobby, professional showcases (Mon-Fri 1-6pm, closed intersession and mid May-mid Sep), 772-4991; at Thomas Hunter Hall,

Lexington Ave. between 68th-69th Sts. (west side), ground fl., students' works (Mon-Fri 1-6pm); at the Center for Puerto Rican Studies, Hunter East, 14th fl., occasional photo exhibits (Mon-Fri 1-6pm), 772-5715/5706; and at the New Gallery, 450 W. 41st St., contemporary art.

Concerts. The Hunter Symphony performances 4 times a year on Wed eves at Hunter Assembly Hall (seats 2,200), 69th St. between Lexington & Park Aves.; the Choir sings out several times on Sun afternoons; Collegium Musicum (pre-Renaissance music), Chamber Music Ensemble and Jazz Band performances throughout the year (some at a fee), 772-5020 or box office, 772-4448.

Dance. The Hunter Dance Co. and visiting troupes perform, 772-5012.

Films. Contact student activities at 772-4261 (day) or 772-4267 (eve).

Lectures. Occasional special lectures, 772-4551.

Special Events. Black History and Women's History Months celebrations, 772-5683/5680; cultural festivities sponsored by the Center for Puerto Rican Studies, 772-5715; and the "Culture Pass," discounts on fee-based Hunter events.

Sports. Intercollegiate games and recreational facilities (fee).

Theater. Student and faculty productions sponsored by the Department of Theater in the Little Theater (seats 125) or the Playhouse (seats 700), 772-4448.

WASHINGTON IRVING HIGH SCHOOL
40 Irving Pl. (16th-17th Sts.).
☎ *(212) 674-5000.*

Free evening high school classes with a guidance center are available on Mon-Thu at 6pm; registration is in late Sep.
Events: *Occasional concerts (fee).*

JOHN JAY COLLEGE OF CRIMINAL JUSTICE (CUNY)
445 W. 59th St. (9th-10th Aves.).
☎ *(212) 237-8000/8628.*

As a quarter of the student body are already police officers, firefighters and corrections officers, the curriculum is heavily geared toward criminal justice, government and administration. A safe place to hang out!

Events

Art Exhibits. At the Wall Gallery & Atrium Gallery, 899 10th Ave., periodic sculpture and painting shows, 237-8628.

Sports. Collegiate basketball games (Nov-Feb), 237-8399.

Theater. Free plays (twice a year) and readings sponsored by the Department of Speech & Theater, 237-8363.

JUILLIARD SCHOOL OF MUSIC ♿
144 W. 66th St. (Broadway & Amsterdam Ave.).
☎ *(212) 874-7515.*
Hours: *Mon-Fri 11am-6pm (Box Office).*

This world-class music school has trained many prominent musicians over the years. Free and genuinely excellent student concerts

(Oct-May) are held at Alice Tully Hall on Wed at 1pm, at the IBM Garden on Wed at 12:30pm, at Juilliard in Paul Hall (times listed in the lobby) and at Juilliard Theater (155 W. 65th St.) or Alice Tully Hall on weekday evenings (tickets can be obtained 3 weeks in advance, first-come, first-served basis). Check the Lincoln Center Calendar of Events.

LIGHTHOUSE FOR THE BLIND
111 E. 59th St. (Lexington & Park Aves.).
☎ *(212) 355-2200.*
This school sets its "sights" on blind and visually impaired students. The cultural outpouring is not affected by their disability.
Events
Concerts. Jazz or solo recitals in Jan, a choral work by the Lighthouse Singers and a fully staged opera by Opera Company; call for free tickets.
Special Events. An Arts Festival with arts & crafts, live demonstrations, drama workshops, readings, dance performances, 2 fashion shows and music (1 week in mid May); and the "POSH Sale" (impressive rummage sale) of great buys on furs, celebrity items, designer clothing (late Oct, free admission).
Theater. The Lighthouse Players stage 5 performances of a drama in mid Mar for 2 weekends (2 consecutive Fri at 8pm, 2 Sat at 2:30pm and 1 Sun afternoon), ext. 1693.

MANHATTAN SCHOOL OF MUSIC
Broadway at 122nd St.
☎ *(212) 749-2802.*
Founded in 1917, this international conservatory strives to provide artistic and personal growth for young musicians with special strengths in opera and contemporary music.
Events
Concerts. Ongoing student concerts in 3 music halls (in spring, there may be 6 a day); operatic scenes with orchestra (fall & spring) and full productions (fee); a contemporary music festival in spring; performances by the in-residence groups (New Music Consort, Groups for Contemporary Music and American String Quartet); and master classes (most at a fee).

MANNES COLLEGE OF MUSIC
150 W. 85th St. (Columbus & Amsterdam Aves.).
☎ *(212) 580-0210.*
For over 70 years, this fine school has provided musical training and encouragement of artistic expression to students. Excellent free concerts on weekdays at 8pm (Oct-May, Mon-Fri in spring) feature professionals, students or faculty. The Mannes Orchestra will be performing regularly at Symphony Space (about 5 times a year). To be kept informed, call to be put on their mailing list.

MARYMOUNT MANHATTAN COLLEGE
221 E. 71st St. (2nd-3rd Aves.).
☎ *(212) 517-0534.*

This small college (90% women) calls itself "one of New York's best kept secrets," although it makes no secret that its strong suit is communication arts and business management.

Events

Art Exhibits. At the Art Gallery in the lobby, in Nugent Hall (possibly) and in front of the Great Hall, interesting professional and student shows, Mon-Sun 1-8pm.

Films. Sponsored by various departments, throughout the year.

Lectures. The "Louis Lefkowitz Series" on international politics and the "Spanish & Latin American Series" featuring writers, poets, musicians and scholars 4 times a year.

Special events. Open house for the Department of Continuing Education's "Life Long Learning" program at semester start.

Theater. The Marymount Manhattan Theater offers occasional free performances, 517-0474; and at the Children's Theater, open to scheduled school groups and the public (suggested contribution), outstanding performances of works by Hans Christian Andersen and Rudyard Kipling.

MATHWORKS
219-1214.

Free introductory workshops for GRE/GMAT exams (about 10 a year) may help you prepare for and better understand the types of questions asked on these standard tests. Classes are held at various locations.

McBURNEY YMCA
215 W. 23rd St. (7th-8th Aves.).
☎ *(212) 741-9210.*

This Y gives free membership to individuals who cannot afford to pay the membership fee. A free "learn to swim" week for adults and children during Easter break (registration required, 741-9224), free community workshops and festivals are offered here. The "uniqueness" prize goes to the Thunderbird American Indian Dancers who stage powwows (and have been doing so for the past 20 years) on the 4th Sat of the month at 8pm (Oct-Apr).

MOUNT SINAI SCHOOL OF MEDICINE (CUNY)
1 Gustave Levy Pl. (100th St. & 5th Ave.).
☎ *(212) 241-9100.*

This fine medical center plays a valuable role in community health education, sponsoring panel discussions on a broad range of medical and societal issues. Courses on preventive medicine are held throughout the city (some at a fee).

NEW SCHOOL FOR SOCIAL RESEARCH
66 W. 12th St. (5th-6th Aves.).
☎ *(212) 741-5353/5630.*

Established in 1919 by a group of leading scholars, the New School has remained a home for leading intellectuals, artists and public figures. In 1970, it teamed up with Parsons School of Design to create the largest college of design and art in the country. It is particularly well known for its wide range of adult education courses in such fun things as films (seeing and making them), advertising, communications, and computers. Undergraduate degrees are taken in the Seminar College. The New School's contribution to the art world is substantial thanks to its New Museum of Contemporary Art, worthy of many visits.

Events: *Consult the "New School Observer."*

Art Exhibits. The New School Art Collection at 65 5th Ave. and the New Museum of Contemporary Art at 583 Broadway (see "For the Culture Vultures"); the outdoor sculpture garden of modern works at 66 W. 12th St.; and the Parsons Art Gallery at 2 W. 13th St.

Film. A legendary film series on Fri at 7:30pm (fee), thanks to their vast film library, 741-8903.

Lectures. An impressive roster of guest speakers and lectures.

Music. Professional concerts (fee), 741-5689.

Performances. At the Bernard Major Aud., readings.

Seminars. Free seminars introducing various Adult Education courses at semester start.

NEW YORK SCHOOL OF INTERIOR DESIGN
155 E. 56th St. (Lexington & 3rd Aves.).
☎ *(212) 753-5365.*
Hours: *Mon-Fri 9am-5pm.*

It's not difficult to figure out what this school's specialty is. With a student body of 90% women, some of the best designers have materialized here. Look for the Annual Student Exhibit with the National Award Winners in Interior Design (Jun) featuring elevations, renderings, models and presentations of outreach renovation programs.

NEW YORK STUDIO SCHOOL
8 W. 8th St. (5th-6th Aves.).
☎ *(212) 673-6466.*
Hours: *Mon-Fri 9am-6pm, Sat-Sun 10am-4pm (Gallery), with open reception on first Fri of show from 6-8pm.*

Once the "salon" of Gertrude Vanderbilt Whitney (where the art elite congregated in the 1920s and 1930s) and then the first home for the Whitney Museum of American Art in 1931, this art school's history is inspiring. Today, the artistic outpouring is not quite so grand, although the 6 shows a year offer a professional outlet for painting and drawing. A lecture series on Wed at 6:30pm draws upon painters, sculptors, philosophers, art historians, critics and poets to create an artistic center.

NEW YORK UNIVERSITY 🍎
Washington Square at W. 4th St.
☎ *(212) 998-1212, 998-2400.*

This large private university in the heart of the village is well known for its arts and business degrees. Its reputation for liberalism dates back to its inception in 1831 when Albert Gallatin (Secretary of the Treasury under Jefferson) and a group of business and professional people were intent on providing schooling for the nonsectarian middle class as an alternative to the Episcopalian and more elite Columbia University. Many distinguished faculty members including Samuel F.B. Morse and students such as Winslow Homer, Walt Whitman and Samuel Colt (as in revolver) spent time at this hallowed institution. Centered around Washington Square Park, the NYU campus consists of a blending of brownstones and modern buildings (the latter by Philip Johnson and Richard Foster).

Places of Interest

Bobst Library, 70 Washington Sq. S. 998-2505.

Loeb Student Center, 566 LaGuardia Pl. Concerts, lectures and films, 998-1212.

NYU Law School, 40 Washington Sq. S. Lectures and panel discussions, 998-6116.

Tisch School, 111 2nd Ave. (near 6th St.) and 721 Broadway at Waverly Pl. Dance, theater and art exhibits, 998-1820.

University Theater, 35 W. 4th St. Theater and recitals, 998-5191.

Vanderbilt Hall, 40 Washington Sq. S. Houses Tischman Aud., 998-6116.

Events: *Consult monthly calendar "Arts & Sciences," 998-8020, or call Info Center, 998-1212.*

Art Exhibits. At 80 Washington Square East Galleries, Grey Art Gallery ♦ and the NYU Photo Center Gallery (see "For the Artists").

Concerts. At Maison Française on 3rd Sun of month for French music or French musicians, 998-8750; and student and faculty recitals at University Theater, 998-4947.

Cultural Societies. The Maison Française and Deutsches Haus (see "For the Society-Goers").

Dance. The NYU 2nd Avenue Dance Co., 111 2nd Ave., 5th fl., performances, 998-1980, or Dance Education Dept., 35 W. 4th St., performances (free and fee), 998-4636/5400.

Exhibits. At Bobst Library in Fales Library, displays of rare books, Mon-Thu 2-5pm, 998-2596.

Films. The Cinemathèque Film Series on Sat at 10am, 1 & 3pm (most weeks) with 3 consecutive feature films at 721 Broadway, 998-1600; and at the Maison Française on most Fri at 8pm (sometimes 6pm), French films.

Lectures. The "Gallatin Lecture Series" at Bobst Library, 12th fl., 998-2505; occasional lectures by individual departments, 995-3336; and the Law School, 998-6116.

Poetry. The "Poets & Critics in Performance" series with monthly poetry readings; contact Poetics Institute, 998-8848.

Theater. At the Tisch School, dance and theater performances, 998-1820; and the Washington Sq. Performers at University Theater, drama, comedy and children's performances.

NYU, INSTITUTE OF FINE ARTS

1 E. 78th St. (off 5th Ave.).

☎ *(212) 772-5800.*

Housed in a splendid 1912 Neoclassical mansion, once owned by

James Biddle Duke (the tobacco magnate), this NYU graduate school in art, architectural history, conservation and museum training offers free lectures on Fri at 4pm (Oct-Dec, Feb-Mar).

NYU MIDTOWN CENTER FOR CONTINUING EDUCATION
11 W. 42nd St. (5th-6th Aves.), 4th & 5th fls.
☎ *(212) 790-1312.*

For credit and noncredit classes in liberal arts, computers and public affairs, this Center is particularly well known for its Real Estate Institute, considered by some to be the best in the country. Thanks to a trompe l'oeil by Richard Haas, the interior design represents a microcosm of N.Y.C. with the corridors representing Broadway, 5th & 6th Aves. Occasional lectures are held here.

PACE UNIVERSITY
Civic Center Campus, 1 Pace Plaza, across from City Hall.
☎ *(212) 346-1200.*

With 3 campuses in Westchester, Pace is highly regarded for its business programs. The Manhattan campus, across from City Hall, resides at the once influential Printing Hall Square, the home of the dozen or so newspapers that flourished from the 1840s to WWI.

Places of Interest

Schimmell Theater, Pace Downtown Theater, on Spruce St. between Nassau & Gold Sts. Music, dance and theater (fee).

Student Union, Pace Plaza, Main Bldg.

Events: *For Monthly Calendar, 346-1360.*

Art Shows. At the Art Gallery in the Student Union level B (room B-2-W), contemporary artists, Mon-Sat 10am-6pm, 346-1590.

Films. At the Student Union (some free), on most Mon at noon, 3 & 9pm, 346-1617.

Lectures. Occasional lectures by individual departments, especially in art, 346-1637.

Special Events. At the Student Union, activities (like lectures and concerts) on some Wed or Thu at noon, 346-1617.

PARSONS SCHOOL OF DESIGN
66 5th Ave. (at 12th St.).
☎ *(212) 741-7572.*

Established in 1896, Parsons merged with the New School in 1970 and now represents the largest college of art and design in the country. Degrees are offered in fine arts, fashion design, communications design, photography, interior design and illustration. As a result, there never seems to be a dearth of artistic work for their galleries at 66th 5th Ave., 5th fl., and 2 W. 13th St.

PRATT MANHATTAN CENTER
295 Lafayette St. (E. Houston St.), 2nd fl.
☎ *(212) 925-8481.*

Part of Pratt Institute of Brooklyn, this Manhattan center offers courses on art and design and is located in the Puck Building (see "For the Artists").

SCHOOL OF T'AI CHI
47 W. 13th St. (at 6th Ave.), 5th fl.
☎ *(212) 929-1981.*
This school of traditional Chinese exercise practiced in slow motion for "relaxation, vitality, health & grace" offers a free introductory class every Tue from 6-7pm (closed Aug) with participatory sessions and a Q&A period. No obligation.

SCHOOL OF VISUAL ARTS
209 E. 23rd St. (2nd-3rd Aves.).
☎ *(212) 670-7350.*
Career-minded students come here to specialize mainly in media arts and computer graphics. The faculty is comprised entirely of business professionals.
Events
Art Shows. In the Museum (see "For the Culture Vultures"); and at student galleries at 209 E. 23rd St. (main & 2nd fls.), at 214 E. 21st St. (2nd & 7th fls.), at 380 2nd Ave. (8th fl.), at 141 W. 21st St. (1st fl.) and at 137 Wooster St. —call for hours.
Lectures. In the Amphitheater, 3rd fl., occasional lectures, slide shows, seminars or readings with guest speakers and well-known artists.
Theater. The SVA Actors' Theater, plays and scenes directed, acted and designed by the students.

SIVANANDA CENTER
243 W. 24th St. (7th-8th Aves.).
☎ *(212) 255-4560.*
Free open houses are given in yoga, inner dance and spiritual and health topics, such as the "role of the spine" and "the world of vegetarianism." Occasional concerts are presented.

THIRD STREET MUSIC SETTLEMENT SCHOOL
235 E. 11th St. (2nd-3rd Aves.).
☎ *(212) 777-3240.*
Since 1890, this school has been welcoming Lower East Side youngsters into the world of music.
Events: *Free faculty concerts on most Wed at 7:30pm; and "A Little Noon Music," at St. Mark's Park, across the street, on Thu at noon (Jun-Jul).*

TRAPHAGEN SCHOOL OF FASHION
686 Broadway (S. of E. 4th St.).
☎ *(212) 673-0300.*
Hours: *Mon-Fri 10am-4pm.*
Founded in 1923, this was the first school to specialize in fashion design, illustration and interior decoration, thanks to Ethel Traphagen. She was instrumental in early fashion education as well as innovative in using American Indian design and color and in her creation of the trouser/skirt, which facilitated the boarding of trolley cars, the new form

of transportation. A wonderful library housing over 14,000 books (some rare) on art, fashion and architecture is available upon appt. only.

TURTLE BAY MUSIC SCHOOL
244 E. 52nd St. (2nd-3rd Aves.).
☎ *(212) 753-8811.*

Begun in 1925 as a community music school, this institution offers a variety of recitals and concerts in its Concert Hall (seats 175). The Adult Chorus meets once a week for 2 hours, and anyone can audition.

THE WESTSIDE YMCA
5 W. 63rd St. (off Central Pk. W.).
☎ *(212) 787-4400/6557.*

This active and well-known Y has a marvelous catalog of courses, athletics, workshops, theater, counseling and community programs, all complementing its holistic approach to health (mind/soul/body). The Center for Arts has a free trial each season for their art classes.

YESHIVA UNIVERSITY
Amsterdam Ave. & W. 185th St.
☎ *(212) 960-5288.*

Although Yeshiva is best known for its Orthodox Jewish program, an excellent secular one is interwoven into the curriculum. For its Museum, see "For the Culture Vultures."

YWCA
610 Lexington Ave. (at 53rd St.).
☎ *(212) 755-4500.*
Hours: *Mon-Fri 11am-7pm (Gallery).*

Day and evening courses include crafts, performing arts, languages, business, women's interests and physical education (for a fee). Adult and youth open houses in Sep offer a free glimpse of the classes and facilities (with use of swimming pool and weight room).

Events

Art Shows. At the art gallery, 1st fl., frequent shows of photography, crafts and painting.

Special Events. The Spring Concert recitals by YMCA finalists (May, fee); Hol events including dance, concerts and sing-alongs; free Career Awareness Night (spring); Holiday Crafts Fair (early Dec); and a spirited Christmas songfest (1st Sun in Dec, fee).

The Bronx

BRONX COMMUNITY COLLEGE (CUNY)
W. 181st St. & University Ave.
☎ *(212) 220-6450.*
Perched overlooking the Hudson River, this 2-year city college's claim to fame is its Neoclassical landmark campus built by McKim, Mead & White around the turn of the century. The highlight is the Hall of Fame, a 600-foot-long semi-circular vaulted arcade with the busts of famous Americans housed under the handsome colonnades by Stanford White. The other landmark buildings include the Gould Memorial Library, the Hall of Languages and the Cornelius Baker Hall of Philosophy.
Events: *For information, 220-6312.*
Concerts. In Schwendler Aud, Club Hours on Thu from noon-2pm; and concerts in Gould Memorial Library Aud. & Hall of Fame Playhouse.
Exhibits. The Hall of Fame of Great Americans, Mon-Sun 10am-5pm (mainly year-round).
Special Events. The annual synchronized swim show in Alumni Gym; and the Health Fair (Apr) with free tests and seminars in Alumni Gym.
Theater. The Theater Workshop's 2 productions (Nov & Mar), for 3-5 days (fee); and the annual modern dance workshop (early May) in the Hall of Fame Playhouse.

COLLEGE OF MOUNT ST. VINCENT
263rd St. & Riverdale Ave.
☎ *(212) 249-8000.*
Undoubtedly one of the most beautiful college campuses in N.Y.C., this 70-acre wooded campus overlooking the Hudson River is a superb harmony of rolling green lawns, trees, flowers, ponds and several landmark buildings. Founded in 1847 by the Sisters of Charity of New York in what is now Central Park, the college moved out of Manhattan in 1857 upon purchasing the Fonthill Castle, the home of Edwin Forrest, the Shakespearean actor. By all means, visit the interior of the Castle, now used for administrative offices. Stressing interdisciplinary learning, this independent college has a strong liberal arts program.
Events
Art Shows. At the Library, 1-2 shows per semester of student and faculty works with an opening reception; call for hours.
Lectures. Sponsored mainly by the Humanities Department; lectures include authors and faculty.
Theater. The Mount St. Vincent Players' student performances (fall & spring, donation).

FORDHAM UNIVERSITY
Rose Hill Campus, Southern Blvd. & E. Fordham Rd., E. of Webster Ave.
☎ *(212) 579-2000.*
Established in 1841 by the Right Rev. John Hughes (N.Y.C.'s first Roman Catholic archbishop) and then headed by John McCloskey (the country's first cardinal), Fordham began as a Jesuit institution, al-

though today it's nonsectarian. With strengths in liberal arts, particularly English and philosophy, this private university encourages its students to be active in the community. The campus is absolutely lovely with its rolling green lawns, small gardens and splendid landmark buildings; it provided a perfect setting for the outdoor "Harvard" scenes in the film *Love Story.*

Places of Interest

Collins Hall. This Beaux-Arts classic with a 350-seat auditorium presents concerts and theater perrformances.

Keating Hall. A fine example of Gothic collegiate, it was built in 1936 by Robert J. Reiley. It features exhibits, concerts and lectures.

McGinley Center. The Student Union, it presents concerts and artworks.

Rose Hill Manor House. This 1838 merchant's house, now a landmark and the administration bldg., is an excellent example of Greek Revival architecture.

University Church. This 1845 landmark (transept, chancel and crossing added in 1929) was built in the Gothic Revival style by William Rodrigue, a teacher at the college. The vibrant stained-glass windows in the nave were a present of Louis Philippe in 1846. The tower bell is believed to have inspired Poe's "The Bells." Check out the impressive interior wooden bas-reliefs in the nave. Concerts are given here.

Events: *Consult "The Ram" or "The Paper." Many special events for Sesquicentennial year, Sep '90-Sep '91.*

Art Exhibits: Outdoor sculpture is dotted around the campus (brochure available, 841-5160); and the permanent collection is on view in McGinley Lobby, 2nd fl.

Concerts. The Bronx Arts Ensemble (artists-in-residence) presents 6 concerts a year with special ones at Christmas and Easter plus a summer series; there are also occasional faculty recitals and chorus concerts, 579-2339.

Films: "Cinevents" presents a classics series on Tue at 8pm and popular recent films on Thu at 8 & 10:30pm in Keating 1st Aud. (seats 400), 579-2339.

Lectures. The American Age Lecture Series (some at a fee) sponsors 3 to 5 lectures per semester with distinguished guest speakers on popular issues in the McGinley Center ballroom or the Gym; there is also an Annual Cervantes Lecture, 841-5616.

Special Events. The Fine Arts Commission, a student group, sponsors art exhibits, dance groups, jazz and chamber music; and the Annual Dean's Day (Apr).

Sports. Athletics include basketball (fee), baseball and soccer games, 579-2447.

Theater. "Mimes & Mummers," an old college drama society, puts on 4 to 5 plays a year at Collins Theater (seats 350), and the Fordham Experimental Theater, student-run in Keating Hall's Little Theater (75), features 3 to 5 productions a year, 579-2339.

HOSTOS COMMUNITY COLLEGE (CUNY)
500 Grand Concourse (149th St.).

☎ *(212) 960-1200.*

This community college for mainly Hispanic and Black students concentrates its efforts on the health sciences and computer studies. A strong Culture & Arts Program offers concerts and workshops for the community.

Events

Art Shows. At the Art Gallery (lobby), good professional and community exhibitions of Third World art with an emphasis on Hispanic, Mon-Fri 10am-7pm; and the Bronx Museum of Art shows (4 of the 9 yearly ones) with gallery talks, 960-1182.

Concerts. Performances including opera, jazz, symphony and classical music by professional groups, like the Bronx Arts Ensemble and graduates of N.Y. Juilliard Chamber Orchestra, 960-1111.

Films. Series of Black and Spanish movies with subtitles on Tue at 12:30pm & 7pm (3 per semester).

Theater. A wide variety of experienced theater groups, 960-1111.

Workshops. An excellent series in writing, drama and crafts for the community (auditions required for writing and drama; open on first-come basis for crafts, Sat from 10am-4pm, fee for materials) with presentations of works at semester end (spring & fall).

HERBERT H. LEHMAN COLLEGE (CUNY)

Goulden Ave. & Bedford Pk. Blvd.

☎ *(212) 960-8211.*

This is a large liberal arts college with popular programs in computers, health, business, music and art. With its blend of Gothic and modern (Marcel Breuer, as architect), the campus offers a hodgepodge of pleasing sites.

Places of Interest

Carman Hall, Speech & Theatre Bldg. Lectures and concerts.

Center for the Performing Arts, Goulden Ave. & Bedford Blvd., 960-8833. This 2,300-seat concert hall has an impressive cultural program of dance, opera, drama and music at a fee. A special subsidy provides some free tickets for Seniors and the disabled.

Events

Art Shows. At the Lehman College Art Gallery in the Fine Arts Bldg., professional, faculty and student shows.

Concerts. In the Theatre, occasional free concerts by the Bronx Symphony, the Bronx Ensemble, the Bronx Chamber Orchestra and the Aeolian Chamber Players (frequently on Sun at 3pm); the Lehman Pop Band's 6 outdoor concerts on Sun at 6pm (summer) in the courtyard near the Speech & Theatre Bldg.; in the Music Bldg.'s Recital Hall, 3rd fl., occasional chamber music or recitals by students or faculty at weekday noontime, 690-8247; and performances by the Children's Free Opera & Dance for school children (1 week, fall & spring), 460-6917.

Special Programs. The "City & the Humanities Program" on Fri at noon (Oct-May, except Hols and school breaks) in Carman Hall, room B-04, lectures, concerts, film or dance.

Theater. At the Speech & Theatre Bldg., occasional plays (some free) by the Drama Department

MANHATTAN COLLEGE
Manhattan College Pkwy., Riverdale.
☎ *(212) 920-0100.*

Despite its name, this small private college is situated very much in the Bronx, in the gorgeous Riverdale-Fieldston section on a handsome American Georgian campus. Founded in 1853 by the Christian Brothers, the first home was in Central Park (hence the name). One of the first ever to feature a peace studies major, this college still waves the flag strongly for engineering and business.

Events: *Consult the "Cultural Calendar" or call campus events, 920-0247.*

Art Shows. At the Rotunda of the Cardinal Hayes Library, commercial artists and student shows occasionally, Mon-Fri 8am-11pm, Sat 10am-9pm, Sun noon-9pm.

Concerts. The Annual Christmas Concert with the symphony orchestra and "Manhattan Singers" during the 1st week of Dec (Thu, Fri nights & Sun afternoon) in the Chapel of De LaSalle & His Brothers; and the Bronx Symphony performances.

Exhibits. At the Engineering Library, room 309, an amazing collection of historical vacuum tubes, undoubtedly the only one of its kind.

Films. An occasional festival; and the "Brotherhood of Visual Drama," student-run films (nominal charge) with "audience participation" about twice a month on Wed at 8pm.

Lectures. An impressive series in Smith Aud., the "Fischbach Lectures," 5 per year on engineering, environmental and societal issues; "Sigma Psi," 2 per year on natural science; "Aquinas," with a big-name speaker (Mar or Apr); "Mulhearn" on business, education or engineering (early Dec); "Olin," with CEO's (3 in spring); and lectures by the Ethics & Peace Studies Centers.

Sports. At Draddy Gym, men's & women's basketball (fee), 920-0227.

Theater. The "Manhattan College Players" student production every semester.

N.Y. MARITIME MUSEUM AND COLLEGE (SUNY)
Fort Schuyler, 10465.
☎ *(212) 409-7200.*
Hours: *Mon-Fri 9am-4pm (year round), Sat-Sun noon-4pm (Sep-May only).*

Begun in 1874 as the N.Y. Nautical School, this is the oldest maritime college in the U.S. and still trains young men and women for careers at sea or in the maritime trade. Jutting out into the Long Island Sound, this college offers excellent views of the Sound and the Throgs Neck Bridge, which passes over the campus. Its landmark Fort Schuyler, now a museum, provides exhibits on the history of the Maritime College, the Alumni Hall of Fame, the U.S. Merchant Marines, the government services of the U.S., and international maritime history. An Adult Education program offers courses for the public in navigation and seamanship, particularly the "Yachtsmen Series."

Brooklyn

BROOKLYN COLLEGE (CUNY)
Bedford Ave. & Ave. H.
☎ *(718) 780-5882.*
Large and academically very good, this city college has a strong Education Department with computer science gaining all the time. A marvelous Humanities Department sponsors excellent free lectures, concerts, workshops and performances at the Occidental and Oriental Lounges at the Student Center.

Places of Interest
Brooklyn Center for the Performing Arts, Nostrand Ave. & Ave. H. Free and inexpensive cultural events at Gershwin Theater, Walt Whitman Hall and New Theater Workshop, 780-5006.

Student Union, North Campus Rd. & E. 27th St., 780-5529.

Events
Concerts. The Composer's Forums with discussions of composers' works, accompanied by student or faculty performances (some free), 780-5286 or write to Conservatory of Music Concert Office, c/o BCBC, Box 163, Brooklyn, N.Y. 11210.

Dance. The Dance Department's workshops and lecture series and 12 student performances (fee) in Brooklyn Dance Theater, 780-5393.

Films. At Brooklyn Center, a mix of classics and sneak previews, 780-5295.

Lectures. An outstanding program presented by the Humanities Department in the Student Union on weekdays from 12:15-2pm (year-round), 780-5847.

Special Events. The "Country Fair" (May) with games, exhibits, international food and festivities.

Sports. Many sporting events on campus (basketball and football with fees), 780-5366.

Theater. The Theater Department's 4 Mainstage Productions a year (nominal fee) at the Performing Arts Center, 780-5666, and for brochure write: Mainstage Productions, P.O. Box 163, Brooklyn, N.Y. 11210.

BROOKLYN CONSERVATORY OF MUSIC
58 7th Ave.
☎ *(718) 622-3300.*
Offering a smorgasbord of classes in music, this Conservatory has something for people of all ages. You can call for their schedule of frequent concerts by students and faculty (donation).

KINGSBOROUGH COMMUNITY COLLEGE (CUNY)
2001 Oriental Blvd.
☎ *(718) 368-5000.*
As the only New York college with its own private beach, this 53-acre campus is like a country club. Modern beige brick buildings are attractively scattered among the green lawns, trees and outdoor sculpture. A walk along the Atlantic Ocean is a sheer joy in warm weather.

In fact, the ocean is a great backdrop for the school's special curriculum in travel and tourism; the school is also known for its communications and management degrees. This campus was built in 1968 on the site of a WWII naval training station.

A special tuition-free Seniors' program called "My Turn" enables those over 65 to participate with younger students in classes and extracurricular activities (this is the only college in the state offering such a program).

Events

Art Shows. At the Art Gallery in the Arts & Science Bldg., professional shows of painting, sculpture, photography and allied fields on contemporary art themes as well as works by the faculty and students, Mon-Thu 9am-4pm, Fri 9am-1pm, 568-5718; occasional shows in the Sculpture Courtyard adjacent to the Gallery; and sculpture in the lobby of the Performing Arts Center.

Lectures. At College Center, 368-5528.

Performances. The Kingsborough Orchestra & Band, the Singing Society & Chorus and the Dance Club performances at the Performing Arts Center (reasonably priced), 368-5528; and at Rainbow Mall, Oriental Blvd., and free Summer Music Festivals on Sat eve (Jun-Jul), 368-5669.

Special Events. "My Turn" Seniors' tuition-free courses (registration fee only), 368-5079; KIPS (public service program) free Annual Health Fair; programs for Seniors and the community, guide books for Seniors and seminars on taxes, 368-5125.

LONG ISLAND UNIVERSITY
Brooklyn Campus, University Plaza, DeKalb & Flatbush Aves.
☎ *(718) 834-6000.*

In the heart of downtown Brooklyn just over the Manhattan Bridge, this 22-acre campus offers a broad liberal arts curriculum as well as business and public administration and health science (including pharmacy) degrees for undergraduates and graduates.

Events

Art Shows. At the Salena Gallery (Salena Library/Learning Center, ground fl.), Resnick Showcase Gallery (Library Learning Center, 3rd fl.) and Paramount Gallery (Metcalfe Bldg., 1st fl.), professional and student works, Mon-Fri 9am-5pm (all galleries), 403-1051.

Concerts. At the Triangle Theatre (Salena Library), the "Jazz Plus Program" on Tue 4-6pm (once a month), performances by jazz instrumentalists and lectures; and at the Athletic Center (the former Brooklyn Paramount), the "Mighty Wurlitzer" organ concerts about 4 times per year, 403-1015.

Lectures. The annual American Literature Lecture series (Feb), 403-1050; and lectures and workshops by different departments.

Special Events. The Honors Program's exhibits from the Smithsonian (twice a year) and lectures on global topics, 403-1006.

N.Y.C. TECHNICAL COLLEGE (CUNY)
300 Jay St. (near Borough Hall).

☎ *(718) 260-5000.*

This N.Y.C. technical college emphasizes a "relevant and employment-oriented career program" for technicians and semi-professionals in business, industry, the professions and government.

Events: *Call for monthly calendar, 260-5195, or visit Info Center in the main lobby.*

Art Shows. At the Grace Gallery, 11th fl., monthly professional and student shows, Mon-Fri 10am-5pm, 260-5176; and yearly sculpture shows in the Quad between 300 Jay & 300 Pearl Sts.

Clinics. Free dental hygiene for adults and children; and ophthalmic dispensing services at moderate cost, by appt. only.

Concerts. Occasional free faculty recitals.

Courses. Occasional free courses open to the community.

Exhibits. At the library, shows featuring arts & crafts, theater memorabilia, photos or books, Mon-Thu 9am-8pm, Fri 9am-5pm, Sat 10am-2pm, 260-5500.

Lectures. The "Presidential Lecture Series" twice a year.

Sports. For team sports viewing, 260-5102.

Theater. At Klit Gord Aud., 285 Jay St., "TheatreWorks" dramatic performances (fall) and a musical (spring), 260-5366.

POLYTECHNIC UNIVERSITY

333 Jay St. (Tillary St., foot of Brooklyn Bridge).

☎ *(718) 260-3600.*

This technical university specializes in engineering, the sciences, management and humanities.

Events: *Forums, seminars, workshops and colloquia in telecommunications, info systems, imaging science, management and engineering.*

PRATT INSTITUTE

200 Willoughby Ave. (DeKalb Ave. & Hall St.).

☎ *(718) 636-3600/3746/3416.*

With a major emphasis on art and design, this Institute also has a strong communications design program (ranking 5th in the nation) as well as an impressive architecture program.

Events: *call for "Gateway" calendar, 636-3635.*

Art Shows. At the Rubelle & Norman Schafler Art Gallery (Chemistry Bldg., 1st fl.), 9 professional, student, faculty and alumni shows a year, Mon-Fri 9am-5pm, 636-3517.

Lectures. At Higgins Hall, the Multi-Media Center, Lafayette Ave. & St. James Pl., the "Visiting Lecture Series" featuring architects, artists and professors on occasional Thu at 6:30pm (sometimes on Mon), 636-3491; occasional lectures by film critics, poets and authors; and the "Art Values Series" of art critics and gallery directors (spring).

Queens

LA GUARDIA COMMUNITY COLLEGE
29-10 Thomson St., Building 3.
☎ *(718) 482-7200.*
Hours: Mon-Fri 10am-4:30pm. For archives, by appt. only.

This 2-year community college has a strong English-as-a-second-language program for its immigrant population as well as vocational training. It has archives featuring records, papers and photos on local history, Fiorello La Guardia, Robert F. Wagner, Steinway pianos and the N.Y. Housing Authority.

QUEENS COLLEGE (CUNY)
65-30 Kissena Blvd. (off L.I.E. at exit 24), Flushing.
☎ *(718) 997-5000.*

Opened in 1937, this city college with its ethnically mixed student body offers degrees in the sciences and liberal arts with excellent music and theater departments.

Places of Interest: Map of campus located at Main Gate.

Colden Center for the Performing Arts, L.I.E. & Kissena Blvd. Free public forums and lectures as well as concerts, dance performances, plays and touring companies (usually fee), 520-7200.

Queens College Theater, at Colden Center for the Performing Arts. Occasional concerts, 793-8080.

Rathaus Recital Hall, behind main gate. Chamber music, opera and ensembles.

Student Union, Kissena Blvd. & Melbourne. Library, lectures, readings, films and videos, Mon-Thu at 12:30-1:30pm (most are free).

Events: *For campus activities, 997-5411.*

Art Shows. At Benjamin Rosenthal Library (6th fl.), Queens College Art Center with monthly exhibits of local artists or faculty, Mon-Thu 9am-9pm, Fri 9am-5pm, Sat-Sun noon-5pm, 997-3770; at Godwin-Ternbach Museum, a general art museum of over 2,000 works in all media from ancient times to the present (currently undergoing construction, reopening in fall 1991 or call for appt., 520-7129); at Kiely Hall, Room 285, occasional shows by the Art Department's faculty and students.

Concerts. At Colden Center for the Performing Arts, occasional free performances by the Queens Symphony or Queens College Wind Ensemble; by the Aaron Copland School of Music, concerts at Rathaus Hall on weekdays and some weekends (frequently at 12:30pm), featuring artists, faculty and music students; and concerts at the Student Union and Queens College Theater.

Exhibits. At the Benjamin Rosenthal Library, main floor, book exhibits, 997-3707.

Lectures & Readings. At the Student Union, the English Department's readings of novels and poetry, book discussions and lectures by authors and critics on weekdays at 7pm.

Sports. The Athletic Department's sporting events (some free).

QUEENSBOROUGH COMMUNITY COLLEGE (CUNY)
56th Ave. & Springfield Blvd., Bayside.
☎ *(718) 631-6262.*

Situated in part on a former golf course, this community college's modern campus offers a picturesque setting par excellence.

Events: *Map of campus in main courtyard.*

Art Shows. At the gallery in the lobby of Oakland Bldg. (the old clubhouse on top of the hill), 3 shows per semester featuring student, community and professional works, Mon-Thu 11am-3pm (with a 1-week break), 631-6396.

Concerts. An impressive Performing Arts Program of performances (some free) by the QCC 90-piece symphonic band or the 60-member chorus, 631-6321; and the Fine & Performing Arts Department's free "Club Hour" on Wed from noon-2pm, 631-6393.

Lecture. The Continuing Education Department's community forums about 4 times a year on literary or current issues, 631-6343.

ST. JOHN'S UNIVERSITY
Grand Central & Utopia Pkwys., Jamaica.
☎ *(718) 990-6161.*

This Catholic commuter college specializes in computer science, communication and criminal justice.

Events

Art Shows. The Chung-Cheng Gallery ♣ of the Institute of Asian Studies (see "For the Artists"), 990-6581.

Lectures. By various departments.

TRUMP VILLAGE CAMERA CLUB
2928 W. 5th St.
☎ *(718) 266-6120.*

Free workshops on slide mounting, cropping and touch-ups are held on some Mon at 8pm.

YORK COLLEGE (CUNY)
94-20 Guy R. Brewer Blvd., Jamaica.
☎ *(718) 262-2000.*

This small liberal arts senior college moved to its new 50-acre campus in 1986; architects Gruzon & Partners designed the pleasing Academic Core with its 5-story atrium with skylights and balconies, and a spacious outdoor plaza. Its curriculum is strong in computers and business as well as in gerontology (aging); 50% of its student body is over 28 years old. Its successful grammar hotline R-E-W-R-I-T-E has received national acclaim.

Events: *Call for monthly calendar, 262-2062.*

Art Shows. At the York Art Gallery (Academic Core, 1st fl.), one-person shows by nationally known or local artists working in all media and all styles.

Concerts. Free concerts (Nov, Dec, Apr & May) by in-residence groups (York College Jazz Workshop, Chorus and Electric Guitar Ensemble); annual free concert in honor of Duke Ellington month (last Fri in Apr or 1st Fri in May) with big-name star; and other concerts at the Performing Arts Center.

Exhibits. At the Library (Academic Core, 3rd fl.), shows featuring books, art and memorabilia; and music history archives by Black American Heritage Foundation-York College.

Lectures. Faculty forum lecture (1 per month, 2nd Mon at 3pm), and a variety of others.

Special Services. Dial R-E-W-R-I-T-E for a grammar hotline (depends on funding); at the York College Health Promotion Center, info on healthy lifestyles and testing for cholesterol, etc., by appt., 262-5205; and the York College Small Business Development Center, for small and minority businesses in Queens, 262-2880.

Sports. Team games at the Health & Physical Education Complex.

Theater. Several free productions.

Staten Island

COLLEGE OF STATEN ISLAND (CUNY)
130 Stuyvesant Pl., St. George.
715 Ocean Terr., Sunnyside.
☎ *(718) 390-7733.*

Formed in 1976 by joining together the borough's 2-year and 4-year schools, this liberal arts and science college still has 2 campuses and continues its 2 separate programs.

Events: Call for possible calendar.

Art Shows. At either St. George campus (6th or 9th fl.) or Sunnyside Art Gallery.

Concerts. At the College Hall (seats 150) at St. George, occasional concerts by students, alumni or visiting artists.

Lectures. Spring & fall symposia with guest speakers.

Special Events. The Int'l Festival (Sep, fee) with entertainment and food.

Sports. Varsity basketball, baseball and soccer games at Sunnyside Gym "D," 390-7607.

Theater. Off-Broadway productions (free or nominal fee) at Williamson Theater (seats 912), Sunnyside campus, 390-7658.

WAGNER COLLEGE
631 Howard Ave., Grymes Hill.
☎ *(718) 390-3100.*

This private liberal arts college is known for its excellent speech and theater departments, although business and nursing degrees are popular. Situated on Grymes Hill (lined with elegant 19th C. mansions), its 86-acre wooded campus has a commanding view of the N.Y.C. harbor, skyline and Verrazano Narrows Bridge (in fact, it is on one of the highest points on the eastern seaboard).

Events

Art Shows. At Kade Gallery in College Union, monthly art exhibitions of professional artists (especially local ones), Tue-Sat 11am-4pm.

Concerts. Occasional student, faculty and guest performers in North Hall, Sutter Hall, the music annex or the new administration building.

Theater. Student performances (fee) in Main Hall Theater, 390-3259.

For the Bookworms

You don't have to be a bookworm to partake in library activities. Our public and private libraries offer some of the most far-reaching and diverse free events for everyone.

> *"Some books are to be tasted; others swallowed; and few to be chewed and digested."*
>
> Francis Bacon

AMERICAN BIBLE SOCIETY
1865 Broadway (at 61st St.).
☎ *(212) 581-7400.*
Hours: *Mon-Fri 9:30am-4:30pm.*

This nonprofit multi-denominational organization has been dedicated to spreading the "word of God" since 1816. Each year the Society publishes, translates and distributes scriptures without doctrinal note or comment. The library has one of the largest collections of reference books and rare, old and new Bibles. Currently the tally is 35,000 Bibles or portions (23 pre-1500 ones), 1,600 translations, 5,000 reference books and periodicals.

AMERICAN IRISH HISTORICAL SOCIETY
991 5th Ave. (at 80th St.).
☎ *(212) 288-2263.*
Hours: *By appt. only Tue-Sat 10:30am-4:30pm (Sat until 4pm).*

This is considered to be the largest collection of Irish and Irish-American history, culture and biography in the U.S. with over 20,000 volumes (1,000 rare books and special editions) and Irish-American newspapers from 1811. The archives and manuscripts include documents and papers of various Irish clubs and religious groups. The splendid 5th Avenue townhouse provides a fine backdrop for the changing exhibits.

AMERICAN KENNEL CLUB FOUNDATION
51 Madison Ave. (26th-27th Aves.).
☎ *(212) 696-8246.*
Hours: *Mon-Fri 8:30-4:15pm.*

This reference library contains 15,000 books, magazines, stamps and pictures exclusively on dogs in English and many foreign languages. Rare, out-of-print editions can be found here. By the way, the foundation will send you free brochures on dogs if you ask them.

AMERICAN MUSEUM OF NATURAL HISTORY LIBRARY
Central Pk. W. at 79th St.
☎ *(212) 769-5400.*
Hours: *Mon-Fri 11am-4pm (Wed til 7:30pm), Sat 10am-3pm (school year). (See "For the Culture Vultures" for details on the Museum.)*

This reference library containing over 385,000 volumes is considered the most valuable resource on natural history in the U.S.

AMERICAN NUMISMATIC SOCIETY
Audubon Terr., Broadway at 155th St.
☎ *(212) 234-3130.*
Hours: *Tue-Sat 9am-4:30pm. (See "For the Culture Vultures" for details on the Museum.)*

This library contains over 70,000 items including books, periodicals, manuscripts and pamphlets on coins and metals. There is also a reference section on non-numismatic subjects such as archaeology, art, history and economics. Reference service is available through the mail and over the phone.

ARCHIVES OF THE COUNTY CLERK & CLERK OF THE SUPREME COURT OF NEW YORK
31 Chambers St., 7th fl., Room 703.
☎ *(212) 374-4376.*
Hours: *Tue & Thu 9am-5pm, researchers on Mon, Wed & Fri by appt.*
   These archives contain records of almost every important N.Y. State court in N.Y. County from colonial to present times. It also houses legal documents of Alexander Hamilton, Aaron Burr, the Roosevelts, Martin Van Buren and John Jay. In addition, you can find immigration and naturalization papers, census data and certificates of incorporation. The wealth of information usually gives rise to an exhibit in the impressive rotunda for all to enjoy.

THE ATLANTIC COMPANIES MARINE LIBRARY
45 Wall St., 10th fl.
☎ *(212) 943-1800.*
Hours: *Mon-Fri 8:30am-4:30pm. By appt. only.*
   This library contains 400 volumes of records on marine subjects, especially vessel disasters between 1857 and 1932; newspaper articles were collected at the time to see if their insured ships were involved. A glass-enclosed display case reveals memorabilia (see "For the Exhibitionists" on the *Mary Celeste*). This is a quiet and cozy spot for contemplating adventures on the high seas.

AUSTRIAN INSTITUTE
(See "For the Society-Goers.")

LEO BAECK INSTITUTE
(See "For the Society-Goers.")

CENTER FOR CUBAN STUDIES
(See "For the Society-Goers.")

CENTER FOR THE STUDY OF THE PRESIDENCY
208 E. 75th St. (2nd-3rd Aves.).
☎ *(212) 249-1200.*
Hours: *By appt. only.*
   The first center dedicated to the study of government, especially the quality of past and present leadership, this library of over 3,000 books elects to specialize in American Presidents and public policy. The center also sponsors lectures at Fordham University, Lincoln Center.

COOPER-HEWITT MUSEUM LIBRARY
(See "For the Culture Vultures.")

DONNELL LIBRARY CENTER (NYPL)
20 W. 53rd St. (5th-6th Aves.).
☎ *(212) 621-0618/0619.*
Hours: *Mon, Tue & Thu 9:30am-8pm, Wed & Fri 9:30am-6pm, Sat*

9:30am-5:30pm and Sun 1-5pm (Adult Section). See "For the Kiddies."
A part of the Central Library Services of N.Y.P.L., this branch specializes in foreign languages, film and video, records and over 100,000 books for children and young adults. The film/video center is equipped with free viewing and audio facilities; it also has the largest collection of circulating films, videos and audiorecordings. The library sponsors exhibitions, like the Annual Glass Month juried competition (Nov).

Events: Concerts on most Mon at 2:30pm; poetry, prose, readings or lectures on occasional Mon at 6pm and/or Tue at 6pm (Sep-May); feature films on Tue & Thu at noon (Oct-Jun); "Collector's Choice" film series on Tue at 2:30pm (Oct-Jun); films for pre-schoolers on Thu at 2:30pm (Oct-Jun); the entertaining and enjoyable "Jazzmen" on Wed at 12:30pm (Sep-Jun); "Meet the Videomaker/Filmmaker" series on some Thu at 6pm; book discussion series (advance registration) on occasional Thu at 6:30pm; stage directors' and choreographers' showcases on occasional Sat at 2:30pm; and concerts, films or performances on some Sun at 2:30pm (Sep-May).

EARLY CHILDHOOD RESOURCE AND INFO CENTER (NYPL)
66 Leroy St. (off 7th Ave. S.), 2nd fl.
☎ *(212) 929-0815.*
Hours: Tue-Fri 1-5:45pm (Thu till 7:45pm), Sat noon-4:45pm and see "For the Kiddies."

Specializing in preschoolers, this Center offers an indoor playground with hobby horses and learning aids galore, while adults can avail themselves of the library facilities on child rearing and the scheduled activities.

Events (For calendar, send a self-addressed, stamped business envelope to ECRIC, 66 Leroy St., N.Y., N.Y. 10014): Films on Sat at 3pm for preschoolers; and a weekday program for adults on early child development.

HENRY GEORGE SCHOOL
(See "For the Knowledge Seekers.")

THE GROLIER CLUB
(See "For the Exhibitionists.")

HAVEN EMERSON PUBLIC HEALTH LIBRARY
455 1st Ave. (at 26th St.).
☎ *(212) 340-4700.*

This library provides information on health sciences for professional people.

THE HISPANIC SOCIETY OF AMERICA
(See "For the Culture Vultures.")

THE HORTICULTURAL SOCIETY OF NEW YORK
(See "For the Birds.")

For the Bookworms

THE INFORMATION EXCHANGE (TIE)
Urban Center, 457 Madison Ave. (50th-51st Sts.), 2nd fl.
☎ *(212) 935-3960.*
Hours: *Mon-Fri 11am-1pm, call for appt.*

TIE, the reference and research arm of the Municipal Art Society, provides information on the environmental arts, urban life in general and New York City in particular. It has over 4,000 books, 160 periodicals and 5,000 files on everything from cultural organizations and government agencies to N.Y.C. parks, buildings and landmark issues. The referral service can guide you to experts in a wide range of environmental and historical fields.

JEFFERSON MARKET LIBRARY

INTERNATIONAL CENTER OF PHOTOGRAPHY LIBRARY (ICP)
(See "For the Culture Vultures.")

ITALIAN CULTURAL INSTITUTE LIBRARY
(See "For the Society-Goers.")

JAPAN SOCIETY LIBRARY
(See "For the Society-Goers.")

JEFFERSON MARKET LIBRARY (NYPL)
425 6th Ave. (at 10th St.).
☎ *(212) 243-4334.*
Hours: *Mon & Sat 10am-6pm, Tue & Thu noon-6pm and Wed noon-8pm, closed Fri.*

This striking red-brick library built by Calvert Vaux (of Central Park fame) and Frederick Clark Withers is a superb example of Victorian Gothic design. Originally it served as a courthouse and the clocktower was the fire lookout. Visit the inside to see some wonderful stained-glass windows. For those with green thumbs, an outside garden can be tended on Sat & Sun during the nice weather.

KOREAN CULTURAL SERVICE LIBRARY
(See "For the Society-Goers.")

MECHANICS INSTITUTE LIBRARY
20 W. 44th St. (5th-6th Aves.).
☎ *(718) 921-1767.*
Hours: *Mon-Thu 9am-7pm (9am-6pm Apr-Aug), Fri 9am-5pm.*

Founded in 1820 and now the 3rd oldest library in N.Y.C., this library has about 140,000 volumes with the main emphasis on nonfiction and out-of-print mystery books.

MERCANTILE LIBRARY
17 E. 47th St. (Madison & 5th Aves.).
☎ *(212) 755-6710.*

Founded in 1820 (a few days earlier than the Mechanics Institute Library), this is the 2nd oldest library in New York and offers refuge to its members only (though lectures are open to the public; call for calendar).

MID-MANHATTAN LIBRARY (NYPL)
455 5th Ave. (40th St.).
☎ *(212) 340-0833.*
Hours: *Mon & Wed 9am-9pm, Tue 11am-7pm, Thu 11am-9pm, Fri-Sat 10am-6pm. Closed Sun & Hol.*
Tours: *Mon, Wed & Fri 2:30pm, 340-0934.*

With 800,000 volumes on art, business, education, history, social studies, literature and science, this is the largest circulating library in the New York Public Library branch system.

J. PIERPONT MORGAN LIBRARY
(See "For the Culture Vultures.")

MUNICIPAL ARCHIVES
N.Y. Surrogate's Court, 31 Chambers St., Room 103.
☎ *(212) 566-5292.*
Hours: *Mon-Fri 9am-4:30pm.*

This government archive contains records of the Mayors' and City Clerks' papers dating back to 1670. Its genealogy collection houses official births, deaths and marriage records dating back to the 19th C. Also available are the Brooklyn Bridge drawings collection, the building records collection and the manuscripts and photos of the N.Y.C. unit from the WPA Federal Writers' Project. All in all, the Archives offers researchers more than 75,000 cubic feet of invaluable N.Y.C. governmental records.

MUNICIPAL REFERENCE AND RESEARCH CENTER
N.Y. Surrogate's Court, 31 Chambers St., Room 112.
☎ *(212) 566-4284.*
Hours: *Mon-Fri 9am-5pm.*

This reference library is the recipient of all official reports and papers published by N.Y.C. government agencies. Besides more than 250,000 reports, books, etc., the center provides old civil service exams (1976 and older), job descriptions, eligibility lists and salary scales for all N.Y.C. positions; biographies and lists of N.Y.C. and state officials and employees; annotated N.Y.C. street name index and neighborhood files; and regulations on N.Y.C. agencies.

THE NEW YORK ACADEMY OF MEDICINE
2 E. 103rd St. (off 5th Ave.).
☎ *(212) 876-8200.*
Hours: *Mon noon-5pm, Tue-Sat 9am-5pm. Closed Sat in summer.*

Founded in 1847 as a private organization to provide a medical research library, today the Academy has about 500,000 books, over 400,000 pamphlets and illustrations, foreign-language textbooks and reference books.
Events: *Occasional exhibits of a medical nature and lectures.*

THE NEW YORK GENEALOGICAL AND BIOGRAPHICAL SOCIETY
122 E. 58th St. (Park & Lexington Aves.).
☎ *(212) 755-8532.*
Hours: *Mon-Sat 9:30am-5pm. Closed on Sat in Jun-Jul, all Aug-Sep and on Hols.*
Suggested donation: *$3.*

If you want to learn about your roots, this is the place to come to do the digging. Founded in 1869, the Society has built its library collection to over 63,000 volumes on genealogy, local history and biography. The reading room itself is a splendid, wood-panelled mecca in the heart of Bloomingdale's country. A small portrait gallery offers many well-known faces, such as FDR, his cousin Teddy, Henry Clay, Washington Irving and Calvin Coolidge.

THE NEW-YORK HISTORICAL SOCIETY LIBRARY
(See "For the Culture Vultures.")
In addition to the Society's superb art shows, historical exhibits and the Jewish Museum, the library contains 600,000 volumes, primarily on American history. Manuscripts, pamphlets and prints are available, including letters of George Washington and the best collection of 18th C. newspapers, genealogical material and local history of each state.

NEW YORK PUBLIC LIBRARY
☎ *(212) 661-7220 (Research), 621-0626/0618 (Branches), 870-1600 (Info). Telephone Reference Service, 340-0849: Answers to questions that can be researched in less than 3 minutes, Mon-Fri 9am-6pm, Sat 10am-6pm.*
The New York Public Library System has 82 branch libraries serving Manhattan, the Bronx and Staten Island with an amazing number of free events and activities for all ages. Pick up a monthly calendar in any library.

THE NEW YORK PUBLIC LIBRARY, 42ND STREET CENTRAL RESEARCH
LIBRARY ♦ ♦ ♦
5th Ave. between 40th & 42nd Sts.
☎ *(212) 661-7220, 869-8089 (Events), 930-0501 (Tours).*
Hours: *Mon-Wed 11am-7:30pm, Thu-Sat 10am-6pm. Hours may vary for special collections.*
Groups: *By appt. only.*
Tours: *Mon-Sat at 11am & 2pm.*
Let Patience and Fortitude, the marble lions, greet the intrepid visitor to this impressive Beaux-Arts landmark and research library, designed by Carrère & Hastings in 1911 to house the Astor, Lenox & Tilden collections. The library's sheer size is staggering, as are its literary offerings. What with 5 million volumes and 11 million manuscripts and periodicals, it's not surprising that the library can brag about its stacks containing 100 miles of books, making this one of the 5 largest research libraries in the world. Its famous books and manuscripts include a Gutenberg Bible, Washington's Farewell Address, Thomas Jefferson's Declaration of Independence and Shakespeare's first folios.

An excursion around the rooms is really a must, either on your own or with the guided tour (see "For the Tourists"). Highlights of this architectural masterpiece are Astor Hall, the impressive classical lobby flanked by marble staircases; Gottesman Exhibition Hall, always offering an interesting literary exhibition of books, prints, photographs and manuscripts; the Map Room (1st fl.) with its carved wooden ceiling; the Periodicals Room (1st fl.) with its fabulous ceiling and paintings by Richard Haas; the 2nd-floor balcony overlooking Astor Hall with an exhibition on the history of the building; the Berg Exhibition Room (3rd fl.) with changing exhibitions of rare books, lithographs, pictures or

manuscripts and the Lenox art collection with many historic paintings, particularly by Gilbert Stuart; and, of course, the 2-block-long main reading room on the 3rd floor with decorative high ceilings, arched windows and antique oak tables. There is so much to see here that you don't have to be a bookworm to enjoy it.

Events: *Occasional readings or lectures on weekdays at 6pm (fee), reservations at 930-0855; and outdoor entertainment at Bryant Park (see "For the Birds").*

NEW YORK PUBLIC LIBRARY FOR THE PERFORMING ARTS 🍎🍎
Lincoln Center, 111 Amsterdam Ave. (at 65th St.). Children's section is moving Sep '91.
☎ *(212) 870-1600/1630.*
Hours: *Mon & Thu noon-7:45pm, Wed & Fri noon-5:45pm, Sat 10am-5:45pm. Closed Tue. Summer hours may vary.*
Tours: *Wed at 2pm, 870-1670.*

Sheltered between the Metropolitan Opera House and the Vivian Beaumont Theater at Lincoln Center, this research and circulating library, dedicated to the performing arts, is deceptively large and quite a find. The 1st and 2nd floors house the circulating library, complete with records and scores along with record players and earphones for your listening pleasure. A children's section (ages 7-13) on the 2nd floor hosts oodles of entertaining books, wall exhibits and a small performance room (occasional Sat at 2:30pm show in Heckscher Oval room, reservation required, 870-1633).

Moving to the 3rd floor, you will discover the Performing Arts Research Center complete with books and periodicals for each of the performing arts. The Billy Rose Theatre Collection has a fantastic archival collection of stage set designs, playbills and manuscripts. Highlights of the Music Division are the original sheet music and notebooks of Beethoven, Brahms and Sousa. The Rodgers & Hammerstein Archives of Recorded Sound offer 500,000 records, now on tape, to which you can listen. The Dance Collection presents an incredible range of rare books, manuscripts, autograph letters, ballet scores, librettos, old programs, playbills, prints and photos. Viewing of dance videotapes is available. Photos and prints of dancers adorn the walls.

Changing exhibitions on the performing arts score high marks in 4 galleries: the Vincent Astor features the library's own collection of prints, photos, costumes, music scores and memorabilia; the Main Gallery on the 2nd floor; and the Plaza and Amsterdam Galleries, both with outside shows. And what would a performing arts library be without live performance?
Events: *Performances of dance, theater or music on most Mon-Fri at 4pm and Sat at 2:30pm (Sep-May) in the Bruno Walter Aud. on the ground floor.*

NEW YORK SOCIETY LIBRARY
53 E. 79th St. (Madison & Park Aves.).
☎ *(212) 288-6900.*
Hours: *Mon 1-5pm, Tue & Thu 9am-7pm, Wed & Fri-Sat 9am-5pm. Closed Sun & Hols and Sat from mid May-mid Sep.*

New York's oldest library was begun as a subscription membership library in 1754. Housed in an attractive 1917 Beaux-Arts Italian palazzo by Trowbridge & Livingston, the Society has 195,000 books on English and American literature, biography, art, history, travel and exploration, books on N.Y.C. as well as rare 19th C. journals, the Hammond collection of fiction from 1750-1830 and the Governor John Winthrop library on chemistry and alchemy. As this is still a membership library, nonmembers are allowed only in the main reading room.

THE PLAYERS CLUB LIBRARY
(See "For the Tourists.")

POETRY SOCIETY OF AMERICA LIBRARY
(See "For the Poets.")

SCHOMBURG CENTER FOR RESEARCH IN BLACK CULTURE (NYPL)
515 Lenox Ave. (at 135th St.).
☎ *(212) 491-2200.*
Hours: *Mon-Wed noon-8pm, Fri-Sat 10am-6pm. Closed Thu. Summer hours may vary.*

One of the world's most important centers on Black culture, this library contains books, periodicals, magazines, photos and personal papers by and about Blacks with a large collection on Caribbean history and culture. The Schomburg also possesses 5,000 hours of historical recordings from interviews and radio programs, 600 TV films and videotapes and 10,000 records from all over.

On the ground floor there's an impressive octagonal main reading room inspired by African "round houses" with listening room facilities off to the right. The 2nd floor has special collections of rare books. The 3rd floor houses a gallery with changing exhibitions of the museum's paintings, sculpture, photographs and other objets d'art. Outside are a sculpture garden and amphitheater.
Events: *Occasional lectures, concerts and recitals.*

SOCIETY OF ILLUSTRATORS LIBRARY
(See Museum of American Illustration under "For the Culture Vultures.")

THE SPANISH INSTITUTE LIBRARY
(See "For the Society-Goers.")

YIVO INSTITUTE FOR JEWISH RESEARCH
(See "For the Society-Goers.")

The Bronx

BRONX COUNTY HISTORICAL SOCIETY
3309 Bainbridge Ave. (at 208th St.).
☎ *(212) 881-8900.*
Hours: *Mon-Fri 9am-5pm, by appt. only.*

Specializing in Bronx history, this research library offers the largest repository of information with an interesting collection of 19th C. postcards and photographic archives. Unique historical recordings of interviews with prominent Bronx business and political leaders reveal hours of tapes to the undaunted listener (as well as manuscripts). A special tour and lecture bureau (fee) makes available top speakers on the Bronx.

NATIONAL MUSEUM OF THE AMERICAN INDIAN LIBRARY
9 Westchester Sq.
☎ *(212) 829-7770.*
Hours: *By appt. only.*
(See "For the Culture Vultures" under Manhattan for museum entry.)

A reference library containing 40,000 items on archaeology, history and culture of North, Central and South American natives.

NEW YORK BOTANICAL GARDEN LIBRARY
Hours: *Mon-Thu 11am-6pm, Fri-Sat 11am-4pm (Sep-Jun), Mon-Fri 11am-4pm (Jul-Aug).*
(For the Harriet Barnes Pratt reference library, see "For the Birds.")

NEW YORK PUBLIC LIBRARY SYSTEM, BRONX DIVISION
Fordham Library, 2556 Bainbridge Rd. (off Fordham Ave.), 2nd fl.
☎ *(212) 220-6565.*

Pick up calendar of events here for all libraries in the NYPL system.

Brooklyn

BROOKLYN BOTANIC GARDENS
(See "For the Birds.")

BROOKLYN CENTRAL PUBLIC LIBRARY SYSTEM
Grand Army Plaza.
☎ *(718) 780-7700/7722/7781 and public service support, 780-7779. Homework Hotline: 780-7766.*

The Brooklyn Public Library System with its 60 branch libraries is separate from the NYPL. It offers a full complement of events throughout the borough; check the monthly calendar of events and the SAGE for Seniors.

The Central Library, housed in a grand 1941 building, is a circulating library with over 1 million books and periodicals. Changing art exhibitions line the balcony.
Events: *Pick up calendar of events.*

BROOKLYN HISTORICAL SOCIETY
(See "For the Culture Vultures.")

BROOKLYN MUSEUM ART LIBRARY
Hours: Wed-Fri 1:30-5pm.
(See "For the Culture Vultures.")

The Art Library on the 2nd floor contains over 100,000 volumes on decorative arts, painting, sculpture and prints. The Wilbour Library of Egyptology on the 3rd floor offers books, periodicals and exhibition catalogs on ancient Egypt and world history.

Queens

LANGSTON HUGHES COMMUNITY LIBRARY & CUL-TURAL CENTER
102-09 Northern Blvd., Corona.
☎ *(718) 651-1100.*
Hours: *Mon-Tue & Thu 10am-6pm, Wed & Fri 1-8pm, Sat 10am-5pm.*

Founded in 1969 to furnish the primarily Afro-American population of Corona-E. Elmhurst with reading material, services and functions, this library provides law and career-training books, basic education study material, juvenile picture books, film strips and film storytelling. The information and referral unit has "survival" info on social and health services, benefits, grants, college brochures, senior citizen data and adult courses. The Black Heritage center services all of Queens with one of the largest and best libraries, workshops, lectures, films, festivals and exhibitions (monthly art shows on the 2nd fl.).
Events: *Homework assistance program for grades 3-7 on Mon-Fri from 3-6pm; and workshops and occasional performances of drama, dance, photography and creative writing.*

QUEENS BOROUGH CENTRAL PUBLIC LIBRARY
89-11 Merrick Blvd., Jamaica.
☎ *(212) 990-0700. Telephone Reference, 990-0714/0781/0728: For facts by phone, Mon-Fri 10am-8:45pm, Sat 10am-5:15pm (mid Sep-May).*
Hours: *Mon-Fri 10am-9pm, Sat 10am-5:30pm, Sun noon-5pm. Closed Sun in Jun-Aug & on legal Hols.*

With 62 branch libraries, Queens has an autonomous public library system. Call for listing of the various library locations and the monthly events.
Events: *At this library, movies for Seniors on Mon at 1:30pm and feature films on Sun at 1pm. Call for listing of events at other locations.*

QUEENS HISTORICAL SOCIETY
(See Kingsland House under "For the Culture Vultures.")

Staten Island

NEW YORK PUBLIC LIBRARY SYSTEM, STATEN ISLAND DIVISION
St. George Library Center, 5 Central Ave., St. George.
☎ *(718) 442-8611/8562.*

Pick up calendar of events here for all libraries in the NYPL system.

For the Listeners

In the hustle and bustle of this city, it can sometimes be quite relaxing (and informative) to spend an hour or so listening to an interesting lecture, gallery talk or forum. And of course, the learning potential is enormous as N.Y.C. has such a wealth of museums, cultural centers, universities and libraries.

> *"Know how to listen and you will profit even from those who talk badly."*
>
> *— PLUTARCH*

Lectures are given at the following universities and schools (see "For the Knowledge Seekers"): Baruch College (CUNY), City College of New York (CUNY), Columbia University, Cooper Union, CUNY Graduate School and University Center, The Educational Alliance, Fordham University, Henry George School, Hunter College (CUNY), Marymount Manhattan College, Mount Sinai School of Medicine (CUNY), New York Studio School, New York University, NYU Institute of Fine Arts and School of Visual Arts.

Lectures are held at the following museums (see "For the Culture Vultures"): American Craft Museum, American Museum of Natural History, The Asia Society, The Center for African Art, The Cloisters, the Cooper-Hewitt Museum, Fraunces Tavern, Frick Collection, The Solomon R. Guggenheim Museum, Metropolitan Museum of Art, J. Pierpont Morgan Library, Museum of American Illustration, Museum of Modern Art, The National Academy of Design, The New Museum of Contemporary Art, The New-York Historical Society, The Studio Museum of Harlem, and Whitney Museum of American Art.

Lectures are held at the following libraries (see "For the Bookworms"): Mercantile Library, The New York Academy of Medicine and the New York Public Library.

HUDSON GROUP
301 W. 53rd St.
☎ *(212) 689-7443.*
Free workshops on emotional aspects of infertility and pregnancy loss (every other month).

NATIONAL ORGANIZATION FOR WOMEN
84 5th Ave.
☎ *(212) 807-0721.*
This New York branch of this women's organization offers free lectures, workshops and seminars on a wide range of subjects pertaining to women, including among others, political action, employment rights, consciousness raising and family relations.

THE NEW YORK ACADEMY OF SCIENCES
2 E. 63rd St. (at 5th Ave.).
☎ *(212) 838-0230.*
Hours: *Mon-Fri 9am-5pm.*
Dedicated to the advancement and appreciation of the sciences, this Academy offers a monthly lecture program (Mon-Fri 8-9:30pm) covering a wide range of scientific subjects, such as math, computers, engineering, science and public policy, not for beginners though! Refreshments are served afterwards. A Junior Academy for high school students interested in science offers a wealth of activities (fee). Occasional changing exhibitions are held in the lobby and meeting areas.

NEW YORK CITY BAR ASSOCIATION
42 W. 44th St. (5th-6th Aves.).
☎ *(212) 382-6600.*

Come here to learn about various legal issues or legislation on Mon-Thu at 7pm (Sep-Jun, approximately 2 per week), with Mar-May as the busiest time with possibly 1 per night. Occasional lectures on art law will draw such influential artists as Christo. An inspiration to all is the statue of Demosthenes, the Greek orator who practiced with a mouthful of marbles to overcome his speech impediment.

NEW YORK MARXIST SCHOOL
79 Leonard St., 1st fl.
☎ *(212) 941-0322.*

This school, which espouses social change, offers a wide variety of lectures on everything from current events to health issues on most Tue-Fri at 8pm (Oct-May, summers at 7:30pm) for a donation. Also, occasional cultural performances on Sat eve (fee) are held as well as works-in-progress programs on 1st Sun of month at 7:30pm (Sep-May).

NEW YORK PUBLIC LIBRARY, 42ND STREET CENTRAL RESEARCH LIBRARY ♣ ♣ ♣
(See "For the Knowledge Seekers.")

This library offers an excellent selection of ongoing lectures.

NEW YORK THEOSOPHICAL SOCIETY
240 E. 53rd St. (2nd-3rd Aves.).
☎ *(212) 753-3835.*

This Society focuses on any philosophies professing to attain a knowledge of God by special relationships or mystical insight.
Events: *Workshops, lectures and classes.*

PLACE DES ANTIQUAIRES
(See "For the Lobbyists.")

Lectures on art or antiques are presented on Wed at 2pm.

VICTORIAN SOCIETY
☎ *(212) 427-2488.*

Founded in 1966, the Society's mission is to increase appreciation of and knowledge about the 19th and early 20th C. Victorian era. The group plays an active role in supporting landmark building legislation as well as sponsoring lectures (at Donnell Library), day trips (fee) and holiday parties.

WETLANDS PRESERVE
161 Hudson St. (Laight St.).
☎ *(212) 966-4225.*

This night club with live music earmarks profits for an environmental program, "Eco-Salon," which sponsors free lectures, slide shows, forums and workshops on a variety of environmental issues on Sun from 5:30-8:30pm. On the 2nd Wed from 5:30-8:30pm, environmental networking features a lecture with a professional. Some music events are also free.

The Bronx

The following universities and colleges feature lectures (see "For the Knowledge Seekers"): College of Mount St. Vincent, Fordham University, Herbert H. Lehman College (CUNY) and Manhattan College.

Also see Bronx Historical Society under "For the Bookworms" and Bronx Museum under "For the Culture Vultures."

Brooklyn

The following universities and colleges feature lectures (see "For the Knowledge Seekers"): Brooklyn College (CUNY), Kingsborough Community College (CUNY), Long Island University, N.Y.C. Technical School (CUNY) and Pratt Institute.

Also see the Brooklyn Historical Society, Brooklyn Museum and Pieter Claesen Wyckoff House under "For the Culture Vultures."

Queens

The following universities and colleges feature lectures (see "For the Knowledge Seekers"): Queens College (CUNY), Queensborough Community College (CUNY), St. John's University and York College (CUNY).

Also see the Jamaica Bay Wildlife Refuge under "For the Birds" and Queens Museum under "For the Culture Vultures."

Staten Island

See College of Staten Island under "For the Knowledge Seekers" and Richmondtown Restoration and Snug Harbor under "For the Culture Vultures."

For the Music Lovers

Probably on any given day in New York, there are at least half a dozen free concerts. And of course the summer brings music into the streets and parks with lunchtime and evening concerts galore. Many of our music schools and universities (with active music departments) offer intimate settings where you can really see the musicians (the future Arthur Rubinsteins and Isaac Sterns). And let us not forget the glorious music making that goes on in our houses of worship, especially active at the holidays.

At Bryant Park (at 42nd St. between 5th-6th Aves.), an outdoor booth sells same-day, half-price tickets to N.Y.C. music and dance performances on Tue-Sun noon-2pm, 3-7pm (11am on matinee days). Bring cash or traveller's checks only, (212) 382-2323/221-0885. See introduction to "For the Matinee Idlers" for info on reduced-priced tickets for same-day theater performances.

"Where there's music there can be no evil."

— CERVANTES

ABYSSINIAN BAPTIST CHURCH
(See "For the Believers.")
A music program on most Sun at 3pm (Oct-Jun).

AFTER DINNER OPERA COMPANY
☎ *(212) 477-6212.*
Along with occasional free operas, this company presents "Meet the Composers" series, dedicated to bringing new operas and composers to N.Y.C.

AMERICAN LANDMARK FESTIVALS
☎ *(212) 866-2086.*
Since 1973 ALF has entertained us with free performances at various Manhattan locations of the National Park Service, especially the Theodore Roosevelt Birthplace, Federal Hall National Memorial, Castle Clinton and Hamilton Grange. Programs include chamber music, recitals, symphony orchestras, dance, mime, opera and lectures.

BARNARD COLLEGE
(See "For the Knowledge Seekers.")
Chamber music on most Tue-Thu from noon-1pm (Sep-early May) at McIntosh Student Center.

BATTERY PARK CITY AUTHORITY
1 World Financial Center.
☎ *(212) 945-0505.*
For a comprehensive calendar of concerts, visit the Winter Garden Ballroom on weekdays at 7pm and Gateway Plaza (Sounds of Sunset) and South Garden in the summer.

BELL PLAZA
41st-42nd Sts., W. of 6th Ave.
This walk-through part of the N.Y. Telephone Co. sponsors a Summer Arts Festival on Tue from noon-2pm.

BLOOMINGDALE HOUSE OF MUSIC
(See "For the Knowledge Seekers.")

BRYANT PARK
(See "For the Birds.")

CARNEGIE HALL ♦
7th Ave. & 57th St.
☎ *(212) 903-9750/247-7800.*
This popular and well-known concert hall, built in 1891 by William B. Tuthill in the Romanesque Revival and Italian Renaissance style for Andrew Carnegie (the steel magnate), attracts top artists at top prices.
However, free concerts are performed by the Youth Symphony Orchestra (3 a year, 581-5933), the All-City High School Band (247-7800) and the Senior Concert Orchestra of New York (239-4802 ext. 266). Also the International American Music Competition (piano, violin and voice)

is held here every other year. At Thanksgiving, free children's concerts are arranged through the Board of Education. Also community outreach programs take professionals into schools, old-age homes and shelters.

CBGB'S
(See "For the Matinee Idlers.")
Offerings include occasional free country, blue grass & blues music.

CENTRAL PARK ♦♦♦♦
(See "For the Birds.")
Concerts at the Dairy on Sun at 1pm (May-Oct); at the Great Lawn, summer concerts by the Metropolitan Opera in Jun and the New York Philharmonic in Jul-Aug; and at the Naumberg 72nd St. Bandshell, the New York Grand Opera's fully staged operas on Thu at 8pm (Jul, 245-8837) as well as dance or music concerts especially in the summer.

CHASE MANHATTAN PLAZA
(See Outdoor Plazas listing under "For the Birds.")
Noontime concerts in the summer and occasional dance performances.

CHRIST & ST. STEPHEN'S EPISCOPAL CHURCH
(See "For the Believers.")
Classical music on Mon-Wed at 8pm and Sun at 3 & 7:30pm (donation).

CITICORP CENTER, THE MARKET ♦
(See "For the Lobbyists.")
Varied concerts at different times during the month.

CITY COLLEGE OF NEW YORK (CUNY)
(See "For the Knowledge Seekers.")
Faculty, student and professional recitals on most Thu at 12:15pm and some Tue at 2pm in either Shepard Hall (Room 200) or at Aaron Davis Hall Theater A or B (Oct-Dec, Feb-May, except Hols); evening performances on some Thu or Fri at 7pm with orchestral or choral offerings.

CITY HALL PARK
(See "For the Birds.")
Noontime concerts on occasional Tue and Thu during the summer.

COLUMBIA UNIVERSITY ♦♦
(See "For the Knowledge Seekers.")
At St. Paul's Chapel on Thu at 12:05pm for organ recitals (Oct-Nov, Feb-Apr); the Bach series on Thu at 8pm (end May-Jun); the "Post-Crypt" coffeehouse on Fri & Sat at 9pm (Oct-Dec, Feb-early May); and at the Maison Française, concerts once a month.

CONTINENTAL INSURANCE BUILDING
180 Maiden La. (Water & South Sts.).

☎ *(212) 269-0320.*
A concert series sponsored by the Lower Manhattan Cultural Council offers good contemporary performances on every other Wed at 12:15pm.

COOPER UNION ✦
(See "For the Knowledge Seekers.")
Concerts on weekdays at 8pm (mid Sep-May).

CORNELIA STREET CAFE
29 Cornelia St.
☎ *(212) 929-9869.*
Hours: *Mon-Sun 8pm-1am. Check summer schedule.*
This supper club offers free evening entertainment on Sun-Thu (though dinner's not free) from 8pm in an intimate and informal setting (holds 35). Shows feature jazz, folk, comedy, new play readings and cabaret revues. And between the acts, you can take in the monthly art exhibitions (photos, watercolors, painting, collages).

CRYSTAL PAVILION
(See "For the Lobbyists.")
Piano music on Tue & Thu from 12:30-2:30pm.

CUNY GRADUATE SCHOOL AND UNIVERSITY CENTER
(See "For the Knowledge Seekers.")
Occasional concerts on Wed at 12:15pm (summer) in the Mall; and chamber music or recitals on some weekdays at 8pm.

CUPPING ROOM CAFE
359 W. Broadway.
☎ *(212) 925-2898.*
Free jazz on Fri & Sat from 9pm-1am is offered at this cafe; dinner and refreshments are optional (fee).

DONNELL LIBRARY CENTER (NYPL)
(See "For the Bookworms.")
Jazz concerts featuring the "Jazzmen" on Wed at noon (Sep-Jun); and occasional concerts on Sun at 2:30pm.

EXPERIMENTAL INTERMEDIA FOUNDATION
224 Centre St.
☎ *(212) 431-5127.*
The organization offers performing artists some fine resources for music and intermedia development; there are over 50 concerts a year ($3).

FEDERAL HALL NATIONAL MEMORIAL ✦
(See "For the Culture Vultures.")
Classical music or recitals on Wed at 12:30pm, sponsored by the American Landmark Festivals.

FORT TRYON PARK
(See "For the Birds.")
   Music and dance concerts on Tue at 7pm (raindate Wed, Jul-Aug).

THE FRICK COLLECTION 🍎🍎🍎🍎
(See "For the Culture Vultures.")
   Free concerts on occasional Sun at 5pm during the year and Wed at 5:30pm (summer).

GALLERIA ATRIUM
(See "For the Lobbyists.")
   Lunchtime concerts on most Tue & Fri at noon.

MARCUS GARVEY PARK
(See "For the Birds.")
   Summer concerts.

GOLDMAN MEMORIAL CONCERT BAND
☎ *(212) 944-1501.*
   This 70-year-old cultural institution sponsors outdoor concerts during the summer at Lincoln Center's Damrosch Park, South Street Seaport, Central Park, and Seaside and Prospect Parks in Brooklyn. These classical concerts feature guest conductors and soloists; consult local newspapers.

ABRAHAM GOODMAN HOUSE
(See Hebrew Arts School under "For the Knowledge Seekers.")
   Student and faculty concerts.

GRACE BUILDING PLAZA
(See "For the Birds.")
   Outdoor concerts on Tue at 12:15pm (Jun-Labor Day).

GRACE CHURCH 🍎
(See "For the Believers.")
   Organ recitals on Wed at 12:30pm (mid Sep-May) and occasional choral readings on Fri at 8pm or Sun at 4pm.

GRANT NATIONAL MEMORIAL (GRANT'S TOMB)
(See "For the Exhibitionists.")
   Summer concerts featuring the Jazzmobile and Dancemobile.

GREENWICH HOUSE MUSIC SCHOOL
(See "For the Knowledge Seekers.")
   Faculty and student concerts.

HAMILTON GRANGE
(See "For the Culture Vultures.")
   Occasional concerts on Sun at 3pm.

DAG HAMMARSKJOLD PLAZA
(See Outdoor Plazas listing under "For the Birds.")
Occasional noontime outdoor concerts and Hol entertainment.

HARKNESS ATRIUM
(See "For the Lobbyists.")
Occasional concerts or performances on Wed from 6-7:30pm.

HARLEM CULTURAL COUNCIL
☎ *(212) 316-6277.*
Since 1964, this community arts council has offered a varied program, including Dancemobile and Jazzmobile; major art exhibitions for museums and universities; Black film festivals; cultural education programs for schools; and assistance to artists and galleries in receiving commissions, grants and special subsidies.

HEBREW UNION COLLEGE—JEWISH INSTITUTE OF RELIGION
(See "For the Knowledge Seekers.")
The "Sunday Afternoon at the College" program on most Sun at 3pm (Oct-Jun, except Jewish Hols) of music and lectures.

HOLY TRINITY LUTHERAN CHURCH
(See "For the Believers.")
Bach Vespers on Sun at 5pm.

IRISH ARTS CENTER
553 W. 51st St. (10th-11th Aves.).
☎ *(212) 757-3318.*
The Irish performing arts center offers a performance of Irish song and dance on some Sun at 7pm (closed Hols & summer). Workshops in Irish culture are held on weekdays at 6pm.

JAZZMOBILE
☎ *(212) 866-4900.*
This nonprofit organization sponsors a roving (mobile) minstrel of outdoor jazz and cabaret performances in parks, streets and community centers throughout the city (Jul-Aug). Possible locations are Grant's Tomb, Union Square or Metropolitan Hospital parking lot.
Events: *Sat jazz workshops at P.S. 201 in Central Harlem for ages 16 and over, school lectures and demos at elementary and junior high schools; young citizens Harlem Arts Program for grades 3-9 on Sat after school and in summer; and semi-annual concerts honoring living jazz greats.*

JUILLIARD SCHOOL OF MUSIC ♠
(See "For the Knowledge Seekers.")
Concerts at IBM Garden on Wed at 12:30pm, at Alice Tully Hall on Wed at 1pm (Oct-May) and student recitals at Paul Hall (listed in school lobby); and weekday evening concerts at Juilliard Theater.

LA MAMA/LA GALLERIA
(See "For the Matinee Idlers.")
   "Meet the Composer" series on 2nd Sat at 8pm and 2nd Sun at 4pm.

LIGHTHOUSE FOR THE BLIND
(See "For the Knowledge Seekers.")
   Jazz or solo recitals, and performances of the Lighthouse Singers and Opera Company.

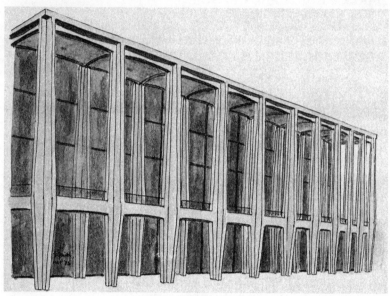

AVERY FISHER HALL

LINCOLN CENTER FOR THE PERFORMING ARTS 🍎🍎🍎🍎
62nd-65th Sts. between Amsterdam & Columbus Aves.
☎ *(212) 877-2011.*
   This 14-acre cultural complex dedicated to music, dance and theater consists of 6 buildings with Avery Fisher Hall, the Metropolitan Opera House and the New York State Theater as the nucleus surrounding the central plaza and fountain.   Built by various architects, including Wallace K. Harrison, Philip Johnson and Max Abramovitz, from 1959 to 1969, this Center initially received criticism ranging from social (destruction of an otherwise residential neighborhood) to architectural (mediocre classicism) to structural (acoustical problems).   Now that acoustical problems have been corrected, Lincoln Center today represents a cultural mecca, acclaimed by most!
   Lincoln Center is adorned with significant artworks, the highlights being the Marc Chagall front murals depicting the Arts at the Metropolitan Opera House and the "Reclining Figure" by Henry Moore

in the reflecting pool in front of the Vivian Beaumont Theater. Home to the New York Philharmonic, the Metropolitan Opera, the New York City Opera, the New York City Ballet, the Juilliard School of Music, the New York Public Library for the Performing Arts and chamber music and film societies, the Center offers a constant cultural menu from which to choose. Although much is not free, there are indeed some wonderful freebies (especially in the summer). A valuable monthly Calendar of Events can be obtained by sending an oversized, self-addressed, stamped envelope to "Calendar of Events," 140 W. 65th St., N.Y., N.Y. 10023.

Free Events:

Damrosch Park (includes Fountain, North & South Plazas). Various types of musical concerts offered in the summer include the incomparable Lincoln Center Out-of-Doors series of concerts (Aug), 360-1333; the Goldman Memorial Band concerts on Wed, Thu, Fri & Sun at 8pm (Jun-Aug), 944-1501; a possible free concert for Kool Jazz Festival (early Jun), 787-2020; and the American Crafts Festival (1st 2 weekends in Jul).

Avery Fisher Hall. The annual fund-raising Radiothon the last weekend in Apr with celebrities and musicians; free theological lectures on Sun at 11am; the annual Mostly Mozart concert series begins with a free outdoor performance on the 2nd Mon in Jul at noon; and the best bargains, open rehearsals of the New York Philharmonic ($3) on occasional Wed at 9:45am with unreserved seating (for listing, send self-addressed, stamped envelope to: Avery Fisher Box Office, Broadway at 65th St., N.Y., N.Y. 10023), 580-8700.

Juilliard School of Music concerts (see separate listing).

The Metropolitan Opera. The company performs several operas at 8:30pm (Jun) throughout the metropolitan area, 362-6000.

THE METROPOLITAN OPERA

New York Philharmonic. The orchestra performs several classical concerts at 8pm (Jul-Aug) throughout the metropolitan area. Bring a blanket and a picnic. Fireworks usually accompany one concert, making it a terrific evening, 580-8700.

New York Public Library for the Performing Arts. Concerts on Mon-Fri at 4pm (occasionally times may vary) and on Sat at 2:30pm (Sep-May), 870-1630/1614 (see "For the Bookworms").

Alice Tully Hall. The Juilliard School of Music offers free concerts on Wed at 1pm (Oct-May) and occasional Tue & Fri at 8pm performances during the school year, 362-1900.

LOWER MANHATTAN CULTURE COUNCIL
☎ *(212) 432-0900.*

This nonprofit arts service organization sponsors cultural events from Houston Street to Battery Park.

MADISON AVENUE PRESBYTERIAN CHURCH
(See "For the Believers.")

St. Andrews Music Society on Sun at 4pm (Oct-May, donation).

MANHATTAN SCHOOL OF MUSIC
(See "For the Knowledge Seekers.")

Ongoing student and faculty concerts during the school year (in spring, up to 6 a day).

MANNES COLLEGE OF MUSIC
(See "For the Knowledge Seekers.")

Concerts on weekdays at 8pm by professionals, students and faculty (Oct-May).

METROPOLITAN OPERA HOUSE
(See Lincoln Center above).

MUSEUM OF THE CITY OF NEW YORK ♦♦♦
(See "For the Culture Vultures.")

Occasional concerts on Sun at 3pm (Oct-May) for adults with informal gathering with the artists afterwards; and special Sun programs at 5pm for adults and children, ranging from jazz, mime, theater and music (fee).

NATIONAL CHORALE
☎ *(212) 333-5333.*

This professional repertory company performs outdoor concerts in the summer at Damrosch Park and Carl Schurz Park and other locations.

NEW YORK FOLK FESTIVAL
☎ *(212) 529-1955.*

A few of the folk festival events in the city (Aug) are free.

NEW YORK GRAND OPERA
☎ *(212) 245-8837.*
Since 1974, this company has been offering excellent, fully staged operatic productions outdoors in the 5 boroughs.

NEW YORK PHILHARMONIC
(See Lincoln Center above.)

OLYMPIC TOWER
(See "For the Lobbyists.")
Pianist on Mon, Wed & Fri from noon-2pm.

ONE LIBERTY PLAZA
(See Outdoor Plazas listing under "For the Birds.")
Outdoor Summer concerts.

PIER 16
(See South Street Seaport Museum under "For the Culture Vultures.")
Outdoor Summer concerts.

PLAZA ON PARK AVENUE
345 Park Ave. (51st-52nd Sts.).
Free summer concerts on Fri at noon.

PORT AUTHORITY BUS TERMINAL PLAZA
8th Ave. at 42nd St., main level in N. wing.
☎ *(212) 466-7255.*
Classics on Thu from 7-9am in South Wing, occasional Hol and summer music and performances; and changing monthly art exhibits in South Wing, main floor.

THE PUBLIC THEATER
(See "For the Film Buffs.")
Occasional free concerts.

RIVERSIDE CHURCH 🍎🍎
(See "For the Believers.")
Carillon recitals on Sat at noon (also Hols) and on Sun at 3pm; summer concerts on Tue at 6:30pm/7pm; and occasional Sun afternoon concerts.

ROCKEFELLER CENTER 🍎🍎🍎
(See "For the Exhibitionists.")
Summer outdoor music including concerts on Tue & Thu at 12:30pm at McGraw-Hill.

THEODORE ROOSEVELT BIRTHPLACE 🍎
(See "For the Culture Vultures.")
Classical music or recitals on every Sat at 2pm, sponsored by the American Landmark Festivals.

ST. BARTHOLOMEW'S CHURCH &
(See "For the Believers.")
  "Great Music" concerts on occasional Sun at 4pm.

ST. MARK'S PARK
(See "For the Believers.")
  "A Little Noon Music" on Thu at noontime.

ST. MICHAEL'S CHURCH
(See "For the Believers.")
  Occasional concerts.

ST. PATRICK'S CATHEDRAL &&
(See "For the Believers.")
  Organ recitals on Sun at 4:45pm.

ST. PAUL'S CHAPEL &
(See "For the Believers.")
  "Noonday Concerts" of chamber music or recitals on Mon & Thu at 12:10pm all year round.

ST. PAUL'S CHAPEL AT COLUMBIA UNIVERSITY
(See Columbia University above.)

ST. PETER'S CHURCH &&
(See "For the Believers.")
  "Jazz Vespers" on Sun at 5pm and concerts on most Sun at 7pm (donation) and "Jazz at Noon" on Wed at noon (Oct-May); and "All Night Soul," a 12-hour celebration on the 2nd Sun in Oct.

ST. THOMAS CHURCH &
(See "For the Believers.")
  Organ recitals on Sun at 5:15pm (4pm, Jun-Sep); a sung evening prayer with full choir on Tue & Thu at 5:30pm & Sun at 4pm (Oct-May); a sung Eucharist on Wed at 12:10pm; and occasional concerts on Tue at 7:30pm (donation).

CARL SCHURZ PARK
(See "For the Birds.")
  Outdoor summer concerts.

SOUTH STREET SEAPORT &&&
(See "For the Culture Vultures.")
  Outdoor summer concerts.

SYMPHONY SPACE
2537 Broadway (at 95th St.).
☎ *(212) 864-1414.*
  In 1978 a group of well-known musicians from the Upper West Side congregated in a run-down movie theater to make free music (in fact, 12 hours' worth) for 7,000 neighbors. That masterful event gave birth

to this nonprofit performing arts center and saved the building from the clutches of demolition. Many local clean-up squads and coats of paint later, this space has seen a symphony of local and international talent in dance, music, drama and film (most at a nominal fee).

This center is probably still most famous for its "Wall-to-Wall" series, 12 hours of continuous free music dedicated to a great composer(s) and performed by great musicians. Wall-to-Walls have featured the music of Bach, Beethoven, Copland/Americana and even the readings of James Joyce's works. The Mannes School Orchestra performs here 5 times for free. A bravo to those brave founding fathers.

THIRD STREET MUSIC SETTLEMENT SCHOOL
(See "For the Knowledge Seekers.")
Faculty concerts on occasional Wed at 7:30pm; "A Little Noon Music" on Thu at noon (Jul) at St. Mark's Park; and the Performing Arts Series of professional concerts (Nov-Mar, fee).

TOMPKINS SQUARE PARK
(See "For the Birds.")
Outdoor summer concerts.

TOWN HALL
123 W. 43rd St. (6th-7th Aves.).
☎ *(212) 997-1003/840-2824 (box office).*
With a full program of professional performances, little is free here, except the Children's Free Opera for 1 week (Fall & Spring), 840-7470.

TRINITY CHURCH ♦♦
(See "For the Believers.")
"Noonday Concerts" of chamber music or recitals on Tue at 12:45pm.

VIETNAM VETERANS PLAZA
(See "For the Birds.")
Concerts on Wed & Fri at noon in Summer.

WASHINGTON SQUARE MUSIC FESTIVAL
Washington Square Pk.
☎ *(212) 431-1088.*
Good outdoor classical concerts on some Tue at 8pm (Jul-Aug) feature the Festival Orchestra with guest conductors and soloists (a 30-year tradition). Bring a blanket or chair. Rainspace at NYU Eisner & Lubin Aud. at the Loeb Student Center, 566 LaGuardia Pl.

WEST BANK CAFE
407 W. 42nd St. (at 9th Ave.).
☎ *(212) 695-6909.*
Free comedy, music and 1-act theater cabaret shows on Sun at 8pm.

WORLD FINANCIAL CENTER WINTERGARDEN ♦♦♦♦
(See "For the Lobbyists.")
An amazing program of arts and events.

WORLD TRADE CENTER PLAZA
(See Outdoor Plazas listing under "For the Birds.")
A wide range of entertainment during Hol and in the summer.

YOUTH SYMPHONY ORCHESTRA OF NEW YORK
☎ *(212) 581-5933.*
This orchestra, comprised of talented musicians aged 12-22, offers full-blown classical concerts during the year, usually 3 at Carnegie Hall, 1 at Merkin Hall, 3 in Greenwich House, 2 at Manhattan Plaza. Also the Chamber Music Players offer 5 concerts at centers for the disabled.

THE BRONX

FORDHAM UNIVERSITY
(See "For the Knowledge Seekers.")
The Bronx Arts Ensemble's 6 free concerts on occasional Sun at 4pm and occasional faculty and chorus concerts.

HOSTOS COMMUNITY COLLEGE (CUNY)
(See "For the Knowledge Seekers.")
Concerts (some fee) of jazz, opera, symphony and classical music by professional groups.

HERBERT H. LEHMAN COLLEGE, CENTER FOR THE PERFORMING ARTS
(See "For the Knowledge Seekers.")
Occasional concerts on Sun at 3pm by the Bronx Symphony Orchestra, Bronx Ensemble or Aeolian Chamber Ensemble; the Lehman Pop Band on Sun at 6pm (6 times in the summer); student and faculty recitals at weekday noontime; and the Children's Free Opera for 1 week.

NEW YORK BOTANICAL GARDENS ♦♦♦
(See "For the Birds.")
Occasional concerts during the year.

VAN CORTLANDT MANSION HOUSE
(See "For the Culture Vultures.")
The oldest building in the Bronx offers concerts (Aug) in its classical garden for a donation.

WAVE HILL HALL ♦♦
(See "For the Birds.")
Occasional concerts (some at a fee); and the availability of the archives of Arturo Toscanini's NBC Symphony Orchestra.

BROOKLYN

BALDWIN PIANO & ORGAN COMPANY
Kings Plaza, Flatbush Ave. & Ave. U.
☎ *(718) 253-3886.*
   Occasional student recitals on Sun at 6pm.

BENSONHURST PARK
Cropsey Ave. & Bay Pkwy.
☎ *(718) 783-4469/3077.*
   Summer outdoor concerts sponsored by BACA.

BROOKLYN ACADEMY OF MUSIC (BAM) 🍎
30 Lafayette Ave. (Ashland Pl. & St. Felix St.).
☎ *(718) 636-4100.*
   This excellent performance center offers a wide selection of concerts, dance and theatrical productions, mainly at a high tariff. However, the Children's Free Opera presents occasional free concerts in the fall & spring.

BROOKLYN ARTS & CULTURAL ASSOCIATION (BACA) 🍎
111 Willoughby St. (Bridge & Duffield Sts.).
☎ *(718) 596-BACA/2222.*
(See "For the Artists.")
   An amazing listing of summer concerts in many Brooklyn parks.

BROOKLYN BOTANIC GARDENS 🍎🍎🍎🍎
(See "For the Birds.")
   Concerts on Sun at 3pm (Jul-Aug).

BROOKLYN BRIDGE ANCHORAGE
☎ *(718) 619-1955.*
   Free concerts, readings by noted writers and poets, and performance art.

BROOKLYN COLLEGE, CENTER FOR THE PERFORMING ARTS
(See "For the Knowledge Seekers.")
   Composer's Forums and student recitals.

BROOKLYN CONSERVATORY OF MUSIC
(See "For the Knowledge Seekers.")
   Occasional free concerts or recitals by students.

BROOKLYN HEIGHTS ESPLANADE
Pierrepont St. Playground.
☎ *(718) 783-4469/3077.*
   Outdoor concerts in the summer on Wed at 7:30pm sponsored by BACA.

BROOKLYN MUSEUM 🍎🍎🍎🍎
(See "For the Culture Vultures.")
BACA concerts on Sun at 2pm (Oct-May, sometimes 3pm) featuring classical music or recitals.

BROOKLYN SOCIETY FOR ETHICAL CULTURE
53 Prospect Park W.
☎ *(718) 768-2972.*
Occasional coffeehouses with music (donation).

CANARSIE PIER
Gateway National Recreational Area, Rockaway Pkwy. at Belt Pkwy. overpass.
☎ *(718) 783-4469.*
Weekend concerts in the Summer sponsored by BACA on Sat at 12:30pm.

CONEY ISLAND
Boardwalk near YM-YWHA.
Summer concerts by BACA on Thu 6-8pm.

EMPIRE-FULTON FERRY STATE PARK 🍎
(See "For the Birds.")
Occasional outdoor concerts in the summer on Tue from noon-2:30pm.

JOHN PAUL JONES PARK
4th Ave. & 101st St.
☎ *(718) 783-4469/3077.*
Outdoor concerts in the summer sponsored by BACA.

MIDWOOD FIELD CONCERT SERIES
East 16th St. between Aves. K & L.
☎ *(718) 469-1912.*
Performances on Thu at 7:30pm (Jul-Aug) featuring big band sound, classical, bebop to comedy (bring your own lawn chair, free bus service for senior citizens from certain neighborhoods, 284-4700) — rain place at Brooklyn College's Whitman Hall, Ave. H. & Flatbush Ave.

OWL'S HEAD PARK
Colonial Rd. & 68th St. (near Park House).
☎ *(718) 783-4469/3077.*
Free summer concerts sponsored by BACA.

PROSPECT PARK 🍎🍎🍎
(See "For the Birds.")
"Celebrate Brooklyn!" at the Bandshell on Fri-Sun at 8pm during the summer featuring jazz, Caribbean and Latin music, classical, folk, pop, funk and dance, 788-0055; concerts at the Picnic and Tennis Houses; and the Metropolitan Opera and N.Y. Philharmonic performances (summer).

REGINA OPERA COMPANY
Regina Hall, 65th St. & 12th Ave.
☎ *(718) 232-3555/236-0909.*
 Every year since 1970, this company has performed 3 fully staged operas with orchestra (Sep-Jun, free for children). Concerts feature opera singers on 1st Sun in Oct, Nov, Feb, Apr & May at 4pm (fee).

SEASIDE PARK
Ocean Pkwy. & Seabreeze Ave.
☎ *(718) 783-4469/3077.*
 At the Asser Levy/Seaside Park Bandshell, outdoor concerts on several evenings (Jun-Aug) by the Goldman Memorial Band and other professionals sponsored by BACA. Bring folding chairs.

WINTHROP FIELD
Kingston & Brooklyn Aves.
☎ *(718) 469-1912.*
 Concerts on Mon at 7:30pm (summer) featuring gospel, Afro-American or reggae music.

QUEENS

BELMONT PARK
Hempstead Turnpike, off Cross Island Pkwy.
☎ *(718) 275-5000.*
 Occasional outdoor summer concerts by Queens Symphony.

BROOKLYN CONSERVATORY OF MUSIC
Queensboro Branch, 140-26 Franklin Ave. (off Kissena Blvd.), Flushing.
☎ *(718) 461-8910.*
 Occasional student recitals; and professional recitals — call to be put on mailing list.

FLUSHING COUNCIL ON CULTURE & THE ARTS
Flushing Town Hall, 137-35 Northern Blvd., Flushing.
☎ *(718) 463-7700.*
 This nonprofit organization is dedicated to cultural activities in Flushing; a wide range of performances take place in their large cultural center.
Events: *Summer outdoor concerts are held at: Alley Pond Park, Springfield Blvd. at 76th St.; Astoria Park, Shore Blvd. & 19th St., adjacent to 23rd Ave.; Crocheron Park, Lakeview Rd., off 35th Ave. & 215th St.; Cunningham Park, Fresh Meadows, 196th St. & Union Turnpike; Flushing Meadow, off Grand Central Pkwy., 111th St. & 54th Ave; Forest Park Bandshell, Woodhaven Blvd. & Forest Park Dr.; Kissena Park, Oak Ave. at 164th St.; and MacDonald Park, Queens Blvd. at Yellowstone Blvd.*

FLUSHING MEADOW, CORONA PARK ♦♦
(See "For the Birds.")

The Queens Symphony performances on some Sun at 6:30pm, sponsored by the Flushing Council on the Arts; and many other free concerts, especially in the summer.

FOREST PARK ♦
Forest Dr. near Woodhaven Blvd.
☎ *(718) 520-5933.*

A bandshell features a wide range of summer outdoor entertainment.

JAMAICA ARTS CENTER ♦
(See "For the Artists.")

The Jamaica Arts Jazz Ensemble concerts on Fri from noon-2pm (Jun-Aug, about 8 times) at the Farmers' Market.

POPPENHUSEN INSTITUTE
114-04 14th Rd. (114th St.), College Point.
☎ *(718) 358-0067.*
Hours: *Mon-Wed & Fri 9am-6:30pm (Tue til 5pm).*

This community cultural center, housed in a landmark building, offers a myriad of programs. Its museum development program presents 4 exhibits each year on local history.
Events: *Classic films, concerts and theater, summer concerts at MacNeil Park, weight training for ages 12-21 and drug and therapy sessions.*

QUEENS BOTANICAL GARDENS
(See "For the Birds.")

Music and dance performances on occasional Sun at 4pm, some sponsored by the Queens Council on the Arts (Jul-Aug).

QUEENS COLLEGE (CUNY)
(See "For the Knowledge Seekers.")

At the Colden Center for the Performing Arts, occasional free performances by Queens Symphony or Queens College Wind Ensemble, the Aaron Copland School of Music concerts at Rathaus Hall on weekdays and some weekends (frequently at 12:30pm), and concerts at the Student Union and Queens College Theater.

QUEENS COUNCIL ON THE ARTS
161-04 Jamaica Ave., Jamaica.
☎ *(718) 291-1100/ARTS.*

This cultural council sponsors musical programs throughout the year at Forest Park Bandshell, Queens Botanical Gardens and Queens County Farm. Call for their comprehensive cultural guide.

QUEENS SYMPHONY, POPS IN THE PARK
☎ *(718) 275-5000.*

This symphony performs at Astoria Park, Baisley Pond Park, Belmont Race Track, Cunningham Park and Forest Park in the summer for free.

QUEENS THEATER-IN-THE-PARK
Flushing Meadow, Corona Pk., across from the N.Y. State Bldg.

SEUFFERT CONCERTS
☎ *(718) 428-1973/566-4076.*
Concerts on Sun at 3pm (mid Jun-Sep) at Forest Park Bandshell; other concerts at 102nd St. & Boardwalk in the Rockaways, Cunningham Pk. and elsewhere.

WOODSIDE ON THE MOVE
☎ *(718) 476-8449.*
This cultural center sponsors free events during the summer, including performances (ethnic music & dance, jazz & theater) on Tue at 7pm (2nd week of Jul-3rd week in Aug) at 3 parks in Queens (call for details); and weekly children's performances (clowns, puppets, storytelling, music and children's theater) on Wed at 1:30pm at Bush Park.

STATEN ISLAND

GREAT KILLS PARK
(See "For the Birds.")
Occasional concerts on Wed or Fri at 8pm (Jul-Aug).

HIGH ROCK ENVIRONMENTAL CENTER ♦
(See "For the Birds.")
Occasional summer concerts on Sun afternoons.

SILVER LAKE PARK
(See "For the Birds.")
Special events and concerts.

SNUG HARBOR CULTURAL CENTER ♦♦♦
(See "For the Culture Vultures.")
At Veteran's Memorial Hall (seats 200), professional concerts (some free); outdoor summer concerts featuring the New York Grand Opera and the Metropolitan Opera (Jun) and the New York Philharmonic (late Jul-Aug); and the Music Hall's opening scheduled for 1992 to feature musical performances.

STATEN ISLAND CHAMBER MUSIC PLAYERS
☎ *(718) 356-2094.*
Since 1972, this small group of music makers has entertained S.I. residents year round (about 60 concerts annually). Their summertime concerts can be heard in parks and diverse neighborhoods. The Encore Series brings workshops and performances to schools. Project Uplift does exactly that to the spirit of physically and mentally disabled S.I. residents through free concerts and entertainment.

STATEN ISLAND COUNCIL ON THE ARTS
One Edgewater Plaza.
☎ *(718) 447-4485.*
Responsible for making S.I. residents aware of the culture in their own backyards, the Council sponsors cultural activities including an information center at St. George Terminal as well as the excellent "Staten Island Arts," a quarterly cultural calendar.
Events: *"Making Waves," program of music and dance on the Staten Island Ferry every year.*

WAGNER COLLEGE
(See "For the Knowledge Seekers.")
Occasional student, faculty and guest performers in North Hall, Sutter Hall, the music annex or the administration building.

For the Dance Cards

Free dance performances are not particularly easy to find. Your best bet is to try the universities and young dance troupes. Occasionally some parks will offer participatory folk dancing or free dance performances in the summer.

At Bryant Park (at 42nd St. between 5th-6th Aves.), an outdoor booth sells same-day, half-price tickets to N.Y.C. music and dance performances on Tue-Sun noon-2pm, 3-7pm (11am on matinee days). Bring cash or traveller's checks only, (212) 382-2323/221-0885. See introduction to "For the Matinee Idlers" for info on reduced-price tickets for same-day theater performances.

"Those move easiest who have learned to dance."

— ALEXANDER POPE

Dance performances are given at the following colleges and universities (see "For the Knowlege Seekers"): Borough of Manhattan Community College, City College of New York (CUNY), Cooper Union, Hunter College (CUNY), New York University and Pace University.

BATTERY DANCE COMPANY
380 Broadway (corner White St.), 5th fl.
☎ *(212) 219-3910.*
This professional dance troupe sponsors the marvelous Downtown Dance Festival (Sep), the 2-week series of outdoor noon performances of classical, ballet, modern and folk dancing accompanied by music at either the World Trade Center, Chase Manhattan Plaza or the South Street Seaport. Call for additional events.

BATTERY PARK
(See "For the Birds.")
Events: *Folk dancing on Sat-Sun at 2-6pm and special Hols, weather permitting.*

CENTER FOR THE DANCE OF ISADORA DUNCAN
The Isadora Duncan Center, 141 W. 26th St. (6th-7th Aves.).
☎ *(212) 691-5040.*
If you enjoy the flowing and flowery dance style of Isadora Duncan, glide over to this center for free workshop performances (mid Jul, at Christmas and in the spring). If you're not familiar with Isadora and her passionate love of life, there are slide lectures held concurrently with the workshops. Monthly exhibits of private collections on Isadora are available for viewing Mon-Fri 2-6pm by appt. only.

CENTRAL PARK ♦♦♦♦
(See "For the Birds.")
Events: *At the King Jagiello Statue at 88th St. E. of Belvedere Lake, folk dancing on Sat-Sun at 2pm-dusk (Apr-fall), weather permitting.*

DANCE THEATRE WORKSHOP
219 W. 19th St. (7th-8th Aves.).
☎ *(212) 691-6500.*
Since 1965, this choreographers' cooperative has been a showcase for choreographers, composers and theater artists, performing at the Bessie Schönberg Theater and others around the city (most at a fee). However, the DTW Gallery features free exhibits every 4-6 weeks for visual artists working in a variety of media.

DANCEMOBILE
☎ *(212) 316-6277.*
Since 1967, the Harlem Cultural Council has sponsored dance performances with full costumes and lights on this self-contained mobile stage in the 5 boroughs and upstate N.Y. during warm weather. Audiences get involved with all aspects of the performance as they watch the setting up of the stage, the warm-up routines and then, of course,

the performance.

MARK GOODSON THEATER
Department of Cultural Affairs, 2 Columbus Circle at 59th St.
☎ *(212) 974-1150.*
Free dance or classical concert on Mon at 12:30pm (Oct-Jun) in this theater (seats 154) on a first-come basis.

SUMMERDANCE
☎ *(212) 269-0320.*
Lunchtime outdoor performances presenting the dances of aspiring choreographers, mainly on Tue & Thu in Jun, are sponsored by the Lower Manhattan Cultural Council. Call for locations.

WASHINGTON SQUARE PARK
(See "For the Birds.")
Folk dancing on Fri at 7:30-10:30pm (mid Jun-Labor Day), weather permitting.

WORLD FINANCIAL CENTER WINTERGARDEN 🍎🍎🍎🍎
(See "For the Lobbyists.")
A fabulous line-up of live entertainment includes many famous dance troupes.

Note: For the **Bronx, Brooklyn, Queens** and **Staten Island,** consult Bronx Community College (CUNY), Fordham University, Brooklyn College (CUNY), Kingsborough Community College (CUNY) and Queens College (CUNY) under "For the Knowledge Seekers" and Coney Island and Prospect Park under "For the Birds."

For the Poets

Those interested in being up to date on all the readings (poetry and otherwise) going on around town (free and otherwise) can subscribe to the NYC Poetry Calendar, 13 E. 3rd St., N.Y., N.Y. 10003, by sending a check for $15 (sorry about that!), (212) 475-7110.

> *"Poetry is the reward of the best and happiest moments of the happiest and best minds."*
>
> — *PERCY BYSSHE SHELLEY*

ABC NO RIO
156 Rivington St. (at Clinton St.).
☎ *(212) 254-3697.*
Poetry readings and open mike on occasional Wed at 8pm (donation).

ACADEMY OF AMERICAN POETS
☎ *(212) 427-5665.*
Free poetry readings or special tributes are sponsored by the group at the Donnell Library Center, the New-York Historical Society (some free) and the Guggenheim Museum (when it reopens).

BACKFENCE
155 Bleecker St. (at Thompson St.).
☎ *(212) 475-9221.*
This folk/rock music club offers free poetry readings on Sun at 4:30pm (Aug-Jan), thanks to the interest of Brigid Murnaghan, a poet. An open reading is on Sun during which any aspiring Byron or Eliot can try out his or her verse; often the better poets then go on to read in later weeks.

BOOKS & COMPANY
939 Madison Ave. (74th-75th Sts.).
☎ *(212) 737-1450.*
Specializing in art, literature and philosophy, the 939 Foundation for the Arts organizes readings on some Tue or Thu at 7:30pm (spring & fall).

BRENTANO'S BOOKSTORE
597 5th Ave. (at 48th St.), N.Y., N.Y. 10017.
☎ *(212) 826-2450.*
This well-known bookstore offers free readings by acclaimed writers every week. To be put on their free mailing list, either come in and sign up or send a self-addressed, stamped envelope to the above address.

CBGB'S
(See "For the Matinee Idlers.")
Readings on Sun at 8pm.

A DIFFERENT LIGHT
548 Hudson St. (Charles & Perry Sts.).
☎ *(212) 989-4850.*
For gay and lesbian literature, attend readings every Wed at 8pm (Sep-mid Jun, occasionally Tue or Thu).

DONNELL LIBRARY CENTER (NYPL)
(See "For the Bookworms.")
Poetry, prose readings or lectures on some Mon at 6pm; poetry and "Writers & Readers" series on some Tue at 6pm; and book discussion series on some Thu at 6:30pm (advanced registration).

ENDICOTT BOOKSELLERS
450 Columbus Ave. (81st-82nd Sts.).
☎ *(212) 787-6300.*
   This west side bookstore's strength is literature; the store sponsors readings with current authors about once a month on weekdays at 8pm (Jan-Nov). Go early as seats are limited; free wine is served.

HUDSON GUILD
441 E. 26th St. (9th-10th Aves.).
☎ *(212) 760-9800.*
   Hudson Guild Book Fair (3rd week in Oct).

JEFFERSON MARKET LIBRARY (NYPL)
(See "For the Bookworms.")
   Poetry workshops on some Wed at 6:30pm sponsored by the Waterways Project.

LA MAMA/LA GALLERIA
(See "For the Matinee Idlers.")
   Poets and Writers night on Fri at 8pm.

LIFE CAFE
343 E. 10th St. (at Ave. B).
☎ *(212) 477-8791.*
   Poetry readings on Tue at 8pm (except in summer).

MONA'S
224 Ave. B (near 13th St.).
☎ *(212) 353-3780.*
   This bar has free readings on Sun at 3pm and an "open mike" on Mon at 9pm when you can read/sing/play guitar.

MOSAIC BOOKS
167 Ave. B (11th-12th Sts.).
☎ *(212) 475-8623.*
Contribution: *$2.*
   Readings on Sun at 4pm on community, Afro-American, Latino and gay issues, and an open reading on 1st Tue at 7pm.

NEW YORK PUBLIC LIBRARY, 42ND STREET CENTRAL RESEARCH LIBRARY ✎✎✎
(See "For the Bookworms.")
   Occasional readings and panel discussions (some fees).

NEW YORK UNIVERSITY ✎
(See "For the Knowledge Seekers.")

NYU POETICS INSTITUTE
☎ *(212) 598-3315.*
   The "Poets & Critics in Performance" series sponsors monthly poetry readings. Call for exact dates and locations.

PEN & BRUSH
(See "For the Artists.")
Monthly prose and poetry workshops or seminars sponsored by this well-established art and literary club.

POETRY PROJECT AT ST. MARK'S
10th St. & 2nd Ave.
☎ *(212) 674-0910/6377.*
This organization is run entirely by poets for the sheer enjoyment of poetry; the general public is always welcome.
Events: *Poetry performances on Mon at 8pm (1st Mon in month open reading) and poetry readings on Wed at 8pm; and occasional workshops on poetry and writing.*

POETRY SOCIETY OF AMERICA
National Arts Club, 15 Gramercy Pk. S. (on 20th St. near Irving Pl.).
☎ *(212) 254-9628.*
Since 1910, this poetry club has provided roots for young and established poets and a forum for those who love poetry. Readings are held weekdays (Oct-May, except Hols). The club's "Writer-in-Residence" program presides over seminars and readings. The Van Voorhis Library houses 6,000 volmes of poetry, biographies and criticism and is open to the public.

SCHOMBURG CENTER
(See "For the Knowledge Seekers.")
Occasional symposia and readings.

SMALL PRESS CENTER
20 W. 44th St. (5th-6th Aves.).
☎ *(212) 764-7021.*
Occasional free poetry and book readings.

SPEAK EASY
107 MacDougal St. (Bleecker & W. 3rd Sts.).
☎ *(212) 598-9670.*
Poetry and open readings on Mon at 7:30pm and music on alternate Sat at 4-7pm (donation).

THREE LIVES & COMPANY
154 W. 10th St. (at Waverly Pl.).
☎ *(212) 741-2069.*
Readings on some Thu at 8pm (Sep-Nov, Jan-Jun) with limited space (no one admitted once reading has begun).

WORLD FINANCIAL CENTER WINTERGARDEN 🍎🍎🍎🍎
(See "For the Lobbyists.")
Occasional readings.

For the **Bronx, Brooklyn, Queens** and **Staten Island,** consult the listings for the borough's universities, schools and cultural centers.

For the Matinee Idlers

There's no better place in America than New York City for theater. The razzle-dazzle of Broadway attracts theatergoers by the droves. It also attracts theater students and aspiring actors by the droves. An amazing number of acting schools, universities, academies, guilds, theaters, repertory companies and churches provide actors, directors and playwrights with a chance to sharpen their skills while audiences enjoy free theater.

> *"You need three things in the theater—the play, the actors and the audience, and each must give something."*
>
> *— KENNETH HAIGH*

For those interested in taking in a Broadway, Off-Broadway or Off-Off Broadway play, there are "two-fers" (one-third discount on tickets in advance bought at Box Office) available at various stores around town as well as at the New York Convention & Visitors Bureau (see Introduction). In addition, same-day discount tickets are obtainable at:

QUIKTIX
The Public Theater, 425 Lafayette St. (E. 4th St. & Astor Pl.).
☎ *(212) 598-7150/7171.*

The Public Theater offers 25% of the tickets for all regular Public Theater attractions at Quiktix prices (reduced price of $10 for Tue-Thu, Sun eve & Sat-Sun matinees or $12.50 for Fri and Sat eve; special events may cost more!). This holds true even for shows already sold out at full prices! Quiktix go on sale at 6pm (1pm matinees) on performance day only. The Public Theater lobby opens at 1pm (noon matinees) and the popularity of any given show should affect your arrival time (call Box Office for suggested time of arrival). No more than 2 tickets will be sold per person. Check to see if credit cards are accepted these days.

TKTS (THEATER DEVELOPMENT FUND)
47th St. & Broadway (Mon-Sat evening performances 3-8pm, Wed & Sat matinees 10am-2pm and Sun matinees & evenings noon-closing).
2 World Trade Center, mezzanine (Mon-Fri 11am-5:30pm, Sat 11:30am-3:30pm).
☎ *(212) 354-5800/221-0885.*
Brooklyn Borough Hall, Court & Montague Sts. (Tue-Fri 11am-5:30pm, Sat 11am-3:30pm).

This invaluable institution has made it possible for many to attend cultural performances (theater, music and dance) without having to pay the prohibitive prices. You show up during office hours to buy tickets at half price (+ small surcharge) for same-day performance (at 2 WTC and Brooklyn locations, matinees and Sun performances are available 1 day in advance). Of course, only those performances not sold out are on the list, so you can probably forget about the most popular shows. However, there always seems to be something worthwhile to see. Prepare to stand on line and pay by cash or traveller's checks (sorry, no credit cards).

* * *

ACTORS PLAYHOUSE
100 7th Ave. S. (Bleecker & Grove Sts.).
☎ *(212) 741-1215/691-6226.*

This small (seats about 150) but cozy theater offers Off-Broadway plays at a fee, except on some Mon at 8pm (Oct-Aug, except Hols) with its free "Actors' Sketchbook." Scenes, monologues, readings or one-act performances (many from well-known plays) are put on by student actors (some quite talented) in a casual and relaxed atmosphere. Wine and cheese reception with the actors follows.

THE AMERICAN MUSICAL AND DRAMATIC ACADEMY
Ansonia Hotel, 2109 Broadway (at 73rd St.).
☎ *(212) 787-5300.*

For over 20 years, this professional school has been offering a total training program combining acting, musical theater and dance. Considered "triple threats," the talented and versatile students are rigorously prepared for it all. And you can bet that their Graduation Showcases in Dec, Apr & Aug are theatrical highlights; the public is invited to attend by reservation only. Thank you, Philip Burton (Richard's father), for starting it all.

AMERICAN STANISLAVSKI THEATER
Sonia Moore Studio of the Theater, 485 Park Ave. (at 58th St.).
☎ *(212) 755-5120.*

Enrolled students learn the Stanislavski acting method, a conscious means to the actor's emotions. Several times a year, open acting classes are given at the NYPL for the Performing Arts (Jan, May, Sep and Nov, usually Mon at 6pm).

AMERICAN THEATER OF ACTORS
314 W. 54th St. (8th-9th Aves.).
☎ *(212) 581-3044.*

Play readings on Tue at 8pm; call for reservation.

AMERICAN THEATER WING
250 W. 57th St. (Broadway & 8th Ave.).
☎ *(212) 765-0609.*

The founders of the Tony Awards sponsor workshops and seminars frequently with top actors mainly at CUNY Graduate School, 33 W. 42nd St., 3rd fl. As they are well attended, reservations are required and by all means get there early.

CBGB'S
313 Bowery (at Bleecker St.).
☎ *(212) 677-0455.*
Hours: *Daily 1-11pm.*

This center for country, blue grass and blues features free performances in all media. The 313 Gallery features diverse monthly art shows in all media.
Events: *Free experimental improvisational theater workshops on Tue*

from 7-9pm, comedy "open mike" on Wed from 6-9, open improvisation on Thu from 7:30-9:30pm, musical performances ($3) on Sat eve; poetry readings on Sun at 8pm (acoustic and blue grass music after each of the above performances).

CENTRAL PARK, DELACORTE THEATER
South of Great Lawn around W. 81st St.
☎ *(212) 861-PAPP/7277.*
    Joseph Papp's New York Shakespeare Festival performs 2 fully staged theatrical productions on Tue-Sun at 8pm from Jul-Labor Day. Tickets are given out at 6pm only to those in line around the Great Lawn. The plays are always worthwhile.

JEAN COCTEAU REPERTORY THEATER
330 Bowery (corner of Bond St.).
☎ *(212) 677-0060.*
    Occasional play readings during the year.

CSC REPERTORY THEATER
136 E. 13th St. (3rd-4th Aves.).
☎ *(212) 677-4210.*
    Play readings series on Mon at 7pm in fall and spring (3 each).

ENSEMBLE STUDIO THEATER
549 W. 52nd St. (at 11th Ave.).
☎ *(212) 247-4982.*
Hours: *Mon-Sun at 7:30pm, Sat-Sun at 2:30pm in Oct. Reservation suggested.*
    Off the beaten track amid warehouses and derelict buildings is this cultural stronghold (including the Interart Theater, (212) 246-1050). Free plays during a month-long Octoberfest celebration take various formats—some are classics, some new, some informal, some staged readings and some full productions. Frequently there is a discussion with the actors afterwards.

GENE FRANKEL THEATER
24 Bond St.
☎ *(212) 777-1710.*
    Occasional free performances of works-in-progress.

FREE THEATER PRODUCTIONS
☎ *(212) 737-0073/721-2309/2323.*
    Since 1982, Stan Tanner has been lining up great theatrical talent to perform for free at St. Bart's, the Donnell Library Center and other locations around town; this enables those who rarely go to the theater or who are financially unable to pay to experience the likes of Eli Wallach, Jason Robards, Colleen Dewhurst, Jeremy Irons, Whoopi Goldberg, Raul Julia and Comden & Green.

HB PLAYWRIGHTS FOUNDATION
122 Bank St. (at Greenwich St.).
☎ *(212) 989-6540.*
Several times during the year, this nonprofit foundation puts on free, fully staged plays, occasionally featuring very well-known actors, e.g., Celeste Holm, Uta Hagen. Shows run for about a week to 10 days. Call to be put on the mailing list.

HECKSCHER THEATER
El Museo del Barrio Bldg., 1 E. 104th St.
☎ *(212) 534-2804.*
This wonderfully decorative 600-seat theater offers occasional free performances (especially at Hols).

HUNTER COLLEGE (CUNY)
(See "For the Knowledge Seekers.")
The Department of Theater presents student and faculty productions (some at a fee).

IRONDALE ENSEMBLE PROJECT
351 E. 18th St. (8th-9th Aves.).
☎ *(212) 633-1292.*
This developmental theatrical company shows its dedication to community outreach by offering free concerts and performances in local schools as well as free workshops and improvisational evenings (generally on Sat). Occasionally complimentary tickets for Seniors are available to other shows.

JOHN JAY COLLEGE OF CRIMINAL JUSTICE (CUNY)
(See "For the Knowledge Seekers.")
Free plays (twice a year) and readings are sponsored by the Department of Theater & Speech.

LA MAMA/LA GALLERIA
6 E. 1st St. (Bowery & 2nd Ave.).
☎ *(212) 505-2476.*
Hours: *Gallery: Wed-Sun 1-6pm.*
This multi-functional art center presents new works in all disciplines. The Gallery features 14 exhibits a year in all the visual arts.
Events: *Free Poets and Writers readings on Fri at 8pm; play readings and "New Voices/New Plays" on 1st, 3rd and last Sat of month at 8pm; Meet the Composer on 2nd Sat at 8pm; and composer series on 2nd Sun at 4pm.*

LIGHTHOUSE FOR THE BLIND
(See "For the Knowledge Seekers.")
The Lighthouse Players present 5 dramatic performances in mid Mar for 2 weekends (Fri at 8pm, Sat at 2:30pm and the last Sun).

MARYMOUNT MANHATTAN COLLEGE THEATER
(See "For the Knowledge Seekers.")

The Marymount Manhattan Theater stages excellent free student productions plus Children's Theater (occasional fee).

NEW DEAL THEATER COMPANY
☎ *(212) 932-1026.*
This theatrical company was founded in 1990 and presents productions around town. Free tickets are available for senior citizens and high school students.

NEW DRAMATISTS WORKSHOPS
424 W. 44th St. (9th-10th Aves.).
☎ *(212) 757-6960.*
This is the oldest playwrights organization in the world (founded in 1949). Funded by theatrical professionals, it gives new playwrights an opportunity to work on and try out their material. Located in a remodelled church, the workshop offers free readings on several weekdays at 7:30pm; reservations are necessary.

NEW YORK SHAKESPEARE FESTIVAL
☎ *(212) 861-PAPP/7277.*
Joseph Papp presents usually 2 theatrical productions (not always Shakespearean) at the Delacorte Theater, Central Park and on the Mobile Theater during the summer. The productions are fully staged and star well-known thespians. See "Central Park, Delacorte Theater."

NEW YORK STAGE AND FILM
McGinn/Cazale Theatre, 2162 Broadway at 76th St.
☎ *(212) 481-5480.*
Free staged readings in spring and fall on occasional Mon at 7:30pm (about 12 a year).

NEW YORK UNIVERSITY
(See "For the Knowledge Seekers.")
The Tisch School and the Washington Square Performers present drama, comedy and children's productions at the University Theater, 35 W. 4th St., 998-1820.

OFF-CENTER THEATER
☎ *(212) 768-3277.*
For "off-center" play readings at different locations, usually satirical and often humorous, make a point to show up on Thu at 8pm (except for breaks in Sep, Oct & at Christmas) in different locations around town (call for details).

PERFORMANCE SPACE 122
150 1st Ave. (at 9th St.), 2nd fl.
☎ *(212) 477-5288.*
This red-brick former schoolhouse has been transformed into a performing arts center by replacing classrooms with artists' studios and offering performances in the auditorium. Although most performances are at a fee, the weekly "open movement series" on Tue at 8pm allows

artists to come in and improvise (contribution). Exhibits of or by performing artists adorn the walls and can be seen independently.

THE PUBLIC THEATER
425 Lafayette St. (E. 4th St. & Astor Pl.).
☎ *(212) 598-7171/7150.*
See chapter introduction for "Quiktix" information.

QUAIGH THEATER
808 Lexington Ave. (at 62nd St.).
☎ *(212) 787-0862.*
Plans to reopen in Spring '91.
Don't miss their lunchtime one-act plays on Mon-Fri at 12:15pm; bring your lunch (suggested donation, Seniors free). They're planning evening productions also (fee).

RED SPOT OUTDOOR SIDE THEATER
Broadway & Spring St., N.W. Wall.
☎ *(212) 925-0143.*
If it's 40 degrees or warmer, you can bet that the show will go on. On Tue-Sat at 9pm (encores on Fri & Sat at 10pm), you can come to this bright spot in Soho and watch a slide and multi-media show outdoors. All slides are artist-made (i.e., not just photos) and are usually accompanied by music (bring your portable cassette player and tune into 98.6 FM).

RIVERSIDE SHAKESPEARE COMPANY
☎ *(212) 369-2273.*
The RSC presents Shakespearean plays in the summer (usually Jun) throughout the 5 boroughs. Possible locations are Co-op City, New York Botanical Gardens or Van Cortlandt Park in the Bronx; Ft. Green, Owl's Head or Prospect Park in Brooklyn; Central, Morningside or Riverside Parks in Manhattan; Astoria, Baisley, Cunningham, Kissena or Highland Parks in Queens; and Richmondtown or Snug Harbor in S.I.

ST. BARTHOLOMEW'S CHURCH ⚭
(See "For the Believers.")
Infrequent theatrical readings by well-known actors sponsored by Free Theatrical Productions; also fine performances in the St. Bart's Playhouse (fee).

SCHOMBURG THEATER (NYPL)
(See "For the Bookworms.")
Performances at the amphitheater.

SCHOOL OF VISUAL ARTS
(See "For the Knowledge Seekers.")
At the SVA Actors' Theater, plays and scenes directed, acted and designed by the students.

FRANK SILVERA WRITERS WORKSHOPS
317 W. 125th St. (near St. Nicholas Ave.), top fl.
☎ *(212) 662-8463.*

Neighborhood Theatrical Workshops (seats about 60) offer free rehearsed play readings (some staged) by new playwrights in the Reading/Critique Series on Mon at 7:30pm, writers' seminar series on Wed from 7-9pm and technical theater on Sat at 3pm (Sep-Jun, check Hols). Discussion and refreshments follow.

LEE STRASBERG THEATER
115 E. 15th St. (Park Ave. S. & Irving Pl.).
☎ *(212) 533-5500.*

This well-known acting school offers occasional free performances as well as free evening "scenes" and "directors" nights critiqued by Anna Strasberg.

THEATER FOR THE NEW CITY
☎ *(212) 254-1109.*

This thespian troupe offers a free ticket program (6-10 tickets) to any civic or community group (senior group, half-way house, etc.) and outdoor street entertainment in the 5 boroughs during the summer by merely closing off the street. A new American musical with a large cast is presented on Sat-Sun at 2pm (Aug-Sep). Call for locations.

UBU REP THEATER
149 Mercer St. (Houston & Prince Sts.).
☎ *(212) 679-7540.*

This dramatic center for contemporary French-speaking playwrights (including Haitians, French Canadians, Belgians, etc.) offers free staged readings in English on most Mon at 8pm (Oct-Jun); call first.

For the **Bronx, Brooklyn, Queens** and **Staten Island,** consult the listings for Bronx Community College (CUNY), College of Mount St. Vincent, Fordham University, Hostos Community College (CUNY), Herbert H. Lehman College (CUNY), Manhattan College, BACA, Brooklyn College (CUNY), N.Y.C. Technical College, Prospect Park, Queens College (CUNY), York College (CUNY) and College of S.I. (CUNY).

For the Film Buffs

Many of N.Y.C.'s museums, universities, libraries and cultural societies present free films and documentaries on a regular basis. Most are shown in rather informal settings and there's no waiting on long lines to be admitted.

Though most television programming is now taped in Hollywood, there are still a few network hold-outs, such as "Geraldo," "The Joan Rivers Show," "Donahue," "Saturday Night Live" and "Regis and Kathie Lee." It's always fun to be part of a live audience!

"A film is a petrified fountain of thought."

— *JEAN COCTEAU*

ABC TV STUDIO
7 Lincoln Sq. (off Columbus Ave. at 67th St.).
☎ *(212) 887-7777.*
    This TV network offers free tickets to "Regis and Kathie Lee," Mon-Fri 9-10am. Call or write to Guest Relations, 36A West 66th St., N.Y., N.Y. 10023.

AMERICAN INDIAN COMMUNITY HOUSE
(See "For the Artists.")
    Occasional films in connection with the Foundation for Independent Video & Film (FIVF).

AMERICAN MUSEUM OF IMMIGRATION ❞❞❞
(See "For the Culture Vultures.")
    A well-done 20-minute film on the making of Ms. Liberty includes some rare footage on the 1880s construction. It should not be missed.

AMERICAN MUSEUM OF NATURAL HISTORY ❞❞❞❞
(See "For the Culture Vultures.")
    Free afternoon and evening films at the Kaufman Theater on natural history subjects; special festivals including films; and the NatureMax Theater with a 4-story screen showing several films throughout the day (though not free, an exceptional experience).

ANTHOLOGY FILM ARCHIVES
32 2nd Ave. (at E. 2nd St.).
☎ *(212) 477-2714/505-5181.*
    This organization presents changing films by a wide selection of directors, especially foreign ones.
Events: *Free screenings on Sun at 2 or 3pm.*

BARNARD COLLEGE
(See "For the Knowledge Seekers.")
    The "Zooprax" Film Society's late show and revivals (some free) on Tue, Fri & Sun at 7, 9 & 11pm at Altschul Hall.

CBS TV STUDIOS
51 W. 52nd St. (corner of 6th Ave.).
☎ *(212) 975-5525 (Joan Rivers), 265-1283 (Geraldo Rivera).*
    This TV network offers free audience attendance for the taping of shows by Joan Rivers on Mon-Wed at 9am & 1pm and Geraldo Rivera on Tue-Thu at 1 & 3pm.

CENTRAL PARK, THE DAIRY
(See "For the Birds.")
    A 30-minute slide show on some aspects of Central Park.

CHELSEA STUDIOS
221 W. 26th St.
☎ *(212) 727-1234.*
    These studios offer occasional free TV tapings with audience par-

ticipation.

COLUMBIA UNIVERSITY

(See "For the Knowledge Seekers.")
At Ferris Booth Hall, films on Thu & Sun at 8 & 10pm; occasional films at Dodge & Earl Halls; at Maison Française for French documentaries on alternate Thu at 8pm; at Casa Italiana, Italian movies with subtitles on Fri at 7pm; and at Furnald Lawn for free films on Wed at 9pm (summer).

DONNELL LIBRARY CENTER (NYPL)
(See "For the Bookworms.")
Feature films on Tue & Thu at noon (Oct-Jun); "Collectors' Choice" films on Tue at 2:30pm; films for preschoolers on Thu at 2:30pm; "Meet the Videomaker/Filmmaker" series on some Thu at 6pm; and occasional films on Sun at 2:30pm (Sep-Jun).

DOWNTOWN COMMUNITY TV CENTER (DCTV)
(See "For the Knowledge Seekers.")
Free media workshops and occasional screenings.

EXPERIMENTAL INTERMEDIA FOUNDATION
224 Centre St. (at Grand St.).
☎ *(212) 431-6430.*
Free multi-channel video and audio art shows; and New Music Composer series (fee).

FEDERAL HALL NATIONAL MEMORIAL
(See "For the Culture Vultures.")
A large collection of historical films is available for on-premises viewing or for loan.

FLOATING CINEMA
☎ *(212) 360-1333/(617) 262-1414.*
In conjunction with N.Y.C. parks, Waterfront Festivals present summer films on a barge with a 30-foot screen moored offshore for nighttime viewing.

FRAUNCES TAVERN
(See "For the Culture Vultures.")
A fairly informative and not too corny 12-minute slide show, "A Colonial Seed Grows a Big Apple," is shown by appt. only.

FRENCH INSTITUTE/ALLIANCE FRANÇAISE
(See "For the Society-Goers.")
First-rate French films with subtitles (nominal fee).

GOETHE HOUSE
(See "For the Society-Goers.")
Free German films with subtitles and film festivals.

MAISON FRANÇAISE
(See "For the Society-Goers.")
French films with subtitles on occasional Fri at 7pm (Oct-May, donation).

METROPOLITAN MUSEUM OF ART ⚹⚹⚹⚹
(See "For the Culture Vultures.")
An impressive array of films at the Uris Center; consult the flyer at the Great Hall Info Desk.

MILLENNIUM FILM WORKSHOP
66 E. 4th St. (2nd Ave. & Bowery).
☎ *(212) 673-0090.*
For those interested in independent filmmaking, there are probably a thousand good reasons for visiting this nonprofit, educational film arts organization, one of which is the free open screenings on Fri at 8pm (monthly, except Aug). Independent filmmakers come and show their films on a first-come basis (contribution). No pre-screening or censorship occurs.
Events: *Free student internships and films on most Sat eve (contribution).*

MUSEUM OF BROADCASTING ⚹⚹
(See "For the Culture Vultures.")
This museum is entirely dedicated to the world of American TV and radio with special shows daily from the library of 7,000 TV and 10,000 radio programs. Also, you can request any program to play on individual consoles (for 2 people). It's great fun for those of all ages.

MUSEUM OF MODERN ART ⚹⚹⚹⚹
(See "For the Culture Vultures.")
Since 1935, MoMA has recognized filmmaking as a modern art form and has been collecting films. With a library of 8,000 films (the strongest international collection in the U.S.), the Film Department presents their offerings all week long (at no extra charge); tickets can be collected at 11am for same-day shows.
Events: *The "Cineprobe" evenings of independent and experimental filmmakers; and "New Directors/New Films" (fee), the works of up-and-coming directors.*

MUSEUM OF THE CITY OF NEW YORK ⚹⚹⚹
(See "For the Culture Vultures.")
An excellent 25-minute multi-media slide show on the Big Apple and its history.

NBC TV STUDIOS
30 Rockefeller Pl. (49th-50th Sts.), N.Y., N.Y. 10112.
☎ *(212) 664-3055/3056 (Groups).*
Tours: *NBC Studio tours leave every 15 minutes, Mon-Sat 9:30am-4:30pm (Sun tours in summer), $7.25. No children under 6 admitted.*
This TV network offers free tickets to the taping of their TV shows.

For "Late Night with David Letterman," requests should be made by mail in Jul & Dec; for "The Cosby Show" and "Saturday Night Live," ticket requests selected in Aug by lottery (taping at Kaufman Astoria Studios); and for "Donahue," requests by mail anytime (wait is about 3-4 months).

Same-day standby tickets are available: for "Letterman," on the morning of show at 8:15am at NBC TV Studios, mezzanine level; for "SNL," on Sat at 9am (same place); for "Cosby," morning of show at 10am at Kaufman Astoria Studio or NBC Studios; and for "Donahue," 1 hour before show at either 1 or 4pm.

THE NEW SCHOOL FOR SOCIAL RESEARCH
(See "For the Knowledge Seekers.")
An excellent film series on Fri at 7:30pm (fee), and occasional films during the school year.

NEW YORK PUBLIC LIBRARY SYSTEM
☎ *(212) 621-0626.*
For an enormous selection of first-rate films shown daily in the branch libraries, consult the monthly calendar, obtainable at any library.

NEW YORK UNIVERSITY
(See "For the Knowledge Seekers.")
Cinemathèque Film Series on Sat at 10am, 1 & 3pm (school year) with 3 consecutive films at 721 Broadway; and the Maison Française's French films with subtitles (fee) on Fri at 8pm (or 6pm, school year).

PACE UNIVERSITY
(See "For the Knowledge Seekers.")
Films on Mon at 3 and 9pm at the Student Union (some free, day may change).

THE PUBLIC THEATER
425 Lafayette St. (E. 4th St. & Astor Pl.).
☎ *(212) 598-7171/7150.*
Once the first N.Y.C. public library (built by friends of John Jacob Astor's estate), this handsome 1849 Italianate building (plus later add-ons) became the home of Joseph Papp's New York Shakespeare Festival in 1967. This company is also responsible for the free Shakespeare at the Delacorte Theater in Central Park every summer (see "For the Matinee Idlers").
Events: The "Public Service" documentaries on Sat-Sun at 2pm (year round) featuring controversial and topical subjects from Iraq to Picasso; additional film and theater programs (fee).

THE SPANISH INSTITUTE
(See "For the Society-Goers.")
Screenings of Spanish films at the Cine Club (possible fee).

STATUE OF LIBERTY
(See American Museum of Immigration.)

WHITNEY MUSEUM OF AMERICAN ART ●●●
(See "For the Culture Vultures.")
Videotape and film exhibits and series; the "Calder Circus" videotape.

The Bronx

FORDHAM UNIVERSITY
(See "For the Knowledge Seekers.")
"Cinevents" classical series on Tue at 8pm and current films on Thu at 8 or 10:30pm at Keating 1st Aud.

HOSTOS COMMUNITY COLLEGE (CUNY)
(See "For the Knowledge Seekers.")
A series of Black and Spanish movies with subtitles on Tue at 12:30 & 7pm (Oct-May).

MANHATTAN COLLEGE
(See "For the Knowledge Seekers.")
The "Brotherhood of Visual Drama" with audience participation about twice a month on Wed at 8pm (Oct-May, nominal charge); and occasional film festival.

NEW YORK PUBLIC LIBRARY SYSTEM
☎ *(212) 220-6565.*
For an enormous listing of first-rate films shown daily in the branch libraries, consult the monthly calendar of events, obtainable in any library.

POE COTTAGE MUSEUM
(See "For the Culture Vultures.")
An 18-minute video of Poe's days in N.Y.C. and the Bronx.

Brooklyn

BROOKLYN ARTS & CULTURAL ASSOCIATION (BACA)
(See "For the Artists.")
   Film and video festivals.

BROOKLYN COLLEGE (CUNY)
(See "For the Knowledge Seekers.")
   A mix of classics and sneak previews on weekdays at 12:15pm at the Student Union.

BROOKLYN HISTORICAL SOCIETY
(See "For the Culture Vultures.")
   Occasional films.

BROOKLYN PUBLIC LIBRARY SYSTEM
(See "For the Bookworms.")
   Consult the monthly calendar of events for the feature films showing in the branch libraries.

Queens

POPPENHUSEN INSTITUTE
(See "For the Music Lovers.")
   Free classic films.

QUEENS BOROUGH PUBLIC LIBRARY
(See "For the Bookworms.")
   Consult the monthly calendar of events for feature films shown in the branch libraries and for this library, feature films on Sun at 1pm; and movies for Seniors on Mon at 1:30pm.

QUEENS MUSEUM ♿♿
(See "For the Culture Vultures.")
   Feature films on Sat at 2pm.

TELEPHONE PIONEER MUSEUM
(See "For the Culture Vultures.")
   Various films on the telephone's history and how to use telephones (mainly for children).

Staten Island

CONFERENCE HOUSE (BILLOPP HOUSE)
7455 Hylan Blvd. (at Satterlee St.), Tottenville.
☎ *(718) 984-2086.*

Once the location of an unsuccessful peace talk during the Revolutionary War, this 17th C. manor is now a museum containing colonial furniture and artifacts.

Events: *Free outdoor films on alternate Wed at 9pm in the summer.*

NEW YORK PUBLIC LIBRARY SYSTEM
☎ *(718) 442-8611/8562.*

Consult the monthly calendar of events, obtainable in any library, for a list of films shown in the branch libraries.

For the Kiddies

A world of goodies awaits young eyes. There are free museums, storytelling, puppet shows, arts & crafts workshops, nature walks, camps, you name it. And don't be intimidated by museums with their "Suggested Contribution" policies. It's hardly worth paying $20 to take a family of 4 to a museum for a half-hour (an hour if you're luckier), but paying $1 or $2 certainly encourages families to visit again and again.

Some museums that allow carriages and strollers include: American Museum of Natural History, AT&T Infoquest, Children's Museum of Manhattan, Metropolitan Museum of Art (Tue-Fri), J. Pierpont Morgan Library, El Barrio del Museo, Museum of American Folk Art, Museum of the City of New York, The New-York Historical Society, Studio Museum of Harlem and the Whitney Museum (downtown branch).

Consult calendar of events on the next page for regularly scheduled free activities for children.

> *"I love these little people and it is not a slight thing, when they, who are so fresh from God, love us."*
>
> — *CHARLES DICKENS*

CALENDAR

MONDAY-FRIDAY

10:30am	Central Queens Y—Storytelling (Tue).
11:30am	FAO Schwarz Toy Store—Entertainment (til 4pm).
1pm	Asphalt Green—Gym program (til 7:30pm, fee).
1:15pm	Central Queens Y—Storytelling ages 2 1/2-5 (Thu).
1:30pm	Abyssinian Ch.—Tutorial (Wed).
	Central Queens Y—Storytelling & art (Thu).
	MMA—Program ages 10-15 (Summer, Tue-Fri).
2pm	Amer. Mus. of Nat. Hist.—Science program (til 4:30pm).
	Brooklyn Children's Mus.—Occ. program.
2:30pm	Donnell Lib.—Film for pre-schoolers (Thu).
3pm	Brooklyn Children's Mus.—Afterschool program.
	Langston Hughes Cultural Ctr.—Homework assistance (grade 3-7).
6:15pm	Central Queens Y—Storytelling & art.
7pm	MMA—Lecture ages 6-12 (Fri).
7:30pm	S.I. Children's Mus.—Family entertainment (3rd or 4th Fri).

SATURDAY

10am	MoMA—Gallery program (fee).
	MoMA—Drop-in classes for H.S. students.
10:30am	Asphalt Green—Puppet show (fee).
11am	MMA—Gallery talk & sketching ages 6-12.
11:15am	MoMA—Family film (fee).
12noon	Amer. Mus. of Nat. Hist.—Discovery Room (til 4:30pm).
	Asphalt Green—Puppet show (fee).
	N.Y. Transit Mus.—Workshop.
	Queens County Farm Mus.—Special program (til 5pm, Apr-Dec).
12:30pm	MMA-Film.
1pm	Asphalt Green—Gym program (fee).
	Queens Mus.—Family workshops (til 4pm).
1:30pm	Amer. Mus. of Nat. Hist.—Program (til 4:30pm).
2pm	Brooklyn Mus.—What's Up workshop ages 8-12.
	New York Hall of Science—Workshop.
	MMA—Film.

2:30pm	MMA-Gallery talk & sketching ages 6-12.
3pm	ECRIC—Film for pre-schoolers.

SUNDAY

11am	Eeyore's westside—Storytelling (Sep-Jun, exc. Hols).
12noon	Amer. Mus. of Nat. Hist.—Discovery Room (til 4:30pm).
	Queens County Farm Mus.—Special program (til 5pm, Apr-Dec).
12:30pm	Eeyore's eastside—Storytelling (Sep-Jun, exc. Hols).
1pm	Queens Mus.—Drop-in workshops (til 4pm, SY).
	New York Hall of Science—Workshop.
1:30pm	Amer. Mus. of Nat. Hist.—Program (til 4:30pm).
2pm	Brooklyn Mus.—What's Up workshop ages 8-12.
	S.I. Children's Mus.—Monthly Meet the Performers.
2:30pm	El Museo del Barrio—Occ. program ages 5-10.
5pm	Mus. of City of N.Y.—Performing arts program.

ABYSSINIAN BAPTIST CHURCH
(See "For the Believers.")
 A tutorial program for children in grades 1-12.

AMERICAN MUSEUM OF NATURAL HISTORY ♦♦♦♦
(See "For the Culture Vultures.")
 Probably one of the best places to take children; a world of discovery awaits the entire family.
Events
 Discovery Room. For ages 5-10, natural history items in creative "discovery boxes" for touching and handling on Sat-Sun noon-4:30pm; free tickets distributed beginning at 11:45am on first-come basis.
 Highlight Museum Tour. An hour-long tour of the main highlights of the fabulous Halls led by excellent guides, appropriate for children 7 and over.
 Nature Science Center. Exploration of wildlife, plants, rocks of N.Y.C., etc., on Tue-Fri 2-4:30pm and Sat-Sun 1:30-4:30pm.

ASPHALT GREEN
555 E. 90th St. (at the East River).
☎ *(212) 289-2448.*
Hours: *Mon-Fri 3:30-6pm, Fri 6-7pm (Oct-Jun).*
 Asphalt Green, a nonprofit neighborhood organization, sponsors weekday afternoon classes in recreational and navigational skills. "Ship 272" is Manhattan's only active sea explorer program for Boy and Girl Scouts working together. There are new athletic facilities, which are terrific; and they're building a sports and training center (completion date 1992).
Events: *Weekday classes for ages 10+ on puppetry, first aid, theater,*

photography, graphic arts, judo and boating; occasional science exhibits at P.S. 190; gymnastic programs on Mon, Wed, Thu & Sat 1-7:30pm (fee); and puppet shows on Sat at 10:30am & noon (fee).

AT&T INFOQUEST CENTER ♦ ♦ ♦
Madison Ave. at 56th St.
☎ *(212) 605-5555.*
Hours: *Tue-Sun 10am-6pm (Tue til 9pm). Closed Mon.*
Groups: *By appt. only.*
Tours: *By appt. only, offered in 6 languages and American Sign Language. Tour can include a program lecture on computer graphics, superconductivity or other scientific subjects.*

Let Gor-don, the 8-foot-high, plexiglass-and-steel robot, introduce you to the high-tech world of communications. Through 40 touch-screen video displays and easy-to-follow guides, information management through fiber optics, microelectronics and software begins to make some sense. Your own personalized access card allows you to activate the exhibits and to make learning fun.

After meeting a voice-activated video of Gor-don, you can watch your name travel in lights down an electronic ticker-tape screen. Then you learn about the importance of laser light; one exhibit demonstrates this by showing how much faster your name can travel when it goes over fiber optic lines (or is digitized) versus being sent by Morse code. You can then "make" hair-thin glass fibers by pressing your finger against a video screen. Telephones allow you to see the person you're talking to.

On the next level, the value of the microchips in our everyday life comes to life. You can "make a microchip" or use a windscope (a 2-person microscope with a larger lens viewer) to examine the electronic circuitry; a video, "Alice in Microchip Land," offers an animated wonderland of electronics.

The favorite lower level is all fun and games about software: a scramble-your-face display; a make-your-own video for which you select the stars, costumes, setting and music; fingerpainting screens; a mouse-in-a-maze voice recognition game; an artificial intelligence game to play against the computer; a talking computer version of "Mad Libs" (supplying key words to an existing story); a controller system for a telephone network; and a famous faces jigsaw puzzle game.

An industrial robot arm can even spell your name. The electronic journey ends at City Views where Checker cabs "take" you through the city to learn about neighborhoods and cultural attractions ("This Week in NYC"). Most of these exhibits and games are appropriate for ages 10 and up, though younger kids can certainly enjoy pushing the buttons. A mini-gallery offers changing exhibits related to technology. An environmental exhibit is in the planning stages.
Events: *For nonprofit groups, free use of the Center's Auditorium; and outreach programs, 605-5140.*

BARNES & NOBLE, SALE ANNEX
122 5th Ave. (at 18th St.), 2nd fl.

☎ *(212) 675-5500.*

This well-known discount bookstore cooks up free entertainment for children (up to 7); call for schedule. Also, special events are available for adults.

BIRD JUNGLE
410 Bleecker St. (at W. 11st St.).
☎ *(212) 242-1757.*
Hours: *Mon-Fri 12:30-6:30pm, Sat 11am-6:30pm, Sun 11am-5:30pm.*
This bird store has over 125 species of feathered friends.

CARNEGIE HALL ♦
(See "For the Music Lovers.")
Free musical performances for children and school classes.

CENTRAL PARK ♦♦♦♦
(See "For the Birds.")
There are so many wonderful things to do here; check under main listing for *Hans Christian Andersen Statue, Belvedere Castle, Carousel, Children's Zoo, The Dairy, Delacorte Musical Clock, Heckscher Puppet House, Swedish Cottage Marionette Theater, Urban Park Rangers* and the *Zoo*.

CHILDREN'S AID SOCIETY CENTERS
Administrative Headquarters, 105 E. 22nd St.
☎ *(212) 949-4800.*
Founded in 1853 by Charles Loring Brace to care for orphaned and destitute children, the centers are considered the pioneers in child care. Their services include placement of children in foster care, free hot lunches, visiting nurse services, free dental care, free nurseries for children of working mothers, inexpensive medical care, arts & crafts workshops, tutoring services and an inexpensive camp.

The various centers include: Dunlevy Milbank Center, 14-32 W. 118th St., 996-1716; Frederick Douglass Center, 885 Columbus Ave., 865-6337; Greenwich Village Center, 219 Sullivan St., 254-3074 (fine visual arts program for a fee); East Harlem Center, 130 E. 101st St., 348-2343; Rhinelander Children's Center, 350 E. 89th St., 876-0500; and Lord Memorial, 150 E. 45th St., 949-4800 (Health Services & Adoption Center). Their camp facilities are at the Goodhue Center, William Osborn Day Camp, 304 Prospect Ave., New Brighton, S.I., (718) 447-2630.

CHILDREN'S ART CARNIVAL
62 Hamilton Terr.
☎ *(212) 334-4093.*
This nonprofit organization offers workshops and after-school programs for ages 4 through young adults (on contribution basis). The "Summer in the Parks" program of free art workshops and classes is conducted on Mon-Thu (Jul-Aug) for children 4-13 in various parks; registration required.

CHILDREN'S FREE OPERA AND DANCE
c/o St. Luke's Chamber Ensemble.
☎ *(212) 840-7470.*

For fully staged operas that are translated into English and reduced to 1 hour, the Children's Free Opera offers performances in fall & spring at the Brooklyn Academy of Music, Lehman College (Bronx) and Town Hall for school children. For reservations, teachers may call Con Edison, 460-6917.

CHILDREN'S MUSEUM OF MANHATTAN (CMOM)
212 W. 83rd St. (Broadway & Amsterdam Ave.).
☎ *(212) 721-1234.*
Hours: *Tue-Fri 2-5pm, Sat-Sun 10am-5pm (Tue-Fri 1-5pm from July 5th-Labor Day).*
Free Admission: *Tue & Thu for public school students. Otherwise $4.*

At publication time of this book, the CMOM was still closed due to a fire in its main exhibition hall. It plans to reopen after renovation.

CITICORP CENTER, THE MARKET 🍎
(See "For the Lobbyists.")
Many programs for children.

CITY COLLEGE OF NEW YORK (CUNY)
(See "For the Knowledge Seekers.")
Monthly children's festivals with films, puppets and mimes.

THE COOPER-HEWITT MUSEUM 🍎🍎🍎
(See "For the Culture Vultures.")
Children's programs on Sat-Sun of puppet shows, workshops or talks (some at a fee).

DONNELL LIBRARY CENTER (NYPL)
(See "For the Bookworms.")
☎ *(212) 621-0636.*
Hours: *For Children's Section: Mon 12:30-8pm, Tue-Thu 12:30-5:30pm, Sun 1-5pm. Closed Fri.*

Besides specializing in foreign languages and film & video, this public library has the largest Children's and Young Adults' sections in the NYPL.
Events: *Films for preschoolers on Thu at 2:30pm; and special Hol and summer programs.*

EARLY CHILDHOOD RESOURCE AND INFO CENTER (NYPL)
66 Leroy St. (off 7th Ave. S.), 2nd fl., N.Y., N.Y. 10014.
☎ *(212) 929-0815.*
Hours: *Tue-Fri 1-5:45pm (Thu til 7:45pm), Sat noon-4:45pm.*

As the name suggests, this center is geared toward the development of preschool children. Its one large room is divided between a library and a playroom. Of course, the books are on such related subjects as childbirth, childrearing and development. The enclosed play area has a potpourri of toddlers' toys and learning aids such as blocks, animals and games. Also dotted around the room are easels, a miniature kitchen, hobby horses, a slide and several playpens. Although there are signs of wear and tear in certain places. it would appear that this is a good socializing spot for both parent and baby alike, especially in the winter. However, this is not a daycare center, as you must stay with your child.

Events: Films on Sat at 3pm for preschoolers; and a program for adults on early child development on weekdays (send a self-addressed, stamped envelope to ECRIC, at the above address).

EDUCATIONAL ALLIANCE
(See "For the Knowledge Seekers.")
   Children's theater.

EEYORE'S BOOKS FOR CHILDREN
1066 Madison Ave. (at 81st St.), East side.
☎ *(212) 988-3404.*
2252 Broadway (80th-81st Sts.), West side.
☎ *(212) 362-0634.*
   These bookstores offer storytelling for children up to age 7 on Sun at 11am at the west side store and on Sun at 12:30pm at the east side store (Sep-Jun, closed Hols). Free juice and cookies.

FAO SCHWARZ 5TH AVENUE TOY STORE ♦♦
767 5th Ave. (at 58th St.).
☎ *(212) 644-9400.*
Hours: Mon-Sat 10am-6pm.
   A fairyland of delights for kids of all ages, this toy store tops them all. You can always find lots of things to play with or marvel at—computer games, stuffed animals, train sets, dolls and even an enlarged piano keyboard on the floor for dancing antics (made famous in the movie *Big*). Look for the "Rainbow of Free Entertainment."
Events: Daily magic tricks from 11:30am-4pm; toy demonstrations; and special seasonal and Hol store decorations and entertainment.

HEADQUARTERS' MUSEUM ♦
(See "For the Culture Vultures.")
   Tours of this "historical" house with "please touch" objects, slide shows and dressing up in colonial costumes.

HOMEWORK HOTLINE
☎ *(718) 780-7766.*
Hours: Mon-Thu 5-8pm (on public school days).
Subject to Board of Education funding.
   This nonprofit service helps elementary through high school students with homework problems (sorry, they don't just give you the answers!).

JEFFERSON MARKET LIBRARY (NYPL)
(See "For the Bookworms.")
Hours for Children's Section: Mon-Thu 2:30-5:30pm, Sat 1-5pm and

summer hours, Mon-Sat 1-5pm. Closed Fri.

Storytelling and films for preschoolers ages 3 1/2-5 on Tue & Thu at 3:30pm (bi-monthly); picture book time for ages 6-8; toddler programs on some Tue at 4, registration required; summer feature films on Thu at 2pm (alternate weeks); and the Reading Club on specific themes (reservation suggested).

MACY'S DEPARTMENT STORE
Herald Sq., Broadway & 34th-35th Sts.
☎ *(212) 736-5151.*
Hours: *Mon, Thu-Fri 9:45am-8:30pm, Tue-Wed & Sat-Sun 9:45am-6:30pm (hours may expand at Christmas).*

Especially well known for its Thanksgiving Day Parade and fireworks display on July 4th, the world's largest department store has other marvelous Holiday programs. And who can forget visiting Santaland at Christmas!

MANHATTAN DOLL HOUSE & HOSPITAL
176 9th Ave. (21st-22nd Sts.).
☎ *(212) 989-5220.*
Hours: *Mon-Fri 11am-6pm, Sat 10am-5pm.*

This commercial store sells dolls of every kind, doll houses and miniatures, and has a repair facility. Looking is certainly free.

MARYMOUNT MANHATTAN COLLEGE
(See "For the Knowledge Seekers.")

The Children's Theater, open to scheduled school groups and the public (suggested contribution), features outstanding performances.

METROPOLITAN MUSEUM OF ART ♦♦♦♦
(See "For the Culture Vultures.")

This world-famous museum can seem daunting to an adult, so you can imagine what children must think. What is recommended are short visits to 1 or 2 galleries. To make the visit more meaningful, pick up the written gallery hunts for young people at the Great Hall Info Desk (there's one for almost every collection). In addition, the museum organizes some of the best cultural activities for children through the *Uris Center for Education.* During the nice weather, there's almost always outdoor entertainment on the museum's steps.
Events: *Gallery talks and sketching for children ages 6-12 + parents on Sat at 11am & 2:30pm and Sun at 11am; films on Sat at 12:30 & 2pm; "Art Adventures" (summer) for ages 10-15 on Tue-Fri 1:30-3pm; member children's workshops; Tally lecture series for children ages 6-12 + parent on Fri at 7-8pm; "First Look" workshops on Sat 11am or 2:30pm (Spring & Fall); for junior and senior high school students, afterschool & Sat classes with gallery talks and sketching, 570-3932; and films for children 5-12 on Tue-Fri at 11am (summer).*

MIDDLE COLLEGIATE CHURCH
(See "For the Believers.")

An "Arts Enrichment Program" for children 8-12.

EL MUSEO DEL BARRIO ♦
(See "For the Culture Vultures.")

This one-of-a-kind museum specializes in Puerto Rican and Latin American culture with bilingual guided tours on Wed 11-2pm.

Events: *Occasional special programs on Sun at 2:30pm for ages 5-10.*

MUSEUM OF MODERN ART (MoMA) ♦♦♦♦
(See "For the Culture Vultures.")

As modern art often is imaginative, whimsical, bizarre and creative, there's an appeal to children of all ages.

Events: *Free programs for N.Y.C. high school classes and teachers; parent/child 3-part workshops on introduction to modern art (fee); family gallery programs on Sat 10am (fee); family film series on Sat 11:15am (fee); and drop-in classes for high school students on Sat from 10am-noon.*

MUSEUM OF THE CITY OF NEW YORK ♦♦♦
(See "For the Culture Vultures.")

This museum is an enjoyable way to learn about N.Y.C. history. An excellent 25-minute multi-media slide show of the Big Apple should be mandatory for all. But the best attraction for children is the collection of antique dolls' houses (or baby houses). The highlights are a 1769 shadow box with waxed dolls by a 14 year old; the Brett House of 1838 (with early silver pieces); the 1845 Goelet brownstone (a replica of the one at 19th St. & Broadway); the 1925 Stettheimer House replete with lace curtains, rich wallpapers, rugs, antiques and even replicas of modern artwork on the ballroom walls; a 1979 stained-glass house and a 1981 fantasy land made of twigs, leaves and magic.

Events: *"Please Touch" workshops on Sat afternoon (mid Oct-Apr); and performing arts programs on some Sun at 5pm.*

NEW MUSEUM OF CONTEMPORARY ART ♦
(See "For the Culture Vultures.")

A special youth program for grades 3-5 in N.Y.C. public schools.

NEW YORK CITY DEPARTMENT OF PARKS & RECREATION
(See "For the Birds.")

To find out about the wide range of activities in all the city parks, ask to be put on the mailing list. Programs include instruction programs, clinics, competitions, workshops, Junior Ranger Naturalist program, play camps for preschoolers, urban day camps and tours with the Urban Park Rangers.

NEW YORK CITY MOUNTED POLICE STABLES
621 42nd St. (11th-12th Sts.).
☎ *(212) 239-9352.*
Hours: *Mon-Fri 9am-5pm by appt.*
Tours: *By appt. only.*

For a chance to frolic with N.Y.C.'s Mounted Police horses, come visit their stables on the west side. During a 30-45 minute tour, you will learn about the Mounted Police, how they groom and care for the horses and what equipment has to be used.

NEW YORK KIDS ON STAGE
☎ *(212) 860-1612.*
Free theatrical training for ages 7-17 is offered in music, dance and acting with performances in touring shows. The Parks Shakespeare Company provides classical training in acting, stage combat, improvisation and speech for those 13-17.

NEW YORK POLICE DEPARTMENT MUSEUM ◆
(See "For the Culture Vultures.")
School Tours: *By appt. only.*

NEW YORK PUBLIC LIBRARY FOR THE PERFORMING ARTS, CHILDREN'S SECTION
(See "For the Bookworms.")
☎ *(212) 870-1633.*
Plans to move in Sep '91.

NEW YORK PUBLIC LIBRARY SYSTEM
(See "For the Bookworms.")
For excellent children's programs, including workshops, arts & crafts, book clubs, films, mime and puppet shows performed in the branch libraries, consult the monthly calendar, "Events for Children," available at all NYPL locations.

NEW YORK STATE OFFICE FOR PARKS, RECREATION & HISTORICAL PRESERVATION
N.Y.C. Region, 1700 Broadway, N.Y., N.Y. 10019, Att: Recreation Staff.
☎ *(212) 977-8240.*
For information on free activities in the state parks located in N.Y.C., including Roberto Clemente in the Bronx, Empire-Fulton Ferry in Brooklyn and Clay Pit Ponds in S.I., write to the above address for a calendar.

RHINELANDER CHILDREN'S CENTER
Children's Aid Society (CAS), 350 E. 88th St. (1st Ave.).
☎ *(212) 876-0500.*
Since 1853, CAS has been sponsoring neighborhood centers, an early childhood parenting center, camps and health services for NYC's children and families. This center primarily supports Yorkville and offers facilities like a "Y."
Events: *Visual and performing arts center classes, free Sat program for deaf and hearing impaired children and birthday parties.*

THE STUDIO MUSEUM OF HARLEM ◆
(See "For the Culture Vultures.")
A special co-op school program; and occasional puppet shows and storytelling.

UKRAINIAN MUSEUM
(See "For the Culture Vultures.")
Workshops at Easter for making Ukrainian Easter eggs.

WORLD FINANCIAL CENTER
(See "For the Lobbyists.")

THE BRONX

THE BRONX ZOO ♦♦♦♦
(See "For the Birds.")
The entire Zoo is great fun. In particular, the excellent Children's Zoo (fee) offers over 40 different species of animals in natural habitats with participatory exhibits, an animal nursery and cutesy picture-taking opportunities with the animals.

ROBERTO CLEMENTE STATE PARK
(See "For the Birds.")
Game room activities for children of all ages; and a wide range of special classes and courses.

CROTONA PARK
(See "For the Birds.")
Many programs for children including a Junior Ranger Program (ages 8-13) in the summer.

NEW YORK CITY DEPARTMENT OF PARKS & RECREATION
☎ *(212) 430-1800.*
Obtain calendar of events for their wide range of monthly activities.

NEW YORK PUBLIC LIBRARY SYSTEM
☎ *(212) 220-6565.*
Pick up a calendar of events at any branch library.

WAVE HILL LEARNING CENTER ♦♦
(See "For the Birds.")
The Educational Department at Wave Hill House organizes a good program for children, including changing exhibitions on the natural history of the Bronx; aquariums; a touch table with natural history items; slide shows, workshops and demonstrations (like maple sugaring); and nature walks.

BROOKLYN

BROOKLYN ACADEMY OF MUSIC (BAM)
(See "For the Music Lovers.")
Children's Free Opera for a one-week engagement (between Feb-Jun), and Backstage Tour.

BROOKLYN BOTANIC GARDENS ♦ ♦ ♦ ♦
(See "For the Birds.")
A wonderful paradise of flowers and plants that every child (big and small) should visit, especially in the spring and summer. At the Chase Manhattan Discovery Center (Tue-Fri 10am-4pm, Sat-Sun & Hols noon-4pm), learn about the world of plants by touching, smelling and exploring the Discovery Boxes.
Events: *Garden plots for children to learn about growing vegetables and flowers (begun in 1914, the first of its kind in the world), starting in the spring and ending with the harvest festivities in the fall (fee, scholarships available).*

BROOKLYN CENTER FOR URBAN ENVIRONMENT
(See "For the Birds.")

BROOKLYN CENTRAL PUBLIC LIBRARY
(See "For the Bookworms.")
For special children's programs, including films, puppet shows and workshops in the branch libraries, obtain a calendar of events.

BROOKLYN CHILDREN'S MUSEUM ♦ ♦
145 Brooklyn Ave. (corner of St. Mark's Ave.).
☎ *(718) 735-4432/4400.*
Hours: *Mon & Wed-Fri 2-5pm, Sat-Sun & Hols 10am-5pm and Mon, Wed-Fri 10am-5pm (summer). Closed Tue & N.Y.C. public school Hols.*
Suggested Contribution: *$2.*
Groups: *For school groups by appt.*
By passing through a 1907 trolley car kiosk and then a neon-lit tunnel with water conduits harnessed for waterpower, you enter the jazzy and high-tech world of BCM. Founded in 1899 as the world's first children's museum to make "serious learning fun," this hands-on museum provides plenty of buttons to push, levers to pull and things to experiment with, thanks to its 10 exhibit rooms filled with interactive displays and multi-media programs covering natural science, cultural and educational subjects.
A clear modular maze winds its way around the museum, offering crawling space for children's play. *Dr. Dimension and the Rulers of the Universe* helps kids learn about measurements through their height and weight. A Music Studio with a plastic "walk-on" piano, like in the movie *Big*, keeps kids in tune with the world. At the *Mystery of Things*, amateur detectives figure out a mystery. The Early Learning Center offers children under 5 a place to romp around and use building blocks.

Events: *Special events and workshops (some at a fee) on occasional weekday afternoons from 2-5pm; ongoing participatory programs on Sat-Sun; film series; "Kids Crew," free after school program without parents; outreach programs; special summer programs for children 7+; June Balloon Festival (early Jun); Halloween Party (Oct); and special Christmas programs.*

BROOKLYN HISTORICAL SOCIETY ●

(See "For the Culture Vultures.")

Excellent free children's programs.

BROOKLYN MUSEUM ●●●●

(See "For the Culture Vultures.")

"What's Up" workshops for children 8-12 on Sat-Sun at 2pm; and special school programs (some at a fee).

BROOKLYN ZOO

Under construction, reopening 1992-93.

CHILDREN'S FARM

Under construction, reopening 1992-93.

GATEWAY ENVIRONMENTAL STUDY CENTER

(See "For the Birds.")

NEW YORK AQUARIUM ●●

(See "For the Birds.")

This marvelous world of undersea life is mesmerizing. Using special viewing platforms, small children can see eye to eye with clownfish, octopus and turtles. A Children's Cove houses goldfish and turtle ponds, a "touch-it" tank with sea stars and urchins and display cases of sponges and conchshells. Thanks to color pictures for identification, maps and informative descriptions, you will find this an educational and enjoyable journey.

Events: *Special educational programs throughout the year.*

NEW YORK CITY DEPARTMENT OF PARKS & RECREATION

☎ *(718) 965-8900.*

PROSPECT PARK ●●●

(See "For the Birds.")

This excellent park features a myriad of activities and places for kids, especially the Carousel, Zoo (when reopened) and Picnic House.

REGINA OPERA COMPANY

(See "For the Music Lovers.")

Three fully staged operas with orchestra, free for children (adults must pay).

QUEENS

ALLEY POND ENVIRONMENTAL CENTER ♠
(See "For the Birds.")

The Center sponsors an extensive program for the appreciation of the natural sciences through nature walks, workshops and slide shows (many free).

BUSH PARK
61st St. & Queens Blvd.
☎ *(718) 476-8449.*

Woodside on the Move, a neighborhood cultural council, sponsors weekly performances designed for children on Tue-Wed at 1:30pm (summer), including clowns, puppets, storytelling, music and children's theater.

CENTRAL QUEENS YM & YWHA
(See "For the Artists.")

Free storytelling and art projects (ages 3-8) on Tue at 10:30am and Thu 1:30 & 6:15pm.

CHILDREN'S ZOO AT FLUSHING MEADOW
111th St. & 54th Ave., Flushing.
☎ *(718) 760-6600.*
Hours: *Mon-Sat 10am-4pm.*

This working farm contains many barnyard animals for children to get acquainted with.

FLUSHING MEADOW, CORONA PARK ♠♠
(See "For the Birds.")

This city park features the "Playground for All Children" at Corona Ave. & 111th St., a 3.5 acre playground for disabled and able-bodied children and a Carousel.

FORT TILDEN AREA
(See "For the Birds.")

LANGSTON HUGHES COMMUNITY LIBRARY & CULTURAL CENTER
(See "For the Bookworms.")

Homework assistance programs for grades 3-7 on Mon-Fri 3-6pm; and on the 1st Mon of month, children's art festivals (school year).

NEW YORK CITY DEPARTMENT OF PARKS & RECREATION
☎ *(718) 520-5900.*

Obtain a calendar of events for the many parks' activities and events.

NEW YORK HALL OF SCIENCE ♠♠
47-01 111th St., Flushing Meadows, Corona Pk., Corona.

☎ *(718) 699-0675/0005.*
Hours: *Wed-Sun 10am-5pm. Closed Labor Day, Thanksgiving, Christmas Eve, Christmas, New Year's.*
Free Admission: *Wed-Thu 2-5pm. Otherwise Adults $3.50, Children & Seniors $2.50.*
Groups: *By appt. only on Mon-Tue 9:30am-2pm, Wed-Sun 9:30am-5pm, 699-0301.*

At New York's only hands-on science and technology museum, young scientists can make enormous bubbles, guide a spinning windmill, pedal an airplane propeller, and swing a 400-pound pendulum with only a string and a magnet, all in the name of learning! By using computers, pressing switches, turning knobs and pulling levers, children can partake in the 150 interactive exhibits. Discover how structures stand up or how to construct arches. Learn about pitch from the pipes of pan. Enter the Realm of the Atom and view the world's first 3-D dynamic model of an atom. Of particular interest is the 2,000-sq.-foot "biggest, smallest show in the U.S.," in which easy-view microscopes examine the world of microorganisms, such as protozoa, viruses and bacteria. An exhibition, *Seeing the Light,* brings the experience of color, light and perception into focus.

As some of the exhibits require the reading of the placards in order to understand the experiment or demonstration, this museum is geared more towards those over 7 years old. A Preschool playroom for ages 6 and under has blocks, toys, books and overstuffed animal pillows to keep the little ones occupied. The Science Access Center, a multi-media library, houses books, videos, periodicals and table-top activities.

Originally built for the 1964 World's Fair, the New York Hall of Science building is itself a work of art. Future plans include an exhibit on the space program and other technological advances of the future.
Events: *DARTS Family workshops on Sat at 2pm & Sun at 1pm and workshops for students, live science demos, weekend use of amateur radio station; annual exhibition of artists working in technology, birthday parties, special festivals and events.*

POPPENHUSEN INSTITUTE
(See "For the Music Lovers.")
Programs for all ages, including free films.

QUEENS BOROUGH PUBLIC LIBRARY SYSTEM
(See "For the Bookworms.")
For special programs for children in the branch libraries, obtain a monthly calendar.

QUEENS COUNTY FARM MUSEUM
(See "For the Culture Vultures.")
This landmark 7-acre farm with an 18th C. colonial farmhouse is the last "authentic working farm in N.Y.C." This is a good place for younger kids to see sheep, chicken, ducks and geese.
Events: *Special programs on Sat-Sun from noon-5pm (Apr-Dec).*

QUEENS MUSEUM é é
(See "For the Culture Vultures.")
Drop-in workshops on Sun from 1-4pm (school year) for the whole family to use materials creatively; an arts enrichment program for Queens children in Jul-Aug; and guided tours and workshops for school classes.

QUEENS ZOO
(See "For the Birds.")

TELEPHONE PIONEER MUSEUM
(See "For the Culture Vultures.")
In addition to containing telephone memorabilia, this is a good place for kids to learn how to use telephones (without running up high phone bills!).

STATEN ISLAND

NEW YORK CITY DEPARTMENT OF PARKS & RECREATION
☎ *(718) 390-8000.*
Obtain a calendar of events for all the wonderful activities in the city's parks.

NEW YORK PUBLIC LIBRARY SYSTEM
☎ *(718) 442-8611/8562.*
Obtain a calendar of events for all the wonderful activities at the city's libraries.

RICHMONDTOWN RESTORATION VILLAGE é é é
(See "For the Culture Vultures.")
This excellent restoration village takes kids on a journey back to colonial days. Of special interest are the ongoing demonstrations of colonial chores, such as candle making, basket weaving, pottery making and baking.
Events: *Special programs, especially at the Hols.*

SNUG HARBOR CULTURAL CENTER é é é
(See "For the Culture Vultures.")
Special programs with a tour, workshop and puppet show (some with a fee) and S.I. Children's Museum.

STATEN ISLAND CHILDREN'S MUSEUM é é
At Snug Harbor, 1000 Richmond Terr., Livingston.
☎ *(718) 273-2060/448-6557.*
Hours: *Wed-Fri 1-5pm, Sat-Sun & Hols 11am-5pm (school year), Tue-Sun 11am-5pm (summer).*
Free Admission: *2nd Fri of the month from 7-9pm and for Children*

under 2 always. Otherwise $2; however, an enormous range of free activities is included in admission fee.

Youngsters can become the captain of Noah's Ark, a TV sports reporter or a "bug" about bugs, thanks to 2 semi-permanent exhibits, 2 changing ones, and an amazing roster of workshops, performance art and special events at this well-designed children's museum. Downstairs, Block Island harbors a small wooden bridge and ship for child's play as well as a cozy cove for building blocks of all sizes and shapes and a stable of plastic animals; a great spot especially for those under 10. The world of bugs can be explored through interactive games, display cases, peek-a-boo doors, a cave and an ant colony. Depending upon your visit, temporary exhibits may include "It's News to Me!" about the world of jounalism, the "Color Arcade" with its spectrum of color questions, "Water" water everywhere, crazy about "Kaleidoscopes" or "Exploration and Discovery." Children's artwork usually hangs in the entrance Atrium.

Events: *Meet the Performers on Sun at 2pm (once a month), Kids' Cabaret of family entertainment on 3rd or 4th Fri at 7:30pm, Stars in the Afternoon (4 times during school year) with major performers at Veterans' Memorial Hall; weekly workshops and classes.*

STATEN ISLAND ZOO ✿
(See "For the Birds.")

This delightful small zoo will enchant those big and small alike.

For the Golden Agers

As many Senior Citizens have much leisure time, they are prime candidates for free events, and what Senior doesn't like a real bargain! Above and beyond the freebies already listed, many Senior Centers offer special programs catering specifically to Seniors' needs and interests.

And some museums and parks are free only to Seniors; they are the Bronx Zoo, Brooklyn Museum, New York Aquarium (Mon-Fri after 2pm, except Hols), Theodore Roosevelt Birthplace, Studio Museum of Harlem (Wed only) and the Staten Island Zoo. However, remember that many museums and parks are either free to all or else free on a given day (or evening); check each chapter.

"To me, old age is always fifteen years older than I am."

— *BERNARD BARUCH*

All Boroughs

CATHEDRAL CHURCH OF ST. JOHN THE DIVINE ♦♦
(See "For the Believers.")
　　A drop-in center on Sat.

CHRIST & ST. STEPHEN'S EPISCOPAL CHURCH ♦
(See "For the Believers.")
　　Special programs include concerts and films.

CHURCH OF THE COVENANT
(See "For the Believers.")
　　Tudor City Adult Day program on Fri from 10am-3pm (exc. Hols) including entertainment, fun & games and a hot lunch ($4).

CHURCH OF THE INCARNATION
(See "For the Believers.")
　　Senior club on Tue from 1-4pm (tea included).

CHURCH OF THE TRANSFIGURATION ♦
(See "For the Believers.")
　　Hot lunches plus special Seniors' programs.

CITY UNIVERSITY OF NEW YORK (CUNY)
☎ *(212) 947-4800/794-5555.*
　　For enrollment at any CUNY college (provided space is available), there's a special tuition fee for Seniors of only $30; see listing below for Kingsborough Community College in Brooklyn for special free programs.

COMMUNITY CHURCH
(See "For the Believers.")
　　Group meeting with socializing and recreation on Wed from noon-2pm.

DEPARTMENT FOR THE AGING
280 Broadway, Manhattan.
☎ *(212) 577-0800.*
　　This city agency is dedicated to serving older adults, 60 and over. With more than 300 Senior Centers located in the 5 boroughs, they provide free comprehensive daytime (Mon-Fri 9am-5pm & some weekends) programs ranging from arts & crafts, exercise and dramatics classes to outings (nominal charge). Hot lunches are always served (small charge); a transportation service for incapacitated Seniors is also available. Contact each borough for a listing of the Senior Centers: the Bronx, (212) 584-1328; Brooklyn, (718) 855-1208; Manhattan, (212) 694-0909; Queens, (718) 544-1265; and Staten Island, (718) 981-1680.
　　In addition, this agency offers a wide range of services including health info, employment training, assistance with filling in forms, a bilingual hotline for Spanish-speaking Seniors (577-0283) and reduced-fare transit passes (577-0819).

DEPARTMENT OF CONSUMER AFFAIRS
☎ *(212) 566-6047/0414.*
Contact the Outreach & Education Division for a wide range of publications on such topics as air conditioning, budget cards, consumer affairs info guide, consumer tips for happier holidays, food additives, generic drug laws, home improvements and how to collect in small claims court.

EMANU-EL MIDTOWN YM-YWHA
344 E. 14th St. (1st-2nd Aves.), Manhattan.
☎ *(212) 674-7200.*
Courses, special events for adults 55+ (some at a fee) and occasional free brown bag concerts at noon.

HUMAN RESOURCES ADMINISTRATION
Senior Center Services, 60 Hudson St., 9th fl., Manhattan.
☎ *(212) 433-5796/2213.*
The Senior Center Services, a division of the city's Human Resources Administration, is responsible for running over 200 Senior Centers in the 5 boroughs. As with the Department of the Aging, membership is free to any adult 60+ or spouse regardless of age, living in N.Y.C. All Centers are open on Mon-Fri from 9am-5pm (some weekends also) and offer Seniors an opportunity for socializing and personal development through an extraordinary program of classes, workshops, arts & crafts, movies and outings (nominal fee). Hot lunches are always served (donation), sometimes breakfast and some Centers offer home lunch delivery. Free transportation is available at some Centers to handicapped Seniors. Contact the Senior Center Services for the Center nearest you.

KINGSBOROUGH COMMUNITY COLLEGE (CUNY), BROOKLYN
(See "For the Knowledge Seekers.")
A special tuition-free program entitled "My Turn" enables those over 65 to participate with younger students in classes and extracurricular activities (this is the only college in the State offering this program).

HERBERT H. LEHMAN COLLEGE (CUNY), THE BRONX
(See "For the Knowledge Seekers.")
The Center for the Performing Arts sponsors an impressive cultural program of dance, opera, drama and music all year round; a special subsidy makes some tickets free to Seniors.

MARBLE COLLEGIATE CHURCH
(See "For the Believers.")
Lunch for Seniors on Wed at 12:30pm (nominal fee).

MIDDLE COLLEGIATE CHURCH
(See "For the Believers.")
Meetings on Tue at 1pm with refreshments, entertainment, lectures and perhaps bingo (nominal fee).

NEW DEAL THEATER COMPANY
(See "For the Matinee Idlers.")
Free tickets for Seniors.

NEW YORK CITY DEPARTMENT OF PARKS & RECREATION
Older Adult Services, 16 W. 61st St., Manhattan.
☎ *(212) 408-0204.*
Since 1979, the Older Adult Services Unit has been responsible for the management of this agency's Senior Centers. With a wide range of recreational activities, the Centers sponsor swimming, sports, games, dancing, music, drama, writing workshops and arts & crafts. For a list of the Centers, contact the unit at the above address.

NEW YORK PUBLIC LIBRARY SYSTEM
(See "For the Bookworms.")
For the public libraries in the Bronx, Manhattan and Staten Island, contact them for special programs including large-print books, reduced-fare cards and homebound services.

ST. BARTHOLOMEW'S CHURCH ♦
(See "For the Believers.")
Special programs for Seniors including an outreach service.

ST. PETER'S CHURCH ♦♦
(See "For the Believers.")
A variety of special programs.

THEATER FOR THE NEW CITY
(See "For the Matinee Idlers.")
Free ticket program (6-10 tickets) for Senior groups.

WASHINGTON HEIGHTS INSTITUTE OF RETIRED PEOPLE
☎ *(212) 942-3573.*
This is a nonprofit membership organization of retired people who love the cultural side of life. Weekly meetings are at the American Academy & Institute of Arts & Letters (155th St. & Broadway) on Fri from 11am-2pm (Oct-May), at which time a member presents a paper on a cultural topic and a discussion follows (bring lunch). Although weekly meetings are free, nominal membership dues are required.

Maps

MAP 1   CITY OF NEW YORK (5 Boroughs)

Museums

1   Statue of Liberty (American
     Museum of Immigration)
2   Ellis Island Immigration Museum

Parks

4   Fort Tilden
5   Jamaica Bay Wildlife Refuge
6   Jacob Riis Park
7   Rockaway Beach

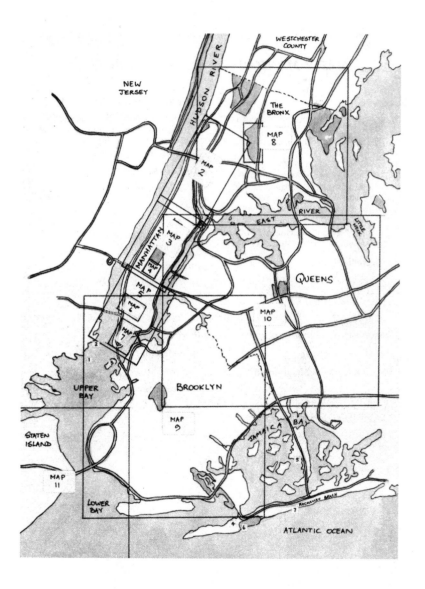

NEW JERSEY

WESTCHESTER COUNTY

HUDSON RIVER

THE BRONX

MAP 8

MAP 2

MANHATTAN

MAP 3

MAP 4

EAST RIVER

LITTLE NECK

QUEENS

MAP 5

MAP 6

MAP 7

2

1

MAP 10

UPPER BAY

BROOKLYN

MAP 9

STATEN ISLAND

JAMAICA BAY

5

MAP 11

LOWER BAY

ROCKAWAY BEACH

7

4

6

ATLANTIC OCEAN

MAP 2 MANHATTAN (Above 125th St.)

Museums

1 American Numismatic Museum (AX)
2 Black Fashion Museum (BZ)
3 The Cloisters (AU)
4 Dyckman House (AU)
5 Hamilton Grange Museum (BY)
6 Hispanic Society of America (AX)
7 Morris-Jumel Mansion (BX)
8 National Museum of American Indian (AX)
9 Studio Museum of Harlem (BZ)
10 Yeshiva University Museum (AV)

Art Galleries

11 American Academy & Institute of Arts & Letters (AX)
12 Arts Interaction (AW)
13 Adam Clayton Powell Jr. State Office Building (BZ)
14 Schomburg Center Gallery (BY)

Special Attractions

15 Grant National Memorial (AZ)

Churches/Synagogues

16 Abyssinian Baptist Church (BY)
17 Church of the Intercession (AX)
18 Riverside Church (AZ)
19 St. Martin's Episcopal Church (CZ)

Cultural Societies

20 International House (AZ)

Parks

21 Fort Tryon (AV)
22 Marcus Garvey (CZ)
23 Inwood Hill (AU)

Schools

24 City College of N.Y. (BZ)
25 Harlem School of the Arts (BY)
26 Manhattan School of Music (AZ)
27 Yeshiva University (AV)

Libraries

28 Schomburg Center (CY)

Theater

29 Frank Silvera Workshop (BZ)

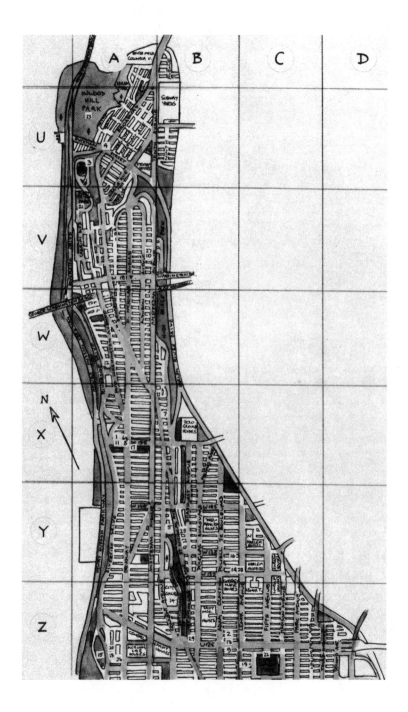

MAP 3 MANHATTAN (34th-125th St.)

Museums

1 American Museum of Natural History (BW)
2 Asia Society (CX)
3 The Center for African Art (CX)
4 The Cooper-Hewitt (CV)
5 The Frick Collection (CX)
6 Guggenheim Museum (CW)
7 Headquarters' Museum (DX)
8 International Center of Photography (CV)
9 Metropolitan Museum of Art (CW)
10 J. Pierpont Morgan Library (CZ)
11 El Museo del Barrio (CU)
    Museum of American Folk Art (BX)
12 Museum of American Illustration (CX)
13 Museum of the City of New York (CV)
14 National Academy of Design (CW)
15 The New-York Historical Society (BW)
16 Nicholas Roerich Museum (AU)
17 Abigail Adams Smith Museum (DX)
18 Whitney Museum of American Art (CW)

Art Galleries

(For Madison Ave. Galleries, consult "For the Gallery Hoppers.")
19 American Institute of Graphic Arts (DX)
20 Board of Jewish Education (BY)
23 High School of Art & Design (CY)
25 International Typeface Corp. (DY)
26 National Urban League (DX)
27 Sculpture Center (CX)

28 Women's Interact Center (AY)

Auction Houses

29 Doyle (CW)
30 Manhattan Galleries (DW)
31 Phillips (DW)
32 Sotheby's (DX)

Special Attractions

33 The Arsenal Gallery (CX)
34 Con Edison Conservation Center (CY)
35 The Dairy (BX)
36 Grolier Club (CX)
37 United Nations (DY)

Special Buildings

38 Ansonia Hotel (AX)
39 Chanin Building (CZ)
40 Chrysler Building (CY)
41 Citicorp Center (CY)
    Crystal Pavilion (DY)
42 Daily News Building (DZ)
    875 3rd Avenue (DY)
43 Empire State Building (CZ)
44 Ford Foundation (DY)
45 Harkness Atrium (BX)
46 Harley Hotel (DZ)
    Place des Antiquaires (DY)

Churches/Synagogues

47 Brick Presbyterian Church (CV)
48 Cathedral Church of St. John (BU)
49 Christ & St. Stephen's Episcopal (BX)
50 Christ Church United Methodist (CX)

335

51 Church of Jesus Christ (BX)
52 Church of the Covenant (DZ)
53 Church of the Heavenly Rest (CW)
54 Holy Trinity Lutheran (BX)
55 Interchurch Center (AU)
56 Madison Avenue Presbyterian Church (CX)
57 St. Michael's Church (AV)
58 St. Peter's Church (CY)
59 Society of Ethical Culture (BX)
60 Temple Emanu-el (CX)
61 Stephen Wise Free Synagogue (BX)

Cultural Societies

62 African-American Institute (DY)
63 American Irish Historical Society (CW)
64 American Scandinavian Foundation (CX)
65 Leo Baeck Institute (CX)
66 Caribbean Cultural Center (BY)
67 Center for Inter-American Relations (CX)
68 China Institute of America (CX)
70 Deutsches Haus, Columbia University (AU)
71 French Cultural Services (CW)
72 French Institute/Alliance Française (CX)
73 Goethe House (CW)
74 Italian Cultural Institute (CX)
75 Japan House (DY)
76 Maison Française, Columbia University (AU)
77 Spanish Institute (CX)
Swiss Institute (BY)
79 Turkish Center (DY)
80 Ukrainian Institute (CX)
81 YIVO Institute (CW)
82 Yugoslav Center (DY)

Tours

83 Gracie Mansion (DW)
84 Seventh Regiment Armory (CX)

Parks

85 Central Park (BW)
86 Morningside Park (BU)
87 Riverside Park (AU)
88 Carl Schurz Park (DW)

Health

89 Lenox Hill Hosp. Health Ed. Center (Tel-Med) (CW)
N.Y. Roadrunners Club (CV)

Schools

90 Barnard College (AU)
91 Bloomingdale House of Music (AU)
92 Columbia University (AU)
93 Fordham University (BX)
94 Hebrew Arts School (BX)
95 Hunter College (CX)
96 John Jay College (BX)
97 Juilliard School of Music (BX)
98 Mannes College of Music (BW)
99 Marymount Manhattan College (DX)
100 Mt. Sinai School of Medicine (CV)
101 N.Y. School of Interior Design (DY)
102 N.Y.U. Institute of Fine Arts (CW)
103 Turtle Bay School (DY)
104 Westside YMCA (BX)

Libraries

105 American Bible Society (BX)
107 Center for the Study of the Presidency (DW)
109 N.Y. Academy of Medicine (CV)
108 N.Y. Public Library for the Performing Arts (AX)
110 N.Y. Society Library (CW)

Lectures

111 N.Y. Academy of Science (CX)

Concert Halls/Music

Mark Goodson Theater (BX)
113 Irish Arts Center (AY)
114 Lincoln Center (BX)
115 Symphony Space (AV)
116 West Bank Cafe (BY)

Theater

117 American Musical & Dramatic Academy (AX)
American Theater of Actors (BY)
American Theater Wing (BY)
118 Ensemble Studio Theater (AY)
120 New Dramatists Workshops (BY)
Quaigh Theater (CX)

Film/TV

122 ABC TV Studio (BX)
N.Y. Stage & Film (AW)

Kiddies

123 Asphalt Green (DV)
Children's Museum of Manhattan (BW)
Eeyore's Books Eastside (CW)
Eeyore's Books Westside (AW)
N.Y.C. Mounted Police Stable (AY)

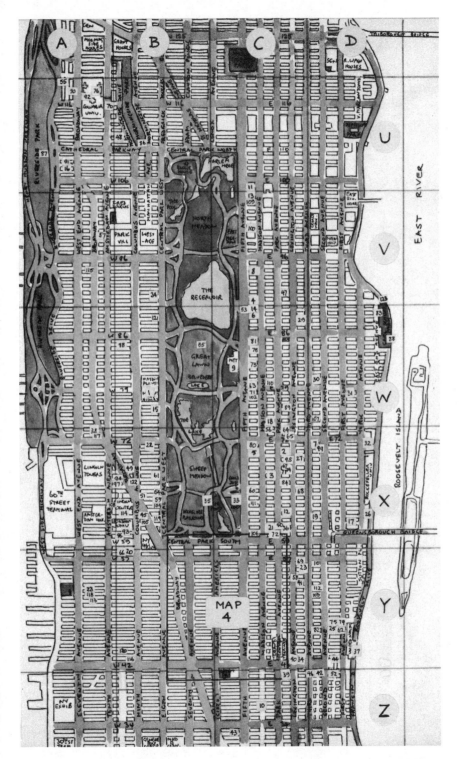

MAP 4 MANHATTAN (Midtown detail)

Museums

1 Amerian Crafts Museum (CV)
3 AT&T Infoquest (DV)
4 IBM Gallery of Science & Arts (DU)
   International Center of
   Photography (BY)
   Lladro Museum (CU)
   Museum of American Piano (AU)
6 Museum of Broadcasting (DV)
7 Museum of Modern Art (DV)
   Whitney Museum at Equitable
   (BW)
9 Whitney Museum at Philip Morris
   (DZ)

Art Galleries

10 Architectural League of N.Y. (DW)
    BMW Gallery (DW)
11 City Gallery (AU)
    Hoya Gallery (DU)
12 Municipal Arts Society (DW)
14 Nikon House (CW)
    PaineWebber Building (BW)
    Steuben Glass (DV)
17 Urban Center (DW)

Auction Houses

18 Christie's (DU)

Special Attractions

19 General Motors Building (DU)
20 Gotham Book Mart (CX)
21 Manhattan Savings Bank (DX)
22 John M. Mossman Lock Collection
    (CY)
24 Rockefeller Center (CW)

Special Buildings

25 Alwyn Court (AU)
26 American Telephone & Telegraph
    (DV)
27 ChemCourt (EX)
28 Equitable Life Assurance (BW)
    575 5th Avenue (DX)
30 Galleria Atrium (EU)
31 Grand Central Terminal (EY)
32 Grand Hyatt Hotel (EY)
33 Helmsley Palace (DW)
34 Hilton Hotel (BV)
35 IBM Garden (DU)
36 Lever House (DV)
37 Olympic Towers (DW)
29 N.Y. Bank for Business (EU)
    Park Avenue Atrium (EX)

38 Park Avenue Plaza (DW)
39 Parker Meridien Hotel (BU)
40 Plaza Hotel (CU)
41 Seagram's Building (EW)
    31 W. 52nd Street (CW)
42 Trump Tower (DU)
43 Warner Communications (CW)

Churches/Synagogues

44 Central Synagogue (EV)
45 Fifth Avenue Presbyterian (CV)
47 St. Bartholomew's (EW)
48 St. Patrick's Cathedral (DW)
49 St. Thomas Church (CV)

Cultural Societies

50 Austrian Institute (DW)
52 Galleria Venezuela (DW)
53 Korean Cultural Service (DU)
54 Nippon Club Gallery (BU)

Tours

55 ILGWU (AV)

Parks/Plazas

57 Bryant Park (CZ)
58 Exxon Mini Park (BW)
    1st Boston Park (BY)
59 Grace Building (CY)
60 Grand Army Plaza (CU)
61 Horticultural Society of N.Y. (BU)
63 McGraw-Hill Mini Park (BX)
64 Paley Park (DV)

Schools

65 Art Students League (AU)
66 CUNY Graduate School (CY)
67 Henry George School (DY)
68 Lighthouse for the Blind (EU)
69 N.Y.U. Midtown Center (CY)
70 YWCA (EV)

Libraries

71 Central Research, the N.Y. Public
    Library (CZ)
72 Donnell Library (CV)
73 The Information Exchange (DW)
74 Mechanics Institute Library (CY)
75 Mercantile Library (DX)
76 Mid-Manhattan Library (DZ)
77 N.Y. Genealogical & Bibliographical
    Society (EU)

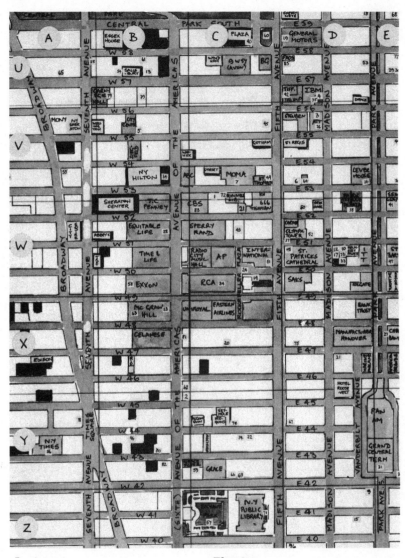

Lectures

78 N.Y.C. Bar Association (CY)

Concert Halls/Music

79 Carnegie Hall (BU)
80 Town Hall (BY)

Readings

Brentano's Bookstore (DX)
Small Press (CY)

Theater

American Stanislavski Theater (EU)

Film/TV

83 CBS TV Studio (CW)
84 NBC TV Studio (CW)

Kiddies

85 FAO Schwarz Toy Store (DU)

MAP 5 MANHATTAN (Below 34th St.)

Museums

1   Con Edison Energy Museum (EW)
    Lower East Side Tenement
    Museum (DX)
4   Museum of Armenian Diocese (DV)
5   New York Police Department
    Museum (DW)
6   Theodore Roosevelt Birthplace
    (CW)
7   School of Visual Arts Museum
    (DW)

Art Galleries

    Castillo Cultural Center (BX)
10 Henry Street Settlement (DX)
11 Master Eagle Gallery (CV)
    MetLife Gallery (CV)
12 National Arts Club (CW)
    National Institute of Architecture
    (CW)

Auction Houses

16 Lubin Galleries (CV)
17 Swann Galleries (CV)

Special Attractions

18 ILGWU Archives (BV)
19 Supreme Court Appellate Division
    (CV)

Special Buildings

20 Bowery Savings Bank (DX)
21 Chelsea Hotel (BW)

Churches/Synagogues

22 Church of the Incarnation (CV)
23 Church of the Transfiguration (CV)
24 Community Church (CV)
25 Marble Collegiate Church (CV)
26 St. Vartan's Church (DV)

Cultural Societies

28 Center for Cuban Studies (DW)
29 Rumanian Society (DV)

Tours

30 Players Club (CW)
31A Shapiro's Winery (DX)

Parks

32 Gramercy Park (CW)
33 Madison Square Park (CV)
34 St. Vartan's Park (DV)
35 Stuyvesant Park (DW)
36 Tompkins Square Park (DX)

Health

37 Blue Cross/Blue Shield (CV)

Schools

38 Baruch College (CW)
39 Center for Media Arts (BV)
40 Educational Alliance (DY)
41 Empire State College (CV)
42 Fashion Institute of Technology (BV)
43 H.S. of Fashion Industries (BV)
44 Washington Irving H.S. (CW)
45 McBurney YMCA (BW)
46 School of Visual Arts (DW)
47 Sivananda Center (BV)
48 Traphagen School of Fashion (CX)

Lectures

49 New York Marxist School (BW)
    Wetlands Preserve (BY)

Concerts

    Port Authority Bus Terminal (BV)

Readings

    ABC No Rio (DX)
    Mona's (DW)

Dance

50 Center for the Dance of Isadora
    Duncan (BV)
51 Dance Theatre Workshop (BW)

Theater

54 Irondale Theatrical Co. (BW)

TV/Film

    Chelsea Studios (BV)
    Experimental Intermedia Foundation
    (DX)

Kiddies

    Manhattan Doll House & Hospital
    (BW)

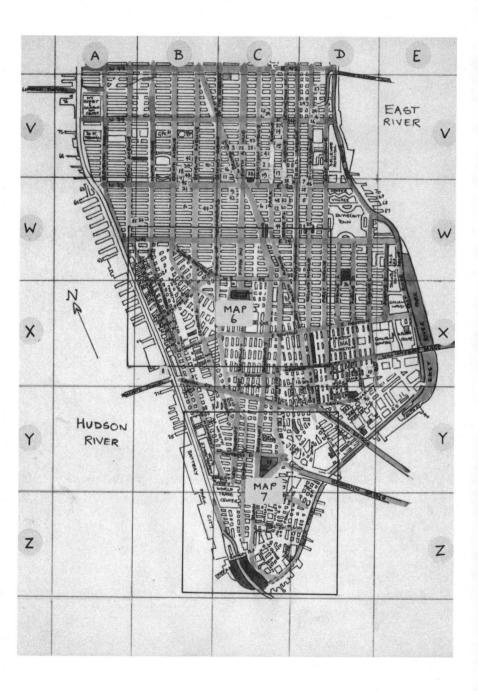

EAST RIVER

HUDSON RIVER

MAP 6

MAP 7

MAP 6 MANHATTAN (Greenwich Village detail)

Museums

   Fire Museum (CZ)
   Forbes Galleries Museum (DW)
2 New Museum of Contemporary Art (EZ)
3 Old Merchant's House (EY)
4 Ukrainian Museum (FW)

Art Galleries

5 American Indian Community House (EZ)
   Camera Club (EW)
   Cinque Gallery (EZ)
6 80 Washington Square East (DY)
7 Emanuel Midtown YM-YWHA (FW)
8 Grey Art Gallery (DX)
   Kampo Cultural Center (EY)
10 New School Art Collection (DW)
11 NYU Photo Center Gallery (EX)
12 Painting Space 122 (FX)
13 Pen & Brush (DX)
14 Puck Building (EY)
15 Salmagundi Club (DW)
16 School of Visual Arts Gallery (DZ)

Churches/Synagogues

17 Church of the Ascension (DX)
18 First Presbyterian (DW)
19 Grace Church (EW)
20 Judson Memorial Church (DY)
21 Middle Collegiate Church (FX)
22 St. John's in the Village (BX)
23 St. Mark's in-the-Bowery (FX)

Cultural Societies

24 Deutsches Haus (DX)
25 Maison Française (DX)

Parks

26 Union Square Park (EW)
27 Washington Square Park (DX)

Sports

28 American Youth Hostels (EZ)

St. Vincent's Hospital (CW)

Schools

29 Cooper Union (EX)
   Empire State College (EX)
30 Greenwich House Music School (CY)
31 Hebrew Union College (EY)
32 New School for Social Research (DW)
33 New York Studio School (DX)
34 New York University (DY)
35 Parsons School of Design (DW)
36 School of T'ai Chi (CW)
37 Third Street Music School (FX)

Libraries

38 Jefferson Market Library (CX)

Music

39 Cornelia Street Cafe (CY)
   Cupping Room Cafe (DZ)

Readings

   Backfence (DY)
   Speak Easy (DY)

Theater

40 Actors Playhouse (BY)
   CBGB's (FY)
   HB Playwrights Foundation (AX)
   La Mama/La Galleria (FY)
41 Public Theater (EX)
   Red Spot Outdoor Theater (EZ)
42 Lee Strasberg Theater (EW)
43 Ubu Rep Theater (EZ)

Film

   Anthology Film Archive (DY)
44 Millennium Film Workshop FY)

Kiddies

   Bird Jungle (BX)
45 Early Childhood Center (CY)

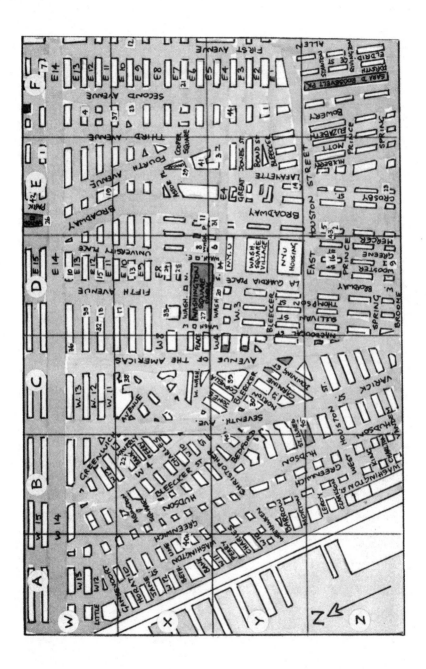

MAP 7 MANHATTAN (Lower Manhattan detail)

Museums

1 Alternative Museum (BU)
2 City Hall Museum (CV)
3 Federal Hall National Memorial (CX)
5 Fraunces Tavern (CY)
   New York Unearthed (BY)
6 South Street Seaport Museum (DX)
7 Trinity Church Museum (BX)
   Whitney Museum Downtown (CX)

Art Galleries

10 The Clocktower (CU)
11 Federal Office Building (CU)
12 Franklin Furnace (BU)
13 Office of Manhattan Borough President (CV)

Special Attractions

16 Castle Clinton (BZ)
17 Mary Celeste Exhibit (CX)
18 Commodities Exchange (BW)
19 New York Stock Exchange (BX)
20 New York Surrogates Court (CV)
22 Supreme court of N.Y. (CU)
23 Tweed Courthouse (CV)
24 U.S. Courthouse (CV)

Special Buildings

25 Woolworth Building (BW)
    World Financial Center (AX)
26 World Trade Center (BW)

Churches/Synagogues

27 Church of St. Peter's (BW)
28 John Street United Methodist (CW)
29 St. Paul's (BW)
30 Trinity Church (BX)

Cultural Societies

31 Asian Arts Institute (DU)

Tours

32 Federal Reserve Bank (CX)
33 New York Police Department (DV)
34 Supreme Court of New York (CU)

Parks

35 Battery Park (BZ)
    Battery Park City (BY)
36 Bowling Green (BY)
37 City Hall Park (CV)
37A Washington Market Park

Schools

38 Borough of Manhattan Community College (AV)
39 Downtown Community TV Center (CU)
40 Pace University (CV)

Concerts

Continental Insurance Building (DX)

Film

41 Collective for the Living Cinema (BU)

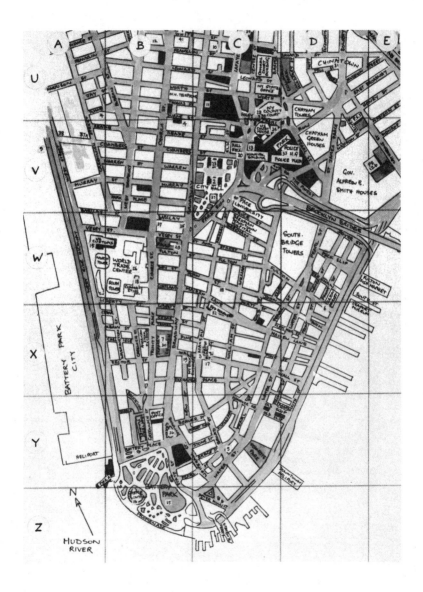

MAP 8 BRONX (Inset: Zoo & Botanical Gardens)

Museums

1 Bartow-Pell Mansion House (DX)
2 Bronx Museum of the Arts (AY)
23 Maritime Museum at Fort Schuyler (DZ)
6 Edgar Allan Poe Cottage (BX)
7 Valentine-Varian House (BX)
8 Van Cortlandt Mansion House (BW)

Parks and Zoos

9 Bronx Zoo (BY)
10 Roberto Clemente State Park (AX)
11 Crotona Park (BY)
12 New York Botanical Gardens (BX)
13 Pelham Bay Park (DX)

14 Van Cortlandt Park (BW)
15 Wave Hill (AW)
16 Woodlawn Cemetery (BW)

Schools

17 Bronx Community College (AX)
18 College of Mount St. Vincent (AW)
19 Fordham University (BX)
20 Hostos Community College (AZ)
21 Herbert H. Lehman College (BX)
22 Manhattan College (AW)
23 New York Maritime College (DZ)

Libraries and Societies

24 Bronx County Historical (BX)

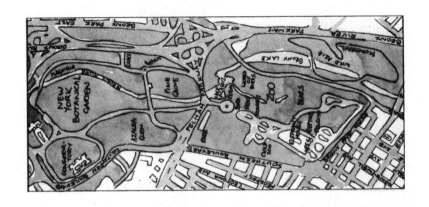

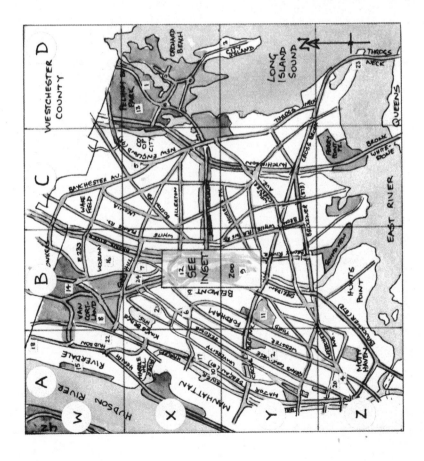

MAP 9 BROOKLYN (Inset: Brooklyn Heights)

Museums

1 Brooklyn Children's Museum (CX)
6 Brooklyn Historical Museum &
Society (FX)
2 Brooklyn Museum (BX)
4 Harbor Defense Museum (AY)
5 Lefferts Homestead (BX)
9 Wyckoff House (CX)

Art Galleries

11 BACA's Downtown Cultural Center
(BW)
Brooklyn Heights Arts Promenade
(EW)
Historic Brooklyn Bridge
Anchorage (FW)
Kings Bay YM-YWHA (CZ)
13 The Rotunda Gallery (FW)
YMCA of Brooklyn (BW)

Church

14 Church of St. Ann & the Holy
Trinity (EX)

Special Tours

Brooklyn Borough Hall (FX)

Parks, Zoos and Beaches

15 Floyd Bennett Field (Gateway) (DZ)
Brighton Beach (CZ)
16 Brooklyn Botanic Gardens (BX)

17 Brooklyn Zoo (BX)
18 Coney Island (BZ)
19 Empire-Fulton Ferry State Park
(EW)
20 Green-Wood Cemetery (BX)
21 Manhattan Beach (CZ)
22 New York Aquarium (BZ)
23 Prospect Park (BX)

Schools

24 Brooklyn College (BY)
25 Brooklyn Conservatory of Music
(BW)
27 Kingsborough Community College
(CZ)
28 Long Island University (BW)
29 N.Y.C. Technical School (FX)
Polytechnic University (FX)
30 Pratt Institute (BW)

Libraries

31 Brooklyn Central Public Library
(BX)

Concert Halls

Baldwin Piano (CY)
32 Brooklyn Academy of Music (BW)
33 Brooklyn College, Center for the
Performing Arts (BY)
34 Regina Hall (AY)

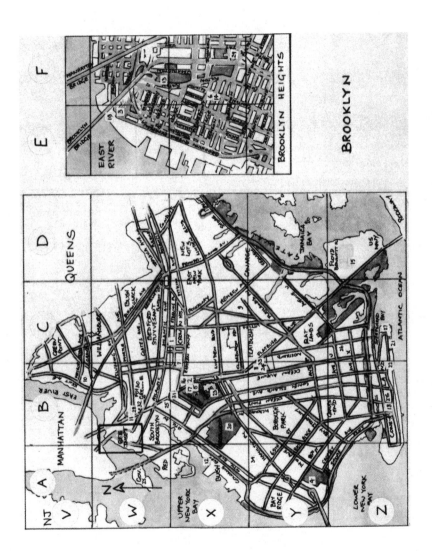

BROOKLYN

BROOKLYN HEIGHTS

MAP 10 QUEENS

Museums

1 American Museum of the Moving Image (AX)
2 Bowne House (CX)
3 Friends Meeting House (CX)
4 Godwin-Ternbach Museum (Queens College) (DX)

5 King Manor Museum (DY)
6 Kingsland House (CX)
  New York Hall of Science (CX)
  Isamu Noguchi Garden Museum (AX)
9 Queens County Farm Museum (EX)
8 Queens Museum (CX)
  Queens Museum at Bulova (CX)
10 Telephone Pioneer Museum (DY)

Art Galleries

  Central Queens YM & YWHA (CY)
11 Chung-Cheng Gallery (St. John's University) (DY)
  Flushing Arts Council (CX)
  Jackson Heights Arts Club (BX)
12 Jamaica Arts Center (DY)

  Ollantay Center for the Arts
13 P.S. 1, Project Studio 1 (AX)

Parks and Zoos

  (See Map 1 for additional listings)
14 Alley Pond Environmental Center (EW)
15 Flushing Meadow, Corona Park (CX)
16 Queens Botanical Gardens (CX)
17 Queens Zoo (CX)
  Socrates Sculpture Park (AX)

Schools

18 Queens College (DX)
19 Queensborough Comm. College (EX)
20 St. John's University (DY)
  York College (DY)

Libraries

22 Langston Hughes Comm. Library (CX)
23 Queens Borough Central Public Library (DY)
24 Queens Historical Society (CX)

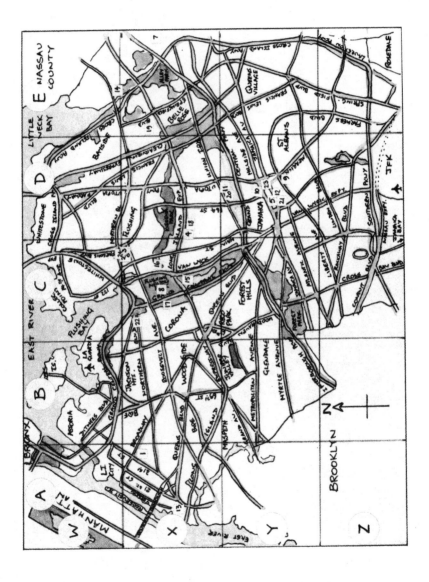

MAP 11 STATEN ISLAND

Museums

1 Alice Austen House (DX)
2 Conference House (AZ)
3 Garibaldi-Meucci Museum (DX)
  Noble Collection (DW)
4 Richmondtown Restoration Village (CY)
5 Snug Harbor Cultural Center (CW)
  Staten Island Children's Museum at Snug Harbor (CW)
7 Staten Island Ferry Museum (DW)
8 Staten Island Museum (DW)

Parks and Zoos

9 Clay Pit Ponds State Park Reserve (AY)
10 Clove Lakes Park (CW)
11 William T. Davis Wildlife Refuge (BX)
12 Great Kills Park (CY)
13 High Rock Park (CX)
   LaTourette Park (CX)
14 Silver Lake Park (CW)
   South & Midland Beaches & FDR Boardwalk (DX)
15 Staten Island Botanical Gardens (CW)
16 Staten Island Zoo (CW)
   Walker Park (CW)
   Willowbrook Park (CX)
   Wolfe's Pond Park & Beach (BZ)

Colleges

17 College of Staten Island, St. George (DW)
18 College of Staten Island, Sunnyside (CX)
19 Wagner College (CX)

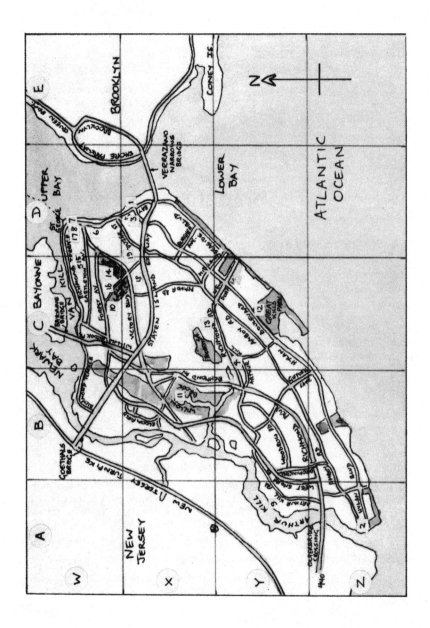

Technical Notes

With the exception of the outside cover, the rest of this book was produced on our personal computer. I thought some of you might be interested in the technical details, so I have included this page.

The current hardware setup is a Gateway 386/33 (IBM clone) with 8 mb memory and 150 mb hard disk. Printing is handled by an 800 dpi resolutionLasermaster board driving an HP Laserjet III. Output was printed at 150% magnification on legal size paper and then reduced to current trim size when film was made. This achieves an effective resolution of 1200 dpi, typesetting quality. Our monitor is a NANAO Flexscan 9500 with Renaissance II board and the scanning is done with an HP Scanjet Plus.

The text was prepared using Microsoft WORD 5.0, with a handful of macros to deal with index entries, ratings, telephone numbers etc. Then the text was imported into Ventura for type-setting. Ventura paginated the whole book and generated the contents and index automatically. It's a publisher's dream as it allowed us to fine-tune so that we came out to an exact number of pages to match 16 page signatures.

Type faces used, in various weights and point sizes, were Bookman for main text, Franklin Gothic for headings, Zapf Dingbats for telephones, Symbol for the apples, and Sans (Helvetica) Condensed for listings and index. Back cover is set in Avant Garde.

I feel that the overall results are very satisfying and are evidence of the enormous potential in desktop publishing.

Index

Notes